queer studies

queer studies

A LESBIAN,

GAY, BISEXUAL

& TRANSGENDER

ANTHOLOGY

Edited by Brett Beemyn and Mickey Eliason

NEW YORK UNIVERSITY PRESS

New York and London

NEW YORK UNIVERSITY PRESS
New York and London
© 1996 by New York University

The editors gratefully acknowledge permission to reprint work
from the following sources:
Amber Ault, "Hegemonic Discourse in an Oppositional Commu-
nity: Lesbian Feminists and Bisexuality," *Critical Sociology* 20,
no. 3 (1994): 107–22.
Alison Bechdel, "Perils of a Midtown Dyke: A True and Caution-
ary Tale," *Dykes to Watch Out For* (Ithaca, NY: Firebrand Books,
1986), 10–11. Copyright © 1986 by Alison Bechdel.
Sherrie A. Inness and Michele E. Lloyd, "G.I. Joes in Barbie
Land: Recontextualizing Butch in Twentieth-Century Lesbian
Culture," *NWSA Journal* 7, no. 3 (1995). Copyright © 1995
NWSA Journal. Reprinted with the permission of Indiana
University Press.
Siobhan Somerville, "Scientific Racism and the Emergence of
the Homosexual Body," *Journal of the History of Sexuality* 5, no. 2
(October 1994): 243–66. Reprinted by permission of the University
of Chicago Press.

Library of Congress Cataloging-in-Publication Data
Queer studies : a lesbian, gay, bisexual, & transgender anthology /
edited by Brett Beemyn and Mickey Eliason.
p.   cm.
Includes bibliographical references and index.
ISBN 0-8147-1257-6 (cloth : alk. paper).—ISBN 0-8147-1258-4
(pbk. : alk. paper)
1. Homosexuality.   2. Bisexuality.   3. Transsexualism.
4. Sexual orientation.   5. Gays—Identity.
6. Lesbians—Identity.   7. Gender identity.
I. Beemyn, Brett, 1966–   II. Eliason, Mickey, 1953–
HQ76.25.Q383   1996
306.76—dc20   96-25709
                              CIP

New York University Press books are printed on acid-free paper,
and their binding materials are chosen for strength and durability.

Manufactured in the United States of America
10 9 8 7 6 5 4 3 2 1

Contents

Acknowledgments

The essays in this anthology represent expanded versions of papers presented at InQueery/InTheory/InDeed: The Sixth North American Lesbian, Gay, and Bisexual Studies Conference, which was held November 17–20, 1994 at the University of Iowa in Iowa City, Iowa. With over 130 panels, discussions, and workshops, and more than 400 presenters, InQueery is the largest queer studies conference convened so far.

This anthology would not have been possible without the conference, and the conference would not have been possible without the tremendous efforts of its steering committee. In addition to ourselves, the steering committee included Ilene Alexander, Meredith Alexander, Rusty Barceló, Bob Brooks, Thea Cooper, Peter Feng, Kevin Floyd, Lori Goetsch, Teresa Konechne, Kevin Kopelson, Theresa Lemire, Jeff Lubsen, Kim Marra, Geeta Patel, William Steven Saunders, Richard Shannon, Mona Shaw, and Kelly Willson.

We would also like to recognize the committee working to establish a sexuality studies program at the University of Iowa, which the two of us cochair. It was this committee which first began discussing the idea of creating a "multicultural" reader to cover areas of diversity typically ignored in past queer studies anthologies.

Introduction

Brett Beemyn and Mickey Eliason

As instructors of undergraduate courses in queer studies, we have continually been frustrated by the fact that, despite the recent queer publishing explosion, few texts in the field cover a broad range of topics around sexual and gender identities. Finding such works that offer more than token inclusions of people of color, bisexuals, and transgendered people, and are also accessible to undergraduate and non-academic readers, has been entirely futile. It is for these reasons that this anthology was born.

Most of the works in lesbian, gay, and bisexual studies or queer studies that have been published in the past few years are high-level theory books, texts focused upon specific disciplines or topics, or practical guides aimed primarily at a heterosexual audience or people just beginning to come out. While there is certainly a place and a need for all these works, the absence of general academic anthologies that are both accessible and inclusive is a glaring omission. For example, The *Lesbian and Gay Studies Reader*, the definitive-sounding anthology edited by Henry Abelove, Michèle Aina Barale, and David M. Halperin, includes many historically important essays, but, in our experience, a significant number are not accessible to undergraduate and non-academic readers. Moreover, as its title indicates, the collection does not include material addressing bisexual and transgender identities, despite the fact that these have been two of the most widely discussed topics in the field in recent years.[1] Similar weaknesses undermine the anthology which came out of the previous queer studies conference, the Fifth Annual Lesbian and Gay Studies Conference, sponsored by Rutgers and Princeton Universities in 1991. Just as the organizers at Rutgers and Princeton chose to remove the word "bisexual" from the title of the conference, their anthology, *Negotiating Lesbian and*

Gay Subjects, contains no essays on bisexuality, even though a number of excellent papers on bisexuality were presented at the conference.[2]

Texts in lesbian, gay, and bisexual studies that are grounded within specific academic disciplines have often been more inclusive of a wide range of sexual and gender identities and more accessible to a broad audience. Among the most significant works that have been published along these lines in the past few years are George Chauncey's *Gay New York: Gender, Urban Culture, and the Making of the Gay Male World, 1890–1940*; Elizabeth Lapovsky Kennedy and Madeline D. Davis's *Boots of Leather, Slippers of Gold: The History of a Lesbian Community*; Anthony R. D'Augelli and Charlotte J. Patterson's *Lesbian, Gay, and Bisexual Identities over the Lifespan: Psychological Perspectives*; William D. Rubenstein's *Lesbians, Gay Men, and the Law*; and Joseph Bristow and Angelia R. Wilson's *Activating Theory: Lesbian, Gay, Bisexual Politics*.[3] For overview classes, though, it is often difficult to adopt such texts because they provide a more detailed analysis than is generally necessary, and requiring more than a few of these books becomes costly for students.

The practical guides aimed largely at readers unfamiliar with lesbian, gay, and bisexual studies, such as Warren J. Blumenfeld's *Homophobia: How We All Pay the Price*, Michael Nava and Robert Dawidoff's *Created Equal: Why Gay Rights Matter to America*, Eric Marcus's *Is It a Choice? Answers to 300 of the Most Frequently Asked Questions about Gays and Lesbians*, and Marshall Kirk and Hunter Madsen's *After the Ball: How America Will Conquer Its Fear and Hatred of Gays in the 90's*, are limiting in other ways for undergraduate instructors in queer studies. Typically, they do not have the academic sophistication necessary for the college classroom and are often best suited for heterosexual audiences that are uninformed and not entirely supportive of queer rights. Some of these texts are also overly simplistic and stress assimilation of lesbians, gays, and bisexuals into straight communities, thereby putting the burden on queers, rather than forcing straight society to face its prejudices. Moreover, with the exception of Blumenfeld's anthology, these books do not adequately address issues of race, gender, transgender, and bisexuality.[4]

In putting together *Queer Studies: A Lesbian, Gay, Bisexual, and Transgender Anthology*, we have sought to fill some of these gaps within existing queer studies texts. We have selected essays which largely meet the following criteria:

- They present new, interesting material or bring new approaches/interpretations to existing material.
- They are not narrowly focused on a particular text (book, movie, etc.), but have wider implications and significances.
- They are inclusive in their approaches and analyses, incorporating discussions of race, gender, and/or sexual diversity where appropriate.
- They are accessible to undergraduates and people outside of the academy, yet put forward sophisticated, intriguing ideas.
- They are, of course, well argued and well written.

We particularly looked for essays that dealt with areas that have often been excluded, marginalized, or ignored by queer studies in the past: race, gender, transgender, bisexuality, and s/m. We also sought to include contributors who occupy different levels of the academy and who are from a wide variety of academic disciplines.

Based as it is upon the papers of the InQueery conference, this volume clearly cannot be exhaustive. But lesbian, gay, bisexual, and transgendered people are so diverse that no one anthology could ever hope to include all possible perspectives. Diversity is a strength of our communities that should be used to the benefit of the burgeoning field of queer studies. We feel that this book presents a wide range of ideas crucial to our progress as a political movement and as an academic discipline, and hope that other works will help rectify some of the omissions of this anthology and expand upon the concepts presented here.

Queer Studies is divided into two overlapping sections. The first focuses upon issues of identity. How do sexual identities form? What do they mean to individuals? How do sexual identities intersect with other identities such as race and gender? How is oppression due to sexual identity similar to and different from other forms of oppression? In what ways are transgender identities similar to and different from sexual identities?

The second section specifically addresses queer theory. What is queer theory? Where and how is it lacking? How does it inform political activism? How can we theorize aspects of sexual performances/behaviors, such as s/m or butch-femme relationships? How do our queer identities/bodies affect our personal lives, our workplaces, the depictions of us in popular culture, and social and political discourses? In other words, how do we as lesbian, gay, bisexual, and transgendered people theorize ourselves within society? Common themes that can be traced throughout these essays include a commitment to inclusivity, particularly the need for queer theory to be flexible enough to accommodate all people who identify as queer, and the recognition that the prejudices which are rampant in Western societies also permeate queer communities and theories.

NOTES

1. Henry Abelove, Michèle Aina Barale, and David M. Halperin, eds., The *Lesbian and Gay Studies Reader* (New York: Routledge, 1993). Examples of this interest include the frequent discussions about transgender and bisexuality on the queer studies listserve and the significant number of books being published in these areas. See Christopher James's essay in this volume for more on the growth of bi texts.

2. Monica Dorenkamp and Richard Henke, eds., *Negotiating Lesbian and Gay Subjects* (New York: Routledge, 1995). Among the papers that could have been included were Stacey Young's "Bisexual Theory and the Postmodern Dilemma," Rebecca Kaplan's "Compulsory Heterosexuality and the Bisexual Existence: Towards a Bisexual-Feminist Understanding of Heterosexism," and Paula Rust's "Neutralizing the Political Threat of the Marginal Woman: Lesbians' Beliefs about Bisexual Women."

3. George Chauncey, *Gay New York: Gender, Urban Culture, and the Making of the Gay Male World, 1890–1940* (New York: HarperCollins, 1994); Elizabeth Lapovsky Kennedy and Madeline D. Davis, *Boots of Leather, Slippers of Gold: The History of a Lesbian Community* (New York: Routledge, 1993); Anthony R. D'Augelli and Charlotte J. Patterson, eds., *Lesbian, Gay, and Bisexual Identities over the Lifespan: Psychological Perspectives* (New York: Oxford University Press, 1995); William D. Rubenstein, ed., *Lesbians, Gay Men, and the Law* (New York: New Press, 1993);

and Joseph Bristow and Angelia R. Wilson, eds., *Activating Theory: Lesbian, Gay, Bisexual Politics* (London: Lawrence and Wishart, 1993).

4. Warren J. Blumenfeld, ed., *Homophobia: How We All Pay the Price* (Boston: Beacon, 1992); Michael Nava and Robert Dawidoff, *Created Equal: Why Gay Rights Matter to America* (New York: St. Martin's, 1994); Eric Marcus, *Is It a Choice? Answers to 300 of the Most Frequently Asked Questions about Gays and Lesbians* (San Francisco: HarperSanFrancisco, 1993); and Marshall Kirk and Hunter Madsen, *After the Ball: How America Will Conquer Its Fear and Hatred of Gays in the 90's* (New York: Plume, 1990).

ISSUES OF IDENTITY

We have chosen to call this a queer studies anthology, even though some people who are attracted to others of the same sex remain opposed to the reclamation of the term "queer," believing that a word hurled at us for decades as an insult cannot be turned around so quickly and used in such a casual manner. The process of ascribing new, positive meanings to the word "queer," though, has to be seen within the context of the ever-changing terminology that same-sex sexual communities use to describe themselves. In general terms, we have moved from the "homosexuals" of the first half of the twentieth century to a small number of "homophiles" in the 1950s; from "gay liberation" in the early seventies to the lesbian and gay movements of the mid-seventies to mid-eighties; and from lesbian, gay, and bisexual organizing in the mid-eighties and early nineties to contemporary lesbian, gay, bisexual, and transgender or "queer" activism. These changes reflect the dynamic nature of both sexuality and the political organizing that has developed around it.

Obviously, no one term or phrase can satisfy everyone. We have chosen to use "queer" because it best characterizes our own personal beliefs, and it potentially leaves room for all people who are attracted to others of the same sex or whose bodies or sexual desires do not fit dominant standards of gender and/or sexuality. Moreover, most of the anthology's contributors use the term "queer," especially in reference to the particular brand of theorizing known as queer theory — a body of work which does not represent a specific kind of theory so much as it does a number of interdisciplinary texts which emphasize the constructedness of sexuality. The concept of "queer" also aptly character-izes our relationship to the academy. The study of same-sex sexual identities and behaviors is seen as out of the ordinary, unusual, odd, eccentric. "Queer" thus describes our position in regards to the mainstream: we don't quite fit in, no matter what labels or terminology we use. Therefore, while there are gaps, exclusions, and other problems within "queer" and "queer theory" — some of which are addressed by the authors in this anthology — we nevertheless see a great deal of potential in their usage.

The essays in this first section explore the concept of identity, which typically serves as the linchpin for social and political organizing in such areas as sexuality. But how stable are sexual identities? Are our organizations built on shaky ground, and does this matter? Identity politics (forming social or political groups on the basis of one or more shared personal characteristics) came under fire in the mid-1980s as a result of the rising prominence of postmodern theory and the growing recognition that lesbian and gay politics, as it had often been constituted, was not very inclusive of the wide range of queer-identified people. In exploring the conflict between postmodernism and identity-based theories, Steven Seidman notes:

> Positing a gay identity, no matter how it strains to be inclusive of difference, produces exclusions, represses difference, and normalizes being gay. Identity politics strains, as well, toward a narrow, liberal, interest-group politic aimed at assimilationism or spawns its opposite, a troubling ethnic-nationalist separatism. Poststructuralism is a kind of reverse or, if you wish, deconstructive logic; it dissolves any notion of a substantial unity in identity constructions leaving only rhetorics of identities, performances, and the free play of difference and possibility. Whereas identity politics offers a strong politics on a weak, exclusionary basis, poststructuralism offers a thin politics as it problematizes the very notion of a collective in whose name a movement acts.[1]

It is clear from much of the work in lesbian, gay, and bisexual studies that there are considerable conflicts between postmodern theory and identity-based politics, and that many of these conflicts stem from the latter's reliance upon dichotomies like assimilation-separation and similarity-difference. The whole notion of a unitary lesbian, gay, or bisexual identity rests on the assumption that people who share a sexual identity will also have similar attitudes, experiences, values, and politics. Moreover, identity-based politics erases or marginalizes areas of identity that are outside of its parameters; organizing around sexual identity, for example, often means that other aspects of identity, including race, gender, and class, are ignored or considered to be secondary issues.

The essays in this part problematize the idea of fixed sexual and gender identities, and thus challenge the basis for a unitary identity politics. Sherrie Inness and Michele Lloyd explore the singular identity of the butch lesbian by dissecting the butch/femme dyad and propose that the term "butch," though hard to define, has historically and culturally bound limits. Their essay raises many interesting questions about butch identity and desire, including: What does masculinity look like on a woman's body? How is butch desire expressed? What does it mean for a butch to desire another butch? Why must gender dualities like butch/femme define lesbian desire? Must opposites always attract?

Vernon Rosario addresses the complexities of gender and sexuality as exemplified through transsexual identities. He begins with the fascinating story of a young biological woman hospitalized on a psychiatric ward who wanted to be a gay man, a female-to-gay-male transsexual, and then examines the medical and psychological literature's "treatment" of transsexualism. Rosario finds that many of those who were described as "sexual inverts," and who were later identified as "homosexuals" by lesbian and gay academics and activists, may actually have been transgendered. Transsexualism, like bisexuality, has largely been overlooked, misinterpreted, vilified, or actively avoided by lesbian and gay scholars because of the challenges that it poses to gender-based sexual identities. People who may have been transsexuals have often been forced into lesbian or gay molds by theorists desperate to make a point.

Amanda Udis-Kessler and Paula Rust explore bisexual identities from two different perspectives. Udis-Kessler provides a history of the bisexual rights movement, outlining how bisexuals, particularly bisexual women, formed identities based upon their experiences in lesbian or lesbian and gay organizations. A common experience for many bisexual women was having to hide their sexuality from lesbian feminists out of fear of rejection. But they began to "come out" in the 1980s to challenge the exclusion and marginalization of bisexuals in lesbian and gay groups and to form political organizations of their own.

Rust, however, cautions that if the bisexual movement seeks to institute bisexuality as a third sexual identity category, it will eliminate bisexuality's radical edge. She begins her essay by stating that the linear models of sexual identity formation proposed by lesbian and gay scholars are too rigid, focus too much attention on individual psychological factors, and are not able to accommodate the dynamic and fluid nature of sexuality. Rust conceptualizes identity instead as "a description of the location of the self in relation to other individuals, groups, and institutions." Identities are thus theorized as dependent on the "sexual landscape." Rust explains that bisexuality is perceived as a threat to monosexuals (lesbians, gays, and heterosexuals) because it challenges the gender-based system of sexual identity, as well as the hetero/homo divide — an idea which is echoed by many of the contributors to this book. Queer theorists have been quick to reject some tenets of Western philosophies that involve dualistic thinking, including the dichotomy of sexual identity. However, many queer theories are still based on a gender duality, since the very definitions of lesbian and gay hinge on gender difference and the presence of two, and only two, genders. For this reason, bisexuality, like transsexualism, may provide a key for understanding sexual and gender identities in radically new ways.

Patricia Duncan interviews "s/m dykes," most of whom are women of color, and explores how they situate themselves in relation to communities that are based around race, sexual identity, and/or sexual practices. Duncan demonstrates that "s/m is a site of *conflict*, both literally and figuratively, for many lesbians who choose to practice it and identify themselves as members of various s/m communities." While critics stigmatize s/m as a "deviant" and "oppressive" sexual practice, the fact that it involves the acting and working out of a conflict or difference for its practitioners often "enables the resolution of seemingly oppositional differences and the renegotiation of identity."

JeeYeun Lee explores how the use of butch/femme styles by bisexual women and lesbians of color is complicated by racial and cultural differences. Specifically, she analyzes the experiences of Asian and Asian American women, stressing that "Asian" is not a monolithic category, but one that represents multiple cultures and what she calls a "coalitional identity." As part of her argument, Lee points to the position in which she is often placed by essentialism and racism:

> I also realize that my use of "we" [to refer to Asian and Asian American lesbians and bisexual women] has the danger of being appropriated by others to view me as a native informant and tokenize me as speaking for a constituency, especially when there is so little on this topic in the legitimated world of research and writing.

Her cautions are appropriate for all of queer theory. Identities are complex and experienced in a variety of different ways, depending, for example, on one's age, gender, sexuality, national origin, class status, and personal history. No individual account should be privileged as representing the views of a diverse group of people.

Gregory Conerly examines the question that is often asked of African American LesBiGays, "are you black first, or are you queer?" Like Lee, he points to some of the weaknesses inherent in attempting to define queer as an issue of sexual identity alone. His discussion of texts by and about African American lesbians and gays also highlights the dangers of creating what Audre Lorde has referred to as a "hierarchy of oppressions" around identities, especially when identities like African American and queer are not uniform or stable.[2]

Whether we accept sexual and gender identities as biologically based essences, social constructions, or some combination thereof, the need for political organizing is still paramount. Warren Blumenfeld ends this part by comparing the negative portrayals of Jews throughout history to the current scapegoating of LesBiGayTrans people by right-wing organizations. He shows the clear connections between different forms of oppression and how dominant groups use stereotypes to legitimate the denial of civil rights to oppressed groups and to keep them from unifying. At a time when open, well-organized hate campaigns threaten the lives of queer people every day, it is imperative that LesBiGayTrans people learn from such histories, reach out to form coalitions like the one that Blumenfeld points to, and create theories of sexual and gender identities that serve practical functions.

NOTES

1. Steven Seidman, "Identity and Politics in a 'Postmodern' Gay Culture: Some Historical and Conceptual Notes," *Fear of a Queer Planet: Queer Politics and Social Theory*, ed. Michael Warner (Minneapolis: University of Minnesota Press, 1993), 135.

2. Audre Lorde, "There Is No Hierarchy of Oppressions," *Interracial Books for Children Bulletin* (1983): 9.

chapter 1

G.I. Joes in Barbie Land:

Recontextualizing Butch in

Twentieth-Century

Lesbian Culture

Sherrie A. Inness and
Michele E. Lloyd

High school years are much harder on butches [than on femmes]. Femmes passed as straight, even to themselves. Butches can't. We stick out like G.I. Joes in Barbie Land.

Straight people call me sir and faggots cruise me, but other butches say: "Aww, you're not so butch." That's cuz I don't go for femmes like I'm supposed to. This confuses people. When I'm out with a femme buddy, everyone assumes we're on a date; when I'm out with a butch date, everyone assumes we're buddies. That's if I can even *get* a date, which isn't easy for someone like me. . . .

To the femmes I'm immediately suspect. They figure if I'm butch and I don't go for femmes, it's because I secretly hate femmes, because I secretly hate women, because I secretly hate myself. Either that or I'm simply a closet femme who's trying to weasel in on the already slim supply of eligible butches. Femmes, on the other hand, are allowed to go for butches — that's normal.

To the butches, I'm the ultimate threat. If you're butch, you gotta have a femme under your arm at all times, that's how you know you're butch. So, when I hit on another butch, it naturally throws her off balance.

The above two quotations, from Jeanne Cordova[1] and Trish Thomas,[2] respectively, point out a number of reasons why an exploration of butchness might be fruitful. Cordova and Thomas's words leave us with more questions than answers about being butch: Why might a butch have conflicting notions of what it means to be butch? Why is the facile assumption made that butches must be attracted to femmes? Can a butch be defined without reference to her "natural" counterpart, the femme? In this essay, we seek to address these and related questions because we believe that butchness has been inadequately described, explained, and theorized by contemporary scholarship.

Butch is a concept that has long permeated lesbian culture: nearly every lesbian, regardless of her self-identification, is at least familiar with the term.[3] JoAnn Loulan writes of her experiences giving talks about lesbian sexuality, "I ask the following: 'How many women here who have been lesbians for longer than two weeks, have *not* ever rated yourself or been rated by others on a butch/femme scale?' At the most, five percent of the audience raises their hands."[4] Current scholarship tends to focus on the butch/femme dyad, usually either emphasizing its historical significance for the lesbian community, or decrying it as an outdated imitation of patriarchal gender roles that fails to embody feminist values.[5] Even within these and other related debates, however, the term "butch" remains ill-defined. Can anyone be a butch just by saying so, or are there certain criteria a woman must meet before she can be called butch? Does a woman need to self-identify as butch in order to be butch? Is a lesbian butch because of how she looks, who she is attracted to, who is attracted to her, or because of what she does in bed? All of these questions have been answered in conflicting fashions by various writers, leading to numerous dissenting concepts of what constitutes butchness. We believe that by examining the context in which butch and butch/femme occur today, and by analyzing current scholarship on the topic, we can unravel some of this confusion.

Our agenda for this essay is to clarify and ultimately to radically reorient our conceptions of butch. We do this by examining the common definitions of butch and showing that the term "butch," despite its flexibility, is not a word with limitless applicability. In this process of redefining the butch, we explode the myth that the butch is characterized by the object of her desire. Examining two common ways that the butch is perceived — as the aggressor in sexual encounters and as desiring femmes — we demonstrate that neither is a fundamental component of butchness. Most importantly, we show that butch is a singular identity position, not a coupled one — that butches should be viewed independently from any possible relationship to femmes. We believe that butch identity and butch/butch relationships have been largely ignored by scholars in favor of concentrating on the more culturally predominant butch/femme relations.[6] Our premise is that "butch" and "femme" are not always interdependent terms, each requiring the other. Rather, butch and femme are simply two expressions of gender that can, but do not necessarily, intersect. We shall, however, need to focus on butch/femme at times, since much of the available material only discusses butch in this manner.[7] Our subject position as butches, and as butches who are primarily attracted to other butches, provides us with experiential knowledge that informs our approach to gender theory: our interest in this topic is derived from an awareness of the gaps in current theory that deny and invalidate our personal experience, as well as the experiences of other butches like us.

What Is a Butch?

A butch is someone no one understands and no one can explain.
— Mike, the main character in Jay Rayn's novel *Butch* (1991)[8]

In heterosexual culture, the term "butch" connotes manliness, but is not often used as a descriptive term, as in, "Jimmy's really butch," nor is it used in reference to women, except in a derogatory sense. But "butch" is an important word in the gay male lexicon, with multiple meanings. Employed as a campy adjective, "Oh, isn't Brian looking *butch* today!," the word has a light-hearted tone; on the other end of the spectrum are the gay men who take their butch identity very seriously, laboring endlessly to achieve and maintain the most masculine physique, bearing, and overall presence. How "butch" is used by male homosexuals deserves a complete article; unfortunately, this issue is beyond the spectrum of the current work.

Among lesbians, "butch" is used to describe a vast realm of attitudes, behaviors, appearances, and actions. For instance, Cherríe Moraga writes, "To be butch, to me, is not to be a woman. The classic extreme-butch stereotype is the woman who sexually refuses another woman to touch her."[9] Another woman states, "Part of identifying as butch stems from a desire to defend, protect, and defy the traditional feminine stereotype."[10] For De Clarke, "being butch is an ethical choice, a choice of resistance. . . . It's more than a preference in clothes, jewelry, shoes; more than a haircut. Butches have a cultural identity that embraces but exceeds mere costumes."[11] These three descriptions show the wide range of ideas that women have about what constitutes butchness. Some women consider being butch to be primarily a matter of one's sexual behavior and, in particular, one's desire to be the dominant individual in sexual activities. Others see butch primarily as a means of resisting the cultural norms for feminine behavior. Given the large number of ways in which a lesbian can appear butch, it is no wonder that lesbians are confused about what exactly makes a butch a butch; as Susan Ardill and Sue O'Sullivan comment,

> The absence of any precise or agreed definition about what butch and femme are produces endless heated arguments among lesbians. One straightforward and fairly widespread view is that they are merely methods of dress and behaviour — roles, in other words. Another view is that butch/femme are metaphors for subject/object in lesbian relationships: that talking about ourselves or others as butch/femme essentially describes how we negotiate desire. . . . [T]hese two words (and their equivalents in other cultures and contexts) have become dreadfully overburdened. They have to be infinitely elastic terms.[12]

Yet, despite the fact that few lesbians can agree on the precise definition of butch, most do seem to agree about who is or is not butch,[13] leading to the conclusion that there must be some specific, observable characteristics that a lesbian must possess before she will be labeled butch. In this part, we elucidate the fundamental components of the butch image today, and show that there are very real limits placed on butch identity, limits that make it impossible for anyone who so desires to claim to be a butch.[14]

The term "butch" has historic specificity: the meaning of butch in the 1950s is not the same as its meaning in the 1990s. To understand butch today, it must be viewed in its proper context. For much of the twentieth century, lesbians, as well as non-lesbians, have perceived the butch largely, although not entirely, in relationship to the femme, the butch's assumed "natural" partner. In the 1940s and 1950s, participation in the butch/femme lifestyle was de rigueur for many lesbians, especially working-class and young women, but such roles fell out of favor in the 1960s and 1970s when many lesbian feminists condemned them as replicating patriarchal relationships. Butch was seen as male-identified, and femme was seen as selling out to the traditional feminine stereotypes of women. Androgyny replaced butch/femme as the cultural imperative in the post-Stonewall lesbian feminist movement. Ironically, many aspects of this androgynous ideal were indistinguishable from butchness: wearing comfortable, non-constrictive clothing such as flannel shirts, jeans, and hiking boots; sporting short, boyish haircuts; and acquiring skills in male-dominated trades such as carpentry and auto repair. While butch/femme roles never completely died out, particularly in rural and working-class communities, there was a resurgence among urban upper- and middle-class lesbians in the 1980s that took an altered form from the butch/femme of the 1950s. In those intervening years, "butch" and "femme" had become broader and more fluid in meaning. More butch styles, such as clothing inspired by the punk movement, were being created and adopted. A sense of the theatrical inspired some women to express their butch or femme images in glamorous and highly visible ways. Instead of being the standard of lesbian identity, butch and femme were two options for the expression of lesbian gender. Butch and femme also became a way for lesbians to challenge the lesbian feminist status quo. "Many young women who claimed butch or femme identities in the 1980s saw themselves as taboo-smashers and iconoclasts," writes Lillian Faderman.[15]

To some women familiar with the butch/femme culture of the 1950s, these neo-butches and -femmes appear to be merely playing with roles that were once an integral part of identifying as a lesbian. Faderman writes that "for most lesbians the roles are not the life-or-death identity they often were in the 1950s, but rather an enjoyable erotic statement and an escape from the boring 'vanilla sex' that they associated with lesbian-feminism."[16] The apparent lack of seriousness attached to these roles leads some scholars, such as Faderman, to argue that butch and femme have ceased to be terms with discrete meaning: "Butch and femme today can mean whatever one wants those terms to mean. A woman is a butch or a femme simply because she says she is."[17] Although there is little doubt that butch and femme roles have become far more flexible today than they were forty years ago, we question Faderman's belief that butch and femme today are entirely subjective terms. We also wonder whether it is accurate to say that the contemporary butch is merely making an "enjoyable erotic statement," since butches still suffer harassment and abuse for stepping outside of the traditional feminine role. Although butches certainly do not comprise the entire lesbian community, they are frequently the ones who bear the brunt of homophobic attacks against lesbians. As Judith Butler notes in *Gender Trouble: Feminism and the Subversion of Identity*, "we regularly punish those who fail to do their gender right."[18] This punishment takes many forms, ranging from overt violence to covert discrimination. All butches endure such castigation — even if a particular butch has not fallen victim to physical violence, she has almost certainly experienced verbal harassment. That butches continue to exist in such an inhospitable environment is a testament to the seriousness of butch identity.

Since the butch is such a prominent figure in lesbian culture, we object to claims that the term has become "infinitely elastic" or "totally subjective" — after all, an infinitely elastic term has no meaning at all. Though definitions of butch may appear to be hopelessly divergent, our research revealed patterns in how butches are usually described. We studied a broad range of texts, including first-person accounts, fictional works, theoretical analyses by writers such as Judith Butler, Eve Kosofsky Sedgwick, Sue-Ellen Case, and Judith Roof, and works of historians such as Lillian Faderman, Joan Nestle, Madeline Davis, and Elizabeth Lapovsky Kennedy, and found that definitions of the butch tended to fall into some configuration of the following four categories: she is a masculine woman; she is like a man; she adopts an active sexual role; and/or she desires femmes. For instance, one of the more complex configurations of these categories can be seen in some accounts of the 1950s bar culture: a butch had to be masculine, had to like femmes, and had to be the "top" in her sexual encounters.[19] Yet must a lesbian fall into all of these categories to qualify as a butch? Some of these categories have been displaced by recent changes in cultural and theoretical conceptions of sex, sexuality, and gender. By examining the meanings and implications of these four categories, we hope to distill some core elements of butchness. The fourth category, we believe, deserves special attention, since it is this relationship between butches and femmes, and how that relationship either does or does not constitute butch identity, that is radically under-theorized and misunderstood today.

"I Just Can't Relate to That Wanting to Look like a Man Trip"[20]

This first category — masculinity — is generally accepted to be an essential foundational element of butchness. A woman who usually expresses herself in a traditionally feminine style is rarely, if ever, thought of as a butch by other lesbians. When one of JoAnn Loulan's audiences declares a lesbian to be butch, it is because this lesbian appears visibly masculine in her dress, physical appearance, or carriage. According to Gayle Rubin, butch is "a category of lesbian gender that is constituted through the deployment and manipulation of masculine gender codes and symbols." She writes: "Butch is the lesbian vernacular term for women who are more comfortable with masculine gender codes, styles, or identities than with feminine ones. The term encompasses individuals with a broad range of investments in 'masculinity.'"[21] Lesbians have associated masculinity with butchness throughout much of the twentieth century, and masculinity continues to be crucial to a butch's self-presentation today. Emphasizing the butch's masculinity over other factors that are typically needed to define butches permits the flexibility needed to account for the "nineties butch," without suffering from Ardill and O'Sullivan's "infinite elasticity," since many lesbians are more comfortable with feminine appearances and attributes than with masculine ones.

But "masculinity" is itself an ill-defined term, one that describes a wide variety of appearances, behaviors, and attitudes that are commonly considered to be expressive of maleness:

> Forms of masculinity are molded by the experiences and expectations of class, race, ethnicity, religion, occupation, age, subculture, and individual personality. National, racial, and ethnic groups differ widely in what constitutes masculinity, and each has its own system for communicating and conferring "manhood." [22]

Various historical periods have different definitions of masculinity, as well. Some traits that are identified as masculine today by the culture at large include physical strength, daring and boldness, emotional non-expressiveness, and straightforwardness. Also, masculinity is always defined in opposition to femininity and femaleness. "Masculine" attire does not include dresses, purses, or pantyhose, and is typically lacking in frills and bright colors. "Masculine" jobs are often ones that require some "masculine" trait, such as physical strength or the ability to think logically, or are occupations that confer "masculine" privilege such as power or leadership. Examples include being a physical laborer, a tradesperson, a stockbroker, a doctor, or a CEO.

Masculinity, in short, is a set of signs that connote maleness within a given cultural moment, and masculinity is as fluid and changing as the society defining it. No one universal presentation of masculinity exists in our contemporary culture. A corporate lawyer presents a different image of masculinity from a rodeo bronco rider. A football player presents a different image of masculinity from President Clinton. An English professor presents a different style of masculinity from a punk rocker. Nor will all these men agree about the masculinity of the others. Class, race, ethnicity, and geography all shape how masculinity is perceived. The rodeo rider, who rides bulls and broncos for a living, may think of the corporate lawyer, with his endless paper pushing and swank office, as a sissy. The lawyer, however, with his wealth, power, and prestige, might consider the bronco rider to be an uneducated hick.

A butch, as we have noted above, is a lesbian who adopts masculine identifiers. Clearly, this fact raises many interesting questions. What does masculinity mean on a female body? How much masculinity does a lesbian need to display in order to be considered butch? How does lesbian masculinity function among lesbians?

Not surprisingly, butches draw much of their style from the culture around them. Clothing is one of the most obvious and notable ways that a butch displays masculinity. Leather jackets, "men's" shirts and suit jackets, pants, ties, and shoes are all part of the butch iconography. But the role of butch clothing is complex. We can better understand the significance of clothing for butches in light of Dick Hebdige's study of punk subcultures in England, in which he refers to the use of mundane objects to form a distinctive punk style:

> On the one hand, they warn the "straight" world in advance of a sinister presence — the presence of difference — and draw down upon themselves vague suspicions, uneasy laughter, "white and dumb rages." On the other hand, for those who erect them into icons, who

use them as words or as curses, these objects become signs of forbidden identity, sources of value.[23]

As do the English punks, butch lesbians use clothing as a way to indicate membership in a group; butches are easily recognized as lesbians because both lesbian and heterosexual cultures typically interpret masculine appearance and clothing, particularly when combined with few feminine signifiers such as lipstick, make-up, long hair, and jewelry, as indicators of homosexuality. Being butch is thus a way to announce to the world, "I am a lesbian." Since lesbians are, for the most part, invisible as a group, the ability to recognize, and be recognized by, other members of the lesbian subculture is vital to creating a sense of belonging, not only for the butch, but also for all lesbians who see and recognize her.

What makes a butch a butch and not just a woman in "men's" clothing is a combination of factors, including her self-presentation and her self-perception. Lesbians identify many different subcategories of butch, all of which are related to masculinity to some degree. The ubiquitousness of the butch/femme scale in lesbian culture is an example of this awareness of diversity, as it allows for several "levels" of butchness. Some extremely masculine women, such as the proverbial "diesel dyke,"[24] are easily labeled butch. The "soft butch" may look less macho than the diesel dyke, but her personal style leans toward the masculine, and she dresses and wears her hair in ways that are coded as butch.[25] An androgynous woman, such as k.d. lang, is trickier to categorize based on appearance alone, but this does not imply that lang cannot be butch, since butchness is dependent on a variety of masculine signifiers.

Being butch is more complicated than merely slipping on a "man's" suit and tie; it also entails adopting behavioral patterns that are typically perceived as non-feminine. The butch's carriage and demeanor are as much a part of her masculine image as her clothing. Dressed in a skirt and high heels, the butch might look ill at ease. She may even strike the observer as somehow "wrong" because her lack of familiarity with the physical bearing that is typically associated with such attire makes her performance of femininity appear awkward. When dressed in a tuxedo or "men's" jeans and a white T-shirt, however, she frequently looks at ease and "natural." The most famous literary example of a butch's masculine image is found in *The Well of Loneliness* (1928). Although she certainly does not represent all butches, Radclyffe Hall's heroine, Stephen, is one idealized image of how a butch should appear: "[Her] figure was handsome in a flat, broad-shouldered and slim flanked fashion; and her movements were purposeful, having fine poise, she moved with the easy assurance of the athlete." Her face is handsome, but there is "something about it that went ill with the hats on which [her mother] insisted — large hats trimmed with ribbons or roses or daisies, and supposed to be softening to the features."[26] Hall's description of Stephen highlights a key component of what distinguishes a butch: the butch is *comfortable* with masculine identifiers, and most likely uncomfortable with feminine ones. She feels attractive and sexual in her pants and boots, and silly in lingerie. Her preferred clothing reflects her perception of herself.

Yet we must also account for the variations that occur in an individual's life. A woman who considers herself butch because she prefers and is most comfortable presenting a masculine appearance may be forced by social and economic necessity to wear a skirt, hose, and pumps to work. Is she a "real" butch? Is a woman who presents a feminine appearance, but who has masculine attitudes and behaviors, a butch? What about the otherwise masculine woman who cries easily and is afraid of bugs? Rubin notes that

> there are at least as many ways to be butch as there are ways for men to be masculine; actually, there are more ways to be butch, because when women appropriate masculine styles the element of travesty produces new significance and meaning. Butches adopt and transmute the many available codes of masculinity.[27]

To further complicate matters, each lesbian is exposed to different ideas, based on a number of cultural variables, about what it means to be butch. The white Harvard graduate might have a different way of showing her butchness than does the Chicano working-class lesbian living in Central Los Angeles, although both might be influenced by similar ideologies about what constitutes a butch. Still, the questions remain: Is there some minimum of masculinity required to be a butch? Which combinations of traits distinguish the butch from the femme who can fix cars? How do we tell the difference between the androgyne and the butch, or explain why the masculine straight woman is not a butch?

Obviously, there are no clear-cut answers to these questions, but there are several factors that help to distinguish the butch. First, it is apparent, after discussing the butch's masculine clothing, image, and attitude, that the butch must repeatedly present/create herself as butch in order to be butch. To borrow Judith Butler's words, "Gender is the repeated stylization of the body, a set of repeated acts within a highly rigid regulatory frame that congeal over time to produce the appearance of substance, of a natural sort of being."[28] Although Butler is speaking primarily about heterosexuals, her words are also applicable to describe the way gender congeals into certain forms for butches and for other non-heterosexual groups. If we apply Butler's definition, butchness is a repeated production of the body's image following certain cultural conventions about what it means to be butch. We concur with Butler that butchness, like any other display of gender, is constituted by regular performance; the butch's butchness is dependent on her adopting various masculine signifiers that identify her as "butch," both to herself and to other lesbians, and it is the repetition of this display that distinguishes the butch from the lesbian (or heterosexual woman) who wears a tuxedo to a party one Saturday night. Second, by claiming masculine identifiers for her own use, the butch sets herself apart from the "average" heterosexual woman by failing to present herself as traditionally feminine in order to appeal to the male gaze. While no woman has control over how a man will look at her, a woman whose appearance is designed to gain the sexual attention of men is not butch, even if she's tough, or has a masculine occupation. Under this view, the heroine of *La Femme Nikita* (1990), an assassin, would not qualify as a butch. Nor would the models crowding the pages of *Vogue, Elle, Glamour,* and other fashion magazines, even when they are wearing "men's" clothing.

Such an approach would seem to rule out the possibility of a heterosexual woman being butch. But what about a figure such as Lieutenant Ripley of the *Alien* films (1979,

1986, and 1987)? She's tough, she's in control, and she's wearing a uniform just like the men are. But because she is a heterosexual, she cannot be called a butch. As Alisa Solomon notes, butches are

> dykes with such objects or attributes as motorcycles, wingtips, money, pronounced biceps, extreme chivalry. Straight women with such objects or attributes are just straight women with motorcycles, cummerbunds, biceps, etcetera. The difference is audience. Butches present their butchness for women. . . . For [the butch], they are not only attributes, but signs.[29]

Earlier, we noted the significance of butch clothing, discussing how attire makes the butch visible to other lesbians, thus helping to engender a sense of community. For butch to exist as a lesbian gender category, its audience must recognize and understand the signs of butchness — out of context, butch has no meaning. This is why heterosexual women, no matter how butch they might act or appear, cannot be butch. Were Ripley to say to her shipmates, "I'm a butch," they likely wouldn't know what she was talking about, since butch is a concept and an identity that has cultural relevance to lesbians, but rarely to heterosexuals. So while Ripley looks butch, and acts butch, Ripley is not a butch.

Still, because the masculine heterosexual woman shares with the butch the rejection of feminine gender roles, she undoubtedly suffers some of the same harassment as does the butch. After all, when a woman adopts a masculine identity, she challenges the association between masculinity and maleness. A female body with masculine carriage and masculine clothing confounds the meanings of terms like "masculinity," "woman," and "male." In discussing the butch, Butler argues in *Gender Trouble*:

> Within lesbian contexts, the "identification" with masculinity that appears as butch identity is not a simple assimilation of lesbianism back into the terms of heterosexuality. As one lesbian femme explained, she likes her boys to be girls, meaning that "being a girl" contextualizes and resignifies "masculinity" in a butch identity. As a result, that masculinity, if that it can be called, is always brought into relief against a culturally intelligible "female body."[30]

As Butler points out, within the dominant conception of gender, the butch makes no sense: her female body ultimately transforms masculinity in a way that makes it non-intelligible to heterosexual society. To the "straight mind," as Monique Wittig calls it, the butch's masculinity comes as a shock. She does not conform to social expectations of what constitutes womanhood, thus throwing into question basic assumptions about people and their place in the world. Given this, we would expect the reaction of straight society to all female masculinity, whether the perpetrator is heterosexual, bisexual, or homosexual, to be hostile. However, this is not the case. Mary Laner and Roy Laner studied which traits of a lesbian were most negatively perceived by a heterosexual audience. Examining people's responses to "hyperfeminine" women, "average feminine" women, and "hypofeminine" women, Laner and Laner found that heterosexual feminine women were the most liked group and were frequently described by such adjectives as normal, agreeable, and nice.[31] The least liked group of women were hypofeminine homosexual women, who were categorized by such words as unappealing, disagreeable, and hostile.[32] The authors concluded:

> Women, it seems, may be either excessively or typically feminine and yet be liked, or at least not disliked, by the majority. Departures toward the masculine end of the continuum of gender-related appearance, interests, or activities are disliked by the heterosexual majority when, and only when, the woman is thought to be a lesbian.[33]

Theorist Judith Roof provides a lucid explanation of this relationship between lesbianism, masculinity, and heterosexual hatred:

> Perceiving lesbians as masculine reveals the threat to masculine supremacy and to a heterosexual system lesbians potentially pose. The representation of the lesbian as masculine is thus two-edged: a put-down, it also encapsulates the very instability of gender prerogatives that undermines heterosexuality. For this reason, attributions of masculinity to lesbians are often expression[s] of anger and anxiety about a de-centering of phallic privilege.[34]

Roof's words are particularly applicable to the butch, the embodiment of this stereotype, and the anxiety that Roof describes is the root of the antipathy expressed by heterosexual society toward the butch. The butch's appearance announces that she does not belong or wish to belong in a society that expects or demands femininity in women, and this upsets the status quo and subverts gender norms. Further, by adopting a conspicuously masculine image, the butch also rejects the role of woman-as-commodity, to be exchanged and bartered by men. As Alisa Solomon explains, the butch refuses "to play a part in the heterosexist binary."[35] She fails to adopt the feminine appearance and behavior (such as flirting with men) that identifies her sexual availability to men. In our society, femininity is frequently "expressed through modes of dress, movement, speech, and action which communicate weakness, dependency, [and] ineffectualness."[36] The butch rejects this vision of womanhood, and in doing so, becomes an outcast in a predominantly heterosexual society.

The Laner study only reflects what most butches recognize from daily experience: the opprobrium of heterosexuals is more likely to be directed at butches than at femmes or lesbians who could be defined as "averagely feminine." Our own experiences of having a passerby sneer, "What are you, a girl or a boy?"; being physically assaulted on the street before a group of bystanders who ignored our plight; having a car full of men, all screaming, "dykes," try to run us over; and numerous other incidents of abuse have shown us firsthand how butches are singled out for harassment because their masculine presentation both challenges feminine gender stereotypes and makes them easily identifiable as lesbians. These encounters show some of the methods, both implicitly and explicitly coercive, by which the dominant society seeks to maintain its version of reality. The fact that she is perceived as such a threat demonstrates that the butch is engaged, however unwittingly, in a radical critique of that reality. Thus butch is more than just a style, it is a political statement.

The Female Man

At first, the second category of the female man[37] — that the butch is like a man or wants to be a man — seems to be little different from category one. However, the two categories are actually quite distinct, since masculinity does not necessarily entail a desire to be a man. The stereotypical perception of a butch as being "like a man," a widely held view that is not limited to the dominant heterosexual culture, arises from her adoption of masculine signifiers. This perception is a manifestation of the larger cultural discourse that defines "woman" as a conflation of "female" and "feminine," and that assumes "woman" and "man" are exclusive opposites.[38] The butch's failure to follow prescribed gender norms means that she is disqualified from the category "woman," just as for Monique Wittig, in her essay "One Is Not Born a Woman" (1980), the lesbian is not a woman because, in refusing heterosexuality, she denies the binary system that defines "woman."[39] Hence, in the dominant heterosexual reality, the butch — a not-woman — must be like a man, though she cannot *be* a man because she does not possess the correct anatomy. As Jacqueline N. Zita points out, in writing about why males cannot be lesbians, "This body is not only a thing in the world, subject to physical gravity, but a thing that carries its own historical gravity, and this collected weight bears down on the 'sexedness' of the body and the possibilities of experience."[40] Applied to the butch, Zita's words suggest that, by virtue of her female body, the butch will have different life experiences and expectations from a man's. For example, a man does not experience the social pressure to be feminine that a butch does. Men are not worried about being raped the way women, even butches, are. As women, butches are still often considered less intelligent and capable than their male co-workers. In sum, butches are raised to be women, are treated like women, and suffer the stigma of not looking and acting the way women are expected to. All of these factors and more shape butches in ways that are radically different from the experiences that constitute men.

While heterosexual society sees the butch as "play-acting" the role of man, and considers her lack of physical maleness to be a failure, in actuality the butch's transgressive behavior exposes the artificiality of social constructs about sex and gender. Thus we can reinterpret a claim such as Moraga's that "a butch is not a woman" as an extrapolation from Simone de Beauvoir's observation that "woman is made, not born"; for Moraga, the butch, while female, is constituted differently from a woman. It could be said that the butch is neither man nor woman, since she fails to fit into society's conventions about how men and women should look and act. We do not wish to suggest, however, that the butch is born "butch"; while there is always the possibility that biological factors may have an influence on her development, the butch is very much constructed through her interactions with other lesbians.

Even so, the butch is raised and lives within a largely heterosexual society, and cannot help but be affected by it. Not only is she inundated with images of masculine males and feminine females — and a cultural obsession with maintaining this congruence — but the butch may occasionally, or even frequently, be mistaken for a man. Even an act as commonplace as going to a public rest room can be a difficult experience for the butch, one that is memorialized in many works of lesbian literature, such as Judy

FIGURE 1. © 1989 by Alison Bechdel

Grahn's poem "Edward the Dyke."[41] Edward's trouble, as she explains, is "chiefly concerning restrooms," such as the day when three middle-aged housewives mistake her for a man invading a department store's powder room. In Lee Lynch's novel, *Toothpick House* (1983), the butch heroine, Annie Heaphy, is sharply admonished by another woman, "This is a ladies' room, sir."[42] The butch, as a result of being frequently mistaken for a man, comes to feel defensive about her right to enter this "women's" space, where sex/gender solidarity is supposedly openly expressed, because though she has the correct anatomy required for entrance, she fails to conform to the social conventions for decorating that anatomy. As lesbian cartoonist Alison Bechdel points out, the butch can become confused about her own sex as a result of constant social misapprehensions (see Figure 1).[43] The experience Bechdel describes is one with which any butch lesbian can empathize.

From these examples of the butch and the bathroom, it becomes clear that a butch is affected by how society views the image that she projects. A discussion of Judith Roof's analysis of how lesbian identity is influenced by cultural configurations can help us to understand better how butch identity is constructed in a similar fashion. Roof writes:

> The relation of [the] cultural imaginary to individual women is complex, as women internalize imaginary configurations while at the same time producing images that confirm the configurations. Configurations help define the lesbian and help the woman identify herself as a lesbian, though like other kinds of stereotype, they never quite succeed in thoroughly containing her. Depending on cultural variables such as class, education, age, race, ethnic group, geographical location, historical context, and even accidents such as whom they know when, women internalize or accept aspects of these configurations.[44]

It is impossible to imagine the butch constructing her image in a vacuum. She, like any other lesbian, constantly discovers that her butchness is shaped and altered by how both lesbian and heterosexual societies perceive her. Some butches internalize the message that lesbians want to be men, and so, for them, being butch is about being like a man. Yet not all lesbians are so profoundly affected by stereotypes of lesbians and butches. For them, the myth of butch-as-man fails to explain fully their own experiences and is a cultural misapprehension. Even so, commonly being mistaken for a man because of her masculinity will likely affect the butch's self-perception to some degree.

The Butch on Top

The third category — the butch as sexual doer who receives her pleasure from giving pleasure to her partner — must be explored if we are going to unlink butch from its connection to desire, a necessary step in altering the perception that butch is only half of a coupled identity. One of the common ways that the butch is defined is by her supposed role as the active agent in sexual encounters, exemplified in Moraga's discussion about the extreme stereotype of the butch, also known as the stone butch. In the 1950s and 1960s, being the active sexual partner was often considered one of the defining characteristics of butchness — a butch who "rolled over" in bed might be called a femme by her peers and suffer a loss in status; the stone butch was the epitome of the 1950s butch, a figure who "became a publicly discussed model for appropriate sexual behavior, and it was a standard that young butches felt they had to achieve to be a 'real' or 'true' butch."[45]

But the stone butch is no longer the exemplar of butchness, nor are there the same kind of cultural sanctions against butches who wish to be the recipients of sexual attention. Personal ads in almost any big city gay newspaper reveal numerous butch "bottoms" (and femme "tops") seeking partners. For these lesbians, the fact that their preferred sexual positioning is an inversion of what was once considered the norm for butches does not affect their sense of gender identification at all. While "butch" still connotes the active sexual partner to many lesbians, the acceptance of the butch bottom is a noteworthy shift in cultural expectations; the years between the "heyday" of butch/femme and its resurgence in the 1980s saw numerous changes in lesbian culture — ranging from the increasing representations of lesbians in mainstream society to the expanding academic debates about gender in the lesbian community to the growth of a more diverse, radical young lesbian culture influenced by AIDS activism — changes that clearly had an impact on lesbians' conceptions of butch. One significant factor that contributed to this shift is the increased visibility and vocalness of lesbian sadomasochists.

When Second Wave feminism became the dominant ideology of middle-class lesbian communities, as Lillian Faderman and other historians argue, their attitudes toward sex changed as well. In the mid-1970s, "feminist sex," many lesbians thought, required equality between partners; butch/femme sex, seen as a replication of unequal heterosexual roles, was thus patriarchal and anti-feminist. In the extreme, butches and femmes were perceived as engaging in what Sheila Jeffreys later called "an erotic communication based on sado-masochism, the eroticising of power difference."[46] But, in the late 1970s, the "real" sadomasochists started coming out of the closet, arguing that there was no conflict between feminism and sadomasochism. The ensuing "sex wars," which periodically resurfaced throughout the 1980s and into the 1990s, had a tremendous influence on many lesbians, affecting their perceptions of sadomasochism, butch/femme, and sex in general. The works of Pat Califia, JoAnn Loulan, Gayle Rubin, Susie Sexpert, as well as others, and the emergence of lesbian erotic publications like *Bad Attitude, On Our Backs,* and *Quim* all helped to expand conceptions of what constituted acceptable, healthy sex for lesbians, though s/m sex has never been accepted by all lesbians as "normal" or desirable.

These "sex wars" affected the butch in at least one crucial way. Over the years, more material became available that portrayed lesbian sadomasochism in a positive light, the most influential being the groundbreaking publication of *Coming to Power: Writings and Graphics on Lesbian S/M* (1981) by SAMOIS, a San Francisco-based lesbian feminist s/m group.[47] Encouraged by these publications, some lesbians, particularly young urban lesbians who felt dissatisfied with "vanilla sex" and who wanted to experiment with sexual power without necessarily embracing the s/m lifestyle, adopted s/m concepts, such as "top" and "bottom," as positive additions to their sexual repertoire. As the negative perception of at least some of the vocabulary of sadomasochism was reduced, the term "top" became available to denote a lesbian who preferred to "run the sex," reducing the burden formerly carried by the word "butch." This transition had an important effect on butch sadomasochists, as well as their "vanilla" counterparts: lesbian masochists and lesbians who simply enjoyed being the recipients of love-making could claim a butch identity without conflict, thus further destroying cultural conflations of sex, gender, sexuality, and desire. Just as the femme lesbian demonstrates the fallacy of theories of inversion, the butch bottom exemplifies the distinction between sexual positioning and gender.

Butch Desire

> *You gotta have a femme under your arm at all times.*
> — Trish Thomas[48]

The fourth way that butches tend to be defined is the one that has received the least critical scrutiny in current scholarship on butch identity: the assumption that butch and femme are interdependent opposites, like the yin and yang of Taoist philosophy, bound together, as Ardill, O'Sullivan, and Thomas all note, by the energy of sexual desire. Under this view, a butch is a butch because she finds femmes erotic and appealing, and a femme is a femme because she is sexually attracted to butches. For example, Loulan writes, "It's impossible for us to get away from the fact that butches and femmes are in opposition. This doesn't mean that they are completely different, only that there is an opposing force in the other that each finds to be an erotic turn-on."[49] Amber Hollibaugh concurs: "butch/femme is an erotic system. It's deeply based in an erotic definition."[50]

But not all butches agree with this assessment. "You're expected to like femmes, if you're butch," one butch lesbian writes, "it's part of the 'like a man' myth, as far as I can see . . . [but] I'm no more comfortable with most femmes than with straight women."[51] We suggest that butch should not be a term that must inevitably and "naturally" appear alongside femme. The conception of butch/femme interdependence has historical roots dating back to the beginning of the century. Turn-of-the-century sexologists, such as

Richard von Krafft-Ebing, Havelock Ellis, and Sigmund Freud, believed that masculine women would typically be attracted to feminine ones. For instance, in "Three Essays on the Theory of Sexuality" (1905), Freud wrote that, among women, "active inverts exhibit masculine characteristics, both physical and mental, with peculiar frequency and look for femininity in their sexual objects — though here again a closer knowledge of the facts might reveal greater variety."[52] Even much later in his career, when he grew less sure that lesbianism always necessitated physical masculinity, Freud continued to insist that a lesbian patient, despite not showing the "bodily traits and mental traits belonging to the opposite sex" that lesbians supposedly possessed, still displayed a "masculine" attitude toward a "feminine" love object.[53]

This idea has been remarkably persistent, and, although we recognize and appreciate the importance of butch/femme relationships, we do not believe that they are the only way to understand butchness (or femmeness). Rather, we maintain that butch can be interpreted more precisely if we divorce it from the butch/femme bipolarity, which has acted as a stranglehold on theorists who have tried to produce new ideas about what it means to be butch in the 1980s and 1990s. Scholars, such as Loulan, Hollibaugh, and Nestle, fall into the trap of limiting their discussions to butch and femme as a dyadic system, failing to recognize that butch can be a signifier that has little to do with femme, or even with sexuality at all. As one butch comments, "If I was celibate for the rest of my life, I would still be butch."

The idea that butches and femmes are a matched set is so predominant even today that many lesbians uncritically assume that butches *must* be attracted to femmes. For instance, Loulan, in her lengthy survey of butch/femme identities, asked her respondents in one question, "If you identify as butch, choose three words to describe aspects of femmes you find erotic," a question which presupposes that butches *will* find aspects of femmes erotic.[54] Yet even Loulan admits that of the butch respondents to her survey, only 50 percent expressed an attraction mainly for femmes, while a full twenty-five percent expressed an attraction mainly for other butches. If Loulan's figures are correct, then the theoretical focus on the butch/femme couple presents a very skewed view of reality.

Loulan's implicit erasure of the reality of butch/butch desire is only one example of this type of elision. On a more theoretical level, Sue-Ellen Case, in her essay "Towards a Butch-Femme Aesthetic," postulates butch/femme as an ideal feminist subject position, one that provides "agency and self-determination to the historically passive subject,"[55] as well as positioning her outside of the dominant ideology. Case writes that

> the butch-femme couple inhabit the subject position together — "you can't have one with-out the other," as the song says. The two roles never appear as . . . discrete. The butch-femme as subject is reminiscent of Monique Wittig's "j/e," or coupled self, in her novel *The Lesbian Body*. These are not split subjects, suffering the torments of dominant ideology. They are coupled ones.[56]

Yet, in building her argument, Case begins with the assumption that butch and femme are linguistically indissoluble, and thereby overlooks the possibility of even more disruptive and powerful constructs than butch/femme. For while butch/femme gains its subversive strength from its parody of heterosexual couplings, "providing [the subject] with at least two options for gender identification," [57] other constructs, such as butch/butch, go a step further by also destabilizing constructs of heterogendered desire and homosexuality as well.

We began with the premise that the individual butch does not require a femme counterpart. While butch and femme are most certainly linked by virtue of the fact that they arise in a culture for which gender is a dyadic system, this does not presuppose that the cultural representation of gender encompasses all variations of gender in existence, nor that the relationships between genders are limited to those that are culturally sanctioned. Indeed, the very existence of homosexuals, bisexuals, intersexed people, butches, and queens is ample evidence of the fallacy of the cultural conflation of sex, gender, and sexuality; the argument that butch and femme are, or should be, symbiotically intertwined ignores reality and only replicates the dominant ideology.

Case, Loulan, and other critics fall into the trap of maintaining the perceived essential heterosexuality of desire itself; as Eve Kosofsky Sedgwick explains, "desire . . . by definition subsists in the current that runs between one male self and one female self, in whatever sex of bodies these selves may be manifested." [58] In such a system, the desire of butches for other butches is impossible, which results in an inaccurate view of what it means to be butch in our culture. To borrow Sedgwick's words, "To alienate conclusively, *definitionally*, from anyone on any theoretical ground the authority to describe and name their own sexual desire is a terribly consequential seizure." [59] By assuming that part of what constitutes a butch is her attraction to femmes, we deny butches this authority; we also deny masculine lesbians who are attracted to other masculine lesbians the right to claim butch as an identity.

Although Biddy Martin writes about the erasure that lesbians in general must face, her words are equally applicable to the erasure that butches experience: "We are not always confronted with direct, coercive efforts to control what we do in bed, but we are constantly threatened with erasure from discursive fields where the naturalization of sexual and gender norms works to obliterate actual pluralities." [60] We must be aware of how sexual and gender norms work within many, diverse lesbian communities to marginalize other lesbians. For instance, the very existence of butches who are passionately attracted to other butches is frequently ignored, if not denied outright. When such butches do become visible, they are often seen as abnormal, as is the case in the novel *Cass and the Stone Butch*, where Jacko thinks Cass, a butch, is "perverted to like [those] butch types." [61] There is no difference between this sentiment and the one that says that lesbianism itself is perverse; both attitudes are designed to maintain the status quo. The absence of butch/butch desire and eroticism is symptomatic of a society that refuses to recognize that sexual desire does not only exist between a self that is gendered masculine and one that is gendered feminine. Butch/butch desire negates the binary oppositions female/male and self/other upon which Western culture is based, and hence is tremendously threatening.

This elision of butch/butch desire is apparent when one looks at lesbian films targeted to a mass audience. *Lianna* (1983), *Personal Best* (1982), and *Desert Hearts* (1986) all star at least one, if not two, stunningly attractive and very feminine women. None of the films features two butches, and two of the films focus exclusively on the relationship between two feminine women who could easily pass as straight. Sexuality between two feminine women is far easier to contain, since such imagery has a long tradition of representation in heterosexual male pornography, in which the illusion always exists that a man will suddenly appear. With two butches, a man seems superfluous, and perhaps even endangered. A related reason that butch/butch desire is not represented in movies or other media forms targeted at a mass audience is that butches fail to fulfill heterosexual ideas about what is attractive and sexually appealing in women. At least up to the present, mainstream lesbian films have been carefully crafted to include lesbians who could be as desirable to heterosexuals as to lesbians and bisexual women, ensuring a broader audience. In addition, butch/butch eroticism raises the spectre of male homosexuality, which might offend and confound the audience.

Given the limited representation of lesbianism in the mass media, it is hardly surprising that butch/butch desire has been largely invisible. What is more curious is how infrequently butch/butch eroticism is represented in the lesbian media. In films, newspapers, magazines, and novels, one sees countless images of the femme/butch couple, but the butch/butch couple is rarely represented. Even in erotic videos produced for the lesbian market, like *Hungry Hearts* (1989) and *Suburban Dykes* (1990) created by Fatale Video, one constantly sees femme with femme or femme with butch, but only rarely butch with butch. This erasure denies that butch/butch relationships are as significant a part of the lesbian community as butch/femme relationships.

A few critics have given attention to erotic relationships between butches. Gayle Rubin provides the most thoughtful commentary in her article "Of Catamites and Kings: Reflections on Butch, Gender and Boundaries":

> Butches are often identified in relation to femmes. Within this framework, butch and femme are considered an indissoluble unity, each defined with reference to the other; butches are invariably the partners of femmes. Defining "butch" as the object of femme desire, or "femme" as the object of butch desire presupposes that butches do not desire or partner with other butches, and that femmes do not desire or go with other femmes.
>
> Butch-butch eroticism is much less documented than butch-femme sexuality and lesbians do not always recognize or understand it. Although it is not uncommon, lesbian culture contains few models for it. Many butches who lust after other butches have looked to gay male literature and behavior as sources of imagery and language. The erotic dynamics of butch-butch sex sometimes resemble those of gay men, who have developed many patterns for sexual relations between different kinds of men. Gay men also have role models for men who are passive or subordinate in sexual encounters yet retain their masculinity. Many butch-butch couples think of themselves as women doing male homosexual sex with one another.[62]

An even more singular view of butch/butch sexuality is Jan Brown's opinion that when two butches "hook up . . . sexually" they are "faggots."[63] Both Rubin and Brown are attempting to do something worthwhile — to show that butch/butch sexuality *does* exist and must be accounted for in a different fashion from butch/femme sexuality. They seem stymied, however, about how to define butch sexuality in a way that exemplifies the butch's lesbian identity. By suggesting that butches who are erotically interested in other butches are modeling their behavior on that of homosexual men, or are actually "faggots" themselves, Rubin and Brown are distancing butches from "normal" lesbians who engage in "normal" lesbian sex. More insidiously, Rubin and Brown are not even classifying butches who are sexually attracted to other butches as lesbians, but as something else completely; while this might be an attitude that some butches would find appealing and alluring, others might find that such a theory positions them as outsiders to the lesbian community. We are critical of such an approach to butch sexuality and argue that when two butches engage in sex, no matter what the practice, it needs to be seen as two women engaging in lesbian sexuality, not gay male sexuality.

For Rubin, Brown, and others, butches who desire other butches are difficult to theorize using lesbian imagery because the numerous social restrictions placed on acceptable forms of desire make it difficult to come to grips with something as multiply transgressive as the butch who desires other butches. Two female bodies having sex violates the myth of "natural" heterosexuality, female bodies in "men's" clothing violates gender restrictions, and female bodies in "men's" clothing having sex with each other is a triple whammy. The butch/butch couple confounds all of these conventions, which is why this form of relationship makes even some lesbians uncomfortable. Trish Thomas describes one such moment when she is pursuing another butch: "She wonders if I've mistaken her for femme. . . . She becomes concerned that she's throwing off femme vibes without even knowing it. . . . And suddenly she gets this overwhelming urge to arm wrestle."[64] Butch/butch sexuality is constantly being assimilated back into familiar categories, like the butch who worries that Thomas must be picking up "femme vibes" or Brown's description of butches having sex with other butches as "faggots."

Despite such overwhelming conceptual erasure, butches, unconcerned with theoretical disputes, continue to desire other butches. Look down Castro Street on any Saturday evening and you are likely to notice a number of butch couples strolling by. Visit a chic lesbian bar in San Francisco, and you are apt to see two leather-jacketed, buzz-cut young women clinging to each other on the dance floor — and they will be far from alone. Might butch/butch even be getting *trendy?* The increasingly apparent presence of butch/butch couples points out the curious location of butch desire today in lesbian communities across the United States. On the one hand, the existence of butch/butch relationships still tends to be ignored, denied, or minimized. On the other hand, butches involved with other butches appear to be moving increasingly into the spotlight. As media overexposure causes other forms of lesbian relationships to become more accepted, lesbians who wish to defy social expectations, whether those expectations originate in lesbian or non-lesbian communities, are seeking new avenues for sexual expression. Butch/butch relationships are one means to that end. But we do not mean to suggest that butch/butch sexuality is merely the trend of the season, which will quickly disappear when a newer trend surfaces. Quite to the contrary, we believe that butch/butch couples, like other sexual radicals, are altering our conceptions of lesbian identity and desire.

Butch and Beyond

Being butch, as we have shown, affects every moment of the butch lesbian's life because she lives in a culture dominated by the myth that gender is a biologically determined behavioral manifestation of anatomical sex. The butch who refuses to pass as non-butch — a "G.I. Joe in Barbie Land" — is, in many situations, a social outcast who might be denied jobs, professional advancement, or social acceptance because of her butch appearance and actions. It is this very real persecution that provided the incentive for us to write this essay.

We have shown that it is masculinity, not sexual desire and choice of sexual object, that should be the chief identifying trait of the butch. As we have argued throughout this essay, masculinity, in one form or another, inevitably identifies the butch. Given the fact that much of what has been said about the butch can be reduced to her adoption of masculine signs, it might be best to simplify how we see her. Associating the butch with her masculine display, rather than with her choice of sexual partner, frees the butch up to have sex with whomever she wants in whatever way she desires, while still avoiding the trap of "infinite elasticity."

Finally, we hope that our essay has exploded the "natural" assumption that butch almost always belongs with femme. This false claim works to negate the experiences of many butches (and femmes). Recognizing that butch/femme is only one of myriad different relationships that function in lesbian communities frees up both "butch" and "femme" as terms that are sometimes, though not always, connected. But questioning the all-too-common linkage of these terms does far more than merely challenge the ways that these terms work in language. It ensures that femme/femme or butch/butch relationships are seen as just as "normal" as butch/femme relationships; a butch, like Trish Thomas, who likes other butches, should not be regarded as "suspect" and "the ultimate threat" because she prefers sexual involvement with other butches. Her sexual expression should not be treated any differently from that of a butch who finds femmes more sexually appealing. As lesbians, we need to make sure that we don't create definitions that function to delineate who is a "proper" lesbian and who is not. Articulating what elements make up various queer identities, from the butch to the femme to the queen to the "clone," is vitally important in order to understand how gender is produced and performed among queers. Exploring the many facets of such images also helps to elucidate the virulent homophobia that some of these individuals, such as butches, experience.

Breaking the linkage of these words also brings to light new thoughts about how gender operates among lesbians. The subversive relationships between butches and butches or femmes and femmes will then be seen as relationships that might say as much about how gender and sexuality function in the lesbian world as do the relationships between butches and femmes. These relationships should not be considered insignificant, and deserve more scholarly attention than they have yet received. Studying such "marginal" relationships will help us better understand the multiplicity of ways that lesbianism is defined and constructed.

NOTES

Acknowledgments: We wish to thank Julie Inness and the anonymous readers from the *NWSA Journal* for their helpful comments on this essay.

1. Jeanne Cordova, "Butches, Lies, and Feminism," in *The Persistent Desire: A Femme-Butch Reader*, ed. Joan Nestle (Boston: Alyson, 1992), 276.

2. Trish Thomas, "Straight People Call Me Sir," *Quim* 3 (Winter 1991): 21.

3. A complete history of butch is beyond the scope of this essay, but a brief explanation is useful. It is impossible to state with great exactness when butch became a clear identity. In " 'They Wonder to Which Sex I Belong': The Historical Roots of the Modern Lesbian Identity," *Feminist Studies* 18, no. 3 (Fall 1992): 467–97, historian Martha Vicinus argues that the "mannish lesbian," a forerunner to the butch, appeared in the early 1800s (480). Vicinus points out that in the nineteenth century, and even in earlier centuries, there were numerous accounts of women who dressed and acted in a mannish fashion, such as George Sand, Rosa Bonheur, and Harriet Hosmer. Some of these women, if not all of them, were undoubtedly precursors of the twentieth-century butch, but they lacked the politicized notion of themselves as both butches and lesbians. By the late nineteenth century, sexologists such as Richard von Krafft-Ebing and Havelock Ellis stressed the masculine appearance of the typical female invert. For example, in *Studies in the Psychology of Sex*, vol. 1 (1897; reprint, New York: Random House, 1936), Ellis wrote, "The commonest characteristic of the sexually inverted woman is a certain degree of masculinity or boyishness" (244). Some historians, such as Lillian Faderman in *Odd Girls and Twilight Lovers: A History of Lesbian Life in Twentieth-Century America* (New York: Columbia University Press, 1991), have suggested that cross-dressed "inverts" in the 1890s were the first "conscious 'butches' and 'femmes' " (59). But can we consider these women "real" butches and femmes? At this point, the answer must be "no," since we have no information about whether these women had a self-conscious perception of themselves as butches and femmes.

We can state with more assurance that butch and femme roles were commonly found in the white working-class lesbian subculture of cities in the 1920s (Faderman, *Odd Girls*, 80). Butches and femmes also existed in the middle and upper classes, with two of the most famous butches in the early twentieth century being Gertrude Stein and Radclyffe Hall. As the century progressed, butch and femme roles became even more prominent in the lesbian communities of the United States. By the 1940s and 1950s, butch/femme roles were essential for many lesbians, particularly working-class and young women. As Elizabeth Lapovsky Kennedy and Madeline Davis write in *Boots of Leather, Slippers of Gold: The History of a Lesbian Community* (New York: Routledge, 1993) about the mid-twentieth-century, working-class lesbian culture in Buffalo, New York,

> butch-fem roles were what we call a social imperative. They were the organizing principle for this community's relation to the outside world and for its members' relationships with one another. . . . [B]utch-fem roles established the guidelines for forming love relationship and friendships. Two butches could be friends but never lovers; the same was true for two fems (244).

Some women did resist butch/femme roles, but they were often made to feel uncomfortable and marginalized by those who did adopt such roles. For instance, in *Zami: A New Spelling of My Name* (Freedom, CA: Crossing Press, 1982), Audre Lorde states that she felt uneasy with the strict roles adopted by many black lesbians in the 1950s: "Their need for power and control seemed a much-too-open piece of myself, dressed in enemy clothing. They were tough in a way I felt I could never be" (224).

4. JoAnn Loulan, *The Lesbian Erotic Dance: Butch, Femme, Androgyny, and Other Rhythms* (San Francisco: Spinsters, 1990), 42–43.

The butch/femme scale is similar to (and possibly derived from) the Kinsey sexuality scale. The scale ranges from one to ten, where one represents an extreme expression of femininity and ten represents the extreme of masculinity (in some parts of the country, the poles are reversed). A rating of five and a half is perfect androgyny.

5. Some exceptions to this rule are Lily Burana, Roxxie, and Linnea Due, eds., *Dagger: On Butch Women* (San Francisco: Cleis Press, 1994); Colleen Lamos, "The Postmodern Lesbian Position: *On Our Backs,*" in *The Lesbian Postmodern,* ed. Laura Doan (New York: Columbia University Press, 1994), 85–103; Gayle Rubin, "Of Catamites and Kings: Reflections on Butch, Gender, and Boundaries," in *The Persistent Desire,* 466–82; and Alisa Solomon, "Not Just a Passing Fancy: Notes on Butch," *Theater* 24, no. 2 (1993): 35–46.

6. Many scholars have focused almost exclusively on butch/femme relationships, with little or no attention to butch/butch relationships. Histories of butches and butch/femme relationships include Vern Bullough and Bonnie Bullough, "Lesbianism in the 1920s and 1930s: A Newfound Study," *Signs: Journal of Women in Culture and Society* 2 (1977): 895–904; Elizabeth Lapovsky Kennedy and Madeline Davis's extensive work that includes: *Boots of Leather, Slippers of Gold;* "Oral History and the Study of Sexuality in the Lesbian Community: Buffalo, New York, 1940–1960," in *Hidden from History: Reclaiming the Gay and Lesbian Past,* ed. Martin Bauml Duberman, Martha Vicinus, and George Chauncey, Jr. (New York: New American Library, 1989), 426–40; "The Reproduction of Butch-Fem Roles: A Social Constructionist Approach," in *Passion and Power: Sexuality in History,* ed. Kathy Peiss and Christina Simmons (Philadelphia: Temple University Press, 1989), 241–56; and " 'They Was No One to Mess With': The Construction of the Butch Role in the Lesbian Community of the 1940s and 1950s," in *The Persistent Desire,* 62–79; Lillian Faderman, *Odd Girls and Twilight Lovers* and "The Return of Butch and Femme: A Phenomenon in Lesbian Sexuality of the 1980s and 1990s," *Journal of the History of Sexuality* 2 (1992): 578–96; Sheila Jeffreys, "Butch and Femme: Now and Then," in *Not a Passing Phase: Reclaiming Lesbians in History 1840–1985,* ed. Lesbian History Group (London: Women's Press, 1989), 158–87; Joan Nestle, "Butch-Fem Relationships: Sexual Courage in the 1950's," *Heresies: Sex Issue* 12 (1981): 21–24; and many of the articles collected in the anthology edited by Nestle, *The Persistent Desire.* Martha Vicinus, in " 'They Wonder to Which Sex I Belong,' " and George Chauncey, Jr., in "From Sexual Inversion to Homosexuality: The Changing Medical Conceptualization of Female 'Deviance,' " in *Passion and Power,* 87–117, both provide excellent overviews of how "wife" and "husband" roles were associated with lesbian behavior before the twentieth century. In addition, Esther Newton describes the importance of the 1920s masculine lesbian in her essay, "The Mythic Mannish Lesbian: Radclyffe Hall and the New Woman," *Signs: Journal of Women in Culture and Society* 9, no. 4 (1984): 557–75. A contemporary analysis of butch/femme roles is found in Kath Weston's thoughtful essay, "Do Clothes Make the Woman? Gender, Performance Theory, and Lesbian Eroticism," *Genders* 17 (Fall 1993): 1–21.   ·

7. Though our focus in this essay is primarily on the butch, we recognize and appreciate the importance of femmes in lesbian culture, and conclusions similar to those we shall draw could probably be arrived at by studying the femme. A number of scholars have produced important accounts of femme identity. See Joan Nestle, "The Fem Question," in *Pleasure and Danger: Exploring Female Sexuality,* ed. Carole S. Vance (Boston: Routledge, 1984), 232–41; Paula Marie-daughter, "Too Butch for Straights, Too Femme for Dykes," *Lesbian Ethics* 2 (Spring 1986): 96–100; and Tracy Morgan, "Butch-Femme and the Politics of Identity," in *Sisters, Sexperts, Queers: Beyond the Lesbian Nation,* ed. Arlene Stein (New York: Plume, 1993), 35–46. Christine Holm-

lund discusses femme identity in the context of mainstream films in "When Is a Lesbian Not a Lesbian — The Lesbian Continuum and the Mainstream Femme Film," *Camera Obscura* 25 (1991): 145–79.

8. Jay Rayn, *Butch* (Boston: Free Women Press, 1991). Other fictional accounts about what it means to be a butch include Antoinette Azolakov, *Cass and the Stone Butch* (Austin, TX: Banned Books, 1987); Leslie Feinberg, *Stone Butch Blues* (Ithaca, NY: Firebrand Books, 1993); Lee Lynch, *Toothpick House* (Tallahassee, FL: Naiad Press, 1983); and Jay Rayn, *Butch II* (Boston: Alyson, 1994).

9. Amber Hollibaugh and Cherríe Moraga, "What We're Rollin Around in Bed With: Sexual Silences in Feminism," in *Powers of Desire: The Politics of Sexuality*, ed. Ann Snitow, Christine Stansell, and Sharon Thompson (New York: Monthly Review Press, 1983), 394–405.

10. Quoted in Loulan, *The Lesbian Erotic Dance*, 34.

11. "Femme and Butch: A Readers' Forum," *Lesbian Ethics* 2 (Fall 1986): 98.

12. Susan Ardill and Sue O'Sullivan, "Butch/Femme Obsessions," *Feminist Review* 34 (Spring 1990): 80.

13. Loulan describes an exercise in which she asks a random member of the audience to come to the front of the room, and then has audience members, most of whom do not know the volunteer, rate the position of this woman on the butch/femme scale. "The fact that the audience is for the most part in agreement indicates to me that there is a collective opinion about where a woman fits on the butch/femme scale" (*The Lesbian Erotic Dance*, 44).

14. We recognize the difficulties of discussing what constitutes a butch — like any lesbian, she is an entity that does not and cannot exist according to the dominant heterosexual reality. As Sarah Hoagland points out, "In the conceptual schemes of phallocracies there is no category of woman-identified-woman, woman-loving-woman or woman-centered-woman; that is, there is no such thing as a lesbian." Quoted in Marilyn Frye, "To See and Be Seen: The Politics of Reality," in *Women, Knowledge and Reality: Explorations in Feminist Philosophy*, ed. Ann Garry and Marilyn Pearsall (Boston: Unwin Hyman, 1989), 77. Marilyn Frye concurs that "Lesbians are outside the [phallocratic] conceptual scheme, and this is something done, not just the way things are" (92). Nevertheless, we wish to attempt to use what words and concepts we have available to describe the phenomena of the butch, rather than enter into an epistemological discussion that could only replicate the work of Frye.

15. Faderman, *Odd Girls*, 263–64.

16. Faderman, "The Return of Butch and Femme," 593.

17. Ibid., 594.

18. Judith Butler, *Gender Trouble: Feminism and the Subversion of Identity* (New York: Routledge, 1990), 140.

19. For information about this culture, see Kennedy and Davis's excellent study, *Boots of Leather, Slippers of Gold*.

20. Quoted in Loulan, *The Lesbian Erotic Dance*, 113.

21. Rubin, "Of Catamites and Kings," 467.

22. Ibid., 470.

23. Dick Hebdige, *Subculture: The Meaning of Style* (New York: Methuen, 1979), 2–3.

24. "Diesel dyke" is a term used to define a lesbian who is domineering, aggressive, brash, hypermasculine, and frequently working class. Stereotypically, she is depicted as driving a Harley motorcycle and spending too much time in lesbian bars, drinking beer and playing pool:

We see her in the image of the 50s and 60s, dressed in her jeans with the pegged legs, motorcycle boots, worn workshirt open at the neck, short hair slicked down, swaggering across the barroom floor with her arm around a sweet young thing ("Femme and Butch," 100).

25. At different points in time, popular boys' haircuts, such as the D.A., the crew cut, and the flat top, have all been adopted by lesbians as butch haircuts. Actually, any short "boy's haircut," which makes no attempt to camouflage itself as a pixie cut or any other "girl's hair style," is a butch look. What constitutes a butch haircut is influenced by the butch's age and her class, ethnic, and racial background. A lesbian who came out in the 1950s might still wear her hair in a D.A., while a young 1990s butch might shave the sides of her head. Butch haircuts are constantly evolving.

26. Radclyffe Hall, *The Well of Loneliness* (1928; reprint, New York: Avon, 1981), 72.

27. Rubin, "Of Catamites and Kings," 469.

28. Butler, *Gender Trouble*, 33.

29. Solomon, "Not Just a Passing Fancy," 37.

30. Butler, *Gender Trouble*, 123.

31. Mary Riege Laner and Roy H. Laner, "Sexual Preference or Personal Style? Why Lesbians Are Disliked," *Journal of Homosexuality* 5 (1980): 349.

32. Ibid., 349.

33. Ibid., 346. Whether heterosexuals perceive a masculine woman as a lesbian or not is a complicated process, which works in a variety of ways. While her masculine appearance alone makes her suspect, there are other factors besides appearance that might make her more or less likely to be identified as a lesbian. For instance, her profession: a masculine physical education teacher is more likely to be thought of as a lesbian than a masculine home economics teacher. A woman's marital status also affects how others classify her, as do her friends and hobbies. For example, a single, masculine woman who rides a Harley-Davidson motorcycle and goes on camping trips with groups of other women is more likely to be categorized as a lesbian than is a masculine woman who lives with a boyfriend and goes on hiking trips with a mixed group of men and women.

34. Judith Roof, *A Lure of Knowledge: Lesbian Sexuality and Theory* (New York: Columbia University Press, 1991), 248–49.

35. Solomon, "Not Just a Passing Fancy," 36.

36. Holly Devor, *Gender Blending: Confronting the Limits of Duality* (Bloomington: Indiana University Press, 1989), 51.

37. With thanks to Joanna Russ, *The Female Man* (Boston: Beacon, 1975). Marilyn Frye makes the following observation: "The term 'female man' has a tension of logical impossibility about it that is absent from parallel terms like 'female cat' and 'female terrier' " ("To See and Be Seen," 86).

38. Although we are focusing in this essay on how the butch is constructed today, we recognize that the perception of the butch as similar to a man has historical roots that go back over a century. The theories of late nineteenth-century sexologists, including Richard von Krafft-Ebing and Havelock Ellis, emphasized a degree of mannishness in the lesbian. For example, Krafft-Ebing wrote in *Psychopathia Sexualis: A Medico-Forensic Study* (1886; reprint, New York: Stein and Day, 1965),

The female homosexual may chiefly be found in the haunts of boys. She is the rival in their play, preferring the rocking-horse, playing at soldiers, etc., to dolls and other girlish occupations. The toilet is neglected, and rough boyish manners are affected. . . .

The masculine soul, heaving in the female bosom, finds pleasure in the pursuit of manly sports, and in manifestations of courage and bravado. (264)

39. Monique Wittig, "One Is Not Born a Woman," *Feminist Issues* 1, no. 1 (1980): 447–54.

40. Jacquelyn N. Zita, "Male Lesbians and the Postmodernist Body," *Hypatia* 7, no. 4 (Fall 1992): 126.

41. Judy Grahn, *Edward the Dyke and Other Poems* (Oakland: Women's Press Collective, 1971).

42. Lynch, *Toothpick House*, 4.

43. Alison Bechdel, *Dykes to Watch Out For* (Ithaca, NY: Firebrand Books, 1986), 10–11.

44. Roof, *A Lure of Knowledge*, 244.

45. Davis and Kennedy, "Oral History," 433.

46. Jeffreys, "Butch and Femme," 179.

47. SAMOIS, ed., *Coming to Power: Writings and Graphics on Lesbian S/M* (San Francisco: SAMOIS, 1981).

48. Thomas, "Straight People Call Me Sir," 21.

49. Loulan, *The Lesbian Erotic Dance*, 125–26.

50. Quoted in ibid., 26.

51. "Femme and Butch," 97.

52. Sigmund Freud, "Three Essays on the Theory of Sexuality," in *Standard Edition of the Complete Psychological Works*, trans. James Strachey (London: Hogarth, 1905), 7:145.

53. Sigmund Freud, "Psychogenesis of a Case of Homosexuality in a Woman," in *Standard Edition of the Complete Psychological Works*, trans. James Strachey (London: Hogarth, 1920–22), 18:154.

54. Loulan, *The Lesbian Erotic Dance*, 250.

55. Sue-Ellen Case, "Towards a Butch-Femme Aesthetic," *Discourse* 11 (Winter 1988–89): 65.

56. Ibid., 56.

57. Ibid., 65.

58. Eve Kosofsky Sedgwick, *Epistemology of the Closet* (Berkeley: University of California Press, 1990), 86–87.

59. Ibid., 26.

60. Biddy Martin, "Sexual Practice and Changing Lesbian Identities," in *Destabilizing Theory: Contemporary Feminist Debates*, ed. Michèle Barrett and Anne Phillips (Oxford: Polity, 1992), 95.

61. Azolakov, *Cass and the Stone Butch*, 46.

62. Rubin, "Of Catamites and Kings," 472–73.

63. Jan Brown, "Sex, Lies and Penetration: A Butch Finally 'Fesses Up," *The Persistent Desire*, 414.

64. Thomas, "Straight People Call Me Sir," 22.

BIBLIOGRAPHY

Ardill, Susan, and Sue O'Sullivan. "Butch/Femme Obsessions." *Feminist Review* 34 (Spring 1990): 79–85.

Azolakov, Antoinette. *Cass and the Stone Butch.* Austin, TX: Banned Books, 1987.

Bechdel, Alison. *Dykes to Watch Out For.* Ithaca, NY: Firebrand Books, 1986.

Brown, Jan. "Sex, Lies and Penetration: A Butch Finally 'Fesses Up." *The Persistent Desire: A Femme-Butch Reader.* Ed. Joan Nestle. Boston: Alyson, 1992. 410–15.

Bullough, Vern, and Bonnie Bullough. "Lesbianism in the 1920s and 1930s: A Newfound Study." *Signs: Journal of Women in Culture and Society* 2 (1977): 895–904.

Burana, Lily, Roxxie, and Linnea Due, eds. *Dagger: On Butch Women*. San Francisco: Cleis Press, 1994.

Butler, Judith. *Gender Trouble: Feminism and the Subversion of Identity*. New York: Routledge, 1990.

Case, Sue-Ellen. "Towards a Butch-Femme Aesthetic." *Discourse* 11 (Winter 1988–89): 55–73.

Chauncey, George, Jr. "From Sexual Inversion to Homosexuality: The Changing Medical Conceptualization of Female 'Deviance.' " *Passion and Power: Sexuality in History*. Ed. Kathy Peiss and Christina Simmons. Philadelphia: Temple University Press, 1989. 87–117.

Cordova, Jeanne. "Butches, Lies, and Feminism." *The Persistent Desire: A Femme-Butch Reader*. Ed. Joan Nestle. Boston: Alyson, 1992. 272–92.

Davis, Madeline, and Elizabeth Lapovsky Kennedy. "Oral History and the Study of Sexuality in the Lesbian Community: Buffalo, New York, 1940–1960." *Hidden from History: Reclaiming the Gay and Lesbian Past*. Ed. Martin Bauml Duberman, Martha Vicinus, and George Chauncey, Jr. New York: New American Library, 1989. 426–40.

Devor, Holly. *Gender Blending: Confronting the Limits of Duality*. Bloomington: Indiana University Press, 1989.

Ellis, Havelock. *Studies in the Psychology of Sex*. 1897. Vol. 1. New York: Random House, 1936.

Faderman, Lillian. *Odd Girls and Twilight Lovers: A History of Lesbian Life in Twentieth-Century America*. New York: Columbia University Press, 1991.

———. "The Return of Butch and Femme: A Phenomenon in Lesbian Sexuality of the 1980s and 1990s." *Journal of the History of Sexuality* 2 (1992): 578–96.

Feinberg, Leslie. *Stone Butch Blues*. Ithaca, NY: Firebrand Books, 1993.

"Femme and Butch: A Readers' Forum." *Lesbian Ethics* 2 (Fall 1986): 86–104.

Freud, Sigmund. *Standard Edition of the Complete Psychological Works*. Ed. and trans. James Strachey. London: Hogarth, 1953–74; New York: Macmillan.

———. "Three Essays on the Theory of Sexuality." 1905. *Standard Edition*. Vol. 7, 125–246.

———. "Psychogenesis of a Case of Homosexuality in a Woman." 1920–22. *Standard Edition*. Vol. 18, 143–70.

Frye, Marilyn. "To See and Be Seen: The Politics of Reality." *Women, Knowledge and Reality: Explorations in Feminist Philosophy*. Ed. Ann Garry and Marilyn Pearsall. Boston: Unwin Hyman, 1989. 77–92.

Grahn, Judy. *Edward the Dyke and Other Poems*. Oakland: Women's Press Collective, 1971.

Hall, Radclyffe. *The Well of Loneliness*. 1928. New York: Avon, 1981.

Hebdige, Dick. *Subculture: The Meaning of Style*. New York: Methuen, 1979.

Hollibaugh, Amber, and Cherríe Moraga. "What We're Rollin Around in Bed With: Sexual Silences in Feminism." *Powers of Desire: The Politics of Sexuality*. Ed. Ann Snitow, Christine Stansell, and Sharon Thompson. New York: Monthly Review Press, 1983. 394–405.

Holmlund, Christine. "When Is a Lesbian Not a Lesbian — The Lesbian Continuum and the Mainstream Femme Film." *Camera-Obscura* 25 (1991): 145–79.

Jeffreys, Sheila. "Butch and Femme: Now and Then." *Not a Passing Phase: Reclaiming Lesbians in History 1840–1985*. Ed. Lesbian History Group. London: Women's Press, 1989. 158–87.

Kennedy, Elizabeth Lapovsky, and Madeline Davis. *Boots of Leather, Slippers of Gold: The History of a Lesbian Community*. New York: Routledge, 1993.

———. "The Reproduction of Butch-Fem Roles: A Social Constructionist Approach." *Passion and Power: Sexuality in History*. Ed. Kathy Peiss and Christina Simmons. Philadelphia: Temple University Press, 1989. 241–56.

———. " 'They Was No One to Mess With': The Construction of the Butch Role in the Lesbian

Community of the 1940s and 1950s." *The Persistent Desire: A Femme-Butch Reader.* Ed. Joan Nestle. Boston: Alyson, 1992. 62–79.

Krafft-Ebing, Richard von. *Psychopathia Sexualis: A Medico-Forensic Study.* 1886. New York: Stein and Day, 1965.

Lamos, Colleen. "The Postmodern Lesbian Position: *On Our Backs.*" *The Lesbian Postmodern.* Ed. Laura Doan. New York: Columbia University Press, 1994. 85–103.

Laner, Mary Riege, and Roy H. Laner. "Sexual Preference or Personal Style? Why Lesbians Are Disliked." *Journal of Homosexuality* 5 (1980): 339–56.

Lorde, Audre. *Zami: A New Spelling of My Name.* Freedom, CA: Crossing Press, 1982.

Loulan, JoAnn. *The Lesbian Erotic Dance: Butch, Femme, Androgyny, and Other Rhythms.* San Francisco: Spinsters, 1990.

Lynch, Lee. *Toothpick House.* Tallahassee, FL: Naiad Press, 1983.

Mariedaughter, Paula. "Too Butch for Straights, Too Femme for Dykes." *Lesbian Ethics* 2 (Spring 1986): 96–100.

Martin, Biddy. "Sexual Practice and Changing Lesbian Identities." *Destabilizing Theory: Contemporary Feminist Debates.* Ed. Michèle Barrett and Anne Phillips. Oxford: Polity, 1992. 93–119.

Morgan, Tracy. "Butch-Femme and the Politics of Identity." *Sisters, Sexperts, Queers: Beyond the Lesbian Nation.* Ed. Arlene Stein. New York: Plume, 1993. 35–46.

Nestle, Joan. "Butch-Fem Relationships: Sexual Courage in the 1950's." *Heresies: Sex Issue* 12 (1981): 21–24.

———. "The Fem Question." *Pleasure and Danger: Exploring Female Sexuality.* Ed. Carole S. Vance. Boston: Routledge, 1984. 232–41.

———, ed. *The Persistent Desire: A Femme-Butch Reader.* Boston: Alyson, 1992.

Newton, Esther. "The Mythic Mannish Lesbian: Radclyffe Hall and the New Woman." *Signs: Journal of Women in Culture and Society* 9, no. 4 (1984): 557–75.

Rayn, Jay. *Butch.* Boston: Free Women Press, 1991.

———. *Butch II.* Boston: Alyson, 1994.

Roof, Judith. *A Lure of Knowledge: Lesbian Sexuality and Theory.* New York: Columbia University Press, 1991.

Rubin, Gayle. "Of Catamites and Kings: Reflections on Butch, Gender, and Boundaries." *The Persistent Desire: A Femme-Butch Reader.* Ed. Joan Nestle. Boston: Alyson, 1992. 466–82.

Russ, Joanna. *The Female Man.* Boston: Beacon, 1975.

SAMOIS, ed. *Coming to Power: Writings and Graphics on Lesbian S/M.* San Francisco: SAMOIS, 1981.

Sedgwick, Eve Kosofsky. *Epistemology of the Closet.* Berkeley: University of California Press, 1990.

Solomon, Alisa. "Not Just a Passing Fancy: Notes on Butch." *Theater* 24, no. 2 (1993): 35–46.

Thomas, Trish. "Straight People Call Me Sir." *Quim* 3 (Winter 1991): 21–25.

Vicinus, Martha. " 'They Wonder to Which Sex I Belong': The Historical Roots of the Modern Lesbian Identity." *Feminist Studies* 18, no. 3 (Fall 1992): 467–97.

Weston, Kath. "Do Clothes Make the Woman? Gender, Performance Theory, and Lesbian Eroticism." *Genders* 17 (Fall 1993): 1–21.

Wittig, Monique. "One Is Not Born a Woman." *Feminist Issues* 1, no. 1 (1980): 447–54.

Zita, Jacquelyn N. "Male Lesbians and the Postmodernist Body." *Hypatia* 7, no. 4 (Fall 1992): 106–27.

chapter 2

Trans (Homo) Sexuality?

Double Inversion,

Psychiatric Confusion,

and Hetero-Hegemony

Vernon A. Rosario II

> One answer to the question "Who is a transsexual?" might well be "Anyone who admits it." A more political answer might be, "Anyone whose performance of gender calls into question the construct of gender itself."
>
> — Kate Bornstein (1994: 121)

In November 1993, I spent a month doing an adult psychiatry clerkship on a locked ward for uninsured patients. On my third day, I started talking by chance with a young female patient in the common room. She wore a black leather jacket and had a short, boyish haircut, yet appeared timid and introverted as she hugged a toy dog. After chatting informally for a few minutes, I matched her up in my mind with the profile of one of the patients we discussed each morning in rounds. She had to be B —, a nineteen-year-old with a history of multiple suicide attempts and accusatory hallucinations who, for the past ten months, had been a patient in nearly all the psychiatric institutions in the area. She bore a dozen diagnoses and was soundly labeled a "diagnostic dilemma."

Once we had moved to an interview room for more privacy, I asked her if the many psychiatrists she had seen in the past months had helped her in any way. After looking down at her dog, she hesitatingly suggested that there was something she knew was recorded in her chart, but which no one really wanted to discuss. She was too embarrassed to come out with it, but with some coaxing, she admitted that she wanted to become a man, and furthermore, she wanted to be a gay man.

Unlike previous interviewers, I was only too eager to listen to B —, so we had daily sessions the rest of the month. B — had quite accurately diagnosed her prior health professionals' discomfort with the subject of transsexualism. The intern, the attending psychiatrist, and the chief of the psychiatric service, while fully aware of B — 's desires, all seemed equally confounded and embarrassed by them. This was a "long-term issue," they warned, and the immediate goal was to treat the suicidality and "psychoses." They also declared that they weren't experts in the matter and a specialist would have to be consulted . . . later, once she had been "stabilized."

They were right — they didn't know much about transsexualism, and I discovered that there is indeed a dearth of information on female-to-gay-male transsexuals (FTGMs) in the medical literature. The field is dominated by research on male-to-female (MTF) transsexuals who want to become heterosexual women, so-called "male *homosexual* transsexuals."[1] There are fewer articles on so-called "female homosexual transsexuals," that is, female-to-male (FTM) transsexuals who want to become heterosexual men. Since the time this chapter was originally written (1993), the classification of "Transsexualism" into homosexual and heterosexual types dictated by the revised third edition of the *Diagnostic and Statistical Manual of Mental Disorders* (DSM-III-R, American Psychiatric Association 1987) has been superseded by the diagnosis of "Gender Identity Disorder," with the specification of sexual attraction to males, females, both, or neither (*DSM-IV*, American Psychiatric Association 1994: 532–38). The new phenomenological classification avoids the confusion involved in the "homosexual" and "heterosexual" subtyping (for example, should B — be classified as "heterosexual" based on her congenital sex, or as "homosexual" based on her self-perceived gender identity?). The *DSM-IV* nevertheless notes that "virtually all females with Gender Identity Disorder will receive the same specifier — Sexually Attracted to Females — although there are exceptional cases involving females who are Sexually Attracted to Males" (534).

B — belonged to this apparently doubly rare breed of humans. After three weeks of discussing B — 's family life, erotic fantasies, and eventual aspirations as a gay man, B — gradually blossomed. B — became one of the most interactive patients on the ward, started talking to others for the first time about transsexualism, and stopped having hallucinations. The treatment team decided that B — was no longer suicidal and could attend a day clinic for troubled adolescents. On the first day there, B — negotiated with the supervisors to be called Sean and be addressed as a male. B — also announced to the other clients that "he" wanted to become a gay man. To all of this, the chief of psychiatry responded with dismay, shaking his head and lamenting that B — 's delusional system was being reinforced at the adolescent day clinic. Clearly, in addition to these psychiatrists' ignorance of the matter, their antipathy to the very notion of "female heterosexual transsexualism" (now "Gender Identity Disorder, Sexually Attracted to Men") was blocking communication and hindering B — 's transition from involuntary psychiatric confinement to an independent, happy life.

While medical science provides an extremely limited understanding of transsexualism (or sexuality in general), this *scientia sexualis* is nevertheless powerful and has the capacity to define and control people's lives in subtle, as well as forceful, ways (cf. Foucault 1976). In this essay, I focus on that medical knowledge and how sexologists since the late nineteenth century have overlooked or buried expressions of transsexualism, which I will define from an existentialist perspective as a subjective feeling of discrepancy between one's gender and one's sex.[2] My definition diverges subtly from a very useful one by Judith Shapiro that transsexuals are

> those who feel their true gender is at variance with their biological sex; more specifically, those who are attempting to "pass" as members of the opposite sex; and most specifically, . . . those who have either had sex change surgery or are undergoing medical treatment with a view toward changing their sex anatomically (1991: 249).

As Shapiro lucidly points out, both the terms "sex" and "gender" are contingent on a number of cultural and scientific factors, and are highly unstable. It should also be understood that I view "sex" and "gender" as *historically* contingent. As will be clear from the rest of the essay, I neither want to attach qualifiers (such as "true" or "biological") to the terms "sex" and "gender," nor further restrict the designation of transsexual to those seeking sex-reassignment surgery (SRS). My definition therefore moves away from an "objective," ontological typology of the "transsexual" to a broad existential distinction of "transsexualism" that is far more independent of "scientific" gender definitions and of psycho-surgical interventions. This subject-centered approach is akin to that proposed by Bornstein (quoted in my epigraph), and permits me to formulate an argument that transgresses into the historic period before SRS became possible, while avoiding any presumptions as to the ontological "truth" of the transsexual's gender or the biological grounding of sex.

I admit in advance that the most important element — the experience of those regulated by biomedical science — is very much beyond my grasp and cannot be defined by my privileged interaction with one "exceptional" FTGM transsexual.[3]

Current Theories of "Transsexualism," or the Flight from Heterosexuality

The new psychiatric criteria for the "diagnosis" of "gender identity disorder" (GID) are basically twofold: (1) "strong and persistent cross-gender identification," or "the desire to be, or the insistence that one is, of the other sex," and (2) gender dysphoria, or "persistent discomfort about one's assigned sex or a sense of inappropriateness in the gender role of that sex," specifically a "preoccupation with getting rid of primary or secondary sex characteristics (e.g., request for hormones, surgery, or other procedures to physically alter sexual characteristics to simulate the other sex)" (*DSM-IV*, 532–33, 558).[4] The definition is exceptional in that it incorporates the demand for medico-surgical intervention as one of the diagnostic criteria. It is as if "appendicitis" could be diagnosed only if lower right quadrant abdominal pain were accompanied by the patient's insistent demand to have an appendectomy. Therefore, the medical definition of "transsexualism" is codependent on its surgical treatment. Not surprisingly then, the word "transsexualism" only gained currency after sex reassignment surgery first came to broad public attention in the early 1950s.[5]

Since then, transsexualism has been described widely in Euro-American societies (*Lancet* 1991) and a diversity of transsexual, transgender, and "third-sex" peoples have been studied and problematized in a variety of cultures (Tsoi 1988, 1992; Herdt 1994). An early estimate of the ratio of MTF to FTM transsexualism was 8:1, but more recent authors have suggested a 1:1 ratio (Blanchard, Clemmensen, and Steiner 1987; Lothstein 1983). This predominance of research on male-to-female (MTF) transsexualism is probably due to many factors: actual disparities in sex distribution; the greater publicity afforded MTF role models (such as Christine Jorgensen, Jan Morris, and Renée Richards, M.D.); better surgical results for MTF sex reassignment; and the psychiatric profession's lack of interest in FTM cases.[6] A significant element is the castration anxiety and horror over forsaken male privilege evoked by the MTF. Richard Green (1967) notes that physicians (who are predominantly male) are "paralyzed by emotionalism" when confronted with MTF transsexuals because of the specter of castration they stir up; therefore, physicians are far more preoccupied with curing MTFs than performing surgery. Physicians' castration anxiety is exemplified by Dr. G. H. Weideman's reaction to Christian Hamburger's published description of the SRS performed on Christine Jorgensen. Weideman wrote to the editor of the *Journal of the American Medical Association* that the patient was castrated not just once but three times: by estrogen hormones, by removal of the testes, and by amputation of the penis (1953).

The etiology of transsexualism (or indeed of gender identification or sexual orientation) remains obscure. In a review of the literature, John Money and R. Gaskin (1971) conclude that no physical laboratory tests have consistently shown transsexuals to be different hormonally, physically, morphologically, or chromosomally.[7] The *DSM-IV* similarly notes that there are no laboratory diagnostic tests specific for GID, nor do these individuals have abnormal genitalia (535).

Phenomenologically, the female-to-male transsexual is typically described as exhibiting tomboyism: a preference for boys' company, games, and clothes; intense physical energy and athleticism; no interest in dolls; little maternal rehearsal; dissatisfaction with the female gender role; desire to be a boy; strong negative reaction to menstruation and breast development; breast binding; and stronger attachment to the father than the mother (Ehrhardt, Grisant, and McCauley 1979).[8] A variety of psychodynamic theories of gender identity have been forwarded to explain these findings.[9]

While Sigmund Freud never discussed transsexualism *per se*, he did propose that girls at the Oedipal or post-Oedipal stage abandoned their innate, natural sense of masculinity and retreated into socially sanctioned femininity once they recognized their castration (1933). Rejecting the Freudian thesis of females' organic inferiority, Karen Horney (1933) postulated the existence of an innate femininity that was based on the girl's awareness of her vagina; penis envy, in contrast, was a result of innate, heterosexual libidinal desire for the father and of the social subordination of women. From this "phase of extremely strong father fixation" at the Oedipal stage, Horney (1926) derived the "masculinity-complex" in women, or the "flight from womanhood."

In his monograph on transsexualism (1975), the respected psychiatrist and sexual psychologist Robert Stoller suggested that FTMs had been ugly, non-cuddly babies whose stereotypically feminine and usually depressed mothers had not received sufficient psychological support from their masculine but distant fathers. The daughter was unconsciously encouraged to play the husband-substitute, both to comfort the ailing mother and to gain her inadequate affection.[10] In adolescence, the female transsexual was described as seeking another female who would support the transsexual's illusion of possessing a penis, which "defends both [girls] against any acknowledgment of a lesbian attachment. Homosexuality is denied" (Volkan and Masri 1989: 98; cf. Socarides 1970). Charles Socarides most clearly elaborated the theory that transsexualism was a delusional defense against homosexuality. "Transsexualism," he claimed,

> is evident in the homosexual who, in attempting to resolve the emotional conflicts of his homosexuality, hits upon the idea of changing his sex through the mechanism of denial . . . and thus alleviates himself of guilt for his homosexual object choice. (Socarides 1969: 1423; cf. Hamburger 1953)

These psychodynamic formulations of transsexualism attempt to explain the "homosexual" type, since, at the time, the authors ignored the possibility of "heterosexual" FTM transsexualism (as in the case of B —). Indeed, "heterosexual" attractions were deemed contradictory to the diagnosis of transsexualism (Bloom 1994: 41; Sullivan 1990).[11] Apparently, it was only in 1983 that the first FTM with sexual attraction to homosexual men was described, a case included by Leslie Lothstein in his monograph, *Female-to-Male Transsexualism*. FTGMs were identified so rarely by psychiatrists that one survey found only one FTGM in a group of seventy-two gender-dysphoric females. The authors promptly discarded the case, declaring, "We do not mention this very unusual case further, and she is not included in any of the statistics that follow" (Blanchard, Clemmensen, and Steiner 1987).

Dorothy Clare (1984) coined the term "transhomosexuality" to describe "individuals who express a strong penchant for, attraction to, and/or idealization of homosexual persons of the opposite sex" (Clare and Tully 1989).[12] Only a few of these individuals were transsexuals or had a desire for sex reassignment. Following these classificatory systems, B — would technically be labeled a "female heterosexual transhomosexual transsexual." As already indicated, the new *DSM-IV* insists that FTGMs are exceedingly rare, thus encouraging any mental health worker to view with extreme skepticism any client's declarations of FTGM sentiments (see Bloom 1994).

In the past fifty years then, the psychiatric profession has focused on MTFs and only recently turned to FTMs. Both forms of "homosexual transsexualism" have traditionally been presented as defenses against homosexual desires, the psychiatric presumption being that the "natural" *heterosexual* drive is so strong that certain individuals flee into gender illusions in order to restore the heterosexual couple in their relationship with either a parental figure or a same-sex lover.

The paradoxically designated "*heterosexual* transsexual" — the female-to-gay-male or male-to-lesbian — poses an enormous problem to this heterosexual paradigm.[13] As several psychiatrists perplexedly exclaimed to me, "If a woman is attracted to men, as normal, why would she want to become male in order to be a homosexual?" This violates their imaginary balance of sexual psychopathologies, which weighs the stigma of transsexualism against that of homosexuality. The hegemonic heterosexual logic seems to be that the female-to-straight-male transsexual is gaining the normalcy of heterosexuality at the cost of her breasts and genitals, while the FTGM is striving for a dysfunctional goal of double social opprobrium.[14]

The psychiatric bias to view so-called psychopathology as an attempt to preserve heterosexuality is not exclusive to the current medical analysis of transsexualism. George Chauncey, Jr. (1982: 118) has pointed out that the medical literature which first described "sexual inversion" in the late nineteenth century also represented the female invert as temperamentally and physically male, which explained her attraction to traditionally "feminine" women. The latter were not inverts, but simply weak women who were deceived by the powerful and cunning female invert.[15] Chauncey and other historians of sexuality, like most psychiatrists, have viewed the "invert" as the genealogical ancestor of the modern homosexual.[16] The few contemporary psychiatrists who have sought similar roots for transsexualism beyond D. O. Cauldwell's coinage of the term in 1949 have cited Magnus Hirschfeld's work on transvestitism (1906 and 1910) as the first discussion of transsexualism. But were "inverts" homosexuals, and were Hirschfeld's transvestites transsexuals?

Transsexual Travesties: The Straightening of "Contrary Sexual Sensations"

If we examine the first descriptions of "Urningen" and "contrary sexual sensation" ("conträre Sexualempfindung") by Karl Heinrich Ulrichs (1864–68), Dr. Carl E. Westphal (1870), and Dr. Richard von Krafft-Ebing (1877), or later descriptions of "sexual inversion" (Tamassia 1878; Charcot and Magnan 1882), the patients' *self*-descriptions are phenomenologically akin to those of "transsexuals." Ulrichs' description of the "Urningen," that is, those with a female soul caught in a male body ("anima muliebris virili corpore inclusa"), primarily suggests the gender sentiments of transsexualism rather than homosexuality.[17] "Our character, the manner in which we feel, our entire temperament is not masculine, it is feminine," wrote Ulrichs, "we only act male. We play the male just as an actress plays a man on stage. . . . It is impossible for us to transform our female instinct into a male instinct."[18]

Similarly, in portraying "congenital contrary sexual sensation in women," Krafft-Ebing in *Psychopathia Sexualis* seems to be describing transsexual inclinations while labeling them as homosexual. "The masculine soul in the female bosom," he wrote,

> announces itself with an Amazonian inclination to manly sports, as well as occupations demanding courage and manly character. There is a strong desire to imitate male hairstyles and attire, and under favorable circumstances even to wear men's clothes and to impose as such. . . . Gynandry represents the severest degree of degenerative homosexuality. In this case, we are dealing with women who possess of the female qualities only the genital organs; in feelings, thought, commerce, and in external appearance they seem thoroughly male. ([1886] 1984: 302)

Jean Martin Charcot and Valentin Magnan, in their article introducing the term "inversion of the genital sense" into French, quoted a French "invert" who confessed,

> I adore female clothing; I love to see a well-dressed woman, because I tell myself I would like to be female to dress so. . . . The ladies are astonished to see how well I judge the relative good taste of their attire, and to hear me speak of such things as if I were a woman myself. (1882: 56)

From our current critical perspective, nineteenth-century descriptions of *Urnings* and inverts seem to confuse "gender identity" and "sexual orientation" (i.e., one's sensed core gender versus one's sexual preference in partners).[19] It has become commonplace to credit Freud (1905) with the first attempt to untangle the various elements of the "libido," thanks to his distinction between "sexual aim" (one's preferred sexual behavior) and "sexual object" (the entity with which one engages sexually) (e.g., Chauncey 1982: 122). Freud's distinction, however, does not touch on the matter of gender identity.[20] It was actually Arrigo Tamassia (the Italian forensic doctor who coined the term "inversion of the sexual instinct") who first recognized that his own term telescoped two separate matters: (1) the feeling that one's psychological gender is the opposite of one's physical sex, and (2) those who "wish to satisfy their sexual instinct with individuals of their same sex" (1878: 99).

So, while confessions of "contrary *gender sensation*" were not absent from the medical record, they were regularly inserted into models of "deviant" *object choice*, particularly homosexuality, in which "contrary gender sensation" delusionally re-created the heterosexual dyad. This was noted and criticized by self-declared homosexuals at the turn of the century, such as Marc-André Raffalovich and André Gide. Raffalovich proposed that the term "unisexuality" be applied to the large subset of "inverts" who, he claimed, were healthy, moral, fully cognizant of their sex, and would still experience same-sex love even if they belonged to the opposite sex (1894: 216). In the name of vindicating the rights of homosexuals and proving their essential normality, Raffalovich and Gide, like many conservative homosexuals today, defended the healthy homosexual by condemning the perverted, pathological, effeminate male or virile female.[21]

Despite these critiques from turn-of-the-century homosexuals, the diagnosis of "sexual inversion," with all of its characteristics of transsexualism, nevertheless evolved into that of "homosexuality." The conflation of these two elements — gender identity and sexual object choice — was further imbricated with a third, transvestitism. In France, Charcot and Magnan, and later Alfred Binet (1887), collapsed "inversion" and cross-dressing into the common category of fetishism, or as they understood it, into various manifestations of a degenerative psychopathology exhibiting deviant erotic attractions. Even to this day, French sexological literature makes no sharp distinction between transvestitism and transsexualism.[22]

It was not until 1910 that Magnus Hirschfeld coined the term "transvestitism" in a monograph subtitled "An Investigation into the Erotic Impulse of Disguise."[23] Hirschfeld, contrary to prior psychiatrists, proposed that "transvestitism" was a sexual phenomenon distinct from homosexuality, but he focused on outward behavior and dress even in those patients who expressed "inverted" sexual feelings.[24] Havelock Ellis perceptively criticized Hirschfeld's formulation of the "impulse to disguise," observing that, "The subject of this anomaly, far from seeking disguise by adopting the garments of the opposite sex, feels on the contrary that he has thereby become emancipated from disguise and is at last really himself" ([1928] 1936: 12).

Despite Ellis's criticism, Felix Abraham labeled as "homosexual transvestites" the two patients upon whom he performed the first "genital transformation" *(Genitalumwandlung)* surgery in 1931 (1931: 223).[25] Likewise, Hamburger, Stürup, and Dahl-Iversen employed the diagnosis of "genuine transvestitism" in their description of the surgical sex change of Christine Jorgensen, which drew enormous media attention in 1953. Further professional interest was brought to the matter with the Symposium on Transsexualism and Transvestitism held in December 1953 by the Association for the Advancement of Psychotherapy. The organizer of the meeting, endocrinologist Harry Benjamin, presented transsexualism as the "extreme degree of transvestitism" (1954: 219). Benjamin went on to dedicate himself professionally to transsexualism and founded the Harry Benjamin International Gender Dysphoria Association. His taxonomy of sexuality would undergo a reversal in the following years, so that in 1967 (at the meeting of the Psychology Division of the New York Academy of Sciences), he hypothesized that there was a spectrum of transsexualism, with transvestitism as its *mildest* manifestation (1967: 429).

While the subsequent medical literature, as I have mentioned, presented transsexualism as an independent diagnosis from that of transvestitism, transsexualism continues to be viewed as a close relative of homosexuality. Even though medical authors in the past twenty years have insisted that the "transsexual syndrome" is distinct from homosexuality, review articles entitled "Reassessment of Homosexuality and Transsexualism," for example, betray a persistent equation of the two in the minds of many medical practitioners, which sexological researchers feel impelled to correct (Friedman, Green, and Spitzer 1976). At the same time, sexologists perpetuate the confusion of transsexualism and homosexuality by creating, for example, research projects that compare FTM transsexuals to lesbians (Ehrhardt, Grisant, and McCauley 1979).

Despite repeated criticisms from a few psychiatrists and their clients that there were a variety of "contrary gender sensations" distinct from same-sex eroticism or from cross-dressing, most sexologists since the mid-nineteenth century have sustained the imbrication of transsexualism with homosexuality and transvestitism.[26] Gay and lesbian scholars have similarly overlooked transsexualism in embracing the "invert" as the Victorian ancestor of homosexuality (Chauncey 1982; Halperin 1990; Newton 1989). Gert Hekma, for example, identifies "uranians" like Ulrichs as "homosexuals," but notes that nineteenth-century sexological research equated "sexual inversion" with gender inversion, which was understood as a "third sex." His meliorist history of homosexuality depicts how the "third sex" or "effeminate male" was increasingly marginalized in the twentieth century and replaced by more self-conscious and more masculine "gay" men. Hekma thereby reproduces the Victorian erasure and condemnation of transgenderism in favor of the "normal," virile homosexual (1994: 238–39).

If other scholars do not completely ignore transsexualism, they often confuse it with cross-dressing or completely vilify it as a reactionary, anti-feminist plot of the patriarchy.[27]

Marjorie Garber, for example, plainly asserts that *"transsexualism, in fact, is one distinctly twentieth-century manifestation of cross-dressing"* (1992: 15; original italics). On the other hand, Janice Raymond epitomizes the radical lesbian-feminist critique of transsexualism as the " 'final solution' of women perpetrated by the transsexual empire. . . . With both [MTF and FTM transsexualism], the biological woman is not only neutralized but neuterized [sic]" (1979: xxv). H. S. Rubin (1994) shows how such lesbian-feminist views in the 1970s led to the marginalization of "butch" lesbians and FTM transsexuals. The popular and gay/lesbian press, as well as a variety of popular cultural representations of transgenderism, also contribute to the elision of transsexualism. Take, for example, Stephan Elliott's film *The Adventures of Priscilla, Queen of the Desert* (1994), which throws together homosexuality, transvestitism, and transsexualism onto the same fabulous, pink bus of "drag queens."[28] Reporting on the film, *Newsweek's* article, "There's Nothing Like a Dame: Hollywood Embraces Drag Queens," first notes that actor Terence Stamp was "frightened of playing a drag queen," and only later goes on to say that he plays a transsexual (Giles and Lee 1994). It is no wonder that the general public continues to confuse transsexualism with homosexuality and transvestitism.[29]

Rediscovering Transsexualism

The early sexological erasure of transsexualism and its subsequent slippage into homosexuality and transvestitism have in common a certain hetero-hegemonic logic: that the "sexual psychopath," through psychic and/or somatic gender "delusions," attempts to restore the "normal" heterosexual pairing. The inability to overcome this model has contributed to the delayed professional and social recognition of transsexualism, particularly the double "inversion" of FTGMs such as B — . As in her case, this has caused a great deal of suffering and psychiatric mismanagement.[30] Although follow-up studies show highly satisfactory outcomes of sex reassignment surgery,[31] and the cumulative evidence indicates that SRS is the treatment of choice,[32] the majority of health professionals (except for clinical psychologists) remain hostile to SRS.[33] Current work, however, suggests that transsexuals can lead as well-adjusted lives as "control" heterosexuals or homosexuals.[34]

Female-to-gay-male transsexuals in a more sexually liberal society such as the Netherlands can also do well by researchers' own standards.[35] A recent Dutch study of nine FTGMs in varying stages of sex-reassignment surgery showed no major differences in sexual satisfaction and psychological adjustment when compared to a "control" group of self-identified gay men (Coleman, Bockting, and Gooren 1993). Most encouragingly, the FTGM's gay-male sexual partners were equally satisfied with their pre-operative FTGM lovers who still had a vagina. Both these Dutch FTGMs and their gay-male partners demonstrate that there is no necessary association between gender identity, gender role, sexual orientation, and sexual aim. Clearly, the union of same-sex genitals is not the *sine qua non* of homosexuality. Likewise, psychiatrists, historians of sexuality, and gay and lesbian theorists might reconsider whether every union of similar genitals, *ipso facto*, is an act of homosexuality. In other words, some people *can* be gender constructivists in the streets and sex constructivists under the sheets.

NOTES

Acknowledgments: This essay is dedicated to B — , who taught me far more about normal human sexuality than her psychiatrists did. I am also extremely grateful to Kent Brintnall, H. S. Rubin, and Susan Stryker for valuable discussions and editorial comments.

1. George R. Brown (1990: 57) and Judith Shapiro (1991: 249) also note that the medical literature largely deals with MTFs.

2. For further reading on existential psychiatry, see Rollo May, Ernest Angel, and Henri F. Ellenberger (1958), and Leston L. Havens (1987: ch. 4).

3. Readers should consult Kate Bornstein (1994) for a poignant analysis of a male-to-female transsexual's personal experiences and confrontations with the medical profession. Those interested in a sociological approach should consult Dave King (1981), who utilizes labeling theory in his analysis of British MTF transsexualism and transvestitism — particularly members of the Beaumont Society. It is nevertheless emblematic of the problems I discuss below that his article is included in an anthology on the "making of the modern *homosexual*." An excellent anthropological perspective on American MTF transsexuals is provided by Anne Bolin (1988, 1994).

4. The *DSM-III-R* further required that these preoccupations had persisted for two or more years and the person had reached puberty (cf. Harry Benjamin International Gender Dysphoria Association 1985: 85). The *DSM-IV* eliminated the specific chronicity requirement, and also created the category of "gender identity disorder in children." The criteria further specify that the "disturbance is not concurrent with a physical intersex condition," and that it causes "clinically significant distress or impairment" (American Psychiatric Association 1994: 538).

5. D. O. Cauldwell coined the diagnosis of "psychopathic transsexuality" in 1949 in a popular, lay sexology journal. While not the first published surgical description of a "sex change operation," the article by Hamburger, Stürup, and Dahl-Iversen received greater professional and public attention since it was published in the prestigious *Journal of the American Medical Association* (1953).

6. Brown (1990) discusses the impact of media coverage of famous transsexuals on the rising number of gender dysphorics who visit psychiatric clinics. Shapiro (1991: 269) also suggests that, from the Freudian perspective of females as castrated beings, all women are fundamentally transsexual; therefore, a woman's desire to become a man is seen as unremarkable and even normal (cf. Horney 1926).

7. Louis Gooren (1990) similarly notes that there were no consistent data explaining the endocrinal determination of transsexualism.

8. These elements would seem to relate more to gender identity than sexual orientation, since the 15 FTMs in the study were all attracted to women rather than men. Also of note in this study was that 40 percent had attempted suicide at least once.

9. See Ethel S. Person and Lionel Ovesey (1983) for a review.

10. Ira Pauly (1974) proposed an explanation similar to Stoller's, the difference being that the father is abusive towards the mother and the daughter becomes the father-like protector of a mother perceived as weak and less admirable. Vamik D. Volkan and As'ad Masri (1989) present Stoller's model with the addition of a suspected actual trauma (usually to the genitals).

11. While the requirement that the patient wishes to acquire a "heterosexual" object choice post-operatively is not formally mentioned in the Standards of Care for gender dysphoria (Harry Benjamin International Gender Dysphoria Association 1985), many individual surgeons have denied SRS to transsexuals wishing to become homosexuals. The legal imposition of heterosexual-

ity is clearer — transsexuals must divorce their spouses before SRS is performed, lest a legal homosexual marriage be produced as a side-effect of surgery (Bolin 1994: 454).

12. Magnus Hirschfeld (1906, 1910) was the first to describe cases of masculine heterosexual women with an attraction to effeminate men (also see Sullivan 1990).

13. By the new diagnostic system, these would be labeled "males with Gender Identity Disorder, Sexually Attracted to Females," and "females with Gender Identity Disorder, Sexually Attracted to Males." Of course, the specific erotic identification "gay male" and the attraction to "gay men" of people such as B — are lost in this new descriptive typology.

14. The former statement actually seems to be in keeping with some sociologists' findings that transsexuals are very conformist and traditional in their views of masculinity and femininity (see Shapiro 1991: 253). Bolin also observes that members of TS/TV organizations in the 1970s and 1980s tended to reify TS/TV and gender dichotomies, and excluded "homosexual" cross-dressers ("drag queens") from TS/TV associations. However, newer organizations for the "transgendered" have adopted more relativist positions that undermine notions of "natural" sex (1994: 477).

15. Elaine Marks (1979: 356) examines the literary antecedents of the "Sappho Model" of older women who prey upon beautiful, young girls in schools and convents.

16. Esther Newton, for example, has described the figure of the "mannish lesbian" as simultaneously a pejorative label used by anti-feminists and as a liberatory identity appropriated by "New Women" of the turn of the century and early twentieth century:

> First, because sexual desire was not considered inherent in women, the lesbian was endowed with a trapped male soul that phallicized her, giving her active lust. Second, gender reversal became a powerful symbol of feminist aspirations, positive for many female modernists, negative for males, both conservative and modernist. (1989: 287)

I do not mean to imply that Newton or Chauncey is *wrong* in applying the label "lesbian" to these representations of women with "trapped male souls" or with "gender reversals"; indeed, Newton and Chauncey's careful scholarship accurately demonstrates that both doctors and the "mannish New Women" themselves made this equivalence. Instead, I want to point out how this equation in nineteenth-century medical literature and contemporary medical and historical texts erases the figure of the "transsexual" (as we have come to understand it).

17. Bornstein (1994: 66) observes that some contemporary transsexuals express the sentiment that "we are trapped in the wrong body." She, however, finds that this is an unfortunate metaphor for the experience of the pre-operative transsexual.

18. From Carl E. Westphal (1870: 92–93) citing Karl Heinrich Ulrichs' *Inclusa: Studien über mannmännliche Geschlechtsliebe* (1864).

19. A useful distinction is made by John Money and Anke Ehrhardt (1972: 4), who define "gender identity" as an individual's private experience and self-perception of being male, female, or ambivalent, while "gender role" includes those behaviors that indicate to others and the self that the individual is male, female, or ambivalent.

20. Sigmund Freud felt that a sharp distinction between masculinity and femininity developed only with puberty and arose from the "natural" distinctions of biological, gonadal difference. Nevertheless, he also mapped the distinction of male vs. female to the culturally traditional dyad of active vs. passive (1905: 219, n. 1).

21. See Marc-André Raffalovich's (1895) denunciation of Oscar Wilde and André Gide's apologia for "normal" pederasty, *Corydon* (1911). For a discussion of Raffalovich and his contributions to the French medical literature on homosexuality, see Vernon A. Rosario (1995). For an

often uncanny recent example of these conservative "gay rights" tactics, see Marshall Kirk and Hunter Madsen (1989).

22. For example, see René Colla's medical thesis on transvestitism (1956), which represents cross-dressing as an expression of transsexualism. More recently, J. Breton, C. Frohwirth, and S. Pottiez, in their medico-legal monograph on transsexualism (1985), review the medical history of transsexualism, transvestitism, and sexual perversion without distinguishing between the terms, and discuss the French law banning public cross-dressing (except during Carnival). They also argue for more humane medical and legal treatment of transsexuals and transvestites, again as if these were interchangeable entities. They do, however, note that the French lack the terminology to make the English-language distinction between sex and gender.

23. Hirschfeld, *Die Transvestiten. Eine Untersuchung über den erotischen Verkleidungstrieb* (1910).

24. Hirschfeld had described masculine-appearing women who claimed to feel like homosexual men and were attracted to young, "beardless" men (1906: 88), which he initially classified under bisexuality, but later reclassified as transvestitism (1910).

25. Genital reconstructive surgery has a longer history than that of "sexual-transformation" surgery, since the former was developed to treat patients with congenital malformations of or traumatic damage to the genitals. Vaginoplasty (the surgical creation of a "vaginal" cavity) was described in 1872 and improved in the early twentieth century for the treatment of congenital vaginal atresia (non-patency or absence of the vagina) (see an early review article by Marshall 1913). Phalloplasty (the surgical creation of a "penis") and penile prostheses were originally developed for the treatment of anatomical malformations and trauma, as well as for impotence secondary to spinal damage. V. Blum (1938) was the first to publish a description of his technique for "plastic restoration of the penis" in a man whose penis was amputated by a jealous rival. Harold Gilles (1948) improved on the technique of using an abdominal pedicle phalloplasty in cases of congenital absence, traumatic loss, or disease of the penis. Also see the first review article on "total reconstruction of the penis" by Jerome Gelb, Maxwell Malament, and Stephen LoVerme (1959).

26. Perhaps the best example of this is Pauly's review of a hundred cases of what he designates "male psychosexual inversion" (1965). While primarily focusing on "transsexualism," Pauly reviews almost every variety of male sexual deviance and proposes that psychosexual inversion is a "spectrum of disorders, from mild effeminacy to homosexuality, transvestitism, and finally transsexualism, each representing a more extreme form, and often including the previous manifestation" (1965: 179).

27. In what may be the first article on transsexualism written by a historian of medicine, Vern Bullough (1975) cautiously suggests that there may have been transsexuals before both the term and SRS were developed in the 1950s. However, he relies on Harry Benjamin's early description of transsexualism as the "extreme form" of transvestitism and therefore only suggests that the most persistent of cross-dressers and "passing" women might have been transsexuals.

28. The press's interpretations of Jonathan Demme's film *The Silence of the Lambs* (1990) similarly betray the failure to differentiate transsexualism, homosexuality, transvestitism, and even psychopathy.

29. Bolin reports that many of her MTF informants felt that most gay men do not understand the difference between gay female impersonators ("drag queens") and MTF transsexuals (1994: 487).

30. On the adverse effects of both popular and psychiatric homophobia on gay adolescents, see A. D. Martin and E. Hetrick (1987), and Richard R. Troiden (1989).

31. Female-to-male transsexuals consistently report greater satisfaction with SRS than male-to-female transsexuals (83–95 percent of FTMs claiming satisfaction vs. 72–85 percent of MTFs) (Gordon 1991). Post-operative FTMs also report increased orgiastic capacity and 85 percent report increased general sexual satisfaction (Lief and Hubschman 1993). Michael Fleming, Daryl Costos, and Brad MacGowan (1985) found that FTMs and their female spouses formed as stable and satisfying relationships as matched control heterosexual couples. These FTMs also showed similar ego development scores when compared with control heterosexual males (Fleming, Costos, and MacGowan 1984).

32. See Leslie Lothstein (1983). Eric B. Gordon (1991) has further argued for Medicaid coverage of SRS in appropriately evaluated cases.

33. See Richard Green, Robert Stoller, and C. MacAndrew (1966), and Louis R. Franzini and Denise L. Casinelli (1986).

34. See Gordon (1991).

35. From an anthropological perspective, Bolin points out the greater variety of interpersonal relationships facilitated in the United States by the gender-relativism of the new "transgendered" identity emerging in the 1990s (1994: 482–85). Bornstein similarly reclaims transgendered subjectivity as a politically/sexually transgressive identity (1994: 134).

REFERENCES

Abraham, Felix. 1931. Genitalumwandlung an zwei männlichen Transvestiten. *Zeitschrift für Sexualwissenschaft und Sexualpolitik* 18(4): 223–26.

American Psychiatric Association. 1987. *Diagnostic and Statistical Manual of Mental Disorders, Third Edition, Revised. (DSM-III-R)*. Washington, D.C.: American Psychiatric Press.

———. 1994. *Diagnostic and Statistical Manual of Mental Disorders, Fourth Edition (DSM-IV)*. Washington, D.C.: American Psychiatric Press.

Benjamin, Harry. 1954. Transsexualism and Transvestitism as Psychosomatic and Somato-Psychic Syndromes. *American Journal of Psychotherapy* 8: 219–39.

———. 1967. The Transsexual Phenomenon. *Transactions of the New York Academy of Sciences* 29(4): 428–30.

Binet, Alfred. 1887. Le Fetichisme dans l'amour. *Revue philosophique* 24: 143–67, 252–74.

Blanchard, Ray, Leonard Clemmensen, and Betty Steiner. 1987. Heterosexual and Homosexual Gender Dysphoria. *Archives of Sexual Behavior* 16: 139–52.

Bloom, Amy. 1994. The Body Lies. *New Yorker* (July 18): 38–49.

Blum, V. 1938. A Case of Plastic Restoration of the Penis. *Journal of the Mount Sinai Hospital* 4: 506–11.

Bolin, Anne. 1988. *In Search of Eve: Transsexual Rites of Passage*. South Hedley, MA: Berger and Degarvey.

———. 1994. Transcending and Transgendering: Male-to-Female Transsexuals, Dichotomy and Diversity. In *Third Sex, Third Gender: Beyond Sexual Dimorphism in Culture and History*, ed. Gilbert Herdt, 447–85. New York: Zone Books.

Bornstein, Kate. 1994. *Gender Outlaw: On Men, Women and the Rest of Us*. New York: Routledge.

Breton, J., C. Frohwirth, and S. Pottiez. 1985. *Le Transexualisme, étude nosographique et médico-légale*. Paris: Masson.

Brown, George R. 1990. A Review of Clinical Approaches to Gender Dysphoria. *Journal of Clinical Psychiatry* 51(2): 57–64.

Bullough, Vern. 1975. Transsexualism in History. *Archives of Sexual Behavior* 4(5): 561–71.

Cauldwell, D. O. 1949. Psychopathia Transexualis. *Sexology* 16 (December): 274–80.

Charcot, Jean-Martin, and Valentin Magnan. 1882. Inversion du sens génital. *Archives de neurologie* 3: 53–60, 296–322.

Chauncey, George, Jr. 1982. From Sexual Inversion to Homosexuality: Medicine and the Changing Conceptualization of Female Deviance. *Salmagundi* 58–59: 114–46.

Clare, Dorothy. 1984. Transhomosexuality. *Proceedings of the Annual Conference of the British Psychological Society*, University of Warwick, U.K.

Clare, Dorothy, and Brian Tully. 1989. Transhomosexuality, or the Dissociation of Sexual Orientation and Sex Object Choice. *Archives of Sexual Behavior* 18: 531–36.

Coleman, Eli, Walter O. Bockting, and Louis Gooren. 1993. Homosexual and Bisexual Identity in Sex-Reassigned Female-to-Male Transsexuals. *Archives of Sexual Behavior* 22: 37–50.

Colla, René. 1956. *Le Travestissement habituel*. Medical thesis, Paris. Thesis director, Justin-Besançon.

Ehrhardt, Anke, Gudrun Grisant, and Elizabeth McCauley. 1979. Female-to-Male Transsexuals Compared to Lesbians: Behavioral Patterns of Childhood Development and Adolescent Development. *Archives of Sexual Behavior* 8: 481–94.

Ellis, Havelock. [1928] 1936. *Eonism and Other Supplementary Studies*. In *Studies in the Psychology of Sex*, vol. 3, part 2. New York: Random House.

Fleming, Michael, Daryl Costos, and Brad MacGowan. 1984. Ego Development in Female-to-Male Transsexual Couples. *Archives of Sexual Behavior* 13: 581–94.

———. 1985. The Dyadic Adjustment of Female-to-Male Transsexuals. *Archives of Sexual Behavior* 14: 47–55.

Foucault, Michel. 1976. *Histoire de la sexualité*. Vol. 1, *La Volonté de savoir*. Paris: Gallimard.

Franzini, Louis R., and Denise L. Casinelli. 1986. Health Professionals' Factual Knowledge and Changing Attitudes toward Transsexuals. *Social Science and Medicine* 22: 535–39.

Freud, Sigmund. [1905] 1962. *Three Essays on the Theory of Sexuality*. In the *Standard Edition*, vol. 7. London: Hogarth Press.

———. [1933] 1964. Femininity. In the *Standard Edition*, vol. 22, 112–35. London: Hogarth Press.

Friedman, Richard, Richard Green, and Robert Spitzer. 1976. Reassessment of Homosexuality and Transsexualism. *Annual Review of Medicine* 27: 57–62.

Garber, Marjorie. 1992. *Vested Interests: Cross-Dressing and Cultural Anxiety*. New York: Routledge.

Gelb, Jerome, Maxwell Malament, and Stephen LoVerme. 1959. Total Reconstruction of the Penis. *Plastic and Reconstructive Surgery* 24: 62–73.

Gide, André. [1911] 1924. *Corydon*. Paris: Gallimard.

Giles, Jeff, and Charles Lee. 1994. There's Nothing Like a Dame: Hollywood Embraces Drag Queens. *Newsweek* (August 15): 69.

Gilles, Harold. 1948. Congenital Absence of the Penis. *British Journal of Plastic Surgery* 1: 8–28.

Gooren, Louis. 1990. The Endocrinology of Transsexualism: A Review and Commentary. *Psychoneuroendocrinology* 15: 3–14.

Gordon, Eric B. 1991. Transsexual Healing: Medicaid Funding of Sex Reassignment Surgery. *Archives of Sexual Behavior* 20: 61–74.

Green, Richard. 1967. Physician Emotionalism in the Treatment of the Transsexual. *Transactions of the New York Academy of Sciences* 29(4): 440–43.

Green, Richard, Robert Stoller, and C. MacAndrew. 1966. Attitudes toward Sex Transformation Procedures. *Archives of General Psychiatry* 15: 178–82.

Halperin, David M. 1990. *One Hundred Years of Homosexuality: And Other Essays on Greek Love.* New York: Routledge.

Hamburger, Christian. 1953. The Desire for Change of Sex as Shown by Personal Letters from 465 Men and Women. *Acta Endocrinologica* 14: 361–75.

Hamburger, C., G. K. Stürup, and E. Dahl-Iversen. 1953. Transvestism: Hormonal, Psychiatric, and Surgical Treatment. *Journal of the American Medical Association* 152: 391–96.

Harry Benjamin International Gender Dysphoria Association 1985. Standards of Care: The Hormonal and Surgical Sex Reassignment of Gender Dysphoric Persons. *Archives of Sexual Behavior* 14: 79–90.

Havens, Leston L. 1987. *Approaches to the Mind: Movement of the Psychiatric Schools from Sects toward Science.* Cambridge, MA: Harvard University Press.

Hekma, Gert. 1994. "A Female Soul in a Male Body": Sexual Inversion as Gender Inversion in Nineteenth-Century Sexology. In *Third Sex, Third Gender: Beyond Sexual Dimorphism in Culture and History,* ed. Gilbert Herdt, 213–39. New York: Zone Books.

Herdt, Gilbert, ed. 1994. *Third Sex, Third Gender: Beyond Sexual Dimorphism in Culture and History.* New York: Zone Books.

Hirschfeld, Magnus. 1906. Vom Wesen der Liebe. Zugleich ein Beitrag zur Lösung der Frage der Bisexualität. *Jahrbuch für Sexuelle Zwischenstufen* 8: 1–284.

———. 1910. *Die Transvestiten. Eine Untersuchung über den erotischen Verkleidungstrieb.* Berlin: A. Pulvermacher.

Horney, Karen. 1926. The Flight from Womanhood: The Masculinity Complex in Women, as Viewed by Men and Women. *International Journal of Psycho-Analysis* 7: 324–39.

———. 1933. The Denial of the Vagina, a Contribution to the Problem of Genital Anxieties Specific to Women. *International Journal of Psycho-Analysis* 14: 57–70.

King, Dave. 1981. Gender Confusions: Psychological and Psychiatric Conceptions of Transvestitism and Transsexualism. In *Making of the Modern Homosexual,* ed. Kenneth Plummer, 155–83. London: Hutchinson.

Kirk, Marshall, and Hunter Madsen. 1989. *After the Ball: How America Will Conquer Its Fear and Hatred of Gays in the '90s.* New York: Doubleday.

Krafft-Ebing, Richard von. 1877. Über gewisse Anomalien des Geschlechtstriebs und die klinischforensische Verwertung derselben als eines wahrscheinlich funktionellen Degenerationszeichens des zentralen Nerven-Systems. *Archiv für Psychiatrie* 7: 291–312.

———. [1886] 1984. *Psychopathia Sexualis. Mit besonderer Berücksichtigung der konträre Sexualempfindung.* Reprint of 14th ed. 1912, ed. Alfred Fuchs. Munich: Matthes and Seitz.

Lancet. 1991. Transsexualism. Vol. 338: 603–4.

Lief, Harold, and Lynn Hubschman. 1993. Orgasm in Postoperative Transsexuals. *Archives of Sexual Behavior* 22: 145–55.

Lothstein, Leslie. 1983. *Female-to-Male Transsexualism: Historical, Clinical and Theoretical Issues.* Boston: Routledge and Kegan Paul.

Marks, Elaine. 1979. Lesbian Intertextuality. In *Homosexualities and French Literature: Cultural Contexts, Critical Texts,* ed. George Stambolian and Elaine Marks, 353–77. Ithaca, NY: Cornell University Press.

Marshall, G. Balfour. 1913. Artificial Vagina. A Review of the Various Operative Procedures for Correcting Atresia Vaginae. *Journal of Obstetrics and Gynæcology of the British Empire* 23: 193–212.

Martin, A. D., and E. Hetrick. 1987. The Stigmatization of the Gay and Lesbian Adolescent. In

    Homosexuality and Psychopathology in Homosexuality, ed. M. W. Ross, 163–83. New York: Haworth Press.

May, Rollo, Ernest Angel, and Henri F. Ellenberger, eds. 1958. *Existence: A New Dimension of Psychiatry and Psychology.* New York: Basic Books.

Money, John, and Anke Ehrhardt. 1972. *Man and Woman, Boy and Girl: The Differentiation and Dimorphism of Gender Identity from Conception to Maturity.* Baltimore: Johns Hopkins University Press.

Money, John, and R. Gaskin. 1970–1971. Sex Reassignment. *International Journal of Psychiatry* 9: 249–69.

Newton, Esther. 1989. The Mythic Mannish Lesbian: Radclyffe Hall and the New Woman. In *Hidden from History: Reclaiming the Gay and Lesbian Past*, ed. Martin Bauml Duberman, Martha Vicinus, and George Chauncey, Jr., 281–93. New York: New American Library.

Pauly, Ira. 1965. Male Psychosexual Inversion: Transsexualism. A Review of 100 Cases. *Archives of General Psychiatry* 13: 172–81.

———. 1974. Female Transsexualism. *Archives of Sexual Behavior* 3: 487–526.

Person, Ethel S., and Lionel Ovesey. 1983. Psychoanalytic Theories of Gender Identity. *Journal of the American Academy of Psychoanalysis* 11: 203–26.

Raffalovich, Marc-André. 1894. Quelques Observations sur l'inversion. *Archives d'anthropologie criminelle* 9: 216–18.

———. 1895. L'affair Oscar Wilde. *Archives D'anthropologie Criminelle* 10: 445–77.

Raymond, Janice. 1979. *The Transsexual Empire: The Making of the She-Male.* Boston: Beacon Press.

Rosario, Vernon A. II. 1995. Pointy Penises, Fashion Crimes, and Hysterical Mollies: The Pederasts' Inversions. In *Homosexuality in French History, 18th–20th Centuries*, ed. Jeffrey W. Merrick and Bryant Ragan, ch. 8. New York: Oxford University Press.

Rubin, H. S. 1994. The Transsexual Experience: Carving the Borders of an Identity. Paper delivered at InQueery/InTheory/InDeed: The Sixth North American Lesbian, Gay, and Bisexual Studies Conference, University of Iowa.

Shapiro, Judith. 1991. Transsexualism: Reflections on the Persistence of Gender and the Mutability of Sex. In *Body Guards: The Cultural Politics of Gender Ambiguity*, ed. Julia Epstein and Kristina Straub, 248–74. New York: Routledge.

Socarides, Charles W. 1969. The Desire for Sexual Transformation: A Psychiatric Evaluation of Transsexualism. *American Journal of Psychiatry* 125: 1419–25.

———. 1970. A Psychoanalytic Study of the Desire for Sexual Transformation ("Transsexualism"): The Plaster-of-Paris Man. *International Journal of Psycho-Analysis* 51: 341–49.

Stoller, Robert J. 1975. *Sex and Gender.* Vol. 2, *The Transsexual Experiment.* New York: Jason Aronson.

Sullivan, Lou. 1990. *Information for the Female to Male Cross Dresser and Transsexual.* Seattle: Ingersoll Press.

Tamassia, Arrigo. 1878. Sull'inversione dell'instinto sessuale. *Rivista sperimentale di freniatria e di medicina legale* 4: 97–291.

Troiden, Richard R. 1989. The Formation of Homosexual Identities. In *Gay and Lesbian Youth*, ed. Gilbert Herdt, 43–73. New York: Harrington Park Press.

Tsoi, W. F. 1988. The Prevalence of Transsexualism in Singapore. *Acta Psychiatrica Scandinavica* 78: 501–04.

———. 1992. Male and Female Transsexuals: A Comparison. *Singapore Medical Journal* 33(2): 182–85.

Ulrichs, Karl Heinrich [Numa Numantius]. [1864–1868] 1898. *"Inclusa": Anthropologische Studien über mannmännliche Geschlechtsliebe. Zweite Schrift über mannmännliche Liebe. Naturwissenschaftlicher Teil, Nachweis, das einer Klasse von männlich gebauten Individuen Geschlechtsliebe zu Männern geschlectlich angeboren ist.* Complete works reprinted in *Forschungen über das Rätsel der mannmännlichen Liebe.* Vol. 2. Leipzig: M. Spohr.

Volkan, Vamik D., and As'ad Masri. 1989. The Development of Female Transsexualism. *American Journal of Psychotherapy* 43: 92–107.

Weideman, G. H. 1953. Transvestitism [letter to the editor]. *Journal of the American Medical Association* 152(12): 1167.

Westphal, Carl E. 1870. Die conträre Sexualempfindung: Symptom eines neuropathischen (psychopathischen) Zustandes. *Archiv für Psychiatrie* 2: 73–108.

Identity/Politics: Historical Sources of the Bisexual Movement

Amanda Udis-Kessler

Consider the following quotes:

Now the version of liberation that I hold is precisely one that would make the homo/hetero distinction irrelevant; for that to happen, however, we shall all have to recognize our bisexual potential. (Altman 1971: 229)

In a society in which men do not oppress women and sexual expression is allowed to follow feelings, the categories of homosexuality and heterosexuality would disappear. (Radicalesbians [1970] 1992: 173)

The main focus of the bisexual movement has been and continues to be the visibility and liberation of all bisexual people. . . . We are just becoming visible to ourselves, coming out as a bisexual pride movement, recognizing that we have a history, a culture, a community. (Hutchins and Kaahumanu 1991: 222)

Quite a change in twenty years — from an implicit universal bisexual potential to an explicit bisexual minority group,[1] from a hope for the end of categories to the creation of a new category and, indeed, a movement claiming "a history, a culture, a community."[2] We have become familiar with the claims of Michel Foucault (1978) and others (D'Emilio 1983a, 1992; Halperin 1990; Katz 1983, 1990; Padgug 1979; Weeks 1979, 1985) that sexual identities are socially constructed, that we must distinguish between the sex act and the sexual actor, and between, as Foucault puts it, the "temporary aberration" of the sodomite and the "species" of the homosexual (1978: 43).[3] Taking Foucault's argument further, we can also consider the ways in which "the bisexual" has been constructed as a "species." Put another way, there is no obvious reason why the bisexual movement and the bisexual identities that fuel it should exist *now*, at this point in history, or why it should be so important to some of us. Consider the recent demands for inclusion of the "b-word" in organizational names and charters, marches, and conferences. Post-Stonewall lesbian and gay groups got along fine for more than a decade without bisexuals insisting on inclusion, and bisexuals did not initially seek such recognition in any politically organized way. What has happened in the past five, ten, or twenty years that has caused some of us to become so invested, not just in our bisexual identities, but in the process of politicizing them? In this essay, I want to take a historical look at part of the social context in which bisexual identities became politicized and in which the bisexual movement arose, and in so doing, hopefully show some of the ways in which the bisexual movement and the identities of many of its members are rooted in feminism and lesbian/gay liberation. Before beginning, though, I need to add the caveat that many crucial aspects of this history, such as the rise of identity politics in the 1980s, go undiscussed here; I hope to do a more complete reading of these events in the future.

There are many points where I could begin this story, but it seems that going back before the late 1960s does not add much to this discussion. The word "bisexual" existed prior to that time, and there were people, including well-known individuals, who lived openly as bisexuals (e.g., Faderman 1991; Greif 1982). However, the focus on bisexuality as a core aspect of one's identity does not seem to have arisen in any patterned way until after Stonewall.[4]

Most of this discussion concerns feminism and lesbian feminism, for while bisexual men have been involved with the bisexual movement since its inception, the bisexual groups that built the current movement have been, and continue to be, led by women — and surprisingly, many women who once identified as lesbian feminists. To a large extent, this difference reflects the way lesbianism was politicized within feminism, such that a culture arose with clearly delineated norms of acceptability, norms which bisexual women — by definition — broke. Such a politicizing of sexuality has not happened within gay male culture, and male bisexuality has never been as politically problematic to gay men as female bisexuality has been to lesbians.[5]

Yet it is worth noting that gay men made a crucial contribution to the bisexual movement during the liberation moment around Stonewall. The opening quotes allude to the idea of "freeing the homosexual in everyone" (Adam 1987: 78) and breaking down sexual categories; a number of radical gays spoke at one time of "the end of the homosexual" (Altman 1971; Escoffier 1985; Jay and Young [1970] 1992; Orlando 1984; Seidman 1993; William 1993; Wolf 1980). Also important was the simple — and utterly radical — emphasis on coming out as the central political act of resistance to lesbian and gay oppression (D'Emilio 1983b, 1992; Marotta 1981). This emphasis on sexual openness would strongly influence bisexuals over the next twenty years.

The situation within feminism was somewhat more complex. The contemporary women's movement developed through women's experiences of sexism in Left political organizations at the end of the 1960s (Echols 1989), with radical feminist groups such as Cell 16 and Redstockings emerging as the theoretical and intellectual wing of the movement at the beginning of the 1970s. It is particularly important to understand that many of these groups offered theories of patriarchy and resistance which belittled lesbianism as a personal cop-out to a political problem. Cell 16 called for celibacy

(Douglas 1990; Echols 1989), while Redstockings acknowledged that most women were in heterosexual relationships and claimed that such relationships should be the site of struggle (Douglas 1990; Echols 1989; Fritz 1979). There were even serious questions as to whether lesbians could be good feminists (Echols 1989). Ironically, many lesbians who had been involved in gay liberation became frustrated with gay male sexism and turned to feminism during this time, only to discover that some heterosexual feminists considered lesbianism a "lavender menace," or at least a "lavender herring" (Abbott and Love 1973; Douglas 1990; Faderman 1991; Marotta 1981; Phelan 1989). The responses of lesbian feminist groups such as Radicalesbians and the Furies turned the tables, arguing that lesbianism was a political choice that indicated their willingness to prioritize women over men, and that such a move was exactly what feminism needed (Abbott and Love 1971, 1973; Atkinson 1973; Bunch 1987; Douglas 1990; Echols 1989; Myron and Bunch 1975; Phelan 1989; Radicalesbians [1970] 1992; Stein 1992; Wilson 1983).[6]

This strategic response opened up a new trend in the relationship between desire and politics. Before the second wave of the feminist movement, it was generally assumed that homosexual desire led to a homosexual identity and whatever degree of political affiliation seemed appropriate. Now, however, the expectation arose among some radical feminists that a woman's political commitment could, and should, lead to her sexual desire for other women. This expectation was tempered by a strong tendency in some circles to downplay the sexual aspect of lesbianism in order to stress the connections, rather than the differences, between women (Adam 1987; Douglas 1990; Stein 1992, 1993).[7] For example, when Alix Dobkin sang, "Any woman can be a lesbian," or when Jill Johnston (1973: 90) claimed that "all women are lesbians," they were referring to a political connection that, theoretically, should ultimately lead to sexual love. Ti-Grace Atkinson had proposed that "feminism is a theory, but lesbianism is a practice"; however, this aphorism spread in a slightly, but crucially, different form: "feminism is *the* theory, lesbianism is *the* practice" (Abbott and Love 1973: 117; Echols 1989: 238). Over time, this idea was adopted among many lesbian feminists, and came to permeate radical feminist culture to such an extent that lesbianism came to be seen as "the only noble choice a committed feminist could make" (Faderman 1991: 207). It became unclear in some circles whether heterosexual women could be good feminists.

The contestation over the sexual identity that "true" or "real" feminists should possess had a number of unfortunate consequences, among them a lesbian-heterosexual split in the early 1970s (Adam 1987; Bunch 1987; Marotta 1981). Most pertinent to the argument presented here, it set up an understanding that feminism was dependent in some way upon sexual practices. Over time, one consequence of problematizing this most intimate form of personal behavior was the development of a sense of resentment and resistance against what was perceived, ironically, as a form of social control. The immediate result of the debate was that most heterosexual feminists dropped out of the women's movement or became involved with its liberal, rather than its radical, branch (joining such groups as the National Organization for Women), and radical feminism became virtually synonymous with lesbian feminism (Echols 1989; Freeman 1975; Fritz 1979).

As heterosexual women went their separate ways, lesbian feminists turned their attention to creating a "women's culture" in the early and mid-1970s (Echols 1989;

Faderman 1991; Taylor and Rupp 1993; Wolf 1980).[8] Feminism was seen as not merely representing values and behaviors; it came to involve goods, services, artistic and intellectual work, and other cultural elements, often in places designated as women-only, such as bookstores, women's centers, restaurants, music festivals, and health clinics. The place of women's culture would later become important when lesbians defended what they defined as "their culture" against bisexuals, claiming that the difference between lesbian feminism and bisexuality was the difference between a way of life, a political commitment, and an entire culture, on the one hand, and a set of sexual practices on the other.[9]

Where were bisexuals at this time? A number were involved in the free love scene, which was in full blossom in a number of cities, and which resulted in the mainstream press running a number of articles depicting bisexuality as the new chic lifestyle ("Bisexual Chic" 1974; Duberman 1991; Highleyman 1994; Klemsrud 1974; Margold 1974; "The New Bisexuals" 1974). Early groups started forming in the mid-1970s: the Bisexual Forum in New York City began in 1975, and the San Francisco Bisexual Center was created in 1976 (Hutchins and Kaahumanu 1991). These groups were generally not politically oriented, at least not in terms of an analysis of bisexual oppression. For example, members of San Francisco's Bisexual Center initially spoke only of the need to recognize and value the natural androgyny of people. The central theme of these early bisexual organizations was human freedom and potential — clearly reminiscent of early gay liberation statements.

By 1978, the year that Chicago's Bi-Ways was founded (Barr 1985), the definition of lesbianism had shifted somewhat. The cultural norms had solidified; "proper" dykes would not be caught dead in a dress, a Burger King, an MBA program — or in bed with a man (D'Emilio 1992; Stein 1992).[10] Rather than being a woman-loving woman, a lesbian at the end of the 1970s was a woman who did not sleep with men. Of course, some lesbians *did* sleep with men, and those who did kept this fact about themselves hidden. These women, it should be noted, were not newcomers to the lesbian fold; some had been lesbian-identified for five years or more. Many had identified as heterosexual prior to the women's movement and had come out as lesbians in the context of the lesbian feminist community and the subtle or not-so-subtle cultural pressure to be a lesbian. While these women did not come to love women grudgingly, they did not necessarily cease to be attracted to men; many simply stopped acting on these attractions, or began to hide the fact that they were acting on them. However, such secrecy was ripe for a new political analysis. Women in this situation in the late 1970s and early 1980s had a language to describe the discomfort, fear, and pain they felt, and it was the language of the closet.

Thus it came to be that women who had grown up identifying as heterosexual, and had come to lesbianism through feminism and through the idea that lesbianism could be a political choice, began to use insights developed by the lesbian and gay rights movement about hiding a disapproved-of sexuality to describe their own heterosexuality.[11] Because they were deeply tied to lesbian feminist communities and had been for years, their values had been deeply influenced by the cultural norms of lesbianism (Wolf 1980). Still, they began to experience the sexual dictates of lesbian feminism as oppressive, and to ask whether both lesbian/gay and heterosexual "communities" had social control over them. Given the entrenched nature of sexism and heterosexism, this may seem like an absurd question. Yet, while these women knew through feminism the ways in which men were oppressive, they also knew that their desires for — or love of — certain men exerted an influence on them with which cognitive arguments and political theory simply could not compete.

Such "lesbians who fell in love with men" were in a bind. They wanted desperately to remain within the community that they had called their own for years, and sometimes had cut themselves off from heterosexual society, yet they were unable to deny their politically proscribed attractions to men. Such women soon became leaders of the political bisexual movement. They "came out" as bisexual and, despite being castigated for doing so, reclaimed pride in their sexuality in ways that were taught to them, ironically, by lesbian feminism and the gay rights movement. For example, in 1980, the year that the New York and Chicago bisexual social groups peaked in popularity (Barr 1985; Mishaan 1985), a lesbian activist in San Francisco went public with her relationship with a man and quietly initiated the process that helped lead us to where we are today. In 1982, she ran an article in a Bay Area women's newspaper calling for bisexuals to become a political force within the women's movement (Kaahumanu 1982); in 1984, she and a small group of bisexuals began engaging in the kind of guerrilla theater now favored by Queer Nation; and in 1987, she wrote a piece on bisexuality for the March on Washington's civil disobedience handbook (Hutchins and Kaahumanu 1991; Kaahumanu 1987, 1994; Tucker 1991).

Lesbians who are critical of bisexual demands have framed the problem as a bisexual desire to invade or infiltrate lesbian space (e.g., Brook 1989; Tait 1991; Wofford 1991), but as this essay makes clear, for many bisexual women, there was no question of invasion. They had been a genuine part of lesbian feminism, and their call for explicit inclusion in the lesbian and gay rights movement as bisexuals was meant to rectify what they perceived as an unjust silencing. That this form of silencing was seen as so problematic indicates the effect that identity politics was having on these women, who had come to understand their situation as a political injustice, and the naming and claiming of their bisexual identity as a political act. And, in a way, this is not surprising: having focused for years on creating a political lesbian identity, these women had, in effect, come to understand their sexual identities as a crucial part of their self-concepts, and as inherently political (Hutchins and Kaahumanu 1991; Ochs 1990).

Elsewhere, "gaydom" was rapidly becoming "lesbian and gaydom." Clearly, there were women in the various "gay organizations" of the 1970s, but this fact became more explicit with the move to include the word "lesbian" in the titles of many gay organizations in the early 1980s, heralding a period of less separation by gender. Lesbian communities were still separated in many ways from "the gay community," but there began to be enough lesbians in "the gay community" who wanted recognition as lesbians for a number of organizations, from college groups to the National Gay Task Force, to change their names (and, where relevant, their charters) to clarify the valued place of lesbians through inclusive language. Both this shift toward linguistic inclusivity, and the reconnection of women and men in the lesbian and gay rights movement, were to have an impact on the bisexual movement's sense of possibilities several years later.

Yet, unlike the lesbian and gay rights movement, bisexual organizing in the early 1980s was primarily a task undertaken by women (Highleyman 1994; North 1990). The bisexual social groups created in the 1970s had ceased to exist (New York's and Chicago's in 1983, San Francisco's in 1984), due primarily to the energy of activists being directed elsewhere and early organizers burning out (Barr 1985; Courtney 1992; Hutchins and Kaahumanu 1991; Mishaan 1985; Rubenstein and Slater 1985; Sheiner 1991). However, bisexual women were beginning to form organizations for support and socializing, groups which would soon turn more explicitly "political" around issues of AIDS and the inclusion of bisexuals within the lesbian and gay community. The Boston Bisexual Women's Network, the Chicago Action Bi-Women, and San Francisco's BiPol formed in 1983, and the Seattle Bisexual Women's Network began in 1986 (Weise 1991). These groups were all composed of explicitly feminist women, in many cases "hasbians" (ex-lesbians). It is worth noting that the Boston group formed partly in response to an ad run in a Boston-based gay newspaper as a joke, which had advised lesbians to acquire "bisexual insurance" so they would not be burned when bisexual women left them for men (Hutchins and Kaahumanu 1991). These early bisexual feminists tried to find ways to stay committed to feminism without excluding men from their beds or drawing rigid lines between their personal and political lives (Morrison 1984; Ochs and Deihl 1994).[12]

As bisexual women were trying to re-imagine ways of explicitly connecting feminism and their relations with (or capacity for relations with) men, the lesbian feminist cultural unity was losing ground and the norms defining "real," "true" lesbians were weakening (Faderman 1991; Phelan 1989; Stein 1992, 1993; Snitow, Stansell, and Thompson 1983; Vance 1984). Some lesbians were voting for Reagan, playing the stock market, and joining other lesbians at power lunches; some lesbians were buying sex toys, joining s/m groups, and subscribing to the sex magazine *On Our Backs*, and some lesbians — including cultural heroes Holly Near (Wofford 1991) and Jan Clausen (Clausen 1990) — were getting involved with men. Put simply, the unified identity required (or thought to be required) was too monolithic and too limiting to be tenable for many women. This exodus and fragmenting of lesbian communities, with the perceived betrayal it involved, caused incredible pain for women who remained within lesbian feminism, a hurt which was dealt with in part through anger at the growing bisexual movement and its "intrusion" into lesbian cultural space.

This brings me to 1987, the point at which the bisexual movement really began to flourish and diversify. In many ways, the story only begins here; new regional networks and a national network were formed, and bisexual identities began to consolidate around cultural artifacts, just as lesbian and gay identities had done earlier. AIDS drew more men into the movement (Alexander 1991), while negative mainstream media coverage of bisexual men as AIDS carriers ironically brought the movement much-needed publicity (Udis-Kessler 1994).[13] During this time, bisexuals also began to publish books (e.g., Geller 1990; Hutchins and Kaahumanu 1991; Weise 1992) and magazines (the Bay Area Bisexual Network's *Anything That Moves*), to organize college courses (Novak 1993) and conferences (Christina 1990; Murray 1990), and to push for inclusion within the growing field of queer studies (Beemyn 1994; Ochs and Ellis 1990/1991). Bisexual activists in newly formed bi political groups (in New York, Chicago, Boston, and elsewhere) adopted a much more aggressive stance on bisexual visibility and inclusion, whether in AIDS information packets, college organizations, media coverage, or titles of national marches (e.g., Kaahumanu 1992). The pent-up anger of bisexual feminists, bisexual AIDS activists, and a range of other bi-identified people found its expression in a concerted effort to change names, charters, and other "exclusive" aspects of lesbian and gay institutions — an effort reminiscent of both early gay liberation and the lesbian push for inclusion in "gaydom" during the 1980s.[14]

Social change movements frequently tell the tale of their inception in such a way as to claim that they burst forth as a natural response to the evils of oppression. While such a strategy may enhance group solidarity, it is, without exception, a simplification of the actual social context in which movements exist. Complicating the story of one such movement, as I have tried to do in this essay, provides a more accurate account of who bisexuals are, where we come from, what resources and limitations we have, and with whom we might — and must — work for justice. I will consider this effort successful to the extent that it keeps these crucial issues alive.

NOTES

1. This chapter is a revised version of a lecture given at Oberlin College in 1992. It draws on several earlier writings of mine (Udis-Kessler 1990, 1991), and appears in an earlier form in *Bisexual Politics* (Tucker 1995).

2. It is interesting to compare some of the pre-Stonewall writing on "homosexuals" as a minority with writing that has come out of the recent bisexual movement. See, for example, Toby Marotta (1981: 6, 9).

3. Jonathan Ned Katz (1990) and Lillian Faderman (1991) offer useful histories of heterosexuality and lesbianism, respectively.

4. But see Paul Berman's (1993: 21) claim that bisexuality was de rigueur in the Weather Underground just before Stonewall.

5. For a recent and not atypical example of gay male hostility toward bisexuals, see Carrie Wofford (1991: 34).

6. Prior to this moment in history, lesbianism had not been seen as a choice that any woman, much less every woman, could make. Rather, it was considered to be the biologically/psychologically fixed inclination of a minority of women. On the tensions between these two perspectives within lesbian feminism, see Barry Adam (1987: 95), and Arlene Stein (1992).

7. See Adrienne Rich (1980) for an excellent example of this tendency taken to its extreme.

8. The ways in which "women's communities" turned out to be resources for white women only has been addressed by Audre Lorde (1984).

9. For analyses of the growth of gay male culture in the "gay ghetto" — a phenomenon that may turn out to have had important effects on the rise of the bisexual movement — see Dennis Altman (1982); Gilbert Herdt (1992); John Lee (1979); Martin Levine (1979); and Stephen Murray (1979).

10. For lesbian feminist perspectives on bisexuality, see Janet Bode (1976: 217–19); Lillian Faderman (1991: 234–35); Jill Johnston (1973: 178–80); and Adrienne Rich (1980). For an early positive perspective, see Sidney Abbott and Barbara Love (1973: 155–57).

11. For examples of bisexual women's fears of — and experiences with — losing their lesbian communities, see Tamara Bower (1991); Sharon Gonsalves (1989, 1994); Julia Klein (1994: 20);

Anastasia Toufexis (1992); Michael William (1993); and many of the essays in *Bi Any Other Name* (Hutchins and Kaahumanu 1991), and *Closer to Home* (Weise 1992).

12. Excellent examples of feminist bisexual political analyses from this period include Lisa Orlando (1984) and Kit Womantree (1986). Such projects were continued by Lenore Norrgard (1990a, 1990b) and in the anthology *Closer to Home* (Weise 1992).

13. For reflection on AIDS reuniting lesbians and gay men, see John D'Emilio (1992: 264–65); Lillian Faderman (1991: 293–95); and Arlene Stein (1992). For commentary on young activists fighting AIDS in gender-mixed (and bisexual-welcoming) settings, see Irene Stroud (1994). The rise of queerdom goes undiscussed in this essay, but is addressed by Allan Bérubé and Jeffrey Escoffier (1991), and Lisa Duggan (1992). See Ann Powers (1993) for the new "queer in the streets, straight in the sheets" phenomenon that is related to, but different from, bisexuality.

14. For further discussion of the bisexual movement and responses to it after 1987, see Lily Braindrop (1992); Elisabeth Brook (1989); Tom Geller (1990); Liz Highleyman (1994); Loraine Hutchins and Lani Kaahumanu (1991); Julia Klein (1994); Steven Seidman (1993); Vanessa Tait (1991); Anastasia Toufexis (1992); Naomi Tucker (1995); Elizabeth Reba Weise (1991, 1992); Michael William (1993); Carrie Wofford (1991); and any issue of the magazine *Anything That Moves*.

REFERENCES

Abbott, Sidney, and Barbara Love. 1971. Is Women's Liberation a Lesbian Plot? In *Woman in Sexist Society: Studies in Power and Powerlessness*, ed. Vivian Gornick and Barbara K. Moran, 601–21. New York: Basic Books.

———. 1973. *Sappho Was a Right-On Woman: A Liberated View of Lesbianism.* New York: Stein and Day.

Adam, Barry. 1987. *The Rise of a Gay and Lesbian Movement.* Boston: Twayne Publishers.

Alexander, Christopher. 1991. Ten Years into the AIDS Epidemic: Bisexuals Battle Invisibility. *Anything That Moves: Beyond the Myths of Bisexuality*, no. 1 (Winter): 34–35.

Altman, Dennis. 1971. *Homosexual: Oppression and Liberation.* New York: Outerbridge and Dienstfrey.

———. 1982. *The Homosexualization of America: The Americanization of the Homosexual.* Boston: Beacon Press.

Atkinson, Ti-Grace. 1973. Lesbianism and Feminism. In *Amazon Expedition: A Lesbian Feminist Anthology*, ed. Phyllis Birkby, et al., 11–14. Albion, CA: Times Change Press.

Barr, George. 1985. Chicago Bi-Ways: An Informal History. In *Two Lives to Lead: Bisexuality in Men and Women*, ed. Fritz Klein and Timothy J. Wolf, 231–34. New York: Harrington Park Press.

Beemyn, Brett. 1994. Toward Bi Inclusivity: The Iowa Queer Studies Conference. *Bi Women* 12 (August/September): 1, 10.

Berman, Paul. 1993. Democracy and Homosexuality. *New Republic* (December 20): 17–35.

Bérubé, Allan, and Jeffrey Escoffier. 1991. Queer/Nation. *OUT/LOOK*, no. 11 (Winter): 12–23.

Bisexual Chic: Anyone Goes. 1974. *Newsweek* (May 27): 90.

Bode, Janet. 1976. *View from Another Closet: Exploring Bisexuality in Women.* New York: Hawthorne Books.

Bower, Tamara. 1991. Coming Out Bi in the Lesbian Community: My Experience. *North Bi Northwest* 4 (October/November): 3–5.

Braindrop, Lily. 1992. Bi and Beyond. *Advocate* (July 30): 52–53.

Brook, Elisabeth. 1989. Lesbians Don't Fuck Men. *Sojourner: The Women's Forum* (July): 6.

Bunch, Charlotte. 1987. *Passionate Politics: Feminist Theory in Action, Essays, 1968–1986.* New York: St. Martin's Press.

Christina, Greta. 1990. The First National Bisexual Conference. *San Francisco Bay Times* (July): 10+.

Clausen, Jan. 1990. My Interesting Condition. *OUT/LOOK*, no. 7 (Winter): 11–21.

Courtney, Autumn. 1992. The Only Thing Constant . . . Is Change. *Anything That Moves: Beyond the Myths of Bisexuality*, no. 4: 30–31.

D'Emilio, John. 1983a. Capitalism and Gay Identity. In *Powers of Desire: The Politics of Sexuality*, ed. Ann Snitow, Christine Stansell, and Sharon Thompson, 100–113. New York: Monthly Review Press.

————. 1983b. *Sexual Politics, Sexual Communities: The Making of a Homosexual Minority in the United States, 1940–1970.* Chicago: University of Chicago Press.

————. 1992. *Making Trouble: Essays on Gay History, Politics, and the University.* New York: Routledge.

Douglas, Carol. 1990. *Love and Politics: Radical Feminist and Lesbian Theories.* San Francisco: Ism Press.

Duberman, Martin. 1991. *About Time: Exploring the Gay Past.* Revised and Expanded Edition. New York: Penguin Books.

Duggan, Lisa. 1992. Making It Perfectly Queer. *Socialist Review* 22 (January–March): 11–31.

Echols, Alice. 1989. *Daring to Be Bad: Radical Feminism in America, 1967–1975.* Minneapolis: University of Minnesota Press.

Escoffier, Jeffrey. 1985. Sexual Revolution and the Politics of Gay Identity. *Socialist Review*, nos. 82/83: 119–53.

Faderman, Lillian. 1991. *Odd Girls and Twilight Lovers: A History of Lesbian Life in Twentieth-Century America.* New York: Columbia University Press.

Foucault, Michel. 1978. *The History of Sexuality.* Vol. 1, *An Introduction.* New York: Pantheon.

Freeman, Jo. 1975. *The Politics of Women's Liberation: A Case Study of an Emerging Social Movement and Its Relation to the Policy Process.* New York: Longman.

Fritz, Leah. 1979. *Dreamers and Dealers: An Intimate Appraisal of the Women's Movement.* Boston: Beacon Press.

Geller, Tom, ed. 1990. *Bisexuality: A Reader and Sourcebook.* Ojai, CA: Times Change Press.

Gonsalves, Sharon. 1989. On Bisexuals in the Lesbian Community. *Sojourner: The Women's Forum* (May): 7–8.

————. 1994. One Bi Woman's Journey. *Bi Women* 12 (October/November): 1, 7.

Greif, Martin. 1982. *The Gay Book of Days: An Evocatively Illustrated Who's Who of Who Is, Was, May Have Been, Probably Was, and Almost Certainly Seems to Have Been Gay During the Past 5,000 Years.* Secaucus, NJ: Lyle Stuart.

Halperin, David M. 1990. *One Hundred Years of Homosexuality: And Other Essays on Greek Love.* New York: Routledge.

Herdt, Gilbert, ed. 1992. *Gay Culture in America: Essays from the Field.* Boston: Beacon Press.

Highleyman, Liz. 1994. The Evolution of the Bisexual Movement. *Anything That Moves: Beyond the Myths of Bisexuality*, no. 8 (Winter): 24–25.

Hutchins, Loraine, and Lani Kaahumanu, eds. 1991. *Bi Any Other Name: Bisexual People Speak Out.* Boston: Alyson.

Jay, Karla, and Allen Young, eds. [1970] 1992. *Out of the Closets: Voices of Gay Liberation.* New York: New York University Press.

Johnston, Jill. 1973. *Lesbian Nation: The Feminist Solution.* New York: Simon and Schuster.

Kaahumanu, Lani. 1982. Bi-phobic: Some of My Best Friends Are . . . *Plexus* 9 (June): 19.

———. 1987. The Bisexual Community: Are We Visible Yet? *National Lesbian and Gay March on Washington CD Handbook:* 47–48.

———. 1992. It's Official! The 1993 March on Washington for Lesbian, Gay and (Yes!) Bisexual Rights and Liberation. *Anything That Moves: Beyond the Myths of Bisexuality,* no. 4: 22–24.

———. 1994. Tippecanoe and Kaahumanu Too. *Anything That Moves: Beyond the Myths of Bisexuality,* no. 8 (Summer): 18–20.

Katz, Jonathan Ned. 1983. *Gay/Lesbian Almanac.* New York: Harper and Row.

———. 1990. The Invention of Heterosexuality. *Socialist Review* 20 (January–March): 7–34.

Klein, Julia. 1994. Pair and Re-Pair. *Philadelphia Inquirer Magazine* (March 6): 18–23, 28.

Klemsrud, Judy. 1974. The Bisexuals. *New York Magazine* 7 (April 1): 37–38.

Lee, John. 1979. The Gay Connection. *Urban Life* 8 (July): 175–98.

Levine, Martin. 1979. Gay Ghetto. In *Gay Men: The Sociology of Male Homosexuality,* ed. Martin Levine, 182–204. New York: Harper and Row.

Lorde, Audre. 1984. *Sister Outsider.* Trumansburg, NY: Crossing Press.

Margold, Jane. 1974. Bisexuality: The Newest Sex-Style. *Cosmopolitan* (June): 189–92.

Marotta, Toby. 1981. *The Politics of Homosexuality.* Boston: Houghton Mifflin.

Mishaan, Chuck. 1985. The Bisexual Scene in New York City. In *Two Lives to Lead: Bisexuality in Men and Women,* ed. Fritz Klein and Timothy J. Wolf, 223–26. New York: Harrington Park Press.

Morrison, Megan. 1984. What We Are Doing. *Gay Community News* (February 25): 13 + .

Murray, Sarah. 1990. Bisexual Movement Comes Out Strong. *San Francisco Sentinel* (July 4): 6.

Murray, Stephen. 1979. The Institutional Elaboration of a Quasi-Ethnic Community. *International Review of Modern Sociology* 9 (July–December): 65–77.

Myron, Nancy, and Charlotte Bunch, eds. 1975. *Lesbianism and the Women's Movement.* Baltimore, MD: Diana Press.

The New Bisexuals. 1974. *Time* (May 13): 79.

Norrgard, Lenore. 1990a. The Myth of Heterosexual Privilege. *North Bi Northwest* 3 (June/July): 3 + .

———. 1990b. The Reality of Heterosexual Privilege. *North Bi Northwest* 3 (August/September): 3 + .

North, Gary. 1990. Where the Boys Aren't. In *Bisexuality: A Reader and Sourcebook,* ed. Tom Geller, 40–46. Ojai, CA: Times Change Press.

Novak, Elizabeth. 1993. Colleges Offer Course on Bisexuality. *The Lavender Network* (January): 20–21.

Ochs, Robyn. 1990. Self-Identifying as Bisexual: A Political Statement. *Gay Community News* (April 8–14): 5.

Ochs, Robyn, and Marcia Deihl. 1994. The Bi-Vocals' Bi-story. *Bi Women* 12 (June/July): 1, 4–5, 7.

Ochs, Robyn, and Pam Ellis. 1990/1991. The Fourth Annual Lesbian, Bisexual and Gay Studies Conference. *Bi Women* 8 (December/January): 1, 4–6.

Orlando, Lisa. 1984. Loving Whom We Choose. *Gay Community News* (February 25): 8 + .

Padgug, Robert. 1979. Sexual Matters: On Conceptualizing Sexuality in History. *Radical History Review* 20 (Spring/Summer): 3–23.

Phelan, Shane. 1989. *Identity Politics: Lesbian Feminism and the Limits of Community.* Philadelphia: Temple University Press.

Powers, Ann. 1993. Queer in the Streets, Straight in the Sheets. *Utne Reader* (November/December): 74–80.

Radicalesbians. [1970] 1992. The Woman-Identified Woman. In *Out of the Closets: Voices of Gay Liberation*, ed. Karla Jay and Allen Young, 172–77. New York: New York University Press.

Rich, Adrienne. 1980. Compulsory Heterosexuality and Lesbian Existence. *Signs* 5 (4): 631–60.

Rubenstein, Maggi, and Cynthia Ann Slater. 1985. A Profile of the San Francisco Bisexual Center. In *Two Lives to Lead: Bisexuality in Men and Women*, ed. Fritz Klein and Timothy J. Wolf, 227–30. New York: Harrington Park Press.

Seidman, Steven. 1993. Identity and Politics in a "Postmodern" Gay Culture. In *Fear of a Queer Planet: Queer Politics and Social Theory*, ed. Michael Warner, 105–42. Minneapolis: University of Minnesota Press.

Sheiner, Marcy. 1991. The Foundations of the Bisexual Community in San Francisco. In *Bi Any Other Name: Bisexual People Speak Out*, ed. Loraine Hutchins and Lani Kaahumanu, 203–6. Boston: Alyson.

Snitow, Ann, Christine Stansell, and Sharon Thompson, eds. 1983. *Powers of Desire: The Politics of Sexuality*. New York: Monthly Review Press.

Stein, Arlene. 1992. Sisters and Queers: The Decentering of Lesbian Feminism. *Socialist Review* 22 (January–March): 33–55.

———. 1993. The Year of the Lustful Lesbian. In *Sisters, Sexperts, Queers: Beyond the Lesbian Nation*, ed. Arlene Stein, 13–34. New York: Penguin.

Stroud, Irene. 1994. Out of the Straight Jacket. *Nation* (July 4): 27–28.

Tait, Vanessa. 1991. The Bisexuality Debate. *Boston Phoenix* (August 16): 6–7.

Taylor, Verta, and Leila Rupp. 1993. Women's Culture and Lesbian Feminist Activism. *Signs* 19 (Autumn): 32–61.

Toufexis, Anastasia. 1992. Bisexuality: What Is It? *Time* (August 17): 49–51.

Tucker, Naomi. 1991. A Bi-Coastal Partnership. *Anything That Moves: Beyond the Myths of Bisexuality*, no. 1 (Winter): 18–26.

———, ed. 1995. *Bisexual Politics: Theories, Queries and Visions*. Binghamton, NY: Haworth Press.

Udis-Kessler, Amanda. 1990. Culture and Community: Thoughts on Lesbian-Bisexual Relations. *Sojourner: The Women's Forum* 16 (December): 11–12.

———. 1991. "A Quiet Stonewall": The Rise of the Bisexual Identity and Movement. Unpublished ms.

———. 1994. Beyond AIDS Vectors, Deluded Closet Cases and LUGS. In *Bound by Diversity*, ed. James Sears, 71–80. Columbia, SC: Sebastian Press.

Vance, Carol, ed. 1984. *Pleasure and Danger: Exploring Female Sexuality*. New York: Routledge and Kegan Paul.

Weeks, Jeffrey. 1979. Movements of Affirmation: Sexual Meanings and Homosexual Identities. *Radical History Review* 20 (Spring/Summer): 164–79.

———. 1985. *Sexuality and Its Discontents: Meanings, Myths, and Modern Sexualities*. New York: Routledge.

Weise, Elizabeth Reba. 1991. The Bisexual Community: Viable Reality or Revolutionary Pipe Dream? *Anything That Moves: Beyond the Myths of Bisexuality*, no. 2 (Spring): 20–25.

———, ed. 1992. *Closer to Home: Bisexuality and Feminism*. Seattle: Seal Press.

William, Michael. 1993. Bisexuality. *Anarchy: A Journal of Desire Armed* 13 (Spring): 34–39.

Wilson, Elizabeth. 1983. I'll Climb the Stairway to Heaven: Lesbianism in the Seventies. In *Sex and Love: New Thoughts on Old Contradictions*, ed. Sue Cartledge and Joanna Ryan, 180–95. London: The Women's Press.

Wofford, Carrie. 1991. The Bisexual Revolution: Deluded Closet Cases or Vanguards of the Movement? *OutWeek*, no. 84 (February 6): 33–39, 70, 80.

Wolf, Deborah. 1980. *The Lesbian Community*. Berkeley: University of California Press.

Womantree, Kit. 1986. Nothing to Lose But Our Illusions. *BBWN* (February/March): 1, 7–8.

Sexual Identity and Bisexual Identities: The Struggle for Self-Description in a Changing Sexual Landscape

Paula C. Rust

As we look back over our lives, we construct them as stories. A story has a conclusion, and the story line leads inexorably to the conclusion; events and details that are irrelevant to the conclusion are irrelevant to the story and distract the listener from the "real" story. When we construct our life stories, we tend to forget the irrelevant details of our pasts. We identify the relevant experiences and interpret them as the building blocks that made us into the people we are today, and we understand our past changes as the twists and turns in the road we took to reach our current selves. Even if we recognize that we have not yet completed our personal journeys and that we will continue to rewrite our stories until we reach the final draft at death, we still perceive our pasts as the paths by which we arrived at our present selves. Most of us who identify our present selves as gay, lesbian, or bisexual have constructed "coming out stories" that explain — to ourselves and to others — how we arrived at our sexual self-definitions.

Social scientists in the 1970s, seeking to redress the scientific sins that had been committed against lesbian and gay people in the past, sought to understand the lives of lesbian and gay people as they (we) understood their (our) own lives. Taking the cue from their lesbian and gay subjects, many sociologists and psychologists set out to study the process of coming out, i.e., the process of lesbian or gay identity formation. Researchers soon discovered "milestone events," or life events that lesbian and gay people had identified as relevant to their development and incorporated into their coming out stories. Typical milestone events were the first experience of a feeling of sexual attraction for someone of the same sex, the first sexual experience with someone of the same sex, the first labeling of one's self as homosexual, the first public expression of one's homosexual identity to significant others, the symbolic switch from a homosexual to a lesbian or gay identity as one's self-acceptance increased and, eventually, the integration of one's private and public identities as one came out of the closet.

Based on these observations, scientists elaborated developmental models of coming out that construct it as a linear process of self-discovery in which a false, socially imposed heterosexual identity is replaced with a lesbian or gay identity that accurately reflects the essence of the individual. These models rarely account for bisexual identity as an authentic identity; when they acknowledge bisexual identity at all, they usually cast it as a phase one might pass through on the way to adopting a lesbian or gay identity.[1] Researchers operating within these linear developmental models of coming out asked respondents for the ages at which they experienced each milestone, and then, reporting the average ages, described coming out as an ordered sequence of events. From this research, we learned that lesbians first experience sexual attraction to other women at an average age of twelve or thirteen, but do not become aware of these sexual feelings until late adolescence. They begin suspecting that they are lesbian at an average age of eighteen, but do not adopt lesbian identities until their early twenties. We learned that gay men experience these events at younger ages and in more rapid sequence than lesbians, and — from the few studies that treated bisexual identity as authentic — we learned that bisexuals come out later and more slowly than gays and lesbians.[2] Based on these findings, researchers began theorizing about why men come out more quickly than women and why bisexuals come out more slowly than monosexuals.

The portrait of sexual identity formation that is painted by these average ages is not only grossly simplified but factually inaccurate. Based on research with lesbian-identified and bisexual-identified women,[3] I have shown that average ages conceal a great deal of variation in the coming out process, both among and between lesbian and bisexual women.[4] In contrast to the linear portrait painted by average ages, lesbian and bisexual women experience each milestone event at a wide range of ages; many women do not experience all of the so-called milestone events; women who do experience these events experience them in various orders; and some women experience some events repeatedly.

Moreover, I discovered that the "finding" that bisexual women come out more slowly than lesbians is an artifact of the statistical methods used in studies based on linear models of coming out. When I calculated average ages for the over 400 women in my first study, the results confirmed earlier findings that bisexual women come out at later ages and more slowly than lesbian women. Bisexual women first felt attracted to women at an average age of 18.1, compared to 15.4 for lesbian women. Bisexual women first questioned their heterosexual identity 1.9 years later, at an average of 20.0 years, whereas lesbians first questioned their heterosexual identity 1.6 years later, at an average age of 17.0. But a closer look at the data revealed that lesbian women were twice as likely as bisexual women to have questioned their heterosexual identity before they felt attracted to women (28% vs. 14%), probably because some women were encouraged by lesbian feminist arguments about the political nature of lesbianism to identify themselves as lesbian even in the absence of sexual feelings toward women. Among women who questioned their heterosexual identities only after feeling attracted to other women, bisexual women actually did so sooner — not later — than lesbian women. In other words, the original finding that bisexual women come out more slowly than lesbian women was an artifact resulting from a failure to recognize variations in the coming out process as equally authentic patterns, rather than as deviations from an underlying linear course.

I also discovered that bisexual women had changed sexual identities more frequently in the past than lesbian women, often alternating repeatedly between lesbian and bisexual identities. Under linear developmental models, this finding would be taken as an indication of the instability of bisexual identity and the sociopsychological immaturity of bisexual-identified individuals.[5] Under more sophisticated, but still linear, social interactionist understandings of the creation of identity, this finding would be taken as evidence of the difficulty of constructing a bisexual identity in a social world that offers only two authenticated categories, heterosexual and homosexual.[6] But I also discovered that, at any given moment, a bisexual woman was as likely to be satisfied with her current sexual identity as a lesbian was with hers. This finding disproves the hypothesis that bisexual women are engaged in a constant struggle to establish a satisfactory sexual identity and suggests instead that bisexual women find different sexual identities satisfactory at different times and under different circumstances. Bisexual women's frequent identity changes do not indicate a state of searching immaturity, but a mature state of mutability.

Previous researchers have attempted to modify the linear model of coming out by introducing feedback loops, alternate routes, and contingencies.[7] Although these modifications produce models with ample room for deviation, they do not effectively describe the formation of sexual identity. They are unable to account for the findings that bisexual women incorporate their same-sex feelings into sexual identities more quickly than lesbians and that bisexual women are as satisfied with their sexual identities as lesbians are. This inability highlights the need to develop a new model of the identity formation process.

To accommodate the empirical reality of identity change processes, linear developmental models of coming out must be abandoned in favor of a social constructionist view of identity as a description of the location of the self in relation to other individuals, groups, and institutions. The individuals, groups, and institutions to which we relate are landmarks on a sexual landscape that is itself socially constructed. From this perspective, identity change would be understood as a process of modifying one's self-description in response to changes in either the location of the self or the socially constructed landscape on which one is located. Identity change would be a necessary outcome of one's efforts to maintain an accurate self-description, not an indication that one has not yet achieved an accurate self-description. "Coming out" would not be a process of essential discovery leading to a mature and stable identity, but merely one story constructed around one of the myriad identity changes we all go through as mature adults attempting to maintain accurate self-descriptions in a changing social environment. Research on the so-called "coming out process" would be reconceptualized as research on the social contexts of identity changes that take place throughout life, and the goal of this research would be to discover the types of contextual changes that motivate individual identity change.

In the spring of 1993, I began a second study guided by the concept of sexual identity as a description of the self in relation to other individuals, groups, and institutions.[8] The overall goal of the study is to document the development of bisexual identity, community, and politics in the United States, the United Kingdom, and other, primarily English-speaking, countries. A specific goal of the study is to explore the types of contextual changes that lead individuals to change their sexual identities, with an eye toward understanding why currently bisexual-identified individuals tend to have changed their sexual identities frequently in the past. The study includes people of all gender and sexual identities, including transsexuals and transgenderists.

Participants in the study were asked several questions about their current and past sexual identities, the first of which was "When you think about your sexual orientation today, what term do you use most often to describe yourself?" This question was followed by response choices ranging from lesbian, gay, straight, and bisexual to polysexual, polyfidelitous, queer, and pansensual and gave respondents the option of writing in other identities or indicating that they preferred not to label themselves or did not know what their orientations were. Respondents who chose or wrote in one or more sexual identities were asked "What does your sexual identity mean to you?" They were also asked to "[t]hink back to the most recent time when you began to think of yourself as _____," to identify the experience, event, or circumstance [that] caused you to decide or realize that this was the term you should use to describe yourself at that time," and to "[d]escribe how this term came to have this meaning for you."

Respondents' answers to these questions provide insights into the social contexts within which their current sexual identities are anchored and in which their identity changes occurred. In particular, they reveal six general types of change that can lead to individual identity change. The first is change in an individual's location on the sexual landscape co[9] inhabits. As individuals' locations shift, so do their relationships to landmarks in the sexual landscape, and they must change their identities to maintain accurate descriptions of these relationships. Second, the landscape itself might alter as the landmarks in it move, change, or fade, and as new landmarks appear. Third, even in the absence of changes in individuals' own locations or in the landscape itself, the language available to individuals to describe their locations might be evolving. As old terms disappear or alter in meaning and new terms develop, individuals find that their sexual identities no longer describe their locations accurately, and they must search the language for new ways to identify themselves. Fourth, the sexual landscape is constructed differently in different social contexts, and a variety of languages for self-description are therefore available: individuals who move from one context to another during the course of their daily lives often use different identities in different contexts. Fifth, if we recognize that people sometimes, intentionally or unintentionally, describe themselves inaccurately to others and to themselves, we find that individuals' sexual identities can change as they become more or less honest about their locations on the sexual landscape. Finally, some individuals change their sexual identities, not in response to changes in their location, landscape, language, social context, or level of honesty, but instead to cause changes in their location, landscape, or language. Within each of these broad categories of change, there are many specific types of change that can lead to identity redefinition, as mature individuals attempt to maintain descriptions of their locations on the sexual landscape. The men, women, and transgendered individuals who participated in my current research provided numerous examples of these various types of sexual identity change.

Changes in One's Location on the Sexual Landscape

The most common type of change reported by individuals is change in their own locations on the sexual landscape. Change is relative, and can only be defined in relation to objects other than the self; these objects might be other individuals, social groups, or social and political institutions. Many respondents recalled that they changed their sexual identities when they developed new relationships with particular people, usually romantic or sexual relationships with people whose genders were different from the genders of the people with whom they had expected to become intimately involved. For example, a White American[10] woman who used to identify herself as a Lesbian[11] explained why she began to identify herself as Bisexual:

> About two years ago, I had been in a sexual relationship with a wonderful woman for one year, and I was identifying as lesbian at the time. I found myself attracted to a man who was interested in me. I had a sense of being at a crossroads: lesbian or "something else." She wanted a monogamous relationship and . . . I didn't want that conservatism. We broke up and I began a sexual relationship with the man.[12]

Her previous Lesbian identity represented her sexual relationship with a woman. It also represented her lack of a relationship with a man, as evidenced by the fact that it had to change when she began to feel attracted to a man. The conflict between her Lesbian identity and her attraction to a man created, for her, a crossroads, i.e., the moment of change. When this attraction led to a sexual relationship with the man, she adopted a Bisexual identity that apparently represents both her (ex-)relationship to a woman and her current relationship to a man. The new identity represents her new location on the sexual landscape, a location that is described in relation to two other individuals, a woman and a man.

Sometimes the new relationship is not an actual sexual or physical one but merely a feeling of attraction toward another person, as was the case with an Irish woman who identified herself as Bisexual when she "[r]ealiz[ed] I was experiencing a sexual fantasy about a female friend." Or the relationships represented by an identity might be potential relationships. For example, a White man explained that he began identifying as a Gay Bisexual when he "recognized the reality of my past (and potential future) relationships."

For some respondents, a single relationship with an individual — whether actual, desired, or potential — is not enough to motivate a complete identity change. These respondents' identities represent their relationships to entire social groups, and they do not change their sexual identities until their relationships with individuals lead them to perceive changes in their relationships to entire social groups. For example, a Jewish Lesbian said that she fell in love with "a woman," but it was not until she realized she "was sexually attracted to women" that she "suddenly saw the possibility and even inevitability of a different (i.e., lesbian) erotic self-definition." In other words, noting that the individual with whom she had developed a relationship belonged to the social group "women," she generalized her feelings to the entire social group by "realizing" that she could potentially be attracted to any member of that group. She then adopted a Lesbian identity to represent her new relationship to this social group. Another woman explained that she did not begin to call herself Bi until her relationship to an individual man led to the realization that she was attracted to men as a social group. She wrote,

> I had been involved with a man for about two years, during which time I identified as "a lesbian who happens to be seeing a man until something else comes along." After a while I realized that I was really deeply committed to my other-sex relationship. . . . Also I became aware that I was starting to feel more generalized attraction to men other than just my lover. So "bi" seemed more accurate.

Many respondents said that their current identities represent a connection to social or political institutions. For example, one American man said that his Gay identity means "not only being attracted to members of the same sex . . . but also identification with an oppressed minority with a distinct identity and culture." Similarly, a White/Native American woman explained that she began calling herself a Lesbian after she became involved with a woman because "I was so immersed in lesbian culture after that, and felt so at home, it felt silly not to call myself a lesbian." In other words, her relationship with a woman led to her involvement in lesbian culture, and her Lesbian identity represents this relationship to lesbian social institutions as much as it represents her relationship to an individual woman.

Despite the fact that many respondents' sexual identities represent their relationships to social or political institutions, very few reported that they had changed their identities in response to changes in their relationships to social and political institutions. This finding suggests that relationships to social and political institutions usually develop after identity change. Identities that are originally adopted because of relationships to individuals or social groups can lead one to develop relationships with social and political institutions, and the identity subsequently comes to represent these institutional relationships as well.

Lesbian-identified, gay-identified, and heterosexual-identified respondents often described their identities as representing a single relationship to either an individual, a group, or an institution, whereas bisexual-identified respondents usually said that their identities represent multiple relationships to various individuals, social groups, and institutions. The larger number of relationships needed to anchor bisexual identity is a function of two facts. First, landmarks in the mainstream Euro-American sexual landscape are gendered. For example, individuals are recognized as either female or male, woman or man. Social groups include "men," "women," and "lesbians," and institutions include "gay male society," "legally recognized marriage," and "the feminist movement." Second, Euro-American sexual categories are defined in reference to gender; heterosexuality is defined in terms of relationships between persons of different gender, and homosexuality is defined in terms of relationships between persons of same gender. Thus, on the gendered sexual landscape, a minimum of one landmark is necessary to anchor a monosexual identity such as lesbian, gay, or heterosexual. But in this system of dichotomous sexuality based on dichotomous gender, bisexuality can only be understood as a hybrid combination of heterosexuality and homosexuality. Thus, to maintain a *bi*sexual self-description on the gendered landscape, one needs to locate oneself with respect to both female and male, or lesbian/gay and heterosexual, landmarks.

For example, a bisexual identity might represent relationships to two individuals of different genders, as it does to the White man who explained that he adopted his Bisexual identity because he "dated a man and woman at the same time." Or, it might represent relationships to two social groups, men and women, as it does to the Asian-American/Caucasian individual who wrote, "I realized I have always loved men. . . . At the same time I did not cease to love or feel attracted to women, so I discovered I was bisexual." Many bisexuals' identities represent an attraction to one gender as a social group and an actual physical or emotional relationship with a particular individual of the other gender. As one man explained, the incident that led him to adopt a Bisexual identity was "My first same-sex experience, but I realized I was still attracted to women." Although the particular landmarks varied, most bisexual-identified respondents were able to support their bisexual identities only by maintaining relationships to multiple landmarks of both genders.

Changes in the Sexual Landscape

Whether or not an individual changes co's location on the sexual landscape, the sexual landscape itself might change, creating new opportunities for self-description while transforming or eliminating existing possibilities. The types of landscape change reported by respondents included the appearance of previously invisible landmarks on the sexual landscape and historical changes in the sexual landscape.

Newly visible landmarks might consist of a single individual. For example, one Heterosexual-identified, Bisexual American woman wrote that she "had to sharpen up my own fuzzy feeling about my own bisexuality" when her daughter came out to her as bisexual. The appearance of a bisexual person in her life forced her to consider her relationship to this person, and in the process, to clarify her thoughts about her own sexuality. Conversely, the disappearance of an individual can eliminate the need for an identity that represents one's relationship to that individual, as it did for this Australian woman:

> I really craved to be a "lesbian" or "bisexual" — but somehow I couldn't take this label unless I had sexual encounters with women. . . . My period of confusion and questioning my heterosexuality passed away [when] the woman I was attracted to left — so I told myself I was hetero. again.

Historical changes, such as the development of social and political movements, create new social groups and institutions and modify or destroy others. As these historical forces transform the sexual landscape, individuals whose identities located them on the old landscape find that they have to relate themselves to their new environment. For example, in the very early days of the second wave of the (predominantly white) feminist movement, lesbianism was labeled a "lavender herring," and feminist lesbians were encouraged to demonstrate their commitment to the feminist movement by remaining in the closet.[13] But the reconstruction of the relationship between lesbianism and feminism in the early 1970s resulted in the creation of the category of the "political lesbian" and led many women to adopt lesbian identities as an expression of commitment to the newly reconstituted feminist movement.[14] One respondent wrote that in 1977 she adopted her Lesbian identity because "Thru feminist politics I began to understand that my primary emotional/energetic commitment was with women." Several years earlier, a lesbian identity would not have served to express her feminist "emotional/energetic commitment" to women.

More recently, the development of a small but growing bisexual culture and social structure has created new social and political landmarks with which individuals can anchor bisexual identities. For example, an American woman mentioned that she had realized that she was bisexual since 1976, but that she only adopted a Bisexual identity "in the last five years since there was a movement." Another woman said that she "had previously identified as a Lesbian," but she "became aware of the Bi option" because "there was a growing, visible Bi community." As the number of bisexual social and political institutions continues to increase, more and more people will identify themselves as bisexual, abandoning the identities that they had considered satisfactory only a few years earlier — identities that became unsatisfactory because the landmarks to which they referred changed and new landmarks arose.

Individuals often experience changes in their personal social contexts. It is only later, when individuals look back over their lives and the lives of others, that they will see the changes they experienced as part of more global, historical contexts that had similar effects on other people. Therefore, few respondents referred to the effect of history on their sexual identities, but this lack of reference to historical change was complemented by an abundance of references to changes in respondents' individual social contexts. These alterations in social context were usually significant because they brought with them changes in the language available for self-description.

Changes in the Language Available for Self-Description

The distinction between changes in the sexual landscape — whether historical or personal — and changes in language is largely theoretical; in practice, they are usually interdependent and virtually indistinguishable. The relevant distinction between different constructions of the sexual landscape is in the language available for self-description, and the relevant distinctions between various languages are the different landmarks and the different relationships to these landmarks that are created by each language, i.e., in the various ways that they construct the sexual landscape.

Some people intentionally put themselves in new social contexts in the hope of finding a new language for self-description. For example, a White American woman said that she went to Coming Out Day in 1990 because she was unsure about her sexuality, but by the time she left, she was a Dyke. Several respondents mentioned that they had read the book *Bi Any Other Name: Bisexual People Speak Out*, and that this book had helped them develop bisexual identities. A Latino-American man explained that he was able to come out as Bisexual after he joined a therapy group in which a bisexual identity was available.

> I joined a bisexual men's therapy group (while still with my female partner). I had always heard the term but never really claimed it until I joined this group. I think I knew that that's what I was but when you're living in a straight environment, you don't talk about it.

Other people, through no conscious intent of their own, find themselves in social contexts where they become involved in new relationships or encounter new identities, and then discover that they can use these identities to describe themselves. For example, a Native American/Caucasian man reexamined his own "repressed bisexuality" when he observed culturally approved intimacy among men while working in the Middle East. A Caucasian man became a "punk" while serving time in a U.S. jail; he explained that he "got used to it and they treated me well so I got emotionally involved with them and dependent on them for security. There was no other term for that role." An Indian woman living in the U.S. was introduced to the Kinsey scale during a seminar on religion and sexuality. She learned that everyone "existed somewhere on this continuum" and scored herself right in the middle. Reflecting on the experience, she stated: "From that moment on, I have thought of myself continuously as someone who is what I would call today 'bisexual.'" An English man explained that he "never really 'began' to think of myself as bisexual, any more than I guess most straights begin to think of themselves as straight." He had begun to use the word "bisexual" after seeing it appear more and more frequently on electronic mail postings.

Because the terms "lesbian" and "gay" are now nearly household words, they are available as self-descriptors even outside lesbian and gay social contexts. In contrast, the concept of an authentic bisexual identity is still limited to particular social contexts, and many bisexual-identified respondents reported that they had adopted their current sexual identities only after encountering the term "bisexual" for the first time when they joined a bisexual support group, therapy group, or political group. Before they encountered the concept of bisexuality, the only terms that were available to them were synonyms for heterosexual and homosexual. Most had chosen one of these two available identities based on their conceptions of the types of relationships that could be represented by each. For example, one man called himself heterosexual, although he had a male sexual partner, because he preferred his wife as a sexual partner. For him, a heterosexual identity was an accurate description of his location on the sexual landscape because it did not deny his relationship to his male lover; it merely indicated that his relationship to his female lover was stronger. When his male partner introduced him to the term "bisexual," he discovered that bisexual identity could also describe his location by representing both of his relationships, and he changed his identity accordingly.

Some individuals discover an identity only to find that they are barred from participating in the context where the identity is available. Lesbian male-to-female transsexuals, for example, are sometimes rejected by lesbian feminists. One lesbian transsexual explained why she calls herself a "Lesbian-identified Bisexual":

I have always been attracted to and loved women only. I thought I was a straight man. Now I'm a woman but still love women and not men at all. Yet lesbians all reject me as one of them because I'm genetically male. Bisexual women, however, fully accept me.

Excluded from lesbian contexts, she adopted an identity that was available in a bisexual context where she was accepted.

Similarly, queer people of color often find themselves excluded from, tokenized by, or ignored within predominantly Euro-American LesBiGay communities, where positive lesbian, gay, and bisexual identities exist. At the same time, they fear exclusion from their racial or ethnic communities of origin, where positive racial and ethnic identities exist. Few have access to social contexts in which the landscape contains the landmarks necessary to anchor both their sexual identities and their racial or ethnic identities simultaneously.

Language also changes when familiar terms take on new meanings or change in meaning. Many respondents reported that they had been familiar with the term "bisexual" for some time but had understood it as a temporary phase that one passed through when coming out as lesbian or gay or as an identity used by those who wish to deny their homosexuality. Once they encountered the term as a reference to a stable set of relationships involving both female and male landmarks, they became comfortable describing themselves as bisexual. For example, one woman encountered a new meaning for "bisexual" when she began associating with a new group of people:

[I] went to a bisexual convention. Though I'd known that I liked women and I like men, meeting a group of people who had chosen this as a viable identity — not just a resting place between gay and straight — gave me a word to use with myself and a sense of legitimacy.

In contrast, another woman felt that the meaning of the word had changed over time, eventually enabling her to adopt it as an identity:

For a long time, I was afraid to say I was bisexual, because it was largely regarded as a term for a lesbian who didn't want to "fess up" and I knew women who were like this and who used the term this way. I've only started calling myself "bisexual" in the last five years because the term seems to have lost the "closeted lesbian" connotation.

Other respondents began identifying themselves as bisexual when they discovered that the term could represent relationships to social and political institutions as well as relationships to individuals. This is a particularly common pattern among previously lesbian-identified Euro-American women, whose lesbian identities represented relationships to lesbian communities and lesbian politics more than relationships to individual women and who were loath to give up their lesbian identities for bisexual identities until they felt that a bisexual identity could connect them to a community and a movement. An American woman who had always "known" that she was bi was unable to identify herself as bisexual until she met Lani Ka'ahumanu, a well-known bisexual activist in the U.S. She said that "hearing [Lani] talk about bisexuality as a 'valid' identity and movement" made it possible for her to "choose this identity wholeheartedly."

For some individuals, a change in the meaning of a term allowed them to maintain an identity that might otherwise have had to change or forced them to change an identity that they might otherwise have been able to keep. An Anglo-American man explained that his concept of "gay" had recently broadened; previously, if he had had a heterosexual encounter, he would have given up his gay identity, but now he says, "If I were to have an occasional heterosexual encounter, I'd still call myself gay, not bisexual." Conversely, a woman who used to identify herself "solely as a Lesbian" was "distressed at the trend of women who used the word Lesbian to be femme, hetero-appearing career women with closet politics." Because of this trend, she no longer feels that the word "lesbian" adequately describes herself; she now calls herself a Dyke, among other things, and is "still sad over the loss of the label Lesbian."

Changes in Social Context

The fact that different relationships and languages for self-description are available in different social contexts means that individuals who live their lives in multiple social contexts — which most people do, particularly those who identify as sexual minorities and/or as members of racial or ethnic minorities — have to describe themselves differently in different social contexts. The act of moving from one context to another entails a change in sexual identity simply to maintain an accurate description of one's location on the sexual landscape. At the very least, an individual might have to use different terms to describe coself in a heterosexual context than co uses in a sexual minority context and different terms in a Euro-American cultural context than in other racial and ethnic contexts.

For example, a Jewish American man explained that he often describes himself as "queer" in gay circles because "it expresses my political identity," but that he "generally use[s] 'bi' in straight circles, since 'queer' is generally considered pejorative." In heterosexual contexts, the term "queer" does not accurately convey his sexual location because the political institution to which it refers — a radical sexual movement — is largely unknown. In contrast to Euro-American sexual culture, which emphasizes the genders of one's sexual partners, the Chicano cultures described by Joseph Carrier incorporate the Mexican cultural emphasis on the role one plays in the sex act over the gender of one's partner.[15] Thus, for Chicanos, the development of a gay identity requires a measure of assimilation to Euro-American culture, and this identity is only viable in contexts in which Euro-American concepts of sexuality operate. A Chicano, therefore, would have to describe his sexuality differently depending on the particular ethnic context he is in.

Even within LesBiGayTrans communities, there are contextual variations that necessitate identity changes as one moves from one part of a community to another. Some women identify themselves as bisexual only among other bisexuals and avoid identifying themselves as bisexual among lesbians, because a positive bisexual identity is often not available in lesbian contexts. Among lesbians, they might identify themselves as "lesbians," or they might call themselves "queer," because they feel that this is the most accurate identity available in that context. An Asian-American woman explained that she calls herself "bi" proudly — but only in certain contexts, because in other contexts her bi identity would be misunderstood and, hence, not accurately describe her location on the sexual landscape:

> [I]n a college environment, there are a few "fakes" — bi women who really do embody lots of bad bi stereotypes. In order not to be lumped in with them, I avoid that term here. However, when I go somewhere more Bi-aware . . . more aware of the diversity of us Bi women, I proudly use the term. . . . I think context is very important.

Changes in the Accuracy of Self-Description

Individuals do not always describe their locations accurately, and identity changes occur as individuals become more accurate or more honest about describing their locations on the sexual landscape. There are many reasons that individuals might intentionally misrepresent their locations, but the most common reason is a belief that other people would disapprove of their true location. Lesbians and gay men often misrepresent their sexual locations when in heterosexual contexts, and bisexual women often misrepresent their location when in lesbian contexts. For example, a White American woman reported that she thinks of herself as a "bi dyke," but until recently, she called herself "queer," because she was afraid "bi dyke" would offend lesbians. She explained that "queer" was a word that she could "use among gay men and lesbians without them knowing I'm bisexual." Unlike the Asian-American woman quoted above, this White woman avoided identifying herself as bisexual in gay and lesbian contexts, not because she thought the term would be misunderstood and hence not accurately represent her, but because she wanted to mislead gay men and lesbians who would disapprove of her true bisexual identity. She also reported that she "just recently felt justified in calling [her]self a 'bi dyke' " among lesbians. In other words, she recently changed the identity she uses in lesbian contexts; this change represented, not a change in her location on the sexual landscape, but a change in her honesty about that location.

Although the politics surrounding bisexual identities are not as intense in gay male communities as they are in lesbian communities, men are also sometimes reluctant to identify themselves as bisexual rather than gay. A Latino man reported that he had known he was bisexual since childhood, but for eleven years he dated women secretly and called himself gay, because he didn't want to lose his friends in the gay community.

It is common for individuals to feel that their previous sexual identities were the result of their own lack of honesty with themselves, even if they did not experience these identities as dishonest at the time. Because "coming out" is traditionally conceptualized as a developmental process of discovering and coming to terms with one's essential sexuality, many people perceive their changes in identity as processes of becoming honest with themselves about their sexuality. For example, a Caucasian man wrote, "I began to question my sexuality and finally admitted that I was in denial about my feelings towards men." Whether the identity changes that these individuals experienced were the result of growing self-honesty, or whether they were the result of actual changes in their relationships or in the languages available to describe their relationships, which in hindsight they interpreted in terms of honesty, is a question that involves a discussion of essential existence that is outside the scope of this article.

The Effect of Changes in Identity on the Sexual Landscape: Identity Change as a Volitional Act

So far, I have been discussing various types of contextual changes that can lead to changes in an individual's sexual identity. But individuals do not merely observe the sexual landscape and passively adopt available terms to describe their locations on this landscape. Individuals also influence the landscape, both unintentionally and intentionally. First of all, the very act of locating oneself on the landscape can alter it. At the very least, describing one's location on the landscape transforms one into a landmark to which other people can relate, such as the daughter, cited previously, who transformed herself on her mother's sexual landscape by identifying herself as bisexual.

Second, individuals who move from one context to another carry with them the memories of each context they have inhabited. Although the landmarks they need to maintain a particular sexual identity might not be readily available in another context, they can import them. In practice, this involves educating people about the existence of the types of people, groups, and institutions with which one has relationships. Coming out to one's parents by introducing them to one's lover is an example of this: the parents become aware of the lover as an individual with which their daughter or son has a relationship. The very act of using an identity term in a context in which it did not previously exist both creates the opportunity to construct for others the landmarks to which it refers and offers the term as a possibility for others in that context.

Third, some people intentionally use their identities to cause changes in particular social contexts. For example, one White American woman explained that she is "working toward the eradication of heterosexism," which she feels "is in part based on the essentialism that says there are relevant, universal differences between men and women." Therefore, in gay and lesbian circles she distinguishes herself by identifying as Bisexual, whereas in straight circles she is content to use the term "queer" and let people assume she is a lesbian. In each context, her identity is chosen for political purposes as a challenge to the identity assumptions usually made by people in that context.

Fourth, some individuals create new identity terms because they find the available ones unsatisfactory. A number of respondents who invented identity terms for themselves later discovered that others had invented the same terms. For example, a woman who calls herself a Bi-dyke said, "I think I made it up for myself (as did many others) out of necessity." Some reported having difficulty using their invented identities to describe themselves to others who are unfamiliar with the identity, so they endeavor to educate others about the meanings of their sexual identities. Through this educational process, they create the language and landmarks necessary to support their newly created identities.

Fifth, individuals who cannot find a context in which a satisfactory identity is available to them sometimes create a context for themselves. Many bisexual support groups have been established by women who found lesbian contexts unsupportive of a bisexual identity. Within these new contexts, a bisexual identity can grow and change in relative freedom from the constraints that are present in established social contexts.

Finally, many individuals are not satisfied with the gendered landmarks that are available for the anchoring of sexual identity, so they create new non-gendered land-marks, such as the non-gendered person or the non-gendered social group. Because there are, as of yet, no widely available terms for the description of relationships not tied to such landmarks, some of these individuals refuse to adopt a sexual identity at all. But doing so means spending considerable energy explaining one's location on the sexual landscape to others, as this Euro-American woman explained:

> [F]or most of those years I rarely used the term "bisexual." Instead I'd say, "I have no sexual preference," or I gave a long-winded explanation about loving the person, not the gender.

Other individuals adapt existing identities, usually "queer" or "bisexual," to the purpose of representing their relationships to non-gendered landmarks. For example, a transgenderist who was unable to describe herself at all in traditional gendered language, discovered that "queer" surmounted her linguistic problems:

> About a year after I accepted my gender identity it was clear that the words "gay," "lesbian," and many others didn't quite work. And I knew I was not a "classic transsexual" since I was reasonably sure I did not want surgery. After getting involved with Queer Nation, the term "Queer transgenderist" seemed to be just right, and still does.

Similarly, an Asian/Pacific Islander woman explained that she calls herself Queer "because it is an inclusive term. . . . I feel that queer is a term broad enough to encompass my range of ideas and actions." A bisexual identity, on the other hand, is often adopted by people who initially use it to describe relationships to both male- and female-gendered landmarks and then find that bisexual identity is flexible enough to withstand the changes that occur when they begin to think in terms of non-gendered landmarks. For example, a Caucasian man explained that his Bi identity "used to mean I would live and date women and have an occasional affair with a man." Over the past fifteen years, however, he has realized that he is "attracted to people — not their sexual identity" and no longer cares whether his partners are male or female. He has kept his Bi identity and now uses it to refer to his attraction to people regardless of their gender.

Bisexual Identity as the Key to Understanding Sexual Identity

Sexual identity has traditionally been conceptualized as a static description of an individual's sexual essence. From this point of view, alterations in an individual's sexual identity are considered evidence of immaturity, and only one type of identity change — a developmental process called "coming out" — is validated. Coming out is conceptual-ized as a process in which individuals become increasingly honest, both with themselves and with others, about the true nature of their essential sexualities.

This conceptualization of sexual identity and sexual identity change is no longer adequate. Sexual identity is more usefully understood as a representation of one's location on the sexual landscape, a location that is described in terms of one's relationships to other people, groups, and institutions on that landscape. From this perspective, identity change that occurs as a result of increasing honesty is only one type among many. Identity changes also occur as mature individuals attempt to accurately describe their locations on the sexual landscape. Sexual identity is thus not a static representation of essential being but a dynamic description of the self in relation to others.

This reconceptualization of sexual identity and sexual identity change calls for a shift in the focus of scientific research. Traditional thinking about sexual identity as a reflection of sexual essence suggests that we should study people who have completed the coming out process, because they are mature individuals whose sexual identities are stable and accurate representations of their essential sexuality. Social scientists working from this perspective studied the process of "coming out" as a topic of interest in its own right, because lesbian and gay people identified it as an important experience in their lives, not because of the light these scientists believed it would shed on the nature of sexual identity. If, however, sexual identity is reconceptualized as a dynamic description of sexual location on a changing sexual landscape, then the key to understanding sexual identity lies in understanding sexual identity change, not sexual identity stability. To understand what sexual identity represents, we have to study the circumstances under which it changes.

But change is relative and can only be perceived in relation to objects other than the self. Therefore, it is the existence of landmarks that makes movement visible; change in an individual's location can be perceived only when that change alters the individual's relationships to defined landmarks. If an individual moves without changing co's relationships to defined landmarks, co's movement will not be perceived as a change, and it will not necessitate a change in self-description.

Herein lies the critical theoretical importance of bisexual identity. Because our sexual landscape is gendered, people who relate to landmarks of only one gender rarely find it necessary to change their sexual identities; a single monosexual identity is often sufficient to carry them through changes in their relationships with individuals, groups, and institutions. The gendered sexual landscape facilitates stable monosexual identities. However, people who relate to landmarks of both genders sometimes find that they have to alter their identities frequently as their relationships change. Traditionally, these identity changes have been interpreted as evidence that bisexual people are more "unstable" than lesbian or gay people or, euphemistically, that they are more "flexible" than either lesbians and gays or heterosexuals. But frequent identity changes do not indicate that people who relate to landmarks of both genders traverse more sexual space than monosexual people do, only that in the course of their movement they are more likely to alter their relationships to the gendered landmarks defined by a culture that favors monosexual identity. Because they change their relationships to the landmarks on the sexual landscape more often, they are the key to understanding that landscape. Consistently monosexual-identified people provide little insight into the texture of the gendered landscape on which they locate themselves, because their movements are not detectable on that landscape and not reflected in their identities, whereas individuals whose relationships to gendered landmarks change provide clues to the locations of those landmarks and to the nature of gender itself. The moment of change reveals the boundaries of gender because the moment of change marks the crossing of those boundaries.

This is not to say that monosexual-identified people necessarily relate to landmarks of only one gender. On the contrary, monosexual-identified people often relate to landmarks of both genders, but their relationships to landmarks of one or the other gender are subsumed, rather than represented, by their monosexual identities. Recall, for example, the man mentioned above who identified himself as heterosexual because he prefers his wife over his male lover; his heterosexual identity subsumes, but does not represent, his relationship to his male lover. Or, consider the fact that substantial research shows that many lesbian-identified women have had heterosexual relationships, a reality which is well known among lesbians themselves.[16] Sometimes lesbians dismiss these relationships as the result of socialization or social pressure, thereby negating any implications that these relationships might otherwise have for perceived essence, and therefore identity. Other times, lesbians acknowledge these relationships as authentic but subsume them under lesbian identity, as in a "lesbian who has sex with men." The fact that monosexual identities subsume relationships with both genders defines bisexual identities — defined here as identities that represent relationships with both genders — out of existence.

If the monosexual construction of the sexual landscape summarily denied the possibility of relating to landmarks of both genders, then the task of creating bisexual identity would be the relatively simple one of demonstrating that such a possibility existed and then proposing a language capable of describing these relationships. But the fact that monosexual constructions subsume relationships with both genders presents bisexuals — defined here as people who wish to create bisexual identities — with the more difficult task of reconstructing the sexual landscape. Individuals who wish to develop a language capable of representing relationships to landmarks of both genders have the formidable task of, not merely creating new relationships or demonstrating the existence of previously unnamed relationships, but also reconstructing/relabeling patterns of relationships that have heretofore been constructed as monosexual.

Another approach to the problem of creating bisexual identities is to construct non-gendered landmarks and then develop a language capable of representing relationships to them, an approach used by some respondents in the current study. Certain kinds of landmarks, such as social and political institutions, can be created anew. But new types of people can be created only by reconstructing existing people and categories of people. Here again, the creation of a bisexual identity implies a reconstruction of the sexual landscape, this time by reconstructing/relabeling the landmarks on it.

The construction of a bisexual identity, whether via the creation of a language capable of representing relationships to landmarks of both genders or via the creation of non-gendered landmarks, is threatening to a monosexual identity. The reconstruction of relationships to landmarks of both genders implies the destruction of the language that provides people with monosexual identities. The reconstruction of gendered landmarks as non-gendered landmarks implies the destruction of the gendered landmarks to which monosexual-identified people relate and with which they anchor their monosexual identities. In other words, bisexual identities are threatening to monosexual identities because they threaten to undermine the bases for monosexual identities. There is, therefore, great resistance on the part of some monosexual-identified people to the construction of bisexual identities. This resistance is born of the fear of existential annihilation, the same existential annihilation that bisexuals experience on the gendered monosexual landscape.

Because bisexual identity is a threat to monosexual identity, bisexuality is often characterized as a challenge to gendered categories and to dualistic thinking in general.[17] Jo Eadie has characterized it as a threat from within, arguing that the bisexuality which threatens lesbians and gay men is really their own bisexuality, with its attendant implication that lesbians and gays are not so clearly different from heterosexuals after all.[18] Bisexuality has also been described as a threat from without — the "double agent" who is dangerous because of co's link to the enemy "camp."[19] Both of these perspectives take dualistic thinking as a given and set up bisexuality as a threat to this thinking by assuming that bisexuality either does not or should not fit into dualistic categories. But, if sexual identity is viewed as a representation of one's relationships to landmarks, then sexual identity is a mature state of dynamic self-description. This conception of sexual identity does not lend itself to the formation of categories, including the monosexual categories that allegedly compose the dualistic thinking against which bisexuality is presented as a challenge. Of course, people can build categories and communities based on sexual identity, and categories and communities have been built on monosexual identities. But the dynamic nature of identity is ill-suited for the formation of these categories and communities, which is why they need constant defense. Therefore, the challenge to monosexual identity is posed, not by bisexuality per se, but by the different understanding of sexual identity that an exploration of bisexual identities in a gendered world can facilitate. Monosexual identities are challenged by the dynamic nature of sexual identity; they are unstable and require constant defense and repair even without the threat of a bisexual identity. Bisexuality merely provides a convenient vehicle for identifying the weaknesses that are already inherent in the effort to create stable categories and communities based on dynamic self-descriptions.

Any attempt to create stable bisexual identities or bisexual communities will eventually encounter the same problems that lesbian and gay identities and communities now face. As David Bell points out, despite the theoretical attractiveness and exciting revolutionary potential of conceptualizing bisexuality as something that exists outside fixed categories, individuals seeking a "home" attempt to create positively defined bisexual identities and communities.[20] Indeed, success within current modes of political discourse might necessitate the creation of a bisexual "ethnicity."[21] Creating a bisexual "home" or "ethnicity" is difficult, and during the formative stage these difficulties are easily attributed to the adverse conditions afforded by the current gendered, monosexual construction of sexual identity. But, if some people eventually succeed in convincing themselves that they have managed to give a specific and definable form to bisexual identity and bisexual community, they will discover that bisexual identity and community, like their monosexual counterparts, need constant defense. At that point, in accordance with the principles of dialectic change, a new antagonist will arise, and the defenders of bisexual identities and communities will be able to attribute their difficulties to the new antagonist, who will be constructed as a threat. But the new antagonist will no more be the real threat to bisexual identities and communities than a bisexual identity is the real threat to monosexual identities and communities. The real threat to all identity-based communities is the dynamic nature of identity itself; the appearance of a new antagonist will merely be the symptom of the tension inherent in attempting to build stable identities and communities on dynamic self-descriptions. The revolutionary potential of a bisexual identity is the potential to expose the dynamic nature of sexuality, and it has this potential only insofar as the current landscape is predominantly monosexual and gendered. If we succeed in reconstructing the sexual landscape to support a bisexual identity, we will have destroyed its revolutionary potential. We will have, in effect, created a new aristocracy and postponed the revolutionalization of sexual identity until the arrival of the next antagonist.

Fortunately, bisexual political ideology is not yet moving toward the solidification of a definition of bisexuality. On the contrary, the current tendency is to resist efforts to agree on a definition.[22] If we continue on this path and refuse to follow in the footsteps of lesbian and gay movements toward the creation of a bisexual ethnicity, then we will preserve the revolutionary potential of bisexuality.

NOTES

Acknowledgments: This research was supported in part by a grant from the Horace H. Rackham School of Graduate Studies of the University of Michigan in Ann Arbor, by research funding from Hamilton College in Clinton, New York, and by a grant from the Society for the Psychological Study of Social Issues. I am grateful to Jackie Vargas, Ana Morel, Sandy Siemoens, and Michael Peluse for their help in tabulating the data. I am solely responsible for the content of this paper.

1. For example, Beata E. Chapman and JoAnn C. Brannock, "Proposed Model of Lesbian Identity Development: An Empirical Examination," *Journal of Homosexuality* 14, nos. 3/4 (1987): 69–80.

2. Alan P. Bell, Martin S. Weinberg, and Sue Kiefer Hammersmith, *Sexual Preference: Its Development in Men and Women* (Bloomington: Indiana University Press, 1981); Pat Califia, "Lesbian Sexuality," *Journal of Homosexuality* 4, no. 3 (Spring 1979): 255–66; Denise M. Cronin, "Coming Out among Lesbians," in *Sexual Deviance and Sexual Deviants*, ed. Erich Goode and Richard R. Troiden (New York: Morrow, 1974), 268–77; Karla Jay and Allen Young, eds., *The Gay Report: Lesbians and Gay Men Speak Out about Sexual Experiences and Lifestyles* (New York: Simon and Schuster, 1979); Harold D. Kooden, Stephen F. Morin, Dorothy I. Riddle, Martin Rogers, Barbara E. Sang, and Fred Strassburger, *Removing the Stigma: Final Report of the Board of Social and Ethical Responsibility for Psychology's Task Force on the Status of Lesbian and Gay Male Psychologists* (Washington, DC: American Psychological Association, 1979); Gary J. McDonald, "Individual Differences in the Coming Out Process for Gay Men: Implications for Theoretical Models," *Journal of Homosexuality* 8, no. 1 (Fall 1982): 47–60; Carmen de Monteflores and Stephen J. Schultz, "Coming Out: Similarities and Differences for Lesbians and Gay Men," *Journal of Social Issues* 34, no. 3 (1978): 59–72; Dorothy Riddle and Stephen Morin, "Removing the Stigma: Data from Institutions," *APA Monitor* (November 1977): 16–28; Siegrid Schäfer, "Sexual and Social Problems of Lesbians," *Journal of Sex Research* 12, no. 1 (February 1976): 50–

69; Richard R. Troiden, *Gay and Lesbian Identity: A Sociological Analysis* (Dix Hills, NY: General Hall, 1988).

3. Henceforth, I will use the terms "bisexual" and "lesbian" to refer to women who were, respectively, self-identified as bisexual and as lesbian at the time of this earlier study.

4. Paula C. Rust, " 'Coming Out' in the Age of Social Constructionism: Sexual Identity Formation among Lesbian and Bisexual Women," *Gender and Society* 7, no. 1 (March 1993): 50–77.

5. For example, Chapman and Brannock, "Proposed Model of Lesbian Identity Development."

6. For example, Philip Blumstein and Pepper Schwartz, "Intimate Relationships and the Creation of Sexuality," in *Homosexuality/Heterosexuality: Concepts of Sexual Orientation*, ed. David P. McWhirter, Stephanie A. Sanders, and June M. Reinisch (New York: Oxford University Press, 1990), 307–20; and Kenneth Plummer, *Sexual Stigma: An Interactionist Account* (London: Routledge and Kegan Paul, 1975).

7. For example, Vivienne C. Cass, "Homosexual Identity Formation: A Theoretical Model," *Journal of Homosexuality* 4, no. 3 (Spring 1979): 219–35; Vivienne C. Cass, "The Implications of Homosexual Identity Formation for the Kinsey Model and Scale of Sexual Preference," in *Homosexuality/Heterosexuality*, 239–66; Eli Coleman, "Developmental Stages of the Coming Out Process," *Journal of Homosexuality* 7, nos. 2/3 (Winter 1981/Spring 1982): 31–43; McDonald, "Individual Differences in the Coming Out Process for Gay Men."

8. I am collecting data via an anonymous self-administered questionnaire containing a postage-paid return envelope inside the U.S. or postal coupons outside the U.S. The cover of the questionnaire tells potential respondents that

> You can fill out this questionnaire if you are bisexual or if you call yourself bisexual, if you are coming out or questioning your sexuality, if you prefer not to label your sexual orientation, if you used to identify as bisexual, if you are lesbian or gay but have felt attracted to or had a sexual or romantic relationship with someone of the other sex at any time in your life, or if you are heterosexual but have felt attracted to or had a sexual or romantic relationship with someone of your own sex at any time in your life.

The cover of the questionnaire encouraged non-eligible individuals to give the questionnaire to an eligible friend. Respondents are, therefore, self-selected. The questionnaire is being distributed through bisexual and bisexual-inclusive social and political organizations; community centers and counseling services for gay, lesbian, and bisexual people and people exploring their sexuality; institutions dedicated to sexuality education and information dissemination; advertisements in bisexual newsletters and alternative community newspapers; fliers in alternative bookstores; conferences on topics related to sexuality and/or gender; electronic mail networks; and friendship networks. More detailed information about the methodology will be forthcoming in later publications.

Distribution began in the U.S. in April 1993 and in the United Kingdom in September 1993. To date, questionnaires have been completed and returned by over 450 individuals in the U.S., 46 in the United Kingdom, and 22 in Australia and New Zealand. Men and women are equally represented in all countries, except the U.S., where women constitute 63% of the sample. Slightly under 4% of respondents are transgendered, including postoperative male-to-female transsexuals, non-transsexual transgenderists, and crossdressers. The age distribution is broader among respondents in the U.S. than the U.K. The ages of U.S. respondents range from eighteen to eighty-two, with 39% in their twenties, 30% in their thirties, 19% in their forties, and 10% fifty years or older.

The oldest respondent from the U.K. is fifty-nine years old, and 67% of respondents from the U.K. are in their twenties. The incomes of respondents in both countries follow normal distribution curves. In the U.S., the median income is in the range $20–29,999 with 18% earning less than $10,000 and 21% earning $50,000 or more. In the U.K., the mean income is £14,000, with 20% earning under £5,000 and 20% earning over £25,000. Eleven percent of respondents from the U.S. are people of color, including African-Americans, Asian-Americans, Indigenous Peoples, and Latinas/os.

9. "Co" is a generic pronoun that refers to a person who might be female, male, or intersexed, and woman, man, or transgendered. It is used in some alternative communities in the United States whose members believe that gendered language, including the use of the masculine pronoun "he" as a generic pronoun, reinforces gender hierarchies. I use it here because it seems particularly appropriate in a paper that discusses the difficulties that gendered language poses for bisexual-identified people. "Co" is less disruptive to the appearance of written language than slashed formations like "s/he" and "his/hers" and avoids the problems of numerical agreement that arise when "they" is used as a generic pronoun for referring to a single individual.

I invite the reader to use this chapter as an exercise in non-gendered language. Observe your emotional reactions to the non-gendered pronoun "co," and notice how it changes your understanding of the written word. Later in this paper, I discuss the importation of non-gendered concepts from one social context to another; the paper itself is an example of this process.

10. The terms used to describe respondents' racial and ethnic identities are the terms used by respondents themselves when they were asked, "What is your race and/or ethnicity?" Throughout this chapter, capitalization of identity terms indicates that these are the terms used by respondents themselves. Some respondents belong to small racial or ethnic groups with only a few representatives in this study; more general terms are used to describe their racial/ethnic identity in order to protect their anonymity. For example, respondents descended from indigenous tribes of North America are referred to collectively as Native Americans.

This is an international study, and respondents are occasionally described in terms of their citizenship or country of residence as well as their racial or ethnic identities. For example, "Irish" indicates that a respondent resides in Ireland, "English" indicates that a respondent resides in England, "Australian" indicates that a respondent resides in Australia, and "American" indicates that a respondent resides in the U.S. This usage of "American" to describe residents of the U.S. is consistent with usage by citizens of other North, Central, and South American countries, who refer to citizens of the U.S. as "Americans" or "Americanos/as," and is not intended to imply that citizens of these other American countries are not also Americans in the continental, rather than the national, sense of the term.

11. Terms representing particular individuals' sexual identities are capitalized. However, when these terms are used to refer to sexual identities in general rather than to the identities of specific individuals, or when they are used as identity descriptors, even if in reference to particular individuals, they are not capitalized. In respondent quotes, respondents' choices regarding capitalization are retained.

12. Quotes from respondents have been edited for space. Identifying personal details have been omitted, and obvious spelling errors have been corrected.

13. Toby Marotta attributed "lavender herring" to Susan Brownmiller, who referred to lesbians as "a lavender herring, perhaps, but surely no clear and present danger." See Toby Marotta, *The Politics of Homosexuality* (Boston: Houghton Mifflin, 1981), 236; and Susan Brownmiller, "Sisterhood Is Powerful!" *New York Times Magazine* (15 March 1970): 140.

14. Paula C. Rust, *Bisexuality and the Challenge to Lesbian Politics: Sex, Loyalty, and Revolution* (New York: New York University Press, 1995).

15. Joseph M. Carrier, " 'Sex-Role Preference' as an Explanatory Variable in Homosexual Behavior," *Archives of Sexual Behavior* 6, no. 1 (January 1977): 53–65; Joseph M. Carrier, "Miguel: Sexual Life History of a Gay Mexican American," in *Gay Culture in America: Essays from the Field*, ed. Gilbert Herdt (Boston: Beacon Press, 1992), 202–24; J. R. Magaña and J. M. Carrier, "Mexican and Mexican American Male Sexual Behavior and Spread of AIDS in California," *Journal of Sex Research* 28, no. 3 (August 1991): 425–41.

16. See Paula C. Rust, "The Politics of Sexual Identity: Sexual Attraction and Behavior among Lesbian and Bisexual Women," *Social Problems* 39, no. 4 (November 1992): 366–86 for data on heterosexual behavior among lesbians who participated in my earlier study of lesbian-identified and bisexual-identified women. Evidence of the prevalence of heterosexual behavior among lesbian-identified women is also provided by Chapman and Brannock, "Proposed Model of Lesbian Identity Development"; Jack H. Hedblom, "Dimensions of Lesbian Sexual Experience," *Archives of Sexual Behavior* 2, no. 4 (December 1973): 329–41; and Marcel T. Saghir and Eli Robins, *Male and Female Homosexuality: A Comprehensive Investigation* (Baltimore, MD: Williams and Wilkins, 1973).

17. Bisexuality has been described as or presumed to be a threat to dualistic or dichotomous thinking, particularly about gender, by numerous authors. Some examples not elsewhere cited in this chapter are Marilyn J. Freimuth and Gail A. Hornstein, "A Critical Examination of the Concept of Gender," *Sex Roles* 8, no. 5 (May 1982): 515–32; Richard J. Hoffman, "Vices, Gods, and Virtues: Cosmology as a Mediating Factor in Attitudes toward Male Homosexuality," *Journal of Homosexuality* 9, nos. 2/3 (Winter 1983/Spring 1984): 27–44; Abraham D. Lavender and Lauren C. Bressler, "Nondualists as Deviants: Female Bisexuals Compared to Female Heterosexuals-Homosexuals," *Deviant Behavior: An Interdisciplinary Journal* 2, no. 2 (January–March 1981): 155–65; Amanda Udis-Kessler, "Present Tense: Biphobia as a Crisis of Meaning," in *Bi Any Other Name: Bisexual People Speak Out*, ed. Loraine Hutchins and Lani Kaahumanu (Boston, MA: Alyson, 1991), 350–58; and the essays by Ruth Gibian, "Refusing Certainty: Toward a Bisexuality of Wholeness," Kathleen Bennett, "Feminist Bisexuality: A Both/And Option for an Either/Or World," and Karin Baker, "Bisexual Feminist Politics: Because Bisexuality Is Not Enough," in *Closer to Home: Bisexuality and Feminism*, ed. Elizabeth Reba Weise (Seattle, WA: Seal Press, 1992).

18. Jo Eadie, "Activating Bisexuality: Towards a Bi/Sexual Politics," in *Activating Theory: Lesbian, Gay, Bisexual Politics*, ed. Joseph Bristow and Angelia R. Wilson (London: Lawrence and Wishart, 1993), 139–70.

19. Clare Hemmings, "Resituating the Bisexual Body: From Identity to Difference," in *Activating Theory*, 118–38.

20. David Bell, "The Trouble with Bisexuality," paper presented at the IBG, Nottingham, U.K., 1994.

21. Paula C. Rust, "Who Are We and Where Do We Go from Here? Conceptualizing Bisexuality," in *Closer to Home*, 281–310.

The term bisexual "ethnicity" refers to the notion of bisexuality as a group identity analogous to racial or ethnic group identities. It involves, for example, the concepts of group heritage and group pride. The concept of sexual ethnicity is drawn from Steven Epstein, "Gay Politics, Ethnic Identity: The Limits of Social Constructionism," *Socialist Review* 93, no. 4 (1987): 9–53, and Richard K. Herrell, "The Symbolic Strategies of Chicago's Gay and Lesbian Pride Day Parade," in *Gay Culture in America*, 225–52. Epstein and Herrell argue that the gay and lesbian movement, which is modeled after earlier racial and ethnic movements, is based on the notion of gayness as an ethnicity.

22. Rust, *Bisexuality and the Challenge to Lesbian Politics.*

BIBLIOGRAPHY

Baker, Karin. "Bisexual Feminist Politics: Because Bisexuality Is Not Enough." *Closer to Home: Bisexuality and Feminism.* Ed. Elizabeth Reba Weise. Seattle, WA: Seal Press, 1992. 255–67.

Bell, Alan P., Martin S. Weinberg, and Sue Kiefer Hammersmith. *Sexual Preference: Its Development in Men and Women.* Bloomington: Indiana University Press, 1981.

Bell, David. "The Trouble with Bisexuality." Paper presented at the IBG, Nottingham, U.K., 1994.

Bennett, Kathleen. "Feminist Bisexuality: A Both/And Option for an Either/Or World." *Closer to Home: Bisexuality and Feminism.* Ed. Elizabeth Reba Weise. Seattle, WA: Seal Press, 1992. 205–31.

Blumstein, Philip, and Pepper Schwartz. "Intimate Relationships and the Creation of Sexuality." *Homosexuality/Heterosexuality: Concepts of Sexual Orientation.* Ed. David P. McWhirter, Stephanie A. Sanders, and June M. Reinisch. New York: Oxford University Press, 1990. 307–20.

Califia, Pat. "Lesbian Sexuality." *Journal of Homosexuality* 4, no. 3 (Spring 1979): 255–66.

Carrier, Joseph M. " 'Sex-Role Preference' as an Explanatory Variable in Homosexual Behavior." *Archives of Sexual Behavior* 6, no. 1 (January 1977): 53–65.

———. "Miguel: Sexual Life History of a Gay Mexican American." *Gay Culture in America: Essays from the Field.* Ed. Gilbert Herdt. Boston: Beacon Press, 1992. 202–24.

Cass, Vivienne C. "Homosexual Identity Formation: A Theoretical Model." *Journal of Homosexuality* 4, no. 3 (Spring 1979): 219–35.

———. "The Implications of Homosexual Identity Formation for the Kinsey Model and Scale of Sexual Preference." *Homosexuality/Heterosexuality: Concepts of Sexual Orientation.* Ed. David P. McWhirter, Stephanie A. Sanders, and June M. Reinisch. New York: Oxford University Press, 1990. 239–66.

Chapman, Beata E., and JoAnn C. Brannock. "Proposed Model of Lesbian Identity Development: An Empirical Examination." *Journal of Homosexuality* 14, nos. 3/4 (1987): 69–80.

Coleman, Eli. "Developmental Stages of the Coming Out Process." *Journal of Homosexuality* 7, nos. 2/3 (Winter 1981/Spring 1982): 31–43.

Cronin, Denise M. "Coming Out among Lesbians." *Sexual Deviance and Sexual Deviants.* Ed. Erich Goode and Richard R. Troiden. New York: William Morrow, 1974. 268–77.

de Monteflores, Carmen, and Stephen J. Schultz. "Coming Out: Similarities and Differences for Lesbians and Gay Men." *Journal of Social Issues* 34, no. 3 (1978): 59–72.

Eadie, Jo. "Activating Bisexuality: Towards a Bi/Sexual Politics." *Activating Theory: Lesbian, Gay, Bisexual Politics.* Ed. Joseph Bristow and Angelia R. Wilson. London: Lawrence and Wishart, 1993. 139–70.

Epstein, Steven. "Gay Politics, Ethnic Identity: The Limits of Social Constructionism." *Socialist Review* 93, no. 4 (1987): 9–53.

Freimuth, Marilyn J., and Gail A. Hornstein. "A Critical Examination of the Concept of Gender." *Sex Roles* 8, no. 5 (May 1982): 515–32.

Gibian, Ruth. "Refusing Certainty: Toward a Bisexuality of Wholeness." *Closer to Home: Bisexuality and Feminism.* Ed. Elizabeth Reba Weise. Seattle, WA: Seal Press, 1992. 3–16.

Hedblom, Jack H. "Dimensions of Lesbian Sexual Experience." *Archives of Sexual Behavior* 2, no. 4 (December 1973): 329–41.

Hemmings, Clare. "Resituating the Bisexual Body: From Identity to Difference." *Activating Theory: Lesbian, Gay, Bisexual Politics.* Ed. Joseph Bristow and Angelia R. Wilson. London: Lawrence and Wishart, 1993. 118–38.

Herrell, Richard K. "The Symbolic Strategies of Chicago's Gay and Lesbian Pride Day Parade." *Gay Culture in America: Essays from the Field.* Ed. Gilbert Herdt. Boston: Beacon Press, 1992. 225–52.

Hoffman, Richard J. "Vices, Gods, and Virtues: Cosmology as a Mediating Factor in Attitudes toward Male Homosexuality." *Journal of Homosexuality* 9, nos. 2/3 (Winter 1983/Spring 1984): 27–44.

Hutchins, Loraine, and Lani Kaahumanu, eds. *Bi Any Other Name: Bisexual People Speak Out.* Boston, MA: Alyson, 1991.

Jay, Karla, and Allen Young, eds. *The Gay Report: Lesbians and Gay Men Speak Out about Sexual Experiences and Lifestyles.* New York: Simon and Schuster, 1979.

Kooden, Harold D., Stephen F. Morin, Dorothy I. Riddle, Martin Rogers, Barbara E. Sang, and Fred Strassburger. *Removing the Stigma: Final Report of the Board of Social and Ethical Responsibility for Psychology's Task Force on the Status of Lesbian and Gay Male Psychologists.* Washington, DC: American Psychological Association, 1979.

Lavender, Abraham D., and Lauren C. Bressler. "Nondualists as Deviants: Female Bisexuals Compared to Female Heterosexuals-Homosexuals." *Deviant Behavior: An Interdisciplinary Journal* 2, no. 2 (January–March 1981): 155–65.

Magaña, J. R., and J. M. Carrier. "Mexican and Mexican American Male Sexual Behavior and Spread of AIDS in California." *Journal of Sex Research* 28, no. 3 (August 1991): 425–41.

Marotta, Toby. *The Politics of Homosexuality.* Boston: Houghton Mifflin, 1981.

McDonald, Gary J. "Individual Differences in the Coming Out Process for Gay Men: Implications for Theoretical Models." *Journal of Homosexuality* 8, no. 1 (Fall 1982): 47–60.

Plummer, Kenneth. *Sexual Stigma: An Interactionist Account.* London: Routledge and Kegan Paul, 1975.

Riddle, Dorothy, and Stephen Morin. "Removing the Stigma: Data from Institutions." *APA Monitor* (November 1977): 16–28.

Rust, Paula C. "The Politics of Sexual Identity: Sexual Attraction and Behavior among Lesbian and Bisexual Women." *Social Problems* 39, no. 4 (November 1992): 366–86.

———. "Who Are We and Where Do We Go from Here? Conceptualizing Bisexuality." *Closer to Home: Bisexuality and Feminism.* Ed. Elizabeth Reba Weise. Seattle, WA: Seal Press, 1992. 281–310.

———. " 'Coming Out' in the Age of Social Constructionism: Sexual Identity Formation among Lesbian and Bisexual Women." *Gender and Society* 7, no. 1 (March 1993): 50–77.

———. *Bisexuality and the Challenge to Lesbian Politics: Sex, Loyalty, and Revolution.* New York: New York University Press, 1995.

Saghir, Marcel T., and Eli Robins. *Male and Female Homosexuality: A Comprehensive Investigation.* Baltimore, MD: Williams and Wilkins, 1973.

Schäfer, Siegrid. "Sexual and Social Problems of Lesbians." *Journal of Sex Research* 12, no. 1 (February 1976): 50–69.

Troiden, Richard R. *Gay and Lesbian Identity: A Sociological Analysis.* Dix Hills, NY: General Hall, 1988.

Udis-Kessler, Amanda. "Present Tense: Biphobia as a Crisis of Meaning." *Bi Any Other Name: Bisexual People Speak Out.* Ed. Loraine Hutchins and Lani Kaahumanu. Boston, MA: Alyson, 1991. 350–58.

Identity, Power, and Difference: Negotiating Conflict in an S/M Dyke Community

Patricia L. Duncan

Sadomasochistic sexual practices represent a site of cultural conflict. Individuals who profess and practice s/m sexuality have faced formidable criticism from many different segments of U.S. culture. Sadomasochistic practices are regarded in the mainstream culture as sick, perverse, and abnormal, while those engaged in such practices are often stigmatized as immoral, abnormal, and in need of psychological treatment. As Gayle Rubin has noted, the sexual preferences and pleasures of these individuals are linked to other so-called heinous sexual misdeeds and crimes, such as promiscuity, cross-generational sex, fetishism, and sex for money; and s/m practices are often equated with coercion, violence, and assault.[1] S/m practices are also stigmatized within less mainstream cultural communities that tend to assume liberal humanistic notions of equality in relation to homosexuality. For instance, within feminist and lesbian-feminist communities, women who practice s/m are frequently accused of perpetuating violence against women and adhering to racist and anti-Semitic stereotypes. Moreover, these women are often accused of coming to s/m as a result of their false consciousness. Their sexual practices are assumed to be related to — in fact caused by — their previous sexual and emotional victimization.[2]

In this essay I argue that s/m is a site of *conflict*, both literally and figuratively, for many lesbians who choose to practice it and identify themselves as members of various s/m communities. The cultural notion of s/m is contextualized in opposition to other institutions and ideologies. Also, the practice of s/m is premised upon a conflict or difference that is acted out and then resolved in the course of a "scene" as a means toward sexual pleasure and expression. In some circumstances (not all), the practice of s/m provides a space for resolving conflict and for reconceptualizing notions of social difference. In such an instance, s/m may become a site in which to question and renegotiate the cultural determinations of "identity." Thus, the practice of s/m becomes a political act.

The practice of s/m as a site of conflict enables the resolution of seemingly oppositional differences and the renegotiation of identity. These negotiations occur through three main processes: (1) In s/m play, identities are not stable, static, or even necessarily clearly demarcated; rather, they are constructed, imaginary, and constantly shifting. (2) Power, in the context of an s/m scene, is also constructed, imaginary, and constantly shifting, and (ideally) is clearly negotiated between participants. (3) S/m play is based on *difference*, whatever form that may take, and the eroticization of that difference. These three processes are clearly related and overlapping. However, the various relationships among these conceptions of identity, power, and difference remain open for interpretation. I will attempt to illustrate these three processes and the ways in which they function within s/m practices, as well as the ways in which they mediate the relationship between s/m play and "reality."

Method

The field work which forms the basis for my analysis was conducted in the summer of 1994 in Atlanta, Georgia and the San Francisco Bay area. What inspired me to undertake this project was my own confusion and sense of conflict regarding my identity as an s/m dyke, a lesbian-feminist, and a woman of color from a working-class background. As I struggled to resolve the ways in which my sexual practices seemed to betray my cultural background and my self-identity as an Asian-American of mixed heritage, I found myself more and more caught *between* an s/m identity and an Asian-American identity. I decided to actively seek out other women of color who practice s/m, in order to explore the different ways in which we might choose to resolve this conflict, to understand the elements of our identities, and to find the forms of sexual and emotional expression and pleasure that we desire.[3]

Identity, here, refers to both individual and collective identities, as complex and multiplicitous sites of conflict. How and why do we make meaning through our identities? What are the ways in which personal and group identities may be constructed, influenced, and transformed? What other processes and political forces are involved in structuring and giving meaning to our experiences? Lisa Duggan describes identity as the narrative of a subject's location within a particular social structure. Collective identities, or narratives, may forge connections among individuals.[4] I would also add that collective identities or forms of identity, such as gender, race, class, or nationality, may also forge connections *within* individuals, who may find themselves to be the very sites of intersection and/or conflict between collective identities. In this instance, these individuals may find it necessary to renegotiate conflicts and to reconceptualize their different relationships to power, in order to make meaning out of their experiences and lives. It is these conflicts and negotiations that focus my attention in this essay.

The eleven interview participants were all women. With the exception of one woman, all identified as lesbian, and all self-identified as "s/m dykes." The term "s/m dyke," as distinct from "lesbian," is used here as a way not only to describe one's identity in relation to s/m practices but also to establish a clearly *political* identity. Lesbian s/m has been viewed as an historical product of the "sex wars" of the 1970s and 1980s. S/m dykes may be seen as agents reacting against the restrictions and prescriptions of feminist analyses which equate pornographic representations with violence and oppression against women.[5] The practice of s/m, then, may be seen as directly opposing a feminist ideology that defines sex as threatening and dangerous for women. According to B. Ruby Rich, s/m also acts as a recuperation of a lesbian "outlaw" status and is linked to an attack on the lesbian-feminism of the 1970s which posited certain desires to be unacceptable and non-feminist.[6]

By predicating identity on eroticism, "s/m dyke" as an identity becomes a way to assert a specific political position and membership within the larger s/m community. This is the way in which most of my respondents used the term. One respondent, a twenty-nine-year-old woman of color named Dru, explained the label in this way:

> I call myself an "s/m dyke" because not only do I perform s/m acts occasionally, sometimes frequently, during sex, but I believe that there's a certain belief system — certain morals and ethics behind s/m practice — and because I have those beliefs, I consider myself to be an s/m dyke.

Although the "morals and ethics" that go along with an s/m identity may vary from community to community, depending on such things as levels of experience and regional, age, and racial differences, several respondents discussed "s/m dyke identities" as political identities involving ethical responsibilities. This political distinction makes it possible for the one respondent who identifies herself as bisexual also to be able to call herself an "s/m dyke" without hesitation. In fact, self-identification became the basis on which participants were included in this study.

My research techniques have been influenced by the growing development of a specifically feminist methodology, which proclaims not only that a purely scientific objectivity can never be obtained, but that the notion of objectivity cannot be separated from its political alignment and affiliation with male dominance, heterosexism, and racial hierarchy. Scientific method is neither neutral nor apolitical in its approach; rather, it implies the existence of a "truth" that can be known through scientific inquiry and documented according to a liberal humanistic claim to social scientific "authority." Because positivist methodological approaches require a distancing of the researcher as "subject" from the "object" of study, such an approach would have required that I deny my respondents (and myself) full human subjectivity by decontextualizing our identities and our specific locations as women of color and as lesbians within particular political structures. Thus, through its upholding of hegemonic cultural values, the ideal of objective and so-called rational inquiry is epistemologically inadequate for feminist research, for research about women of color, and for lesbian/gay/bisexual inquiry.[7]

My own research is based upon a belief that the varied experiences of the participants in this study and the ways in which they are interpreted by the subjects themselves should be central to the analysis; thus the theories that develop follow from and are generated by the narratives. Intrinsic to this method is a belief in the agency and subjectivity of the respondents, who create meaning for their lives from their narratives and, in so doing, actively make choices regarding their sexual practices, identities, and beliefs. For these reasons, I rely heavily upon the voices and narratives of participants.

Of the eleven participants, all but two were women of color. I actively sought the participation of women of color because many of the issues I intended to explore dealt specifically with racial difference as a site of conflict in the negotiation and construction of an s/m identity. Two women who do not identify as women of color were included in the study, however, because both articulated extremely insightful and sophisticated conceptualizations of racial and class identity, and they also offered valuable perspectives on the history of the San Francisco lesbian s/m community. The participants varied in class backgrounds, by their own determinations, from poor and working-class to professional/upper middle-class. They ranged in age from twenty-three to fifty, clustering predominantly in the late twenties and early to mid-thirties. The amount of experience in s/m communities and groups varied from two to twenty years. The amount of formal education varied among respondents, from the completion of a high school equivalency course to a graduate degree in psychology. The majority of the participants had attained at least some college education, and all were extremely knowledgeable about current theoretical discourses concerning feminism, sexuality, and power. Most of the participants are relatively open about their identities as lesbians and/or s/m dykes; however, in light of the social stigmatization of both of these identities, I feel the need to be protective about the names of the participants. I use pseudonyms wherever this was deemed necessary by the participants themselves.

I use the term "s/m" to refer to the institutionalized practice of consensual sadomasochistic sexual acts, which the participants themselves label s/m. The term "s/m" is generally understood, by individuals who profess an "s/m identity," to include a variety of practices in addition to sadism and masochism, such as play with dominance and submission, bondage and discipline, the use of roles, and age play, among other things.

Although I may use the terms "leather" and "s/m" interchangeably in parts of this essay, I recognize, in specific instances, how these two terms denote very different meanings for a number of the respondents in regard to their sexual practices and sexual communities. For instance, one respondent, Annette, claims that:

> s/m *is* my dyke identity in a lot of ways. It's not separate from that at all. [But] I don't think of myself as a leatherwoman, like I never use the word "leather" when I think about my identity, or about my practices, because I really don't identify in that way.

For Quinn, the distinction between "leather" and "s/m" has to do with visual cues:

> Well, basically, I think in the gay men's community there's a lot of old guard leathermen who wear the leather. They go to the bars; they may get as far as doing some bondage, but that's basically it. It's just kind of a visual [thing] — the fetish is the leather. And then there's the s/m scene where you have people that may never put leather on, but they do s/m practices. They practice scenes. They do all kinds of stuff around sadomasochism; but like I said, they never put on the leather 'cause that's not their fetish. . . . And of course there's a lot of overlap.

The distinction between the two terms "leather" and "s/m" was the most pronounced for Dru, who, in discussing San Francisco's s/m community, said:

When I came into the community [six years ago] there were all these play parties. . . . There was this very tight-knit s/m — not leather, s/m — community. That's the difference for me — there used to be an s/m community, now there's a leather community, and they're different. The s/m community turned into the leather community because instead of play parties — people who were throwing play parties weren't able to make their money back so they had to stop — you went to leather bars. . . . And you go to a leather bar, and there is no playing, so what you do is observe. So we all observe each other. And we start to become critical about what we look like, what we're doing, who we're with. And all the things that were the least important in the s/m community become the most important in the leather environment. . . . That sense of self is lost, I think, in the leather community.

Rather than identifying two discrete communities which overlap, Dru suggested the metamorphosis of the San Francisco s/m community into the leather community. This development was based on changes in social activities and meeting environments, from "play parties" in private homes or rented spaces (the s/m community) to public leather bars with an emphasis on the visible and the public (the leather community).

A "scene" is a carefully constructed interaction between participants, described by Ami, a twenty-nine-year-old woman of Polynesian descent, in the following way:

Formal scenes are where you use a language that people who are experienced in s/m use. You use a sort of convention, that you've learned about or been taught by someone else, such as establishing safe words, talking about beforehand what it is that you want to happen, discussing any roles that you want to do, like "you be the mailman and I'll be the bored housewife," that kind of thing.

Although many of the women in this study described their s/m practices in terms of scenes, others do not necessarily employ this convention.

Another word frequently used by respondents was "hapa," a term which designates mixed heritage or mixed race. This term was used by respondents in San Francisco and not by those in Atlanta. Also, "hapa" was used in very different ways by different participants. The word "hapa" comes from Hapa Haole, Hawaiian for half/mixed Hawaiian and white. It implies the reclaiming of a mixed-race identity and attempts to highlight the structures and processes of colonialism and hybridization. By my respondents, however, it was used to refer to Asian/Pacific Islander women of mixed heritage, African-American women of mixed race, or any person of color who might be part white. The term brought to my attention the relatively large number of women in this study who claim a mixed-heritage racial identity and the different issues that such an identity raises for many of them, a point to which I will return later.

Community Formation and the Construction of Identity

The practice of s/m, as an ideological institution, is engaged in persistent, perpetual conflict with other institutions and ideologies. Informed by a medical/psychological model of mental health and influenced by conservative, conventional religious values, mainstream American culture views s/m as a degraded form of sexuality: psychologically unhealthy and morally wrong. The development of communities based upon sexual identities provides the means to identify and conceptualize a shared difference from the rest of society. It is also a way to establish relatively safe spaces for marginalized groups of people who choose to identify themselves in particular ways and to seek others like themselves. Popular cultural representations and media images portray s/m communities and other marginal sexual worlds as "bleak and dangerous . . . impoverished, ugly, and inhabited by psychopaths and criminals."[8] Individuals who have been involved in the formation of s/m communities describe the process as a combination of empowerment, clarity, and pride, on the one hand, and conflict and guilt, on the other.[9]

Pat Califia, a founding member of the San Francisco lesbian s/m community, has described her early feelings of terror and guilt about having sadomasochistic fantasies within the context of the 1970s feminist movement. She recalled her need, in the 1970s, to break from the mainstream women's community in order to create a space in which lesbians who wanted to learn about s/m could find one another and where s/m fantasies could be discussed and explored:

> Despite my vigorous participation in the women's movement, my S/M fantasies had not been "cured," [despite] my attempts to renounce my "sick" sexuality. . . . I was desperate for change, for relief, for a sex life without self-hatred. I began to realize that I had been lied to. S/M *was* a part of women's sexuality. . . . I began to tell everyone I knew that I was into S/M and looking for partners and support. I figured if I made myself visible enough, if there were other S/M lesbians in San Francisco, they would be able to find me.[10]

Dossie, a fifty-year-old white lesbian who was also involved in the early years of organizing, described a similar sense of conflict with the women's movement regarding her sexuality:

> In the early years of feminism — because I'm old enough that I sort of became a feminist rather than getting to have that available to me when I was a teenager or something like that — it wasn't something that was out there that I could kind of *find*. You had to create your own, especially if you were . . . I mean the dykes hadn't even come out in 1969. So it was kind of inventing it, and I had always been, well, I had always been a slut, basically. And so when I came into feminism, part of my agenda was to grasp my sexuality, and I was not finding that to be a high agenda in women's C-R groups — that wasn't something that was so big for them. As a matter of fact they were all talking about their husbands, and I didn't have one of them. I couldn't figure out why they didn't just leave. So I was kind of separated from the mainstream in that way.

The idea of an s/m community, however, is problematic. Because there are so many different communities based around s/m practices, it is becoming increasingly difficult to talk about *the* lesbian s/m community. In addition, the concept of a coherent community, while allowing a certain level of group cohesion, tends to ignore and gloss over differences among individuals.[11] Many of the women I interviewed expressed radically different conceptions of their own communities and of "the lesbian s/m community" as a whole. Moreover, a significant number of participants seemed to identify one aspect of their identity as more salient than others. They would then seek a sense of community based on this particular identity.

A number of participants discussed negative experiences where their various identities were called into question. Some of the respondents who identify as feminist remembered feeling alienated from their feminist communities, either because of their lesbianism, their affiliation with s/m, or both. Several women of color recalled experiences of being exoticized by other lesbians (both white women and other women of color) and of being accused by others in their racial and ethnic communities of perpetuating damaging racial myths, and as a result, being exiled from those communities. Women of color described feelings of isolation within the leather community because of the perceived absence of other women of color. And all respondents discussed feelings of being forced to choose among various communities.

Initially, what this conflict might look like is a choice among three potential "communities": a racial/ethnic community (which might include men and women, both queer and straight), a lesbian-feminist community (which in most cases, for these women, would be predominantly white), and a leather-fetish community (which might include gay men, lesbians, bisexuals, and other "queer" people who practice s/m or identify as sexually radical in some way). Yet the sense of conflict was actually much more complex for the participants in this study. In some cases, this conflict involved more than just having to choose a community with which to align oneself, at the risk of losing contact with (or being distrusted by) members of the other communities. More often participants reported conflict over how to avoid a feeling of betraying oneself, one's racial identity, one's integrated sense of self.

Several women of color described their hesitations to "come out" as s/m dykes to other women of color, for fear of not being accepted. Ami, for instance, described her frustration over a negative interaction with another woman of color, because of her sexual practices:

> She tried to tell me that s/m was violent, and that was just ridiculous to me, you know. I mean her definition of s/m had nothing to do with what I do in my bedroom, and what I call s/m. . . . It was disappointing because [she] was another woman of color — not just a woman of color but an A.P.I. [Asian/Pacific Islander] woman who grew up in [the south] and had similar experiences of cultural displacement.

Michelle, who identifies as a Black lesbian of mixed race (half African American and half white), stated that it is generally much easier to come out to white women about her s/m practices than to other women of color. "I have found that dealing with other women of color I have more reluctance than dealing with women of non-color. It's much easier to say to a woman of non-color, 'oh yeah, I'm a leatherdyke,' whatever." J.D., a Black lesbian living in San Francisco, discussed the ways in which she has been treated by other Black women because of her identification with s/m:

> I've been to a few Black women's gatherings [and] it's like I'm looked at like I've got some kind of rare disease. . . . The women of color community in general, I just have gotten the feeling that it's more taboo, like we're having a hard enough time being a lesbian of color without having this extra stigma stuck to it. . . . They're like, "How can you do this as a woman of color?"

However, for all of these women, finding a community of women of color was extremely important. Veena, a young South Asian/Anglo lesbian in Atlanta, described a strong need to identify with other Asian and South Asian people around her. Yet she experienced ambivalence about her own place within a South Asian community because of her lesbianism, and because she chooses to practice s/m:

> There's always that accusation that you're just Americanized completely and you're totally western, and that this is a western thing. There's a sense of being outcast from people of your own race and culture. And white women just don't confront that in the same way because they aren't members of a community of racial "others" in this country.... I just feel so much more comfortable with women of color when I know that basic understanding is there ... that your racial identity and your cultural identity are so important, and yet you feel totally marginalized within that community, and how hard that is. I feel that way. Because that's a really big thing for me, and that's such a big loss, in a way. A loss of community because I feel like most South Asians — you know that they would hate me, you know, essentially. I'm hated, not only by American society at large, but within that community that I identify with to a certain extent. And that's a loss that I don't feel a white woman could feel in this country.

For Veena, an identity as an s/m dyke contradicts her identity as a South Asian woman, creating an embattled location between notions of feminism, Indian womanhood, and s/m sexual practices. The concept of making a choice among potential communities does not adequately describe the experiences of many of the women I interviewed, because the options available to them are not always clear-cut. Choosing to belong to a community of predominantly white lesbians, gay men, and bisexuals who practice s/m is not the same thing as being rejected from one's racial and cultural community.

Because practicing s/m is an important part of Veena's identity, and she does not wish, or even believe that it would be possible, to separate it out from her sense of self, making connection with other queer women of color who are interested in s/m is crucial:

> The people that I find myself most comfortable with or who I feel most strongly connected to in a community way are women of color.... [W]hen it comes to s/m I'm really much more interested in being with women of color, and much more wary of white women, and I think that's because s/m is so much more close to what I want to be sexually.... [I]t's really important to me to have a community or to know women of color who are into s/m.

A distrust of white women, for many of the participants, involved a fear of being exoticized and/or reduced to racial/ethnic stereotypes. Because white women are not "members of a community of racial 'others' in this country," to Veena they simply do not or cannot understand her cultural positioning. This sense of distrust is also connected to the threat of losing some sense of community with others of the same racial or cultural background, or with other women of color. Many participants reported feeling isolated within the more mainstream lesbian community because of their racial difference and because of their affiliation with s/m. Finding a community of s/m dykes of color seemed to be a priority for many of the women I interviewed.

For L.B., a woman of mixed heritage — Chinese, Korean, and Anglo — this wariness of white women involved a conscious decision to practice s/m and form intimate relationships only with other women of color:

> Two girlfriends ago I was with this white woman, and after we broke up — while we were breaking up — I remember [thinking] "That's it. No more white girls." Because it was really hard, because she was just laden with white guilt, you know, and would get into these racial conversations . . . and she would try to tell me about racial issues and stuff. . . . And this is wrong, I admit it, but it's easier [for me] to accept a person of color's racism than it is an Anglo person's racism, and I don't believe that's fair but . . . for me, one of the things that I absolutely refuse to engage in, in an intimate relationship, are issues of race. I mean, that is not negotiable. Certainly that's the last game that I'm going to deal with in a relationship, you know, is to have to listen to my lover make racist comments. . . . Oh man, I'd have to kill her in the middle of the night [laughs].

Similarly, Mariana, a twenty-seven-year-old woman of mixed heritage in San Francisco, claimed that although she has not actually made the rule for herself to be with only women of color, when asked by a white woman if she only practices s/m with other women of color, her response was:

> I don't remember ever saying that, but I thought that was pretty intense. I never said that, but I'm kind of caught, because it's kind of true. What it has to do with is speaking a similar language. I'm impatient — I don't have the time to teach people a new language every fucking time I get near them.

Many participants felt an intimate sexual relationship would be impossible without a basic understanding of the complexities of racial and sexual identities. Interestingly, several women attributed an understanding of these processes to an identity as a woman of color. For instance, Veena claimed that for her it is easier to hear racist remarks from other women of color: "there's just a different dynamic." Even though it may be frustrating, she is more apt to engage in dialogue with other women of color than with white women.

Donna, a thirty-one-year-old African-American lesbian, expressed a different viewpoint, in that although she desires a sense of community with other women of color and with other s/m dykes, she does not base her alliances solely on these distinctions:

> I really have not allowed social, political, [and] personal relationship-related anything to get in the way of me being okay about what I do, or about who I am. . . . I do not, I have not ever, and I don't think I ever will become a person who is so stratified. I refuse to reverse-segregate myself. . . . I want women of all persuasions in my life. . . . And I am not going to only hang out with s/m dykes. That's boring. . . . Going away isn't the answer, which is why I'm not going away.

Annette, a Latina woman from Spanish Harlem who now lives in San Francisco, comments:

> While I have a community with some women of color here, yet socially, like in terms of the club scene and stuff, like the clubs are *white*, that I go to. . . . It comes down to a personal style choice for [me]. And [these white women] — I don't feel alienated, you know. Certainly I don't feel like them — I feel like there's an essential difference, but I like that

difference. I feel comfortable with that difference. It's not a difference that makes me uncomfortable. . . . It's just style.

Several women expressed a sense of community with gay and bisexual men who practice s/m, indicating that a common interest in s/m might be more salient than gender or lesbianism in the formation of community. And when forced to choose between an "s/m culture" which might be predominantly gay and bisexual male and a lesbian community which might be anti-s/m, a few women, such as Veena, noted that they feel more comfortable in a gay and bisexual male space, where their identities as s/ m dykes are accepted:

> It's really interesting that the only leather bar I've been to in Atlanta is a gay male bar, but I like that better than Revolution, this dyke bar that's not s/m. I feel like a freak there, you know — and at the Eagle [a gay male leather bar], I don't feel like a freak; but I'm very conscious of the fact that I'm one of the seven women among hundreds of men. But I don't feel like a pervert in the way that I do at Revolution. And that's much more comfortable for me in some ways. . . . I feel so frustrated when I go to Revolution where I see a lot of these women — I feel like they're just living double lives, you know — and we have in common that we're lesbian or bisexual, but beyond that nothing. *Nothing.* And I feel like they just hate me there. I feel like a lot of women just would hate me. And I think that's because I remind them, to a certain extent, that if you're queer then you're *different*, and they don't want to be reminded of that.

And according to Mariana, "I don't actually think the women's community is as advanced as they make it out to be — I do find that it's easier to go to a men's leather bar than it is for me to hang out at Cafe San Marcos [a lesbian bar]."

However, such an alliance with gay and bisexual men was not unproblematic for any of these women. Although they might choose to go to a gay male leather bar rather than a lesbian bar, in order to avoid "feel[ing] like such a pervert," several participants expressed ambivalence about becoming part of a predominantly white, gay and bisexual male community. Annette commented on the fact that many of her early feelings about her own sexuality were influenced by gay male culture. More and more, however, this has become something from which she would prefer to dissociate:

> I see a lot of stuff lifted from gay male sexuality, which initially when I was younger I was very into, but a lot of this sort of Tom of Finland-derived cop worship, you know, and military worship, like Nazi worship, you know, depending on my mood either really pisses me off or just bores me. . . . When I was coming into my sexuality I got really hooked on gay male eroticism, and this was like when I was thirteen or fourteen years old, you know — it was like "homosexuality," like a dictionary or something. And it was like the word "lesbian" didn't exist at all, and two women — that didn't exist. Homosexuality was a man fucking another man, and I was completely fascinated by that.

For Annette, claiming a lesbian identity necessitated, in part, moving away from her early association with gay male culture, which she now identifies as sexist and as disregarding complex issues of race: "But I don't really see women being that slack about race." And for her, the issue of race is inseparable from class privilege, which may be more easily assumed by gay men than lesbians.

Quinn, a white lesbian from England who is in her early thirties, also made the point that there are privileges assumed by white gay men who practice s/m which may not be as easy for women to claim:

> "The community" is a very strange thing — it's certain bars and certain people. . . . [It's] very much based around the men's community. It now *incorporates* women. Leatherwomen and leathermen have a community together, but I think it's still set up in the structures of the old guard leathermen's way.

In this way, lesbians who practice s/m are seen as being incorporated into an already existing structure, in which they remain marginalized. Rather than challenging or changing the structure in order to center lesbian identities and experiences, several respondents reported feeling that their own communities have been heavily influenced by gay male s/m cultural frameworks. What this means for women of color who practice s/m is often their incorporation into a white lesbian s/m community, based on a white gay male community, which may tokenize or marginalize them. This frequently results in the separation and compartmentalization of identities.

In the United States, where there is a history of racial difference defined by "other"-ness, "raced" groups of people are marginalized in racially distinct ways. Whiteness is taken as the norm — central, neutral, colorless — in effect, raceless. Racialized "others" carry the signifying marks of race and ethnicity — color, history, culture — and these signifiers are believed to delineate certain beliefs and values specific to racial and ethnic groups and the sociohistorical events that have functioned to create and to maintain "otherness." The lesbian s/m community is no exception. Whiteness is the norm, and according to Dru, women of color are seen as "novelties."

Western liberal ideology, which often fails to deal with issues of power, offers a pretense of universality by engulfing difference, in fact obliterating different identities. Taking the dominant group as its point of reference, liberal humanistic hegemonic discourse attempts to contain difference by compartmentalizing it. In the words of Trinh T. Minh-ha:

> Difference does not annul identity. It is beyond and alongside identity. . . . The idea of illusory separated identities, one ethnic, the other woman (or more precisely female) again, partakes in the Euro-American system of dualistic reasoning and its age-old divide-and-conquer tactics. Triple jeopardy means that whenever a woman of color takes up the feminist fight, she immediately qualifies for the possible "betrayals": she can be accused of betraying either man (the "man-hater"), or her community ("people of color should stay together to fight racism"), or woman herself ("you should fight first on the women's side").[12]

The women in this study identified this constant splitting as a source of anxiety in their lives. This sense of betrayal induces many of us to separate and compartmentalize ourselves and to identify one aspect of our identities as more salient, more *different*, than the others. As Donna Haraway has suggested, "the feminist dream of a common language, like all dreams for a perfectly true language, of perfectly faithful naming of experience, is a totalizing and imperialist one."[13]

Annette discussed the ways in which, for her, racial identity cannot be separated or compartmentalized from the rest of her sense of self. In fact, her race has everything to do with her identity, as a woman and as an s/m dyke, and even with her conceptualization of butch and fem:

> I think I'm butch by default. I remember when I was growing up feeling like femininity belonged to white girls, and that it didn't belong to me, that I couldn't live up to that; I wasn't equal to that. I wasn't capable of that kind of performance, or being that kind of object, you know. I see a lot of women of color get classified as butch, you know, Chicano women, African-American women especially, and that we each — women of color — have such a different relationship to fem, what it is to be fem, and femininity, that isn't problematized for blond white girls. . . . For me it doesn't feel like butch is like this big transgression, I guess that's really it. It's not a big transgression, you know, 'cause you're always told that you're not as good as the cute blond girl. She's better at being a girl than you are, whatever the fuck that means; she's cuter, she's better. So it's easier to turn your back on something like that.

Because the construction of femininity is based on and defined by a model of white womanhood, the meaning of femininity might vary according to one's racial or ethnic identity, or the ways in which this identity is perceived by others. For Annette, a butch identity is determined by and contingent upon a racial identity as a Latina woman. Her identities as butch and Latina are inseparable, however, in that they are constantly in the process of constructing one another.

In the practice of s/m, many participants described a feeling of resolving issues around their identities — precisely because they are able to *construct* their own identities and personae. Ami is a Pacific Islander who was adopted by white parents. She is from a working-class background but feels that it is increasingly difficult for her to identify as a working-class woman, as she is now in graduate school. She eloquently described her position as constantly moving between identities:

> And I'm used to those — the kinds of identities that are more within the borders of various categories. I mean I don't feel like I fit into any categories really easily. . . . I always felt different racially when I was growing up. That framework of identity has sort of become my way of identifying sexually as well. . . . [I]t's sort of a framework and structure that structures my entire identity — *difference*.

In s/m play, differences in race, ethnicity, class, and sexual identity do not have to be mutually exclusive, hierarchized, or negated. Rather, in the creation of a cultural space that is imaginary — a space that is increasingly unfixed, unsettled, porous, and hybrid — plurality is acceptable and "constructable" in the context of a scene.

Dossie, who was involved in the formation of the San Francisco lesbian s/m community twenty years ago, talked about Cynthia Slater, an early s/m activist who formed the Society of Janus. Dossie recalled Slater's distinction between s/m and "real life":

> [Cynthia] said, "My feminism doesn't end just because I'm a masochist," and so she put forth the idea really very strongly that we all rely on now, which is that what happens within the boundaries of a scene, the boundaries of when we are in roles in s/m, is very different from what may happen in the rest of our lives, and that the roles that we choose to play in

S and M may not be the roles that we choose to play, or enact or be or whatever you want to call it, full-time in your life. I mean I consider the persona that I explore as a bottom as essential to my sense of identity, as much me as what I do when I'm sitting here being a therapist or whatever — all those are very essential roles to me, and they're very essential parts of me, but [Cynthia's] sense of boundaries about that, that we can be things in scenes that we may not want to be the rest of the time, that may be different from who we are the rest of the time, kind of defined a "scene."

Within the rhetoric of s/m, roles are not necessarily arranged in binary opposition. Sadism and masochism are not necessarily different or opposing concepts but are recognized as elements of the same concept. Roles such as butch, fem, top, bottom, dominant, and submissive do not necessarily relate to one another in predictable con-figurations. For example, L.B. identifies as a butch top and described her "dyke daddy" role as a submissive one, in the way that she may sometimes choose to play that role. Other respondents described their experiences as fem tops, butch bottoms, masochistic but not submissive bottoms, and so on. Seemingly conflicting and contradictory identities are constructed and negotiated. Within such a framework, and in the context of a scene, an identity as a woman of color and an s/m dyke identity may seem perfectly harmonious, whereas outside of that space resolution seems impossible.

Annette discussed the ways that s/m operates, for her, as a space to explore different identities and personae:

> Sometimes it's so hard to pull apart the assumed cultural role from the physical manifesta-tion of that assumed cultural role, and to turn it on its head, and to sort of play with it in that way; and for me it's not about living something, or having something be a part of your character. It's about how you want to *perform* something; and what's intriguing or exciting about performing something a certain way, you know, like there are things that are attractive about masculinity, and how do I want to play with it . . . and there are things that are really attractive about culturally-coded femininity, and how do I want to play with that? It's when you think about it in terms of *drag*, in a really broad sense, that it becomes really fun. But when you think about it in terms of like what you have culturally been pushed into or defined as by someone else, then that's when you resist that perspective. . . . It depends on the context that it all is happening in. That's what makes it so empowering, that we all understand what we're talking about, you know, like when it's a common language, then it works.

Many participants discussed the roles that they take on in play. For Dossie, who has always felt ambivalent about her class background, class identities in s/m scenes can operate in significant ways:

> I actually like playing with class . . . because I'm not really the class I sound like — I was just educated to it. And pushed into it in this doggedly, upwardly-mobile family, and I have enormous questions about it in the real world. But I do love to pretend to be the lady being dragged in the dirt, 'cause I get to pretend to be a lady.

In this way, "playing with class" allows Dossie to rethink and revise rigid class boundaries and distinctions and to try out identities that are based on class backgrounds, while recognizing the shifting cultural meanings of "class."

Donna discussed the ways in which different roles may take on different meanings depending on the context.

> I can play any number of roles. I can't stand when people want me to just be one thing. And, of course, when you play a role, and you're a butch and you're a top, there are going to be women who come to you specifically so that they can live the fantasy of being dominated by this Black butch whatever — it might be male, female, whatever their fantasy is, you know, it doesn't matter. It doesn't matter to me because if I decide that I want to play that role then I will. Most of the time I try to keep them from objectifying me without knowing it. I try to force them to admit that what we're doing here is you want to do this scene where you get shoved around by this — like I'm gonna put my baseball cap on backwards and I'm going to start plugging into your media conception because that's what you want. . . . I don't feel like it's insulting unless they're asking me to participate without my knowing that I'm participating, or letting me give permission to participate. . . . This is for play.

What is significant to Donna is her awareness and consciousness of what she is doing, and her ability to make independent choices regarding her sexual practices. In this way, she controls various aspects of her identity that culture, history, and society may tell her are stable, uniform, and beyond her control. Michelle, who identifies as a switch and plays both butch and fem roles, described the personae that she employs in scenes:

> There are several. I have a couple boys that I really enjoy. . . . I like that ability to be comfortable with that different type of energy. My male energy is just as present as the feminine energy that I have available, and s/m allows me to live that in its time.

Another type of play that is integrated into the practices of several of the participants for this research is referred to as "age play" and involves the conscious adaptation of roles such as parental figures or infants. Three of the women I interviewed identify as "daddies" and play these roles in different ways. For L.B., a daddy role does not conflict at all with her identity as a woman: "I identify very strongly as a woman. . . . [E]ven though I'm butch, and even though I play Daddy roles, and I can play male agenda roles, it's quite evident that I'm a woman, and I have no desires to be a man." For Quinn, a daddy role is structured in relation to someone else, and does not conflict with her identity as a woman and a lesbian:

> I've had people say to me, people who don't understand the dyke daddy thing, well like, "You're taking on a male figure. If you're going to take on a parental role, why not be a mama?" And I'm like, well because I'm butch. . . . [But] I'm a woman, very happy to be a woman, and doing the role of Daddy as a woman.

"Daddy" creates a space in which Quinn can explore emotions and relationships in a carefully controlled, formally structured environment:

> I didn't have a healthy relationship with my father, and this is a way for me of undoing some of that, and actually coming back in a really positive way of saying, we can create this as women. . . . For me it's not about recreating something old, or recreating bad times. It's about making something new, as a woman, because as women we don't really have much safety in our lives, you know . . . so to find a place where you can just break down, where

you can cry, where you can be really young, where you can be nurtured — I mean where there's *boundaries*. You know the rules and you have some kind of structure to kind of heal the little one that most of us got damaged as a child. For me, that's why I do what I do, and that's the place I come from. I think it's a really healthy thing, and it's not everybody's thing, but for me it really works well.

For many of the women to whom I spoke, the possibility of choosing roles within s/m, constructing a scene with clearly demarcated boundaries, and controlling the parameters of the scene through mutual decision-making, all function to create a space in which anything seems possible. On a day-to-day basis, our identities as women of color, lesbians, s/m dykes, are constantly being separated and compartmentalized. What the world tells us is impossible, irresolvable, and unnegotiable becomes possible in s/m, within the context of a scene. Identity becomes not only mutable but malleable.

Conceptualizations of Power and Difference

Proponents of lesbian s/m have been engaged in conflict with a segment of the feminist movement, primarily because s/m is perceived as eroticizing inequality and a power dynamic that feminism has fought to destroy. Several participants recalled being accused by other lesbian-feminists, specifically other women of color, of not recognizing power differences and/or the reality of women's oppression in this culture. The argument goes something like this: S/m eroticizes power differences and inequality, and s/m dykes get off on women's oppression. S/m sexual practices, therefore, have no transformative value; rather, they represent the ways in which women have been duped by a patriarchal society.

For instance, in *Toward a Feminist Theory of the State*, Catharine MacKinnon purports to discuss and analyze "male" power (or the power maintained by male supremacy and the hegemony of "the male perspective"). Hers is a bleak view of the patriarchal system in which we live and the means we have at our disposal to transform it. Because "male" power is so deeply ingrained and male supremacy the very foundation on which our culture is grounded, and because sex, and sexuality itself, is premised on this idea of dominance and submission (male dominance, female submission), what we may think of as consensual sex looks like (and is) rape. And what may appear to be subversive sexual acts and practices are really the results of false consciousness on the part of women who do not understand feminism and are merely perpetuating a patriarchal system of male supremacy.

> When women engage in ritualized sexual dominance and submission with each other, does that express the male supremacist structure or subvert it? . . . Lesbian sex, simply as sex between women, given a social definition of gender and sexuality, does not by definition transcend the eroticization of dominance and submission and their social equation with masculinity and femininity.[14]

Sexuality, in this sense, may be so gender-marked that it carries the dynamic of dominance and submission with it, no matter what the sex of either participant. For instance, lesbian culture's butch-fem roles, according to MacKinnon, simply serve to reiterate the male-female dichotomy and the power imbalance inherent in heterosexual relations; and sexual practices such as sadomasochism, in which "the basic dynamic . . . is the power dichotomy . . . do not even negate the paradigm of male dominance, but conform precisely to it."[15] In arguing that there is virtually no difference between consensual and nonconsensual sex, MacKinnon effectively writes "woman" out of sexual practice. What any individual woman desires is of no consequence. In fact, a woman is not even a subject, according to MacKinnon's radical theory of experience, which, Donna Haraway notes, "does not so much marginalize as obliterate the authority of any . . . [woman's] political speech or action." The eventual result is "MacKinnon's intentional erasure of all difference through the device of the 'essential' non-existence of women."[16] As Mariana Valverde has argued, in constructing sexuality as monolithic and uniformly oppressive, MacKinnon effectively erases differences between women. Not only are race and class differences ignored, and the ways in which they may constitute and influence sexual and gender expression, but also individual variations in desire, fantasy, and consent: "Resistance, subversion, and pleasure are written out of the account."[17]

The women I interviewed were much more critical of conceptualizations of power and difference than MacKinnon would suggest. The respondents were very aware of s/m as *play*. Although they recognized the way power differences are based in reality and in our culture, they also made it very clear to me that power, in their s/m practices, is a dynamic process, exchanged between two or more partners within the parameters of a scene. It is not the failure to recognize oppression and structural power differences that has led these women into s/m culture and practices but the constant and everyday reminders of their own positions within a system that often ignores, marginalizes, and exploits them. Many of the respondents choose to explore the concept of difference and the dynamics of power, and attempt to transform these dynamics in their own lives. Ami described this position of difference, and what it means for women of color, in the following way:

> I think that being different racially and socially, being a dyke, being a dyke of color, is really hard. I think that one can become very, very embattled, and it's very confusing. We have to think about things that white dykes don't have to think about, but certainly other white women don't have to think about, and *certainly* white men don't have to think about. And *we do* — we have to deal with those things on a daily basis.

Mariana, a twenty-seven-year-old woman of mixed race in San Francisco, discussed the concept of power as a dynamic process in her s/m practices, based in the reality of our culture but separated nonetheless by the parameters of a scene:

> There are so many issues around equality and women — in the women's community they always say that associating or affiliating yourself with power is a negative thing. And in s/m you're playing with power, and that's one of the reasons I think that s/m is so thrashed, it's because hey — I'm willing to say that power gets me off. Or a lack of it gets me off. And either way you're stuck. Because in the women's community it's like just enough power is the right place to be — self-empowered, and really what it is is a reaction to abusive power.

... I recognize that I haven't always been empowered. What really gets my goat is when people who were raised with at least power around money, or power around color, are so insensitive to me.... I have access to my desires; I have access to who I am and what I want to be; and I believe in it; and I'm willing to pay the price for my choices, and I'm willing to have boundaries, and I'm willing to be responsible for all of me. So, that allows me to indulge my perversions, because I recognize and I'm safe with myself about them; whereas other people have to draw those really thick boundaries.

Nearly all of the women I interviewed explained their s/m practices as sites of transformation in their lives. Again and again, they described the concept of power in their s/m practices as a shifting, polyvalent dynamic. Thus, they articulated a concept of power in terms similar to Foucault's theory about relations of power-knowledge and "the omnipresence of power":

not because it has the privilege of consolidating everything under its invisible unity, but because it is produced from one moment to the next, at every point, or rather in relation from one point to another. Power is everywhere; not because it embraces everything, but because it comes from everywhere.... Relations of power-knowledge are not static forms of distribution, they are "matrices of transformation" ... subject to constant modifications, continual shifts.[18]

The ways in which s/m was used to transform lived events, experiences, and identities varied for the participants. For Ami, s/m does not involve ignoring power differences; rather, it is a conscious attempt to confront discourses and processes of power. After recognizing sadomasochism as part of her sexual pleasure, she decided to more consciously pursue, explore, and experiment with power dynamics. For her, "s/m is one way to be more aggressively me, and to choose to be me." At the same time, she recognizes the risks involved and the fact that the ways in which she eroticizes power may be rooted in cultural forms of inequality:

Because sexual violence by men on my body is an issue that I have to think about and fear on a regular basis. . . . I mean for a while it was like I'm taking back my sexuality, and it was really unclear to me what I meant by that. I just meant like I'm taking it back from "the patriarchy," you know. But then the more I sort of got into my own personal stuff, the more I realized that I was taking it back, you know, from my grandfather who molested me when I was a child; from my mother who insisted that I be whoever she wanted me to be, and made it very difficult for me to express myself; taking it back from the Christian church, who told me that I was bad and sinful; you know, taking it back. As a Pacific Islander woman there are many stereotypes about who I am supposed to be sexually, culturally. . . . S/M has been part of a journey toward feeling empowered about my own sexuality, being really clear about what other people are projecting onto me, and what's my own stuff.

Several women emphasized the important distinction between consensual and nonconsensual sexual practices. "Healthy" s/m, for them, involves clearly negotiated scenes or interactions, where power is exchanged, rather than being placed in the hands of one participant. For Dru, who became involved in s/m following a three-year-long violently abusive relationship, s/m provided a space where she could create her own rules and make conscious choices about what she would do or have done to her. Annette discussed s/m as a source of empowerment in her life, because she could be in control:

> There's definitely a part of me that is over being told by people that I think are pretty fucked up that my practices are fucked up. And the whole issue of women, well, you're just doing that because you're a survivor of sexual abuse; well, maybe I am a survivor of sexual abuse and maybe that is related to my — I mean, I was raped, and yes, I can separate my sex life and my history of being a rape survivor, but why should I have to? Like there's a better way and a worse way to work out your history and your experiences, and to deal with your experiences, and I should be in therapy and I should be having a certain kind of sex? And if I'm not having a certain kind of sex, then I'm sick or still recovering from something, and still damaged in some way? Wait, to me that is just taking my power away. So a man did it, and now you're going to do it to me too — you're going to tell me that my sexuality is wrong *again*. I don't need that. . . . If it's empowering to you then you should explore it.

And for Dossie, who is also a survivor of sexual and physical abuse, s/m creates a space to play the role of a victim where it may be possible to explore its meanings, to choose a different outcome, to experience her feelings in a safe space:

> All the times I was dealing with that, I couldn't afford to see myself as pathetic because I was too busy feeling guilty, like I was somehow responsible or at fault for the fact that my father was abusing me. . . . It was a great luxury to just sit there and be really pathetic. There was this honesty because on a most profound level it brings me back in sympathy with child parts of me that I've rejected in order to empower myself, and is needy and victim-y [sic] and whatever — is a part of me that I rejected, and that I'm only now being able to accept and own. . . . To me, it's about an exploration toward more wholeness through s/m by reclaiming parts of me that were lost to the abuse.

S/m provides for Dossie a way to integrate many different experiences and the many different parts of herself and to accept them all. It is a way to transform the events she has lived through, while at the same time recognizing the very real manifestations of power in her life: "It's very true that in a society with different power dynamics that the myths about power would be different and so our s/m might look different. But, as it stands, we are in this culture, and so our myths about power come out of this culture." For these women, s/m provides one means to exist in a preexisting cultural framework, while at the same time attempting to transform that framework. The key to understanding how s/m may provide critical and self-conscious moments of subversion for some individuals is a recognition of the role of fantasy. S/m may be based in reality, to some extent, but it involves the manipulation of that reality in order to create fantasy.

Michelle, who is an incest survivor, and has spent the last eight years of her life in substance abuse recovery, described s/m as a powerful healing tool:

> Before I got clean and sober, I had no idea what boundary meant. It was through my s/m that I learned about boundaries, and I learned about needs, and I learned about respect and about self-worth and value. And being able to work out some of my own issues — my own recovery issues and my incest issues . . . [s/m] has been a tremendous recovery tool for me in my life, and it's equally a tremendous tool of pleasure.

Because s/m allows her to create personae and construct boundaries, Michelle is able to actively confront painful issues and experiences in her life and consciously transform them into pleasure.

Several women discussed s/m as a way to explore their identities as women of color in relation to specific sociohistorical events. J.D., an African-American woman of mixed race who has been practicing s/m for nine years, identifies as a top and as a daddy:

> As a Black woman you are raised with this entire background of hearing horror stories about slavery. And you hear from day one . . . how awful the practices were. We were brought here against our will, and the concept of being whipped, or chained to something, or anything that even looks like it might be against your will, is extremely taboo. . . . [T]he fact that I am a top — I'm considered a perpetrator. I'm considered someone who's advocating and perpetrating violence against women, specifically as a Black woman because I engage in this type of activity. As a Black lesbian you don't even discuss it.

Donna, who is also an African-American s/m dyke in San Francisco and is in her mid-thirties, made an important distinction between the history of slavery in the U.S. and her sexual practices. These practices may be influenced by the history and by the current marginalization and stereotyping of Black women in this country; however, she consciously chooses her practices and her roles, and the dynamics that she creates in her s/m play do not adhere to any strict formula of power difference:

> This one sister-woman used the phrase "my people" and kept talking about "whips and chains" and "my people" and I was going, "oh my god, you can't do this." This is not the same argument. This is a different case. This is a *fantasy* that we're creating . . . and it's not wrong. Why in the world would they try to pull this argument out and say "I can't believe that you're doing this when our ancestors were bound up in chains." And I'm like, you know, that would make a great scene too, especially between people who really understood what it was about, to be able to reclaim something of that. . . . The history is real, but this is *play*. . . . I think that the thing that people get hung up on is that they think that the power has to be invested in one person. And I don't think that that's really true. I don't play that way. . . . Nobody has their power stripped away from them. Even if the negotiation says symbolically we are going to strip you of your power . . . it's still symbolic. . . . The power is shared. . . . I mean I'm not naive enough to think that I don't live in this world and politics, and you know. . . . But I also live inside this body, and what happens here is the first thing that I worry about. . . . These women who put down s/m and say this is harkening back to slavery — I just can't support it, I can't at all. It's just nuts.

Not everyone in this study would agree with Donna that because s/m is play, history can be recuperated and transformed. For Quinn, certain practices do not have any transformative value; Nazi play, for example, and the use of images such as swastikas, are terrifying and difficult to reclaim:

> To take a symbol like that [a swastika] and play with it, when it's as oppressive as it is to so many people — it's very hard to reclaim it. . . . Race scenes and Nazi scenes are not okay scenes for me. . . . What you do privately in your bedroom is up to you . . . but bringing it into public spaces where I have to look at it — that's nonconsensual. . . . Yes, you can look

away, but you've already seen it, it's already affected you.... For me, s/m is not about forcing stuff in people's faces or forcing people to face their fears.

Annette, while recognizing the different meanings certain practices may have for different individuals, also feels that there are some practices which are not necessarily transformative:

> Things do have different contexts for people, [but] there are some things I feel can't be recuperated, and shouldn't be recuperated. But first and foremost I really need to hear from the person themself [sic] what it means to them. And I have to take that into account — I can't dismiss that.

Creating boundaries and being able to make choices about what is and is not acceptable content for play is a component that makes s/m appealing to many of the participants in this study. Because they are able to construct the power dynamics in a scene in any form that they wish, they may explore different issues and conflicts in safe spaces, without the risks that such power exchanges would entail in "real life." Dru explains s/m in terms of the construction of boundaries:

> The result of what I think is a really healthy formula that we're taught in s/m is about boundaries, because before I found s/m I had no boundaries. Or at least I didn't recognize them as boundaries.... Suddenly you have this option and you want to exercise it as much as you possibly can.... [L]ike I never realized I had a *choice*, so I'm going to exercise that choice every single time I play.

Because power in s/m is constructed and never fixed or absolute, "scenes," for many of the women I interviewed, represent contained, microscopic sites of conflict and power exchange. They operate as "matrices of transformation" in which constructed identities and shifting power exchanges are possible.[19] Whether a transformation entails reclaiming parts of oneself that may have been affected by abuse, victimization, or oppression, or simply rethinking the role of fantasy in one's life in relation to an individual or collective identity, s/m play may provide liberatory spaces where power is not erased or ignored but employed by conscious participants in a dynamic of pleasure and fantasy.

The practice of lesbian s/m conflicts with and is often critiqued by an ideology that is based on a liberal humanistic notion of equality. S/m practices acknowledge and, in some instances, eroticize difference: racial difference and/or forms of racialized power, gender difference, and class difference, among other things. In addition, s/m play often employs roles that may seem like stereotypes: for instance, racial stereotypes or stereotypes about racial relationships and other types of constructed images. In this way, s/m practices to some extent "de-essentialize" racial and other structures of identity, while at the same time calling attention to these differences and making them salient in the context of a scene. For this reason, s/m ideology conflicts with a liberal notion of universal equality that is premised on a belief in our inherent sameness. S/m not only acknowledges difference that may already exist; it also *creates* difference. Identities in an s/m scene are neither fixed nor stable. Rather, roles may be imaginary and constructed, based perhaps in the reality of sociohistorical events but clearly neither essential nor determined.

However, women of color who practice s/m do not necessarily attempt to fit racial stereotypes, live by them, or eroticize them. On the contrary, many participants noted the damaging effect of racial stereotypes in their own lives. L. B., for example, commented on how stereotypes affect her racial identity:

> We all hate to hear the exotic thing. . . . One that really makes me afraid is when people say "Oh, I love Asian women." You know, to me, as I look on my maternal side, all of the women are married to white servicemen. And so, I come from a place where what does that mean? All these white servicemen went out to marry "Orientals," you know, because they knew that they would be demure and quiet and clean their house and keep it nice. So, when I hear people say "Oh I love Asian women" it brings up a whole bag of stuff.

Veena discussed the ways in which stereotypes of South Asian women have affected her own self-concept:

> There are these stereotypes hanging over my head . . . and I think that the stereotypes of Asian women have affected me like, now that I'm identifying as a top, I feel that just clashing with these stereotypes that I've always lived up to, and the identity of an Indian woman, which is really central [for me], you know. I feel like I'm getting farther and farther away from what my father always told me I was supposed to be as a woman — as an Indian woman, and it's like *fuck* — it's scary.

Several respondents articulated clear conceptualizations of the distinction between stereotypes which serve to maintain the marginalization of women of color and play that acknowledges racial difference in order to explore its parameters.

The ideology which argues that we are all equal because we are all the same puts forth the idea that, on the one hand, race is essential and determined, in the same way that sex is believed to be. On the other hand, in order to be equal we must erase difference (race, color) in order to be the same (read: white). To be "equal," for many people in this country, means to assimilate, not only by ignoring the visible markers of difference that may be inscribed on our bodies, but also by attempting to erase or obliterate different cultural values or histories. Feminist theory that attempts to unite women by claiming that we share common values and goals, while ignoring the vast differences between women, results in what Adrienne Rich refers to as "white solipsism": the tendency "to think, imagine, and speak as if whiteness described the world."[20] By assuming an equal status based on a shared identity — "as if commonality were a metaphysical given, as if a shared political viewpoint were not a difficult political achievement" — western feminist theory often fails to distinguish "woman" from "white," yet never forgets that blackness and womanness, for instance, or Indianness and womanness are "discrete and separable elements of identity."[21]

In some instances, s/m play may acknowledge differences, and in fact, make them apparent and salient; at the same time, by constantly constructing and deconstructing difference, s/m questions the very concept of difference by "playing" with it. Rather than assuming a notion of equality that would universalize and engulf difference — a totalizing force which in fact erases difference — s/m acknowledges and, in some instances, even eroticizes difference. For those who choose to play, the goal of s/m is liberatory. It operates as a positive process for many of us by offering a space to resolve conflict, make choices, explore and exchange power. In addition, s/m, for some women, fuels fantasies and provides a means toward sexual expression and the experience of pleasure.

A number of the respondents, however, do not simply accept s/m practices and membership in various s/m communities uncritically or without question. In play, identities may be constructed, and difference can be acknowledged and manipulated, but within their communities, difference sometimes remains fixed and hierarchized, with women of color often incorporated in marginal, tokenistic ways. For example, several respondents who are of mixed race pointed out the ways in which women of color may face different issues depending on how "colored" they are or are perceived to be and how they are recognized as women of color. These participants expressed feelings of invisibility because they are often assumed to be white. They may find themselves existing along the borders of two or more racial/cultural identities: although they are not white, they are also not recognized as women of color. According to Mariana, one's experiences as a woman of color often depend on the concept of visibility:

> Hapa women [women of mixed heritage] have completely different experiences as women of color than like African-American women. It's like those who are visible and those who are invisible is really how the break-up goes, right? Because really for an Asian woman, really it has nothing to do with color; it has everything in the world to do with the shape of your eyes. But we don't talk in terms of symmetry, or facial structure; we talk in terms of color....
>
> Issues that we carry are very different.... I'm struggling with issues of access. I'm struggling with issues of invisibility, not too much visibility.

Other women discussed the ways in which they struggle with feelings of complicity with a racist system because they are so often assumed to be white. L.B. discussed the way racism functions differently in her life than for women of color who are clearly visible as women of color:

> When it comes down to who are you, what are you, well — okay, I am a woman of color, because I am half colored. When it comes down to writing something on an application, it's always hard for me because I think, why are they asking me this question? Will I be rejected or accepted on the basis of this? And for me it's particularly hard because I — well, half of me is *white*. . . . For women of mixed heritage, especially women of mixed heritage that pass for being white, issues are so much different from women of color who are obviously women of color. Because all of my racial issues stem not so much from being racially objectified myself, but come from having to be a part of racist remarks and conversations that are carried on by my Anglo counterparts who don't realize . . . you know, they just think that they're talking to another Nazi or another like-minded white, you know, and to me that's the hardest thing.... The racism that I find in the community has to do with the fact that I hear [racist comments] because people feel free to make racist comments in all Anglo settings, you know, and I happen to be there, and they see me as part of that.

When asked about conflict in her life regarding s/m and her racial identity, L.B.'s response was "No, never — I've been very accepting of it [laughs]." Yet, when asked whether or not she participates in the San Francisco Asian/Pacific Islander lesbian community, she said:

No, because passing as an Anglo, I generally don't feel welcome. And there is a group here that advertises, you know, "look, mixed-heritage people come, even if you look white — it's okay." And I just never got around to going, you know — I'm so afraid of being rejected by it. And I tend, very consciously, to put myself in environments that are conducive to my behavior, so for me, being in a cotton-and-wool community [a non-s/m, or anti-s/m community] isn't something that I venture into very much.

Both passing (or being passed) for white and practicing s/m function to maintain some women of color in positions of invisibility within what is then perceived to be a predominantly white lesbian s/m community. As Dru points out, there are many women of color in the leather community who are not counted as women of color:

People are fighting to move the leather community into a more interracial atmosphere, but because of what I believe about how some races are seen and some races not seen, I don't think that their numbers are right. I think that plenty of us are out there that consider ourselves of color, and they're not counting us. So even the people who are trying to integrate us aren't being fair, 'cause they don't count the people who they don't see as being a person of color. They don't count me. They don't believe me; so I'm like, "Well, I don't believe you either." I don't believe the people who say "We don't want any people of color," and I'm not believing the people who say "Well, we want people of color 'cause we don't have any" because they're both wrong. They're both wrong.

Because of the invisibility of many s/m dykes who identify themselves as women of color, the politics of race and integration in the lesbian s/m community are skewed. Mixed-race identities necessitate new subject positions and frameworks of racial difference which are capable of acknowledging the complexities of racial identities and can articulate multiplicitous and sometimes conflicting sets of meanings and values.[22]

In addition, many respondents recognized the ways in which issues of race are intricately connected to those of class. They related issues of racial identities to class positions, as both serve similar functions in the erasure of difference. Several participants discussed the ways in which, not only for s/m dykes but within the lesbian community more generally, there has been a trend toward downward mobility, where members of a young, urban, mostly educated community of lesbians attempt to "de-class" themselves in order to remove privilege and difference. Mariana discussed the function of class in relation to "finding" s/m:

What I recognize is that people who have been raised in the upper-class, or in the mid- to upper-class, have a sense of entitlement, that they are more likely to find the s/m in themselves because they have the space; they recognize their right to engage in behaviors that are not culturally or socially sanctioned. . . . I think that issues of color sort of figure in here; color and class are sometimes hard to separate. But when you struggle with issues of color as you're being raised, because they are visual cues that allow people to oppress, or create oppressive environments, that again, you have less strong of a sense of entitlement, and so your choices come a little bit more thoughtfully, and maybe slowly.

Annette discussed the role of class in relation to arguments within the lesbian s/m community regarding the acceptability or unacceptability of certain practices, and also in relation to the arguments made by anti-s/m feminists:

I think a lot of the arguments around porn and s/m are really middle-class arguments, about like propriety, and what sex is about. Like sex is about love, and we shouldn't be hurting each other — it just shouldn't be happening. And yeah, some naiveté. I think there's a lot of other criticisms around s/m that I think are more challenging, more engaging, more interesting, and they tend to come from women who aren't very privileged, and are more about calling people on their shit, like this is fucked up, you know, swastikas are fucked up; or look around you, why are all the women white? That kind of thing, and I think that the bourgie [sic] arguments get heard more than the other arguments, and I really think that's a function of class, that those women get heard. The women who say, "Oh, you're enacting childhood abuse," get heard a lot more than the women who say "This community isn't inclusive," or "These practices aren't inclusive."

In regard to the move toward "de-classing" the lesbian s/m community, Mariana explored the implications of glossing over difference and privilege in order to create a false sense of unity. Coming from a working-class background, but working now in a middle-class environment, Mariana asserts that "de-classing" not only glorifies poverty but also fails to recognize and confront privilege:

I watch the women in the community and I hear the snide remarks — what do they call them? Foundation kids, or something, like where they have an inheritance that they live on; they have the freedom to indulge in more of a punk look or a leather look or a dirty look, a baggy look, a pierced look; and they take on attitudes about class, like when you have money or when you have a "straight job," that is somehow bad or somehow negative. I get a lot of flack for looking "straight"; I always have. And what I recognize, or what I carry as my sort of grudge against these women who can afford and choose to look that way, the grudges I carry are that — that's when I say they are proud of being downwardly mobile. That's my way of saying they can choose it; and I resent the glorification of poverty. I think that much as they think that they're doing some good because they're trying to take away from empowered classes, they're trying to take away from them, take away their power and their sense that they deserve by saying, "I don't want." I think that it is naive, and it is not very sensitive. . . . How dare they judge me for choosing what they were given and take for granted.

For Mariana, "de-classing" the lesbian community functions like the liberal ideology that assumes a sameness by ignoring racial difference. The glorification of poverty, to her, does nothing to change the status quo or weaken empowered classes; rather, it denies certain aspects of individual identities and fails to adequately acknowledge power differences created by class identities. The issue of class came up for many of the respondents in different contexts and often associated with racial difference. In the construction of sexuality and in cultural understandings of s/m practices, the functions of class and race are inextricably intertwined, as exemplified by the narratives of respondents.

Lesbian s/m practice conflicts with several dominant forms of discourse in this culture. It gains its cultural significance from this conflict, however, and the conflict itself serves as a site or a space for the resolution of seemingly oppositional differences and the renegotiation of identity. S/m provides this site of conflict through three main processes. First, identities in s/m play are not stable or essential; rather, they may be constructed as dynamic "roles." As a result, they are often partial, fragmented, fluid, and changing, and may also be performative. Second, power, as it is constructed in the context of an s/m scene, is also subject to constant modification, manipulation, and control. And finally, s/m play is based on *differences,* whether recognized or constructed, and the eroticization of these differences. Difference, as a social concept, is therefore recognized, yet also acknowledged as a construction.

In thinking about a participant, or "persona," in an s/m scene, I use Donna Haraway's image of the cyborg: a fictional mapping of social and bodily reality in "an argument for pleasure in the confusion of boundaries and for responsibility in their construction." The cyborg, as she explains, is "resolutely committed to partiality, irony, intimacy, and perversity. It is oppositional, utopian, and completely without innocence." It is constructed within the transgressions of boundaries, and it is not afraid of "permanently partial identities" or contradictory standpoints. As a postmodernist identity, it is constructed from "otherness, difference, and specificity," and it is consciously political.[23]

The differences created by race in self-conceptualization and self-representation draw attention to the limitations of current theoretical discourses on queer identities and sexualities and contest the usefulness of political strategies intended to draw us all together by blurring the lines between us. In a space where the boundaries are constantly being pushed and expanded, where identities are not only contestable and multiplicitous but hybrid, mosaic, *cyborg,* and where difference can be explored, I see great possibilities for reconceptualizing the very notions of "identity" and "difference." More than anything, the experiences of the women I interviewed highlight the need for new frameworks of conceptualization that are able to acknowledge the indivisibility of complex cultural identities.

NOTES

Acknowledgments: Thanks to Gayle Rubin for the many introductions in S.F., to Kath Weston for putting me in contact with some of the respondents, and especially, to Ami Mattison, who accompanied me on a number of interviews, offered constructive comments and criticism from the start, and, through our many discussions, helped me to formulate the ideas and implications of s/m as a site of conflict. Also, thanks to all the women who have participated in the project thus far. This research was made possible by summer funding from the Institute for Women's Studies, Emory University.

1. Gayle Rubin, "Thinking Sex: Notes for a Radical Theory of the Politics of Sexuality," in *Pleasure and Danger: Exploring Female Sexuality,* ed. Carole Vance (London: Pandora, 1984), 267–319.

2. For a more complete discussion of these viewpoints, see Robin Ruth Linden, Darlene R. Pagano, Diana Russell, and Susan Leigh Star, eds., *Against Sadomasochism: A Radical Feminist Analysis* (San Francisco: Frog in the Well, 1982); Irene Reti, ed., *Unleashing Feminism: Critiquing Sadomasochism in the Gay Nineties* (Santa Cruz, CA: HerBooks, 1993); and Sheila Jeffreys, *The Lesbian Heresy: A Feminist Perspective on the Lesbian Sexual Revolution* (Melbourne: Spinifex, 1993).

3. The term "woman of color" is used strategically here. I employ this term, not in an attempt to blur distinctions between different racial and ethnic identities, or to assume a false sense of

unity among women of different cultural backgrounds and experiences, but rather as a politically useful tool which may foster alliances and understandings, while recognizing differences. In some ways, the term is also a conscious attempt to resist the "divide and conquer" tactics of the New Right, which attempt to pit different cultural communities against one another, divide us on issues of class, and persuade us that queerness is a white/western concept. The term "woman of color," as it is used here, is always consciously political.

4. Lisa Duggan, "The Trials of Alice Mitchell: Sensationalism, Sexology, and the Lesbian Subject in Turn-of-the-Century America," *Signs: Journal of Women in Culture and Society* 8, no. 4 (1993): 791–814. Duggan describes identities as

> stories rather than mere labels ... [which] constitut[e] a central organizing principle connecting self and world. Individual identities, usually multiple and often contradictory, structure and give meaning to personal experience. Collective identities — of gender, race, class, or nation — forge connections among individuals and provide links between past and present, becoming the basis for cultural representation and political action.

5. Pat Califia, "A Personal View of the History of the Lesbian S/M Community and Movement in San Francisco," in *Coming to Power: Writings and Graphics on Lesbian S/M*, ed. SAMOIS (Boston: Alyson, 1987), 245–83; Julia Creet, "Daughter of the Movement: The Psychodynamics of Lesbian S/M Fantasy," *differences: A Journal of Feminist Cultural Studies* 3, no. 2 (Summer 1991): 135–59.

6. B. Ruby Rich, "Feminism and Sexuality in the 1980's," *Feminist Studies* 12, no. 3 (1986): 532.

7. For more discussion of specifically feminist methodological techniques which attempt to center the experiences of women, of lesbians, and of women of color in particular, see Evelyn Fox Keller, *Reflections on Gender and Science* (New Haven: Yale University Press, 1985); Liz Stanley and Sue Wise, "Method, Methodology and Epistemology in Feminist Research Processes," in *Feminist Praxis: Research, Theory and Epistemology in Feminist Sociology*, ed. Liz Stanley (New York: Routledge, 1990), 20–60; Celia Kitzinger, *The Social Construction of Lesbianism* (London: Sage Publications, 1987); and Patricia Hill Collins, *Black Feminist Thought: Knowledge, Consciousness, and the Politics of Empowerment* (London: HarperCollins, 1990).

8. Rubin, "Thinking Sex," 295.

9. Califia, "A Personal View," 247.

10. Ibid., 247.

11. See Audre Lorde, "The Master's Tools Will Never Dismantle the Master's House"; "Age, Race, Class, and Sex"; and "Eye to Eye: Black Women, Hatred, and Anger," all in Lorde, *Sister Outsider* (Freedom, CA: Crossing Press, 1984).

12. Trinh T. Minh-ha, *Woman Native Other: Writing Postcoloniality and Feminism* (Bloomington: Indiana University Press, 1989), 104.

13. Donna Haraway, "A Cyborg Manifesto: Science, Technology, and Socialist-Feminism in the Late Twentieth Century," in *Simians, Cyborgs, and Women: The Reinvention of Nature* (New York: Routledge, 1991), 173.

14. See Catharine MacKinnon, *Toward a Feminist Theory of the State* (Cambridge: Harvard University Press, 1989), 119.

15. Ibid., 142.

16. Haraway, "A Cyborg Manifesto," 149.

17. Mariana Valverde, "Beyond Gender Dangers and Private Pleasures: Theory and Ethics in the Sex Debates," *Feminist Studies* 15, no. 2 (Summer 1989): 242.

18. Michel Foucault, *The History of Sexuality*, vol. 1 (New York: Vintage Books, 1978), 93, 99.
19. Ibid., 99.
20. See Adrienne Rich, "Disloyal to Civilization: Feminism, Racism, Gynephobia," in *Lies, Secrets, and Silence: Selected Prose, 1966–1978* (New York: Norton, 1979), 299. In this essay, Rich writes:

> I used to envy the "colorblindness" which some liberal, enlightened, white people were supposed to possess. . . . But I no longer believe that "colorblindness" — if it even exists — is the opposite of racism; I think it is, in this world, a form of naiveté and moral stupidity. It implies that I would look at a black woman and see her as white, thus engaging in white solipsism to the utter erasure of her particular reality.

See, in particular, pages 299–300 and 306–10.
21. Elizabeth V. Spelman, *Inessential Woman: Problems of Exclusion in Feminist Thought* (Boston: Beacon Press, 1988), 13. Spelman introduces the term "boomerang perception" — "I look at you and come right back to myself" (12) — and discusses white solipsism and the feminist movement in the context of a critique of Kenneth Stampp's book, *The Peculiar Institution: Slavery in the Ante-Bellum South* (1956), in which he argues that "We're the same, because underneath that black skin is a white man." In her critique of the universalizing mechanisms of the feminist movement, she echoes Cherríe Moraga's preface to *This Bridge Called My Back: Writings by Radical Women of Color* (1981), in which Moraga makes the argument that "sisterhood" with other women of color (and with white women) is a political achievement, not something to be assumed. Both Biddy Martin and Donna Haraway have commented on the political significance of Moraga's words, in that her language and her identity are fragmented, partial, and often engaged in conflict. See Biddy Martin, "Lesbian Identity and Autobiographical Difference[s]," in *The Lesbian and Gay Studies Reader*, ed. Henry Abelove, Michèle Aina Barale, and David M. Halperin (New York: Routledge, 1993), 274–94; Haraway, *Simians, Cyborgs, and Women*.
22. At the same time, as I was reminded by a close friend, it is important to consider the negative impact of common representations of "confused, conflicting" mixed-race identities. Anti-miscegenation sentiment often portrays mixed-heritage individuals as tragic "products of clashing cultures," representing the idea of mixed race as something to be feared and/or denied. Mixed-race individuals who recognize the processes and effects of racism, colonialism, and imperialist intervention may occupy complex subject positions; we are not simply victims of oppressive interlocking systems. My friend described her own process of coming to critical consciousness regarding her identity as a biracial woman:

> [At one time] I felt like my two racial and cultural backgrounds could not be reconciled and that I could never know who I was on any significant level. . . . I realized that those feelings [are] influenced by racism — fear of racial mixture which makes people of mixed race out to be eternally internally confused. . . . This stereotype is enforced and strengthened by the invisibility of people of mixed race, race being characterized most often as black and white or as consisting of discrete categories like the ones on applications. (Tara Mulay, letter to the author, November 1994)

23. Haraway, "A Cyborg Manifesto," 150, 155–56. Haraway discusses the cyborg in the context of a "border war," where "the relationships for forming wholes from parts, including those of polarity and hierarchical domination, are at issue" (151). She uses the term specifically to refer to the political location of women of color in a postcolonial setting. Also, Haraway relies on Chela

Sandoval's theory of "oppositional consciousness": a postmodern model of political identity that refers to contradictory locations — not pluralisms — in the production of anti-colonialist discourse. See Chela Sandoval, "Oppositional Consciousness in the Postmodern World: United States Third World Feminism, Semiotics, and the Methodology of the Oppressed," diss., University of California, Santa Cruz, 1993.

chapter 6

Why Suzie Wong Is Not a Lesbian: Asian and Asian American Lesbian and Bisexual Women and Femme/Butch/Gender Identities

JeeYeun Lee

Lately, some commentators of lesbian life have noted the prevalence of what Lillian Faderman calls "neo-butch/femme," where women appear to be playing with femme and butch roles "with a sense of lightness and flexibility."[1] These writers are worried by the seemingly de-politicized nature of this carefree attitude:

> [T]he "fluidity" school seems to champion a celebratory approach, a refusal to consider any deeper, or problematic, elements. "Gender play" is all the rage, but, in all this, where is a feminist consciousness and challenge to gender divisions and inequalities?[2]

This characterization of femme/butch as an apolitical lifestyle is itself somewhat glib. While it is true that many lesbian and bisexual women in certain regions of the U.S. do describe their gender/sexual styles as play, the reasons that women play with gender have deeper significance than just frivolous masquerade and have more to do with living the complex intersections of sex, appearance, anatomy, sexuality, race, and culture. In particular, for women of color who "play" with gender, relationships to gender identities are complicated by racial and cultural differences that affect both how their genders are perceived and how they shape their genders. In this essay, I specifically want to explore some of these factors that affect Asian and Asian American lesbian and bisexual women.

First, let me clarify some terms that form the bounds of my discussion. I use "gender" to address both femme/butch dynamics and ideas about femininity and masculinity. These two frameworks are not quite the same, and the definitions of these terms are highly contested. Let me make a working definition here: I use "femininity" and "masculinity" to talk about the alignment of behavior with anatomy in a framework of compulsory heterosexuality; that is, I use these terms to refer to heterosexually based gender norms. I use "femme" and "butch" to refer to gender/sexual styles among lesbian and bisexual women, styles that have historical and cultural variations and roots.[3] The two frameworks are not absolutely distinct, yet neither are they exactly similar. Indeed, the crux of the debate about femme/butch dynamics is precisely the extent to which they are imitations (or appropriations) of heterosexual genders. I do not intend to engage in this debate here; for the purposes of this article, I will use "femme/butch" when discussing lesbian and bisexual women's communities and "feminine/masculine" for heterosexual contexts.[4]

Another clarification concerns my interchangeable use of both "Asian" and "Asian American," although I do restrict my analysis to women of Asian descent living in the U.S. On the one hand, since the 1960s, Asian American groups have insisted on being recognized as "American," in order to defy dominant views of Asians as perpetual foreigners as well as to provide an alternative to the loaded term "Oriental." On the other hand, many first-generation Asian Americans do not identify as Americans. Also, many people of all generations who originate from nations that have endured colonial subjugation in the past and/or neo-colonial relationships in the present, such as the Philippines, reject Americanness: to a certain extent, these people have already been forcibly made "American" in their own homelands. In addition, racial stereotypes do not distinguish between Asian and Asian American, as they are based on phenotype and imagined cultural traits. For all these reasons, I will use both "Asian" and "Asian American" interchangeably. I also debated whether including women of Pacific Islander descent would be truly inclusive or merely tokenizing. Since much of my analysis involves specifically Orientalist constructions of Asian women that are substantially different from those of Pacific Islander women,[5] I decided it would be hypocritical to extend my discussion to include Pacific Islanders in name only. However, I do believe that many of the other factors that I discuss here also affect Pacific Islander lesbian and bisexual women.

Related to this issue is my use of "we" and "our" throughout this article to refer to Asian and Asian American lesbian and bisexual women. I do this in order to deconstruct the myth of objectivity in the social sciences, but I realize that this has the danger of falling into an identity politics that relies on some mythic vision of a monolithic "community" that comes together naturally. This is hardly the case, either in theory or in fact; as the APLN (Asian Pacifica Lesbian Network)[6] 1989 national retreat and 1993 West Coast retreat showed, there is still an implicit center that marginalizes many people. As was stated at the latter retreat, this "community" can only work as a coalition, and it is in this sense that I use "we": to acknowledge those who are joined by common political agendas. However, I also realize that my use of "we" has the danger of being appropriated by others to view me as a native informant and tokenize me as speaking for a constituency, especially when there is so little on this topic in the legitimated world of research and writing. This is a risk that I consciously face and can only hope to deflect through a constant reiteration of the diversity in this coalitional identity.

In this essay, I want to explore some factors that affect Asian and Asian American lesbian and bisexual women's femme/butch/gender identities. I am particularly interested in those factors that reflect the racial and cultural differences that influence how we shape gender and how our genders are perceived by mainstream and lesbian communities. One of these factors is a particular strain of Orientalist discourse in the U.S. that constructs Asian women of various ethnicities as hyperfeminine, exotic, passive objects of white heterosexual male desire.[7] In an environment where we are constantly confronted by such expectations, our presentations of gender are decidedly not neutral. Another factor is the prevailing image in lesbian communities of what a lesbian looks like, an image that is constructed as white and butch, making invisible lesbian and bisexual women of color and femme women of all races. This invisibility is compounded especially for femme and feminine-looking Asian women, who often find themselves judged in light of the above-mentioned Orientalist discourse that can only construe them as heterosexual. In addition, all of this is complicated by our awareness of different cultural norms for gender. For Asian and Asian American women, ideas about what it means to be masculine or feminine are influenced not only by dominant U.S. norms but also by our perceptions of various Asian cultural standards of gender.

I do not want to present these forces as having all-powerful effects on Asian women's gender identities, and in fact, some of the women I interviewed for this work were not aware of the existence of some of these factors. However, gender is not an individual choice that lies completely outside of societal discourses and practices. I want to examine these various forces in a way that accounts for both determination and agency; while not all women experience these pressures to equal degrees, they form part of the terrain on which our genders are mapped.

I want to emphasize that these are only a few of the many forces that affect gender identities. I focus on these to show how the consideration of racial and cultural differences affects analyses of gender and femme/butch identities for lesbian and bisexual women. Whether Asian and Asian American lesbian and bisexual women consciously respond to these forces or not, our gender identities do not resonate solely in the context of compulsory heterosexuality: they are also affected by histories and practices of racialization and ethnocentrism and differences in cultural standards. Critics must also start to investigate the particularities of white women's gender identities; white lesbian and bisexual women's concepts of femme and butch are also specifically shaped and interpreted in light of what is deemed appropriate for white women in mainstream and lesbian/bisexual communities.[8]

Part of my research for this article consisted of interviews with ten Asian and Asian American lesbian and bisexual women. These women are in no way representative of the diversity of all those who identify as such. I tried to interview a group diverse in age, immigration status, ethnicity, mixed-race heritage, bisexual/lesbian identification, and femme/butch identification but did not have sufficient resources to achieve the diversity and outreach I would have liked. I am of course not trying to generalize these women's responses as representative of all Asian American lesbian and bisexual women; I do not view these interviews as subject matter to be dissected or as proof of my views, but rather as anecdotal illustrations of the kinds of factors that I am examining.

Lotus Blossoms and American Orientalisms

> Images of Asian women, however, have remained consistently simplistic and inaccurate. . . .
> There are two basic types: the Lotus Blossom Baby (a.k.a. China Doll, Geisha Girl, shy
> Polynesian beauty), and the Dragon Lady (Fu Manchu's various female relations, prosti-
> tutes, devious madames). . . . The Lotus Blossom Baby, a sexual-romantic object, has been
> the prominent type throughout the years. These "Oriental flowers" are utterly feminine,
> delicate, and welcome respites from their often loud, independent American counterparts.
> Many of them are the spoils of the last three wars fought in Asia.[9]

> In the world's media, the stereotypes are being perpetuated. We're geisha girls, we're Suzie
> Wong, or whatever, just somebody to exploit sexually. And also somebody really sexual in
> bed. That we're really meek and passive but once you get us in bed, we're wildcats (O.M.).[10]

Many of the women I spoke to were familiar with the above stereotypes, citing not
only their encounters with film images but also with male strangers on the streets who
hailed them as "mama-san" or "china girl." However, before I discuss these images and
the impact they have on Asian lesbian and bisexual women's gender identities, I want to
utter a word of caution. In *Critical Terrains: French and British Orientalisms*, Lisa Lowe
argues persuasively that there are a multiplicity of discourses about the East that can all
be called Orientalist while differing wildly in their purposes, their referents (which part
of the East they are talking about), and the reasons for their development.

> [M]uch as I wish to underscore the insistence of these power relations, my intervention
> resists totalizing orientalism as a monolithic, developmental discourse that uniformly con-
> structs the Orient as the Other of the Occident. . . . I argue for a conception of orientalism
> as heterogeneous and contradictory; to this end I observe, on the one hand, that orientalism
> consists of an uneven matrix of orientalist situations across different cultural and historical
> sites, and on the other, that each of these orientalisms is internally complex and unstable.[11]

My analysis of Orientalist constructions of Asian women is thus not only specific to
twentieth-century U.S. dominant discourses — what I call American Orientalisms, following Toni Morrison's coining of "American Africanism"[12] — but also points to the
internal diversity of these constructions. Not only is there the "Lotus Blossom," but also
the "Dragon Lady," as Renee E. Tajima and others note, as well as news anchors,
Olympic figure skaters, model minorities, store owners, and other variations.

Here I want to focus on American Orientalist constructions of the Lotus Blossom
image, primarily of East and Southeast Asian women, as it is depicted in and reified
through various representations, institutions, and practices. This is obviously a very
broad topic, so I will only discuss a few aspects here. It has been noted that many
Orientalist discourses portray the East as feminine in and of itself, with the men
emasculated and the women hyperfeminized.[13] For instance, David Henry Hwang's play
M. Butterfly turns on this notion; in a much quoted passage, the character Song Liling
comments: "The West thinks of itself as masculine — big guns, big industry, big money —
so the East is feminine — weak, delicate, poor . . . but good at art, and full of inscrutable
wisdom — the feminine mystique."[14] This type of Orientalist discourse constructs Asian
women of various ethnicities as hyperfeminine, passive, eroticized objects of white

heterosexual male desire.[15] Similarly, one assessment of portrayals of Asian women in mainstream film mentions "Hollywood's skewed representations of Asian women: sleek, evil goddesses with slanted eyes and cunning ways, or smiling, sarong-clad South Seas 'maidens' with undulating hips, kinky black hair, and white skin darkened by makeup. . . . If we are 'good,' we are childlike, submissive, silent, and eager for sex . . . or else we are tragic victim types."[16]

Aside from representations in film, literature, and other media, other U.S. institutions and practices that participate in this discourse are the sectors of the sex industry that sell racialized sex and the mail-order bride business.[17] Hwang comments on some of these practices:

> "Yellow Fever" — Caucasian men with a fetish for exotic Oriental women. I have often heard it said that "Oriental women make the best wives." . . . This mythology is exploited by the Oriental mail-order bride trade which has flourished over the past decade. American men can now send away for catalogues of "obedient, domesticated" Asian women looking for husbands. Anyone who believes such stereotypes are a thing of the past need look no further than Manhattan cable television, which advertises call girls from "the exotic east, where men are king; obedient girls, trained in the art of pleasure."[18]

In addition, U.S. involvement in Asia helps to reinforce these American Orientalist constructions; this includes the sex industry around U.S. military bases, sex tourism in Thailand, the Philippines, South Korea, and other parts of Asia, and wars in Asia and the consequent phenomenon of Asian war brides.[19] Connie Chan describes this historical context:

> During the U.S. involvement with the Philippines wars, Japan and China in World War II, and more recently, the Korean and Vietnamese Wars, Asian women were perceived by American soldiers as prostitutes and sexual objects who provided rest and recuperation from the war zones. This perception was not restricted to Western soldiers overseas, but was portrayed and perpetuated through film and other media in the United States and Europe. . . . As a result of these war and media images, Asian women have suffered from a cultural stereotype of being exotic, subservient, passive, sexually attractive and available.[20]

Although I do not agree with this strict cause-and-effect model, it does appear that U.S. participation in wars has been significant in reifying this particular American Orientalist image of Asian women.

How does this construction of Asian women as models of heterosexual femininity par excellence impact on Asian lesbian and bisexual women? How do we deal with and/or challenge the stereotypes of passivity, hyperfemininity, and eroticization that are meant to be in service of white heterosexual male desire? Among the women I interviewed, those who were familiar with this discourse thought that it affected their lives whether they conformed to it or not. For example, one feminine-looking woman states:

> I hate seeing Asian women with a white man. I hate it, I just hate it. . . . I guess it feels especially weird, because every time I see that, I know that's what I'm looked as. That's how people see me, as somebody who should be with a white man. Which means I'm heterosexual. Which means I can't possibly want my own brothers, let alone my own sisters. Or that [I can possibly be] butch. I mean, you know, shit. (O.M.)

This woman finds that she is circumscribed by a narrow conception of "the Asian woman," where her appearance alone is enough to trigger very specific and limited expectations about her behavior, her sexuality, and her gender attributes. Some of the consequences of fulfilling certain aspects of this particular Orientalist construction can be significant:

> To go back to the exoticism of Asian women, even in a domestic violence situation with an Asian woman, you get race-baited. . . . I think that I'm seen as someone who can be beaten on, as an Asian woman, 'cause the stereotype that I'm weak, I'm passive, that I'm sort of like a lily flower, and I can be beaten on, and stomped on, and attacked and abused. And that is seen by, I'm sure it's seen by men, I know it's seen by men, I know it's seen by women, I know it's seen by sisters, other sisters. That's happened. I also see, I do see, that maybe Asian women do experience a lot of violence because of that stereotype of us, in the heterosexual world, in the queer world, you know, we'll get raped because we're exoticized, abused because we're seen as weak and passive, and silent. (O.M.)

> I think women who are feminine get harassed a lot, every day on the street. I mean I used to have long hair, you know, when I was in high school, and I would get shit all the time. . . . Course that was in Denver too, and there aren't that many Asians. But women get a lot of shit, just walkin' the streets, just being out there, just being out there; it's constant and it never stops. (L.D.)

Being femme and feminine seems to lead to greater vulnerability to harassment from men. Because this Orientalist image is so strongly heterosexual, Asian women are viewed as a more-than-appropriate object of male attention, and because the image is so passive and docile, Asian women are seen as an easy target. Yet equally significant are the reactions when a woman does *not* fulfill these stereotypes.

> Growing up as a butch, or as a Chinese butch, and what that means as far as when people see Asian women and the stereotypes of them being docile, submissive, long hair, kind of, like, eroticized, demoralized — I don't fit those descriptions as far as being Asian, so it's very different. When I talk butch/femme, I also have to talk about my Asian identification. Because it all plays into that. Because — I'll give you a typical day: I'm walking down the street, Southern California. Because I'm also mixed, I also get this assumption by people in the military that my father is a soldier who went over to Vietnam and fell in love with, or captured, a Vietnamese woman. . . . Then they trip on the fact that it wasn't just a Vietnam story, and then they trip on the fact that, all of a sudden, through the conversation, they figure out that I'm in a woman's body, and then it goes like, men, if they can't come on to you, then they want to kick your ass. If you challenge them, then you're in a fist fight, and you know, you're subjected to a lot of violence because you don't feel like being mentally, emotionally, or physically oppressed. So, I also have to bring race into that. I get a lot of "you slant-eyed slut," blah, blah, blah. (J.M.)

How does that translate into people's choices, to the extent that they have a choice, about marking themselves as gendered beings? I think considerations like this often have much to do with our gender presentations. Being feminine might mark one as an easy target, but it is apparent that being more butch isn't necessarily safer or easier: people are beaten up for defying, as well as for complying with, the dominant stereotypes. This is true for women in general, but the discourse that casts Asian women as particularly feminine, weak, and passive leaves us more vulnerable to both violence and backlash.

I present these stories about harassment from men because they seem to constitute a significant aspect of the American Orientalist image of Asian women. However, I do not want to make it sound as if we are always and solely reacting to this image. Our gender identities have many aspects and are shaped by many forces; and how we are viewed by men is often the least of our concerns. In fact, one woman, an immigrant from Singapore, stresses that her gender identification has nothing to do with reacting to these images:

> I've never seen this Suzie Wong image; I don't even know what it means. . . . I've never thought of, like, "Oh, Asian women are supposed to be passive or whatever," you know, so it doesn't affect [me]. Even without knowing that, I'm still butch, you know. It's not because I'm trying to fight off this stereotype that I'm butch. (J.U.)

Yet I discuss this Orientalist discourse here as an example of how gender is always racialized; any analysis of femme/butch and gender identities must be complicated by a consideration of racial specificities. These images affect us to varying degrees — whether we react to them, choose to ignore them, or are simply unaware of them — but they do form part of the environment in which our gender identities are perceived and judged.

Looking like a "Lesbian"

> If you're really, really, really, really, really stupid, and think the whole world is completely heterosexual, and that every single woman with long hair, no matter how she acts, is heterosexual, then you could probably assume that I'm heterosexual. . . . And I think it has a lot to do with, not only because I have long hair, but because I'm an Asian woman, and the stereotype of an Asian woman with long hair. In their eyes, I cannot be anything but a heterosexual woman. Which is fucked up, you know, because I can be many things, and I am. (O.M.)

Another factor that affects Asian lesbian and bisexual women's gender identities is the archetypal figure of the lesbian as butch. Although this image varies in different lesbian and bisexual women's communities, butchness usually serves as the visible marker of lesbian difference.[21] As Arlene Istar states:

> In the lesbian community, though, butches *are* our image of dykes. Butchness is the hub of our lesbian universe. Lesbians are never described as women who wear dresses and high heels, or have long nails or hair, or as women who dislike sports. Oh, we all know there are lesbians like that, but somehow they are different, not like "us," somehow not authentic.[22]

Even in the era of "neo-butch/femme," where there is more flexibility in and tolerance for a range of lesbian styles than in earlier decades, the butch is still more recognizable and is accepted as the typical lesbian. People know and rely on the butch image as the visual definition of lesbian even as they question it.

I don't think I have anything, show anything, or wear anything that makes me look like a lesbian. . . . That's kind of a weird thing to say, because what does a lesbian look like? . . . [T]hey look like us! How do you look like a lesbian? But there is a definite distinct thing that people are saying. You know, "She doesn't look like a lesbian": she's not wearing Birkenstocks, she's not carrying a backpack, her hair's too long, or she's not wearing triangle earrings. You know, there's always something. (S.U.)

The image of the butch also serves to define a queerness that is conflated with lesbianism, since the stereotypical representation of bisexual women is as femmes. That is, the usual equation is queer = lesbian = butch, excluding self-defined femmes, feminine-looking women, and bisexual women of all genderings. Many stereotypes associated with femme women are also applied to bisexual women: that they are inauthentic lesbians who want to pass as straight, that they are not feminists and not politicized, that they are indeed weak, duped, apolitical, and traitorous. Many femme-identified women describe their encounters with this exclusion and devaluation, both in the past and also sometimes in the present, in the anthology *The Persistent Desire: A Femme-Butch Reader*.[23] Lisa Walker, in an article decrying these assumptions, addresses the accusation that femme women want to pass as straight women, supposedly garnering some heterosexual privilege as a result of fulfilling traditional visual norms of femininity:

> The glorification of the butch as authentic lesbian is based on her "blatant" representation of sexual deviance, and this in turn implies ambiguity and confusion around the femme's sexual identity. The femme's adaptation of what has been historically defined as a "feminine" sexual style is tacitly constructed as evidence of her desire to pass for straight and not of her desire for other women.[24]

Bisexual women offer similar accounts of exclusion and denigration in anthologies such as *Bi Any Other Name: Bisexual People Speak Out* and *Closer to Home: Bisexuality and Feminism*.[25] I want to make clear that bisexuality and femme styles *are* accepted to varying degrees by lesbians, and that the attitudes described above are not held by a monolithic bloc of lesbians. However, it is equally clear that these attitudes still exist.

For Asian American lesbian and bisexual women, these stereotypical assumptions are compounded by various racialized discourses. The American Orientalist construction of Asian women as Lotus Blossoms, as subservient, feminine, heterosexual women, influences both femme and butch identities. L.D. notes that in the shadow of this image, it is often hard for Asian butches to be recognized as butch:

> [Y]ou talked about the subservient Asian woman, I think that definitely carries over in the mainstream dyke community. I don't think that a lot of people take us seriously. . . . [I]f you talk about, like, butch and femme, it's like Asian women aren't real butches, we're just pretending to be, but we could never aspire to gain that recognition because we're still considered followers.

For femme Asian women who look recognizably feminine and Asian, this confluence of various discourses works to almost completely erase their existence as lesbians and bisexuals. One explanation for this dynamic is offered by Walker, who views this as the result of the intersection of various erasures: not only are femmes invisible as lesbians, but in addition, the sexualities of women of color are often not seen or differentiated.

> If we pursue the racist logic of this layered invisibility and add to it the invisibility of the lesbian femme, it follows that the woman of color who identifies as femme may be triply erased. That is to say, while a butch woman of color might not be recognized as a lesbian because she is not white, she might be perceived as lesbian because her sexual style is considered "blatant." A femme woman of color, on the other hand, will probably not be recognized as lesbian, first because she is not white and then because she is not butch.[26]

Although this analysis is seductive in its logic, it is a little simplistic when one considers the prominent stereotype of black lesbians as butch bulldaggers. The gender identities of bisexual and lesbian women of color are not formed by a simple addition or layering of racist, *then* sexist, *then* homophobic logic. Discourses do not work as sums, they work as particularities. For femme Asian women, it is a *specific* racializing discourse of gender that constructs them as feminine and heterosexual and serves to make them invisible. One woman stated:

> I guess that's one reason why I'm so in your face and out about being a dyke. . . . It's just, like, the eye of the other looking at me; they always see a heterosexual woman, and that *pisses* me off like nothing else. And a lot of it has to do with how I carry myself in a cultural context. I'm a Cambodian lesbian, and this is how I look. And I'm invisible as a lesbian because I look in a cultural way — that is, where I have long hair, you know — and I *despise* that invisibility, because it's their ignorance that makes me invisible. And not the way I look, necessarily, you know. I think even if you have short hair and you're an Asian woman, you have a hard time, because the idea of being anything but heterosexual is so far from anybody's mind. You have long hair, it's doubly that way. . . . I know other sisters of color . . . who have the same problem. Pushed into [a femme role] by the lesbian world, labeled a femme, when they might not be, and always assumed heterosexual by the straight world. So you're invisible both in the gay world and in the straight world. You know? So we make a lot of noise. To compensate. (O.M.)

Asian women who are both bisexual *and* feminine or femme occupy an even more overdetermined position that renders them extremely invisible as queers. The assumption of normative heterosexuality embedded in American Orientalist discourse colludes with the image of the lesbian as butch and the stereotype of bisexuals as swinging straights to virtually erase the very existence of femme bisexual Asian women.

Cultural Norms of Gender

J.L.: [So] when you identify as a butch, it's more from a different cultural stance than white American?
J.M.: It's got a different "slant" to it.

Another factor that affects the gender identities of Asian and Asian American lesbian and bisexual women is our awareness of various Asian cultural norms of gender. I do not wish to imply that there are monolithic, unchanging norms for any given "culture" that Asian lesbian and bisexual women know "correctly" and authentically, but rather that we experience pressures that we feel are different from those exerted by the dominant standards of the U.S. white middle class. It is our *perceptions* of these cultures and their gender norms that we respond to. These different ideas about masculinity and femininity intersect in complicated ways with U.S. norms, sometimes contradicting them, sometimes overlapping with them, and differ according to specific class backgrounds, occupations, U.S. regional differences, and a host of other factors. They affect not only how we are perceived as masculine or feminine by the mainstream but also how we are viewed as butch or femme in lesbian communities. Thus, as Lyndall MacCowan notes, "we need to be aware of the nuances that arise from different classes and cultures. What is butch to a Jewish lesbian is not necessarily butch to a lesbian from Philadelphia's mainline [sic], a lesbian from Harlem, or a lesbian from Thailand."[27] Yet most lesbian communities make evaluations according to white American hegemonic norms for gender and white lesbian standards for femme/butch identities, thus distorting, or simply being unaware of, the cultural differences. For some of my interviewees, certain behaviors or appearances that they felt were masculine, feminine, or not gendered according to their Asian cultural backgrounds were rendered femme or butch in mainstream lesbian contexts and thus interpreted in ways that they hadn't intended.

For example, J.M. states that, as a butch, her models for masculinity include those of her Chinese culture:

> And for me, I also wanted to put out, because I'm Asian, I don't necessarily have all of the — although I do, I would say I do have more of a macho defense mode towards men — [but] I don't have the same butch thinking that perhaps a white dyke butch would have. 'Cause, for one, in my culture, the Asian men, they cook. So I cook . . . because the men in my family cook. . . . And I would also say that in my culture . . . when I say my culture, I mean mostly my Chinese culture — the Cantonese heterosexual roles, the men are much softer. They're more softer, very family-oriented. . . . It's not the same [as white western heterosexual roles]. It's just not the same. So therefore butch/femme isn't the same. In my head.

B.T., on the other hand, feels that since her models for femininity are those of a southern Philippine culture with standards that she cannot fulfill, she never feels truly feminine.

> I have a different reality about being female, based on my size. I think that it really does affect my perception of myself as feminine or masculine, you know, it makes me never believe that the feminine comes off perfectly. . . . I know that my image of myself as not a successful femme is *very* much tied into being culturally Filipino and genetically mixed. . . . If I were raised as culturally Filipino from Manila, I also wouldn't have as much of a problem. Because there's more Spanish blood in the North, and there's more European blood in general up there, because it's a big city, and there's more milk, so people are growing taller. And, in general, there's like at least a one to two inch height difference between people from the North and people from the South. But I'm from the South. . . . In some part of my head I equate grace and femininity with petite. And so it's not just, like,

height; it's petiteness, it's everything about it. And so, when I'm in a room full of women, I cannot perceive myself that way. I cannot perceive myself as feminine. I feel like a drag queen.

Others adhere to a culturally significant form of gender that they consciously embrace as expressing their cultural differences but find that, in U.S. lesbian contexts, their cultural differences are interpreted as reflecting a femme identity. For example, Kaushalya Bannerji writes:

> As a lesbian of Indian origin with an active relationship to India and to my family, I was struck by the conformity to androgyny that appeared to be the norm of white lesbian beauty. . . . My breasts, hips, and long hair were not seen by everyone as symbols integral to my identity as an Indian woman; they were reinterpreted by white lesbians as manifestations of my being a "femme."[28]

Similarly, O.M. expresses her dissatisfaction with being labeled femme for traits that she experiences as being more "cultural" than "gendered":

> Long hair is a stereotypical femme look, but void of the cultural context. For me, as a Cambodian immigrant, to have long hair is a cultural identity. It's also something I like. But it doesn't mean I'm femme, based on the way I wear my hair. . . . I'm very nurturing . . . and very affectionate — . . . of course, all that being me, being the individual that I am — but I think that it has a lot to do with my culture. You know, Cambodian people are very affectionate people. Of course I'm gonna be affectionate, and of course, you know, Cambodian women, a lot of women, are very nurturing, and my mother's very nurturing, and I learn from my mother to be a nurturer, and I see that as a very powerful powerful thing, very creative and very powerful female thing to be a nurturer. But I think it's pegged as femme.

Some women feel that there are differences in cultural norms, not only for gender in general, but also for what constitutes appropriate femme/butch roles in same-sex relationships. For some Asian lesbian and bisexual women who are closely tied to Asian communities or lived until recently in Asia, it appears that their gender identities respond not so much to white lesbian femme/butch roles as to their own norms for femme/butch and how these identities resonate in Asian communities.[29]

> I've heard that sometimes, from this one woman, for her [femme/butch] is a construction. It's definitely heterosexually based; she totally acknowledges that. It's partially based on familial acceptance. . . . That she expects that because she's butch, her family will accept her going out with a femme. And because in her family, there're basically very masculine men and very feminine women, she sees herself, if she's gonna be dating women, she's identifying with a masculine role. So, that kind of construction, it fits into her family. (B.T.)

Moreover, in their conscious reasons for not wanting to be traditionally feminine, Asian women may be reacting more to what they perceive to be Asian cultural norms of femininity than to white mainstream standards, which might actually be perceived as more liberating.

[In] a lot of cultures that are from Asia or perhaps even from other of color cultures, I think women's roles and women's identities are still very much . . . placed in a very, more clearly defined, sexist context. . . . You don't want to be in that more traditional role. It's like a box. It's like you suddenly don't have arms, you know? You wanna be able to walk around with these arms, and you really need to move them and to use them. And from an identity perspective it's, like, in order to do that, what do you do? You reject, you reject, you push away any perception . . . of you being perceived as being like this objectified, passive, Asian female woman. (G.M.)

Although such descriptions of Asian cultures may seem a little extreme, I cannot compare them to some "objective" view to see how "correct" they are. Instead, I assume that, insofar as these are conscious interpretations, such perceptions of Asian gender norms have a distinct impact on gender identities. This awareness of different cultural standards for gender constitutes another part of the environment that affects how Asian lesbian and bisexual women shape gender identities. In these and myriad other ways, we react to what we perceive to be Asian norms for femininity and Asian ideas about femme/butch roles. Yet, inevitably, we also react to the myopia of mainstream heterosexuals and white lesbians and bisexuals, who interpret our appearances and behaviors according to white hegemonic standards for femininity and masculinity and white lesbian ideas about femme/butch identities. It is important for analyses of gender not to fall into the same shortcomings, but to examine closely how the specificities of cultural differences affect gender, not only for women of color, but also for white women.

Conclusion

What I have discussed here are a few of the factors that affect the gender identities of Asian and Asian American lesbian and bisexual women, in terms of how we shape them and how they are perceived in the U.S. by mainstream and lesbian/bisexual communities. I have specifically focused on those factors that reflect racial and cultural differences, to show that gender analyses *must* include a complex account of racialization. Asian women are affected by American Orientalist images that portray us in a specifically racialized construction of gender: as hyperfeminine, submissive, eroticized objects of white heterosexual male desire. This "heterosexualization" and the forces of femme invisibility and devaluation work to exclude us from the dominant visual definition of lesbians as butch and converge to make femme and feminine-looking Asian women especially invisible. In addition, our adherence to or rejection of what we perceive to be Asian cultural standards are often misinterpreted and compared to mainstream U.S. standards of masculine/feminine and lesbian standards of femme/butch. Asian American lesbian and bisexual women interact with these forces in different ways, sometimes consciously responding to them, sometimes choosing to ignore them, sometimes simply being unaware of them.

However we respond or not, I believe that these factors form a significant part of the environment in which our gender is perceived and judged. Because they intersect in different ways and resonate differently in different circumstances, our gender identities have no simple or single meanings. Thus, when we "play" with gender, our playing has significant effects. Due to discourses around race and our lack of white privilege, we have less room to maneuver; we thus often end up challenging serious societal forces that are meant to control our appearances and behaviors, and ultimately our place in society. Our playing with gender disrupts, not only compulsory heterosexuality and traditional gender norms, but also discourses of race and racialized gender.

> I like to challenge people's idea of what things are, because I feel like my whole existence has been constant, constant contradiction to a lot of different things. The role of me being with a white man, I contradicted that a long time ago. I date women of color! That's the total opposite. Of having long hair, whatever, of being seen as whatever way of being with women, the way I am being femme in a different way, I challenge that, being very outspoken and loud Asian woman, as opposed to being quiet and passive, you know? I figure if you can't see me as a lesbian, I don't need to change the way I look to fit your definition of a lesbian. *You* need to change your definition of what a lesbian looks like to include me, with my hair, or Jee, with short hair, you know? And I think that's revolutionary. To challenge other people's ideas and not conform to their ideas is revolutionary. So if a butch with short hair says to me, "Well, you're just being a white man's woman," you know, I'm like, "No, I'm challenging your idea of what a lesbian looks like, of what a lesbian is." (O.M.)

I believe that the specification of racial and cultural differences and how they impact on gender must be more fully explored not only for other women of color but also for white women and white femme/butch identities. Just as there are discourses that construct images of Asian women and other women of color, there are specific discourses that construct white women in certain ways. The gender identities of white lesbians and bisexual women are also shaped by racially specific forces that prescribe how they should act out their gender and affect how they are perceived. This changes the ways in which hegemonic norms of gender can be challenged; since the limits of what is seen as allowable are different, strategies to resist them must also be different.

I want to end by stating that despite the heavy emphasis I have placed on some of the specific factors that affect the gender identities of Asian lesbians and bisexual women, these forces are neither monolithic nor all-powerful. They may constitute certain limitations and pressures, but they are also permeable, self-contradictory, and multiple. Indeed, were they not so, there would be no possibility of challenging them. The gender identities of Asian lesbians and bisexual women often use these contradictions and are formed in the gaps of these discourses and practices. I do not believe that our challenges to dominant structures of race, gender, and sexuality are formed fully outside these structures; that would be to imagine some pure space of marginality that is somehow untainted by all dominant discourses. Yet neither do I believe that this dooms us to the impossibility of changing them. The possibilities for resistance lie in the inconsistencies inherent in the multiple and self-contradictory nature of discourses. Our interventions in our gender identities do not completely destroy the hegemonic Orientalist constructions of Asian women, of femme Asian invisibility, of white standards for femme/butch, but they do shift the ground on which these are built.[30]

Appendix: Backgrounds of the Interviewees

I would like to thank the women I interviewed; although I did not use all of their interviews directly, they were all extremely generous with their time and honesty and helped me to clarify many of my ideas. I hope that our conversations and this essay will spark more discussions of this topic within the community. The following are descriptions of the interviewees by age, ethnic background, approximate class background, immigration status, bisexual/lesbian identification, and femme/butch identification.

A.D. is a second-generation, butch-identified Chinese American lesbian and describes her class background as upper middle class. She is twenty-six years old.

B.T. is twenty-six years old and of Filipino and white heritage, the white part being "English, Irish, Welsh, and Scottish, American white mix, mutt." Her class background in the U.S. is middle to upper middle class; she was born in the U.S. but lived in the Philippines until the age of six. She identifies as bi, as opposed to bisexual, and thinks she is both femme and butch in different ways.

C.H. is a thirty-nine-year-old Indian lesbian who came to the U.S. from India at the age of seventeen. She describes her class background as upper middle class in India and immigrant working class in the U.S. She does not identify as either femme or butch.

C.W. is a forty-three-year-old third-generation Chinese American lesbian who identifies as neither femme nor butch.

G.M. is a twenty-eight-year-old second-generation Chinese American lesbian, who does not identify as either femme or butch.

J.M. is a butch-identified lesbian of mixed Cantonese and Polish/English/Germanic heritage. The Cantonese side of her family has resided in the U.S. for three generations. She is twenty-nine years old.

J.U. is twenty-two years old. She is of Chinese heritage and came to the U.S. from Singapore when she was seventeen. She describes her class background as having been middle to upper middle class in Singapore. She identifies as a lesbian and views herself as fairly butch.

L.D. is thirty-three years old, a second-generation American of Chinese and Mexican heritage. She is lesbian-identified, of working class background, and a tradeswoman. She identifies as a top, but not as a butch.

O.M. is a twenty-seven-year-old Cambodian lesbian who came to the U.S. as a refugee when she was nine. She identifies as working-class and does not identify as either femme or butch.

S.U. is a second-generation American of Asian Indian and Japanese heritage. She is thirty-three years old and states that her class background is working to middle class. She is a lesbian who describes herself as fairly femme.

NOTES

1. Lillian Faderman, "The Return of Butch and Femme: A Phenomenon in Lesbian Sexuality of the 1980s and 1990s," *Journal of the History of Sexuality* 2, no. 4 (1992): 592. The writers I refer to are Arlene Stein, "All Dressed Up, but No Place to Go? Style Wars and the New Lesbianism," in *The Persistent Desire: A Femme-Butch Reader*, ed. Joan Nestle (Boston: Alyson, 1992), 431–39; Inge Blackman and Kathryn Perry, "Skirting the Issue: Lesbian Fashion for the 1990s," *Feminist Review* 34 (Spring 1990): 67–78; and Susan Ardill and Sue O'Sullivan, "Butch/Femme Obsessions," *Feminist Review* 34 (Spring 1990): 79–85. Sue-Ellen Case's "Towards a Butch-Femme

Aesthetic," *Discourse: Journal for Theoretical Studies in Media and Culture* 11, no. 1 (1988–89): 55–73, also characterizes femme/butch roles as play and camp, but defends it as such.

2. Ardill and O'Sullivan, "Butch/Femme Obsessions," 79.

3. For more detailed and complex self-definitions and histories of femme/butch identities, see Nestle, *The Persistent Desire*; Lillian Faderman, *Odd Girls and Twilight Lovers: A History of Lesbian Life in Twentieth-Century America* (New York: Penguin Books, 1991); Madeline Davis and Elizabeth Lapovsky Kennedy, "Oral History and the Study of Sexuality in the Lesbian Community: Buffalo, New York, 1940–1960," *Feminist Studies* 12, no. 1 (1986): 7–26; and Davis and Kennedy, *Boots of Leather, Slippers of Gold: The History of a Lesbian Community* (New York: Routledge, 1993). For a brief historical overview of the changing practices of femme/butch in U.S. lesbian communities since the 1970s, see Faderman, "The Return of Butch and Femme," although I am uncomfortable with some of its totalizing generalizations.

4. I deliberately use "femme/butch," as opposed to the usual "butch/femme," following the subtitle of Joan Nestle's anthology, *The Persistent Desire: A Femme-Butch Reader.* Of this decision, she states in her introduction:

> As feminists, we continue to fight back with a femme proclamation of independence. I subtitled this anthology "A Femme-Butch Reader" to herald this new voice in identity politics and break the traditional rhythms of the phrase and image. Femmes are the Lavender Menace within our community. (18)

I believe this reclamation of femme is long overdue, of which this deliberate change in terminology is a modest but important part.

5. See J. Kehaulani Kauanui and Ju Hui "Judy" Han, " 'Asian Pacific Islander': Issues of Representation and Responsibility," *Moving the Mountains: Asian American Women's Journal* (1993): 24–25.

6. The name of this network has subsequently been changed to "Asian and Pacific Islander Lesbian and Bisexual Women's Network," or APLBN.

7. Suzie Wong, a character in the 1960 film "The World of Suzie Wong," is a Chinese prostitute in Hong Kong who falls in love with a white man from the U.S. I invoke her here as the paradigmatic image of the submissive, exotic Asian woman.

8. See Ruth Frankenberg, *White Women, Race Matters: The Social Construction of Whiteness* (Minneapolis: University of Minnesota Press, 1993), although she focuses more explicitly on race than gender.

9. Renee E. Tajima, "Lotus Blossoms Don't Bleed: Images of Asian Women," in *Making Waves: An Anthology of Writings by and about Asian American Women*, ed. Asian Women United of California (Boston: Beacon Press, 1989), 309.

10. Initials refer to interviewees. See appendix for background descriptions of the interviewees.

11. Lisa Lowe, *Critical Terrains: French and British Orientalisms* (Ithaca, NY: Cornell University Press, 1991), 4–5.

12. Toni Morrison, *Playing in the Dark: Whiteness and the Literary Imagination* (New York: Random House, 1992).

13. This dynamic is also found rather blatantly in gay men's communities, where gay Asian men are often feminized in this way. See Daniel Tsang, "M. Butterfly Meets the Great White Hope," *Informasian* 6, no. 3 (1992): 3–4; and Richard Fung, "Looking for My Penis: The Eroticized Asian in Gay Video Porn," in *How Do I Look? Queer Film and Video*, ed. Bad Object-Choices (Seattle: Bay Press, 1991), 145–60.

14. David Henry Hwang, *M. Butterfly* (New York: Penguin Books, 1986), 83.

15. L. Hyun-Yi Kang, "The Desiring of Asian Female Bodies: Interracial Romance and Cinematic Subjection," *Visual Anthropology Review* 9, no. 1 (1993): 5–21, discusses the representations of relationships between Asian women and white men in three mainstream Hollywood films, noting how the alleged focus on the Asian women characters is deflected by their portrayal as objects of white heterosexual male desire.

16. Jessica Hagedorn, "Asian Women in Film: No Joy, No Luck," *Ms.* 4, no. 4 (January 1994): 74.

17. See Alice Mayall and Diana E. H. Russell, "Racism in Pornography," in *Making Violence Sexy: Feminist Views on Pornography*, ed. Diana E. H. Russell (New York: Teachers College Press, 1993), 167–77; and Venny Villapando, "The Business of Selling Mail-Order Brides," in *Making Waves*, 318–26.

18. Hwang, *M. Butterfly*, 98.

19. See Brenda Stoltzfus and Saundra Pollock Sturdevant, *Let the Good Times Roll: Prostitution and the U.S. Military in Asia* (New York: New Press, 1993); and Elaine Kim, "Sex Tourism in Asia: A Reflection of Political and Economic Inequality," *Critical Perspectives* 2, no. 1 (1984): 214–32.

20. Connie S. Chan, "Asian-American Women: Psychological Responses to Sexual Exploitation and Cultural Stereotypes," *Women and Therapy* 6, no. 4 (1987): 34–35.

21. The hegemonic heterosexual imagination also subscribes to this lesbian-as-butch image but, in addition, often portrays lesbians as very feminine, usually in order to make lesbianism either titillating or unthreatening or both. This is apparent in many film representations and in heterosexual pornography. Thanks to Caroline Streeter for bringing this to my attention.

22. Arlene Istar, "Femme-Dyke," in *The Persistent Desire*, 378.

23. See especially Joan Nestle, "Butch-Fem Relationships: Sexual Courage in the 1950's," *Heresies* 12 (1981): 21–24; Amber Hollibaugh and Cherríe Moraga, "What We're Rollin Around in Bed With: Sexual Silences in Feminism," in *Powers of Desire: The Politics of Sexuality*, ed. Ann Snitow, Christine Stansell, and Sharon Thompson (New York: Monthly Review, 1983), 394–405; and the following articles in Nestle, *The Persistent Desire*: Nestle, "The Femme Question"; Madeline Davis, Amber Hollibaugh, and Joan Nestle, "The Femme Tapes"; Lyndall MacCowan, "Re-Collecting History, Renaming Lives: Femme Stigma and the Feminist Seventies and Eighties"; Paula Austin, "Femme-inism"; Mykel Johnson, "Butchy Femme."

24. Lisa M. Walker, "How to Recognize a Lesbian: The Cultural Politics of Looking like What You Are," *Signs: Journal of Women in Culture and Society* 18, no. 4 (Summer 1993): 882.

25. Loraine Hutchins and Lani Kaahumanu, eds., *Bi Any Other Name: Bisexual People Speak Out* (Boston: Alyson, 1991); and Elizabeth Reba Weise, ed., *Closer to Home: Bisexuality and Feminism* (Seattle: Seal Press, 1992).

26. Walker, "How to Recognize a Lesbian," 886.

27. MacCowan, "Re-Collecting History," 323.

28. Kaushalya Bannerji, "No Apologies," in *A Lotus of Another Color: An Unfolding of the South Asian Gay and Lesbian Experience*, ed. Rakesh Ratti (Boston: Alyson, 1993), 60–61.

29. See also Marivic R. Desquitado, "A Letter from the Philippines," in *The Persistent Desire*, 295–98, for a description of femme/butch identities in the Philippines.

30. My understanding of this theory of hegemony comes from Lowe, *Critical Terrains*.

REFERENCES

Ardill, Susan, and Sue O'Sullivan. "Butch/Femme Obsessions." *Feminist Review* 34 (Spring 1990): 79–85.

Austin, Paula. "Femme-inism." *The Persistent Desire: A Femme-Butch Reader.* Ed. Joan Nestle. Boston: Alyson, 1992. 362–66.

Bannerji, Kaushalya. "No Apologies." *A Lotus of Another Color: An Unfolding of the South Asian Gay and Lesbian Experience.* Ed. Rakesh Ratti. Boston: Alyson, 1993. 59–64.

Blackman, Inge, and Kathryn Perry. "Skirting the Issue: Lesbian Fashion for the 1990s." *Feminist Review* 34 (Spring 1990): 67–78.

Case, Sue-Ellen. "Towards a Butch-Femme Aesthetic." *Discourse: Journal for Theoretical Studies in Media and Culture* 11, no. 1 (1988–89): 55–73.

Chan, Connie S. "Asian-American Women: Psychological Responses to Sexual Exploitation and Cultural Stereotypes." *Women and Therapy* 6, no. 4 (1987): 33–38.

Davis, Madeline, Amber Hollibaugh, and Joan Nestle. "The Femme Tapes." *The Persistent Desire: A Femme-Butch Reader.* Ed. Joan Nestle. Boston: Alyson, 1992. 254–67.

Davis, Madeline, and Elizabeth Lapovsky Kennedy. "Oral History and the Study of Sexuality in the Lesbian Community: Buffalo, New York, 1940–1960." *Feminist Studies* 12, no. 1 (1986): 7–26.

———. *Boots of Leather, Slippers of Gold: The History of a Lesbian Community.* New York: Routledge, 1993.

Desquitado, Marivic R. "A Letter from the Philippines." *The Persistent Desire: A Femme-Butch Reader.* Ed. Joan Nestle. Boston: Alyson, 1992. 295–98.

Faderman, Lillian. *Odd Girls and Twilight Lovers: A History of Lesbian Life in Twentieth-Century America.* New York: Penguin Books, 1991.

———. "The Return of Butch and Femme: A Phenomenon in Lesbian Sexuality of the 1980s and 1990s." *Journal of the History of Sexuality* 2, no. 4 (1992): 578–96.

Frankenberg, Ruth. *White Women, Race Matters: The Social Construction of Whiteness.* Minneapolis: University of Minnesota Press, 1993.

Fung, Richard. "Looking for My Penis: The Eroticized Asian in Gay Video Porn." *How Do I Look? Queer Film and Video.* Ed. Bad Object-Choices. Seattle: Bay Press, 1991. 145–60.

Hagedorn, Jessica. "Asian Women in Film: No Joy, No Luck." *Ms.* 4, no. 4 (January 1994): 74–79.

Hollibaugh, Amber, and Cherríe Moraga. "What We're Rollin Around in Bed With: Sexual Silences in Feminism." *Powers of Desire: The Politics of Sexuality.* Ed. Ann Snitow, Christine Stansell, and Sharon Thompson. New York: Monthly Review, 1983. 394–405.

Hutchins, Loraine, and Lani Kaahumanu, eds. *Bi Any Other Name: Bisexual People Speak Out.* Boston: Alyson, 1991.

Hwang, David Henry. *M. Butterfly.* New York: Penguin Books, 1986.

Istar, Arlene. "Femme-Dyke." *The Persistent Desire: A Femme-Butch Reader.* Ed. Joan Nestle. Boston: Alyson, 1992. 378–83.

Johnson, Mykel. "Butchy Femme." *The Persistent Desire: A Femme-Butch Reader.* Ed. Joan Nestle. Boston: Alyson, 1992. 395–98.

Kang, L. Hyun-Yi. "The Desiring of Asian Female Bodies: Interracial Romance and Cinematic Subjection." *Visual Anthropology Review* 9, no. 1 (1993): 5–21.

Kauanui, J. Kehaulani, and Ju Hui Han. " 'Asian Pacific Islander': Issues of Representation and Responsibility." *Moving the Mountains: Asian American Women's Journal* (1993): 24–25.

Kim, Elaine. "Sex Tourism in Asia: A Reflection of Political and Economic Inequality." *Critical Perspectives* 2, no. 1 (1984): 214–32.

Lowe, Lisa. *Critical Terrains: French and British Orientalisms*. Ithaca, NY: Cornell University Press, 1991.

MacCowan, Lyndall. "Re-Collecting History, Renaming Lives: Femme Stigma and the Feminist Seventies and Eighties." *The Persistent Desire: A Femme-Butch Reader*. Ed. Joan Nestle. Boston: Alyson, 1992. 299–328.

Mayall, Alice, and Diana E. H. Russell. "Racism in Pornography." *Making Violence Sexy: Feminist Views on Pornography*. Ed. Diana E. H. Russell. New York: Teachers College Press, 1993. 167–77.

Morrison, Toni. *Playing in the Dark: Whiteness and the Literary Imagination*. New York: Random House, 1992.

Nestle, Joan. "Butch-Fem Relationships: Sexual Courage in the 1950's." *Heresies* 12 (1981): 21–24.

———. "The Femme Question." *The Persistent Desire: A Femme-Butch Reader*. Ed. Joan Nestle. Boston: Alyson, 1992. 138–46.

———. "Flamboyance and Fortitude: An Introduction." *The Persistent Desire: A Femme-Butch Reader*. Ed. Joan Nestle. Boston: Alyson, 1992. 13–20.

———, ed. *The Persistent Desire: A Femme-Butch Reader*. Boston: Alyson, 1992.

Stein, Arlene. "All Dressed Up, but No Place to Go? Style Wars and the New Lesbianism." *The Persistent Desire: A Femme-Butch Reader*. Ed. Joan Nestle. Boston: Alyson, 1992. 431–39.

Stoltzfus, Brenda, and Saundra Pollock Sturdevant. *Let the Good Times Roll: Prostitution and the U.S. Military in Asia*. New York: New Press, 1993.

Tajima, Renee E. "Lotus Blossoms Don't Bleed: Images of Asian Women." *Making Waves: An Anthology of Writings by and about Asian American Women*. Ed. Asian Women United of California. Boston: Beacon Press, 1989. 308–17.

Tsang, Daniel. "M. Butterfly Meets the Great White Hope." *Informasian* 6, no. 3 (1992): 3–4.

Villapando, Venny. "The Business of Selling Mail-Order Brides." *Making Waves: An Anthology of Writings by and about Asian American Women*. Ed. Asian Women United of California. Boston: Beacon Press, 1989. 318–26.

Walker, Lisa M. "How to Recognize a Lesbian: The Cultural Politics of Looking like What You Are." *Signs: Journal of Women in Culture and Society* 18, no. 4 (Summer 1993): 866–90.

Weise, Elizabeth Reba, ed. *Closer to Home: Bisexuality and Feminism*. Seattle: Seal Press, 1992.

chapter 7

The Politics of Black Lesbian,

Gay, and Bisexual Identity

Gregory Conerly

Are you black first, or are you queer? This question embodies a central conflict many African-American lesbians, bisexuals, and gays (lesbigays) experience in dealing with two identities that are often at odds with each other. The answer to this question varies. For example, in his documentary *Tongues Untied*, Marlon Riggs argues that the two identities are inseparable.[1] Others, however, see one identity as being more important than the other and have organized their social and sexual lives, as well as their political activism, around their choice. Hence, African-American lesbians, gays, and bisexuals have responded to the conflict between their racial/ethnic[2] and sexual preference identities by situating themselves in cultures where both identities are centered, where one identity or the other is marginalized, where both identities are marginalized, or some variation of these.

The choices for African-American bisexuals are more complex because our society sees sexual orientation as an either/or homosexual/heterosexual proposition. Bisexuals generally lack institutional and communal supports that are specific to them. Therefore, they are often forced either to emphasize a preference for one gender over the other and socialize in those cultural spaces that support that gender preference or to go back and forth between straight and lesbian or gay communities. African-American gays and lesbians usually have the option of socializing in a community where their specific sexual identity is centered, whereas bisexuals frequently do not.

Julius Johnson has done the most extensive research that explores the dynamics of primary group affiliation and the justifications for that choice among African-Americans.[3] His study, like the general academic discourse on this issue, has unfortunately focused only on gay men thus far. Using questionnaires, Johnson sampled sixty black gay men to see whether they saw their black or gay identities as more central to them. He called those black gays who chose a predominantly heterosexual black culture as their primary communal affiliation "black-identified" gays. These men were generally less open about their sexual preference (though they still felt positively about it), were uncomfortable about expressing any form of intimacy with other men in public, had greater social and political involvement with other blacks, and preferred black lovers. They felt that their black identities were more important because skin color was more visible than sexual orientation, which they could hide. Hence, skin color had a greater influence on how others interacted with them.

Johnson labeled those black gays who chose a predominantly white gay culture as their primary communal affiliation "gay-identified" blacks. They were generally more open about their sexual preference, were more comfortable expressing affection for other men in public, had greater social and political involvement with whites, and preferred white lovers. Their gay identity was more important to them because they believed that the gay community was generally more tolerant than the black community, that sexual orientation affected their social lives more than race, and that they were more oppressed on account of their sexual preference than on account of their race.

While Johnson's study is useful for identifying two groups of black gays, there were other potential groups that he chose not to analyze. For example, there were some black gays in his sample who felt that both identities were equally important, but he did not identify their characteristics. The same was true of those gay men who believed that other identities, such as ones based on religion or class status, were more important to them. Johnson also did not examine whether his subjects' primary identity choice had changed over time, giving the impression that once a choice is made, it is fixed. In contrast, Marlon Riggs suggests in *Tongues Untied* that the primary communal affiliation for some black lesbigays changes over time. In the documentary, Riggs depicts how he moved among three communities at various times in his life: mostly heterosexual black spaces, mostly white gay spaces, and black gay spaces.

Other academics, such as John Peterson and Darryl Loiacano, have also examined this issue.[4] But, like Johnson, none have analyzed the social and political implications of choosing to affiliate oneself with one culture or another. One major consequence of having a primary communal affiliation is that conflicts have arisen between black lesbigays who have chosen to affiliate with different primary cultures, and between them and the larger black and/or lesbian and gay cultures within which they are marginalized. In particular, many blacks criticize those who have chosen a largely white lesbian and gay culture as their primary social world, because they see them as denying their black cultural heritage.[5] While some heterosexual blacks see all black lesbigays as denying their blackness — because to them, homosexuality is something they associate with white culture — many black lesbigays are much more aware of the divisions among themselves.

In this article, I focus on power relationships among black lesbians, gays, and bisexuals who choose different primary communities. First, I examine the context for this antagonism by exploring some of the reasons why black lesbians, gays, and bisexuals often feel that their racial/ethnic and sexual orientation identities are in conflict. Then I focus on a central theme of the debate on primary community choice, the politics of what it "really" means to be black. I conclude by looking at how African-American lesbigays might move beyond the "blacker-than-thou" debate — or at least recast it in different terms. I examine the politics of blackness by looking at the major anthologies produced thus far that have focused, either in whole or in large part, on the writings of black lesbians and gay men: Essex Hemphill's *Brother to Brother: New Writings by Black Gay Men*; Barbara Smith's *Home Girls: A Black Feminist Anthology*; Joseph Beam's *In the Life: A Black Gay Anthology*; Michael Smith's *Black Men/White Men: A Gay Anthology*; Makeda Silvera's *Piece of My Heart: A Lesbian of Colour Anthology*; Cary Alan Johnson, Colin Robinson, and Terence Taylor's *Other Countries: Black Gay Voices*; B. Michael Hunter's *Sojourner: Black Gay Voices in the Age of AIDS*; and Cherríe Moraga and Gloria Anzaldúa's *This Bridge Called My Back: Writings by Radical Women of Color*.[6] These texts are part of a larger discourse and represent one of the more prominent ways in which black lesbians and gays have tried to create a distinctive culture of their own: through creative works. As Essex Hemphill has argued, it has been through these works that they have left affirmative "evidence of being" about their lives and cultures.[7] Unfortunately, the editors of these anthologies generally have not included African-Americans with bisexual identities. "Evidence of [their] being" is, for the most part, still lacking.[8]

I chose to focus on anthologies because they feature a multiplicity of black gay and lesbian voices, and their editors usually claim to speak to and/or for them. Barbara Smith, for example, writes in her introduction to *Home Girls* that she sees the anthology as a space where the "girls from the neighborhood and from the block, the girls we grew up with" could be themselves.[9] Colin Robinson notes in his introduction to *Other Countries* that this anthology "is a celebration of the importance of difference. Not only the difference [black gay men] share, but [their] own internal diversity as a community."[10] And Joseph Beam proclaims that he and the other contributors to *In the Life* speak for, among others, "the brothers whose silence has cost them their sanity" and "the [then] 2500 brothers who have died of AIDS."[11] Sometimes, editors will note gaps in the range of voices they present. Essex Hemphill, for example, states in his introduction to *Brother to Brother* that the anthology does not address topics such as older gays and interracial relationships.[12] These anthologies all feature a multiplicity of voices, but with the exception of *Black Men/White Men*, they present an overwhelmingly black-identified vision of what it means to be black and lesbian or gay.[13] Hence, the same discourse that has been instrumental in fostering a collective African-American lesbian and gay identity has itself alienated and marginalized some who claim such an identity.

This discourse began in earnest in the late 1970s, for two reasons.[14] One is the politicization of sexual and gender identities brought on by the lesbigay and feminist movements. As a result, women and those attracted to others of the same sex achieved greater visibility. They also were able to provide a social context in which they could create a discourse that centered on their experiences and countered dominant, oppressive discourses around their identities. Through their activism, they tried to end a variety of oppressive cultural practices and to force people to rethink what it meant to be a woman/man and lesbigay/straight — with varying degrees of success. They also created their own cultural institutions, such as music festivals, publishing companies, bars, and community service centers.

The other reason for the rise of this discourse relates to racial/ethnic and gender divisions within the movements themselves. Increasingly, there was an awareness among lesbigays of color that the larger movements were not addressing the multiple oppressions they faced, nor other kinds of identity-specific experiences. In fact, the movements often perpetuated these oppressions. Joseph Beam expressed this sentiment in his introduction to *In the Life*, an anthology of African-American gay male fiction, poetry, and essays:

> It is possible to read thoroughly two or three consecutive issues of the *Advocate*, the national biweekly gay newsmagazine, and never encounter, in words or images, Black gay men. It is possible to peruse the pages of *212 Magazine*'s special issue on Washington, D.C. and see no Black faces. It is possible to leaf through any of the major gay men's porno magazines, *In Touch, Drummer, Mandate, Blueboy,* or *Honcho,* and never lay eyes on a Black Adonis. Finally, it is certainly possible to read an entire year of *Christopher Street* and think that there are no Black gay writers worthy of the incestuous bed of New York's gay literati. We ain't family. Very clearly, gay male means: white, middle-class, youthful, nautilized, and probably butch; there is no room for Black gay men within the confines of this gay pentagon.[15]

The Combahee River Collective raised similar criticisms of "the white women's movement." They argued that white feminists have made little effort to deal with their racism or develop a comprehensive knowledge of racial politics and the cultures of people of color.[16]

African-American lesbigays responded to this in two major ways. One was to pressure the leaders of these movements to go beyond single identity politics and address multiple oppressions. The other was to create a discourse that focused on their own experiences. A major focus of this discourse has been the conflict between their sexual preference and racial/ethnic identities.

Sources of Identity Conflict

This conflict exists for several reasons. One is that, for the most part, cultural, social, and political institutions specifically for black lesbians and gays are rare. There are only a handful of bars, churches, and social and political organizations that serve primarily black lesbians and gays, and they are all to be found in just a few major cities — Atlanta, Chicago, and Washington, D.C. There is a growing black lesbian and gay press, with magazines like *BLK* and *SBC* attaining national distribution. But most of these publishing efforts are short-lived or come out irregularly. Institutions specifically for African-American bisexuals are virtually nonexistent.

Another reason many African-American lesbigays experience conflict between the two identities is that they perceive racism among white lesbigays and homophobia among heterosexual blacks. As I have already noted, a number of black lesbians and gays have described the discrimination, sexual stereotyping, and other injustices they have faced from white lesbigays. They have also focused on the homophobic remarks made by many African-American political leaders and intellectuals, the ostracization from family, friends, and neighbors, and the verbal and physical assaults perpetrated against them by heterosexual blacks. Since their racial/ethnic identity is often marginalized by the white lesbigay culture and their sexual orientation identity by the black heterosexual culture, many black lesbigays do not feel fully accepted in either.

A third reason for the conflict in identities is the lack of overlap between mostly white lesbigay cultures and mostly heterosexual black cultures. They tend to be separated culturally, politically, and, in those areas where black and lesbigay cultures have a spatial presence, geographically. Sometimes, there is overt antagonism between the two groups. One area of tension has been white gay male involvement in gentrifying some lower-class, predominantly black neighborhoods in several major cities. This has reduced the amount of low-income housing available to blacks.[17] While some black organizations and leaders, such as the NAACP, bell hooks, Jesse Jackson, and most members of the Congressional Black Caucus, have come out in favor of lesbigay rights, there is still a long way to go toward full acceptance.[18] This is especially true regarding white lesbigays building coalitions with African-American leaders over political issues that affect all blacks, not just those affecting black lesbigays. This separation between the two cultures forces many African-American lesbians, gays, and bisexuals to choose a primary affiliation with one of the cultures or go back and forth between them. To solve this dilemma, they have also created their own spaces, usually reflecting the larger cultures within which they are marginalized. For example, many of the black lesbigay churches started by the late Dr. James Tinney and others are rooted in traditional African-American ways of worship.[19]

The social movements to end discrimination based on race, gender, and sexuality have had a major impact on the ability of black lesbigays to choose a community or to move back and forth between communities. Anti-discrimination legislation, enhanced public awareness of the issues, and a (slow) decline in the acceptability of prejudice have led to greater access to public accommodations, greater social and economic independence, and a growing number of businesses and organizations geared toward lesbigays. Barriers remain for black lesbigays, however, when trying to negotiate their marginalized identities in community spaces. But African-American lesbigays now live in a social context in which their concerns must be given at least some consideration, even if it is token. They also have a variety of legal and political weapons at their disposal.

The Politics of Blackness

There are many different kinds of black-identified lesbigays and lesbigay-identified blacks. However, the political and social animosity between them has centered on two subgroups: black-identified Afrocentrists and gay-identified interracialists. The Afrocentrists focus on what they identify as African-American cultural traditions, values, and practices. Interracialists are known primarily for their sexual attraction to whites — in spite of the fact that other kinds of interracial relationships, such as those between blacks and other people of color, are possible. For the most part, this antagonism has been explicit only in black gay male textual discourses. Perhaps this is because, as L. Lloyd

Jordan argues, "men are more prone to convert difference into dispute."[20] Perhaps it also reflects the more marginalized status of black lesbian discourses. It should be noted, for example, that while most of the anthologies that featured the writings of black gay men did so exclusively, the anthologies that featured black lesbians were usually presented within some larger context, such as the writings of black feminists *(Home Girls)*, feminists of color *(This Bridge Called My Back)*, or lesbians of color *(Piece of My Heart)*.

In the anthologies I examined, constructions of African-American lesbian and gay identity were overwhelmingly black-identified. This was particularly true among black lesbians, where discussions of interracialists were virtually nonexistent. In those instances where interracialist voices were heard, they were tokens, and the emphasis was on black self-hatred. For example, Makeda Silvera, editor of the lesbians of color anthology, *Piece of My Heart*, published a letter from one of the contributors, Judy Nicholson. Nicholson wanted to withdraw some of the poems she had submitted for publication because

> They are poems of naiveté from my paler lesbian days. They reflect a period in my life when I stayed hidden in my own writing and instead lauded the "beauty" of my White lovers. . . . I do not know me enough to love me, to love my blackness, and to love other Black lesbians.[21]

Within this discourse, it has been the interracialists who have had to defend themselves. Black-identified gays and lesbians, many of whom have had to hide their sexual identities to appease homophobic black communities, have not been forced to question their commitment to lesbigay politics. It has been interracialists who have had to question their blackness and their commitment to black politics.

Central to a black-identified definition of blackness is to have roots in "the" black community and to place a supreme value on one's home of origin. Barbara Smith, in her introduction to *Home Girls*, warns against transforming "cultural beliefs and habits that may characterize many [Black women] into requirements and use them as proof of [their] own and others' full membership in the race."[22] But her selection of stories, poems, and essays contradicts this. All the pieces in *Home Girls*, and in the other major anthologies featuring black lesbians, focus on black communities.

Jewelle Gomez's essay reviewing black lesbian literature most clearly reveals this bias. She praises Audre Lorde's *Zami: A New Spelling of My Name* because it "advances the theme of women-loving-women within a recognizable context of Black life."[23] For Gomez, a "recognizable context" is one that "takes place in the bosom of the Black community which Black Lesbians recognize as the place of their beginnings."[24] Praising Lorde's work for these reasons is odd, because, as Lorde recounts in *Zami*, she became open about her sexuality only after moving out of the black neighborhood in which she grew up and beginning to live and socialize in the mostly white and/or lesbian spaces of Greenwich Village. Here, she felt disconnected from other blacks, including other black lesbians:

> During the fifties in the Village, I did not know the few other Black women who were visibly gay at all well. Too often we found ourselves sleeping with the same white women. We recognized ourselves as exotic sister-outsiders who might gain little from banding together. Perhaps our strength might lay in our fewness, our rarity. That was the way it was

Downtown. And Uptown, meaning the land of Black people, seemed very far away and hostile territory.[25]

While Gomez praises Lorde, she criticizes writer Ann Allen Shockley because her novel *Say Jesus and Come to Me* fails to represent black lesbians in the appropriate cultural context: "The main character, the Reverend Myrtle Black, is egotistical and self-centered. She lacks any kind of anchor in Black culture. Neither her language nor her posture say anything about the complex society which spawned her."[26] Gomez claims that although Shockley did deal with black issues, such as racism in the music business and the whiteness of the women's movement, as well as black male sexism, "[s]he skims the surface of these complicated issues and of the characters themselves, leaving no lasting literary or human sensation in her wake."[27]

In the same anthology, Shockley, reviewing literary representations of black lesbians, makes similar claims about what it means to be black. She argues that "Black women writers *live* in the Black community and *need* the closeness of family, friends, neighbors, and co-workers who share the commonality of ethnicity in order to survive in a blatantly racist society."[28] Consequently, she found a paucity of black lesbian characters (when she wrote the essay in 1979) since, in her view, black women by necessity belonged in black society, where they were under tremendous pressure to conform to homophobic black cultural norms. Because she sees "being black" as having roots in the black community, she also criticizes white author Rita Mae Brown for having an "inauthentic" black lesbian in her novel *In Her Day*: "[T]he bourgeois professor Adele, a Ph.D. in pre-Colombian art, is hardly recognizable as Black. . . . Adele talks white without any of the intentional or unintentional breaks into Black English which are commonly made by all Blacks, regardless of education, at some time or another. Adele acts white, thinks white, and apparently has no significant Black friends."[29]

For Shockley and the others, a black lesbian whose primary social world, whose "home" of origin or of choice has been among whites, or who has internalized Euro-American values and patterns of behavior, is an impossibility, even though a growing number of blacks are living and working outside of predominantly black communities.[30] As a result, the lives of lesbian-identified blacks are erased — as is the diversity among African-Americans — and a black-identified lesbian life is presented as the only viable way to be an African-American lesbian.

Black-identified gay men acknowledge that gay-identified black men exist, but they use black nationalist "blacker-than-thou" rhetoric to discredit them. Gay-identified blacks either do not have strong roots in black communities or have severed most of their connections to them. Also, many of them prefer whites in sexual relationships. Because of this, they are portrayed by black-identified gays as oblivious to the racism that exists in white gay culture and as hating their blackness. For example, in his description of an interracialist, Joseph Beam writes: "Maurice has a propensity for white people, which is more than preference — it's policy. He dismisses potential Black friendships as quickly as he switches off rap music and discredits progressive movements. He consistently votes Republican. At night he dreams of razors cutting away thin slivers of his Black skin."[31]

While there probably are interracialists who fit these characterizations, it is a mistake to attribute these qualities to most of them. If the essays and stories in *Black Men/White Men*, the only major anthology of interracialist experiences produced thus far, are any indication, interracialists are only too aware of the racism that exists in the "home" they have chosen. The sexual stereotyping; the discrimination in bars, baths, employment, and housing; the prevalence of white male standards of beauty; the racist ads that appear in gay newspapers; and the gay white gentrification that has displaced lower-income blacks pervade the pages of the anthology. Interracialists are no more unaware of white gay racism than Afrocentrists and other black-identified gays are of heterosexual black homophobia, a theme that pervades their work.

Both groups are aware of the limitations of the primary communities they have chosen, and of the ones they have not. It is ironic that Afrocentric black gays have used black nationalist rhetoric to discredit the interracialists, since many heterosexual black nationalists have used the same rhetoric to discredit black gays. Homosexuality is a "white thang," according to these nationalists, and those blacks who practice it have "sold out." Haki Madhubuti, for example, has argued that getting black men to practice homosexuality is one way in which whites systematically "disrupt black families and neutralize black men."[32]

Ultimately, choosing a primary community when you do not have access to one that accepts both your racial/ethnic and sexual preference identities is an intensely personal decision that, for many, centers around these questions: Which do you find to be more oppressive or important politically, racism or homophobia? Which identity is more important in your social life, race/ethnicity or sexual preference? How much value do you place on your home of origin? Which community is more conducive to sexual relationships with those who have the qualities you desire? The answers to these questions will depend on, among other things, each black gay, bisexual, or lesbian's personal history, the meanings they have attached to their experiences, whether their home of origin is in fact a black community, the nature of their sexual desires, and their politics. The answers to these questions may also change over time. Because of this, interracialist black lesbigays should not be made to feel that they are not really black simply because they prefer white lesbigay communities as their homes of choice. In fact, as L. Lloyd Jordan has argued, having black lesbians, gays, and bisexuals in both cultures can be beneficial politically. Many lesbigay-identified blacks have battled racism among white lesbigays, just as many black-identified lesbigays have challenged homophobia in black communities.[33]

Conclusion

Afrocentric black lesbians, gays, and bisexuals need to de-essentialize their ideas of what it means to be black. As black cultural critic Michael Dyson has argued, "[There are] distinct black cultural characteristics that persist over space and time. . . . They do not, however, form the basis of a black racial or cultural essence. Nor do they indicate *the* meaning of blackness will be expressed in a quality or characteristic without which a person, act, or practice no longer qualifies as black."[34]

A major consequence of the essentialist notion of blackness promoted by Afrocentric lesbigays and other blacks is that interracialists and other lesbigay-identified blacks are forced to question the authenticity of their black identities. And for those who find aspects of what has been promoted as "being black" to be problematic, the only solution to their dilemma sometimes seems to be to reject what they perceive as "being black" altogether, rather than to forge a new kind of black identity. Reginald Shepherd, the token "tortured" interracialist in *In the Life*, writes about this dilemma in relation to the anti-intellectualism promoted in the black neighborhoods he grew up in:

> Too much of what I've seen of black society simply assumes . . . that black people should have no interest in these words [of culture and education], that these words are irrelevant to or destructive of "black culture." . . . I've had notions, negative each one, images of what it is to *seem* black: to look black, to talk black, to dress black. . . . The language of culture and education was not among these seemings. I've shaped for myself a manner of appearing quite other than those seemings.[35]

As a result, Shepherd and others like him are forced to live a contradiction. On the one hand, they have the physical characteristics generally associated with African-Americans — and hence, others interact with them as such. At the same time, they have a sense of themselves as being something other than black, because they or others perceive them as not exhibiting the "right" cultural characteristics. And the ones they do exhibit are those generally associated with whites.

While black lesbigay identities need to be de-essentialized, this does not mean that various socially constructed definitions of blackness should be immune to criticism. All meanings of blackness have social, cultural, and political implications, and these implications change, depending on the historical context. Therefore, these meanings must continually be reevaluated and reshaped.

What I am suggesting here is that the silences and the "blacker-than-thou" rhetoric that has characterized the conflicts between Afrocentric and interracialist black lesbigays need to be cast in different terms. What should be at issue is not who is or is not "really" black, but the social, cultural, and political implications of adopting various definitions of blackness. This changes the debate in several ways. One, the emphasis is on exploring what qualities are desirable or undesirable in various definitions of blackness, rather than on racial essence. Two, there is an acknowledgment that there are a multiplicity of potentially valuable black lesbigay identities, rather than just one "right" one. And finally, there is the recognition that there are advantages and disadvantages to all potential definitions of blackness.

This does not, however, resolve the issue of who sets the political agenda for African-American lesbigays and who benefits most from it. L. Lloyd Jordan is correct in noting that a central part of the debate about primary community choice is "who gets to call the shots, lobby the politicians, get funding and mug for the media in *your* name."[36] Efforts by lesbigay-identified blacks to stop racist practices by white lesbigay cultural institutions, such as bars and the press, may not be a major concern for black-identified lesbigays, since they do not participate in these cultural spaces. Similarly, many lesbigay-identified blacks may not see it as crucial to link black lesbigay issues to those of the larger African-American community as being most important. It needs to be recognized that African-American lesbigays have multiple and often conflicting values and political agendas. But with contending groups of African-American lesbigays battling over limited resources, who is going to be listened to by those who control the resources?

There is also a danger in identifying with either community. In both, African-American lesbigay voices risk being usurped, co-opted, and/or silenced to serve the ends of the larger communities. This was evident in the sole anthology that focused on interracialist experiences, *Black Men/White Men*. The editor, Michael J. Smith, was a white gay man who was one of the founders of the interracialist organization, Black and White Men Together. Because he was the editor, black gay men were not in a position of power to control how they were represented in an anthology that primarily was supposed to be about them. If the anthology was about "the Black and interracial gay experience in White America," as the back cover announced, why did not blacks, at the least, share editorial control over how these experiences were to be represented? And why were a significant number of the articles about blacks written by whites? Regardless of whether his representation was "fair" or "accurate," that he was using his white male privilege to speak for and about African-American gays at a time when there were so few speaking for themselves is problematic.

Both black-identified lesbigays and lesbigay-identified blacks must be aware of and deal with the paternalism, racial essentialism, and other kinds of power relationships that exist — both among themselves and between them and the larger black and lesbigay communities within which they are marginalized. Only then can there be a constructive dialogue on black lesbigay identity. The goal is not to have a social world in which all black lesbigay identities are equally valid. That is neither possible nor desirable. It is not possible because history and existing power relationships cannot be ignored. Through historically determined power relationships, some discourses on, and cultural meanings of, black lesbigay identity are more dominant than others. That is, they are more widely available, felt by more people, and asserted with greater authority (either through persuasion or force). But even if it were possible to give all black lesbigay identities equal validity and weight, it would not be desirable because there are some constructions of black lesbigay identity that should be discouraged, such as those rooted in internalized racism or homophobia. The goal, then, is to have multiple non-oppressive black lesbigay identities that take into account the diversity that exists among us.

NOTES

1. *Tongues Untied*, directed by Marlon Riggs (Frameline, 1989).

2. I will use both terms because, in contemporary common usage, people of African descent are referred to as both a racial group (black) and an ethnic group (African-American). Although there are differences in meaning, the two terms are often used interchangeably — as they will be in this chapter.

3. Julius Maurice Johnson, *Influence of Assimilation on the Psychosocial Adjustment of Black Homosexual Men* (Ann Arbor: UMI, 1982).

4. John L. Peterson, "Black Men and Their Same-Sex Desires and Behaviors," in *Gay Culture in America: Essays from the Field*, ed. Gilbert Herdt (Boston: Beacon Press, 1992), 147–64; Darryl

K. Loiacano, "Gay Identity Issues among Black Americans: Racism, Homophobia, and the Need for Validation," *Journal of Counseling and Development* 68 (September/October 1989): 21–25.

5. L. Lloyd Jordan, "Black Gay vs. Gay Black," *BLK* 2, no.6 (June 1990): 25–30.

6. Essex Hemphill, ed., *Brother to Brother: New Writings by Black Gay Men* (Boston: Alyson, 1991); Barbara Smith, ed., *Home Girls: A Black Feminist Anthology* (New York: Kitchen Table: Women of Color Press, 1983); Joseph Beam, ed., *In The Life: A Black Gay Anthology* (Boston: Alyson, 1986); Michael Smith, ed., *Black Men/White Men: A Gay Anthology* (San Francisco: Gay Sunshine Press, 1983); Makeda Silvera, ed., *Piece of My Heart: A Lesbian of Colour Anthology* (Toronto: Sister Vision Press, 1991); Cary Alan Johnson, Colin Robinson, and Terence Taylor, eds., *Other Countries: Black Gay Voices* (New York: Other Countries, 1988); B. Michael Hunter, ed., *Sojourner: Black Gay Voices in the Age of AIDS* (New York: Other Countries, 1993); Cherríe Moraga and Gloria Anzaldúa, eds., *This Bridge Called My Back: Writings by Radical Women of Color* (New York: Kitchen Table: Women of Color Press, 1983).

7. Essex Hemphill, Introduction to *Brother to Brother*, xxi–xxviii.

8. For an essay addressing African-American bisexual experiences, see Brenda Marie Blasingame, "The Roots of Biphobia: Racism and Internalized Heterosexism," in *Closer to Home: Bisexuality and Feminism*, ed. Elizabeth Reba Weise (Seattle: Seal Press, 1992), 47–53.

9. Barbara Smith, Introduction to *Home Girls*, xxii.

10. Colin Robinson, Introduction to *Other Countries*, 1.

11. Joseph Beam, Introduction to *In the Life*, 18.

12. Hemphill, Introduction, xxx.

13. I should acknowledge here that my preliminary survey of black lesbigay discourse suggests that this bias may be limited to the anthologies. For example, most of the non-anthologized fiction and autobiographies I have examined have focused on interracialist experiences. It is unclear why the polyvocal anthologies are mostly black-identified, while single author works are mostly gay-identified. But since the anthologies supposedly represent many different African-American lesbigay voices, their bias is of greater concern.

14. John D'Emilio, "After Stonewall," in *Making Trouble: Essays on Gay History, Politics, and the University* (New York: Routledge, 1993), 234–74.

15. Beam, Introduction, 14–15.

16. Combahee River Collective, "The Combahee River Collective Statement," in *Home Girls*, 281.

17. John V. Soares, "Black and Gay," in *Gay Men: The Sociology of Male Homosexuality*, ed. Martin P. Levine (New York: Harper and Row, 1979), 263–74.

18. Don Thomas, "Liberty and Justice for All," *Advocate*, 5 October 1993, 5; bell hooks, "Homophobia in Black Communities," in *Talking Back: Thinking Feminist, Thinking Black* (Boston: South End Press, 1989), 120–27; Paul Horowitz, "Beyond the Gay Nation: Where Are We Marching?" *OUT/LOOK* 1 (Spring 1988): 19.

19. James S. Tinney, "Why a Black Gay Church?" in *In The Life*, 70–86.

20. Jordan, "Black Gay vs. Gay Black," 25.

21. Judy Nicholson, "Dear Sisters," in *Piece of My Heart*, 106.

22. Smith, Introduction, xl.

23. Jewelle L. Gomez, "A Cultural Legacy Denied and Discovered: Black Lesbians in Fiction by Women," in *Home Girls*, 118.

24. Ibid., 119.

25. Audre Lorde, *Zami: A New Spelling of My Name* (Freedom, CA: Crossing Press, 1982), 177.

26. Gomez, "A Cultural Legacy Denied and Discovered," 114.

27. Ibid., 113.

28. Ann Allen Shockley, "The Black Lesbian in American Literature: An Overview," in *Home Girls*, 86.

29. Ibid., 88.

30. Joe R. Feagin and Melvin P. Sikes, *Living with Racism: The Black Middle-Class Experience* (Boston: Beacon Press, 1994), 226–27.

31. Joseph Beam, "Brother to Brother: Words from the Heart," in *In the Life*, 240.

32. Quoted from Ron Simmons, "Some Thoughts on the Challenges Facing Black Gay Intellectuals," in *Brother to Brother*, 215.

33. Jordan, "Black Gay vs. Gay Black," 30.

34. Michael Dyson, *Reflecting Black: African-American Cultural Criticism* (Minneapolis: University of Minnesota Press, 1993), xxi.

35. Reginald Shepherd, "On Not Being White," in *In the Life*, 48–49.

36. Jordan, "Black Gay vs. Gay Black," 25.

BIBLIOGRAPHY

Beam, Joseph. "Brother to Brother: Words from the Heart." In *In the Life: A Black Gay Anthology*. Ed. Joseph Beam. Boston: Alyson, 1986. 230–42.

———. Introduction to *In the Life: A Black Gay Anthology*. Ed. Joseph Beam. Boston: Alyson, 1986. 13–18.

Blasingame, Brenda Marie. "The Roots of Biphobia: Racism and Internalized Heterosexism." In *Closer to Home: Bisexuality and Feminism*. Ed. Elizabeth Reba Weise. Seattle: Seal Press, 1992. 47–53.

Combahee River Collective. "The Combahee River Collective Statement." In *Home Girls: A Black Feminist Anthology*. Ed. Barbara Smith. New York: Kitchen Table: Women of Color Press, 1983. 272–82.

D'Emilio, John. "After Stonewall." In *Making Trouble: Essays on Gay History, Politics, and the University*. New York: Routledge, 1993. 234–74.

Dyson, Michael. *Reflecting Black: African-American Cultural Criticism*. Minneapolis: University of Minnesota Press, 1993.

Feagin, Joe R., and Melvin P. Sikes. *Living with Racism: The Black Middle-Class Experience*. Boston: Beacon Press, 1994.

Gomez, Jewelle L. "A Cultural Legacy Denied and Discovered: Black Lesbians in Fiction by Women." In *Home Girls: A Black Feminist Anthology*. Ed. Barbara Smith. New York: Kitchen Table: Women of Color Press, 1983. 110–23.

Hemphill, Essex. Introduction to *Brother to Brother: New Writings by Black Gay Men*. Ed. Essex Hemphill. Boston: Alyson, 1991. xv–xxxi.

hooks, bell. "Homophobia in Black Communities." In *Talking Back: Thinking Feminist, Thinking Black*. Boston: South End Press, 1989. 120–27.

Horowitz, Paul. "Beyond the Gay Nation: Where Are We Marching?" *OUT/LOOK* 1 (Spring 1988): 7–21.

Hunter, B. Michael, ed. *Sojourner: Black Gay Voices in the Age of AIDS*. New York: Other Countries, 1993.

Johnson, Cary Alan, Colin Robinson, and Terence Taylor, eds. *Other Countries: Black Gay Voices*. New York: Other Countries, 1988.

Johnson, Julius Maurice. *Influence of Assimilation on the Psychosocial Adjustment of Black Homo-sexual Men*. Ann Arbor: UMI, 1982.

Jordan, L. Lloyd. "Black Gay vs. Gay Black." *BLK* 2, no. 6 (June 1990): 25–30.

Loiacano, Darryl K. "Gay Identity Issues among Black Americans: Racism, Homophobia, and the Need for Validation." *Journal of Counseling and Development* 68 (September/October 1989): 21–25.

Lorde, Audre. *Zami: A New Spelling of My Name*. Freedom, CA: Crossing Press, 1982.

Moraga, Cherríe, and Gloria Anzaldúa, eds. *This Bridge Called My Back: Writings by Radical Women of Color*. New York: Kitchen Table: Women of Color Press, 1983.

Nicholson, Judy. "Dear Sisters." In *Piece of My Heart: A Lesbian of Colour Anthology*. Ed. Makeda Silvera. Toronto: Sister Vision Press, 1991. 106–7.

Peterson, John L. "Black Men and Their Same-Sex Desires and Behaviors." In *Gay Culture in America: Essays from the Field*. Ed. Gilbert Herdt. Boston: Beacon Press, 1992. 147–64.

Riggs, Marlon, director. *Tongues Untied*. Frameline, 1989.

Robinson, Colin. Introduction to *Other Countries: Black Gay Voices*. Ed. Cary Alan Johnson, Colin Robinson, and Terence Taylor. New York: Other Countries, 1988. 1.

Shepherd, Reginald. "On Not Being White." In *In the Life: A Black Gay Anthology*. Ed. Joseph Beam. Boston: Alyson, 1986. 46–57.

Shockley, Ann Allen. "The Black Lesbian in American Literature: An Overview." In *Home Girls: A Black Feminist Anthology*. Ed. Barbara Smith. New York: Kitchen Table: Women of Color Press, 1983. 83–93.

Silvera, Makeda, ed. *Piece of My Heart: A Lesbian of Colour Anthology*. Toronto: Sister Vision Press, 1991.

Simmons, Ron. "Some Thoughts on the Challenges Facing Black Gay Intellectuals." In *Brother to Brother: New Writings by Black Gay Men*. Ed. Essex Hemphill. Boston: Alyson, 1991. 211–28.

Smith, Barbara. Introduction to *Home Girls: A Black Feminist Anthology*. Ed. Barbara Smith. New York: Kitchen Table: Women of Color Press, 1983. xix–lvi.

Smith, Michael, ed. *Black Men/White Men: A Gay Anthology*. San Francisco: Gay Sunshine Press, 1983.

Soares, John V. "Black and Gay." In *Gay Men: The Sociology of Male Homosexuality*. Ed. Martin P. Levine. New York: Harper and Row, 1979. 263–74.

Thomas, Don. "Liberty and Justice for All." *Advocate*, 5 October 1993, 5.

Tinney, James S. "Why a Black Gay Church?" In *In The Life: A Black Gay Anthology*. Ed. Joseph Beam. Boston: Alyson, 1986. 70–86.

chapter 8

History/Hysteria: Parallel Representations of Jews and Gays, Lesbians, and Bisexuals

Warren J. Blumenfeld

One day, when I was very young, I sat upon the knee of my maternal grandfather, Simon. Looking down urgently, but with deep affection, he said to me, "Varn" (he always pronounced my name Varn), "you are named after my father, Wolf Yusel Mahler, who was killed in Poland by the Nazis, along with my mother and most of my thirteen brothers and sisters." When I asked why they were killed, he responded simply, "Because they were Jews." Those seemingly simple words have reverberated in my mind, haunting me ever since.

In this country, my own father suffered the effects of anti-Jewish prejudice. One of only three Jews in his high school, he returned home many afternoons injured from a fight. To get a decent job, his father, Edmond, was forced to anglicize the family name, changing it from Blumenfeld to Fields.

My parents did what they could to protect my sister and me from anti-Semitism, but still I grew up with a constant and gnawing feeling that I somehow didn't belong. It was the early 1950s, the so-called "McCarthy Era"—a conservative time, a time when difference of any sort was suspect. By the time I reached the age of seven or eight, I was increasingly becoming the target of harassment and attack by my peers, who perceived me as someone who was different. Names like "queer," "sissy," "little girl," and "fag" were thrown at me like the large red ball that the children hurled on the school yard when they played dodgeball. Not knowing what else to do, my parents sent me to a child psychiatrist for seven years beginning at the age of five because they feared I might be gay (or to use the terminology of the day, "homosexual"). And, as it turned out, their perceptions were indeed correct.

My journey of "coming out" in the succeeding years was often difficult and painful, though looking back, I conclude that it has been worthwhile in that it has been the prime motivator for the work I am doing. Though I have experienced a double stigma growing up gay and Jewish, I truly believe that I am "twice blessed" (Blumenfeld 1992).

Making the Links

Throughout history, many agent or dominant groups (sometimes called "majorities") have depicted or represented target groups (sometimes called "minorities") in a variety of negative ways in order to maintain control or mastery. The oppression of target groups is expressed through myths and stereotypes in proverbs, social commentary, literature, jokes, epithets, pictorial depictions, and other cultural forms. Stereotypes of lesbians, gays, bisexuals, and transgendered people (LGBTs) were exemplified at the 1992 Republican National Convention when presidential candidate Pat Buchanan announced that a cultural war was being fought in this country. The war he spoke of is currently being waged by the political and theocratic Right to preserve what Buchanan termed "traditional family values." He characterized the enemy as "homosexuals," who are supposedly attempting to undermine the foundations of this country with their "gay agenda."

Why are segments of the Right so vehemently anti-gay now? While there are a number of possible explanations, political scientist Matthew Moen argues in *The Transformation of the Christian Right* that the primary reason is that the Right "didn't have any more agenda items on their plate" (Solomon 1993: 34). Before the 1994 elections, in which Republicans gained control of both houses of Congress, they had been losing ground on issues like abortion, school prayer, and tuition tax credits for private schools, and, most importantly, the far Right had lost what Loretta Ross of the Center for Democratic Renewal calls their "ideological glue": world Communism. Therefore, they needed a new "enemy" to unite around and scapegoat, and LGBTs have become a common target (Solomon 1993: 34).

We are now seeing this played out. Recently, on the floor of the U.S. Senate, Joseph Broadus, a professor at the George Mason University School of Law, urged legislators to defeat the Employment Non-Discrimination Act of 1994, a measure which would have protected lesbians and gays from job discrimination, by arguing that "It [would] result in special privileges for an elite group that has unjustly played the victim card to advance." Upon hearing this, Senator Paul Wellstone (D-MN), barely controlling his rage, responded: "As a Jew, I have a real problem with what you say. That is precisely the kind of argument that has been made . . . on behalf of the worst kind of discrimination against Jewish people" (Roehr 1994: 10).

This incident highlights what many of us have noticed for some time: the many clear and stunning connections between historical representations and oppressions of Jewish people and LGBTs. As John Boswell notes in *Christianity, Social Tolerance, and Homosexuality*:

> The fate of Jews and gay people has been almost identical throughout European history, from early Christian hostility to extermination in concentration camps. The same laws which oppressed Jews oppressed gay people; the same groups bent on eliminating Jews tried to wipe out homosexuality; the same periods of European history which could not make

room for Jewish distinctiveness reacted violently against sexual nonconformity; the same countries which insisted on religious uniformity imposed majority standards of sexual conduct; and even the same methods of propaganda were used against Jews and gay people — picturing them as animals bent on the destruction of the children of the majority. (Boswell 1980: 15–16)

Because Jewish people and LGBT people have suffered similar injustices, they are, or at least can be, natural allies. However, primarily in the West, a Christian and heterosexual cultural hegemony has prevented such alliances from forming to the extent that is possible.

Qualifications

By highlighting the parallel representations and manifestations of oppression of Jews and LGBTs, I am not asserting (or even attempting to imply) that members of these groups encounter oppression similarly. The experiences of Jewish people with institutional and societal anti-Semitism and the experiences of LGBTs with forms of homophobia/biphobia/transphobia and heterosexism are often very distinct. Indeed, experiences also differ *within* these groups. Many aspects of social identity have an influence on experience, including biological sex, race, class background, religion, sexual orientation and identity, age, geographic residency, and degree of assimilation into the dominant culture. The daily realities for most Jews in the U.S. today, for example, are not identical to those of their European ancestors in the 1930s. Likewise, societal reactions to lesbians, gays, bisexuals, and transgendered people have become less repressive to an extent since the advent of a visible modern rights movement. In addition, experiences certainly differ between individuals within a given time frame.

Many forms of oppression, while unique in many respects, run parallel to each other; others actually intersect. My primary goal in this essay is to unearth some of the intersections between homophobia/heterosexism and anti-Semitism, for it is at these points of intersection that there is the greatest potential for the development of alliances. Although I have chosen to compare these two specific forms of oppression, I believe that all the various spokes on the wheels of oppression are connected to some degree. I have therefore written and conducted workshops about the links between such forms of oppression as racism and homophobia/heterosexism, racism and anti-Semitism, and sexism and racism. Thus, while my discussion here is limited to anti-Semitism and homophobia/heterosexism, no assumption should be made that these are the only forms of oppression that are in some way connected.

Parallel Representations of Jews and LGBTs

I divide the interconnections between historical representations of Jews and LGBTs into five basic categories: "Religious Condemnations," "Immature Developmental Stage," "Immutable Biological Types," "Abuse and Recruitment of Children," and "Domination and Destruction of 'Civilized' Society."

Religious Condemnations

Fundamentalists often cite certain biblical passages to justify their denial of legal protections for LGBTs, even though there is great disagreement among scholars over the interpretation of these passages. From the Hebrew Bible (the "Old Testament"), references are frequently made to Genesis 19:1–25 (the story of Sodom and Gomorrah), Leviticus 18:22 ("Thou shalt not lie with mankind, as with womankind: it is an abomination"),[1] and Leviticus 20:13 ("If a man also lie with mankind, as he lieth with a woman, both of them have committed an abomination: they shall surely be put to death; their blood shall be upon them"). Another often quoted text is 1 Kings 22:46: "And the remnant of the Sodomites, which remained in the days of his father Asa, he took out of the land." In the Christian scriptures (the "New Testament"), four passages in particular have been interpreted as condemnations of homosexuality. Paul is said to have denounced women who were involved in same-sex sexual relationships in Romans 1:26 ("For this cause God gave them up unto vile affections; for even their women did change the natural use into that which is against nature") and to have extended this rebuke to men in the following chapter ("And likewise also the men, leaving the natural use of the women, burned in their lust one toward another, men with men working that which is unseemly, and receiving in themselves that recompense of their error which was meet"). Other passages referred to by fundamentalists include Timothy 1:10 ("For whoremongers, for them that defile themselves with mankind, for menstealers, for liars, for perjured persons, and if there be any other thing that is contrary to sound doctrine") and 1 Corinthians 6:9 ("Know ye not that the unrighteous shall not inherit the kingdom of God? Be not deceived; neither fornicators, nor idolaters, nor adulterers, nor effeminate, nor abusers of themselves with mankind").

Often forgotten in current debates are demeaning depictions of Jews in the New Testament. For example, in 1 Thessalonians 2:15–16, Paul proclaims that the Jews "killed the Lord Jesus and the prophets and drove us out," and that they "are heedless of God's will and enemies of their fellow man, . . . All this time they have been making up the full measure of their guilt, and now retribution has overtaken the good of all." Writing to the Galatians, Paul also warns Christians to refrain from the Jewish practice of circumcision:

Christ set us free, to be free men. Stand firm, then, and refuse to be tied to the yoke of slavery again. Mark my words: I, Paul, say to you that if you receive circumcision, Christ will do you no good at all. Once again, you can take it from me that every man who receives circumcision is under obligation to keep the entire law. When you seek to be justified by way of law, your relation with Christ is completely severed: you have fallen out of the domain of God's grace. For to us, our hope of attaining that righteousness which we eagerly await is the work of the Spirit through faith. If we are in union with Christ Jesus, circumcision makes no difference at all, nor does the want of it; the only thing that counts is faith active in love. (5:1–6)

In his letter to Titus, Paul lists Jews among the ranks of the disbelievers:

Do not give heed to Jewish fables and commandments of merely human origin that turn men from the truth; to the pure all things are pure, but nothing is pure to the tainted minds of disbelievers, tainted alike in reason and conscience. They profess to acknowledge God, but deny him by their actions. Their detestable obstinacy disqualifies them for any good work. (1:14–16)

In Matthew 27:24–25, Jews are also blamed for the death of Christ:

Pilate could see that nothing was being gained, and a riot was starting [among the Jews]; so he took water and washed his hands in full view of the people saying, "My hands are clean of this man's blood; see to that yourselves." And with one voice the people cried, "His blood be on us, and on our children."

Not until 1962, at the Second Vatican Council under Pope John XXIII, were Jews exonerated for the death of Jesus.

Throughout the ages, the citations from Paul and Matthew have been used to justify Jewish persecution. During the late fourth and fifth centuries, for example, Jews residing in Christian societies had most of their communal and legal rights taken away. They were not permitted to hold state office or enter the army, and proselytism and intermarriage with Christians were capital offenses. The leading Greek theologian of the time, John Chrysostom (354–407), delivered eight "Sermons against the Jews at Antioch," which featured diatribes such as: "Their synagogue is not only a brothel and a theater, it is also a den of robbers and lodging for wild beasts. The Jews themselves are demons. They are a common disgrace and infection of the whole world" (Meeks and Wilken 1978: 97).

Other religions leaders were no less anti-Semitic. Pope Gregory the Great (590–604) created an ideology of Christian anti-Judaism which was to lead directly to physical attacks on Jews. What he argued, in effect, was that Jews understood the claims of Christianity; they knew that Jesus was the Messiah and the Son of God. But they had rejected him, and continued to reject him, because their hearts were corrupt. Similarly, Pope Innocent III (1198–1216) enacted a series of anti-Jewish decrees at the Fourth Lateran Council in 1216, arguing that Jews had corrupted and reversed the "natural order" with their unscrupulous use of money and power, and that the "free Christian" had essentially become the servant of a Jewish master. He concluded that government must restore nature by penalizing Jews (Grayzel 1966: 108). Previously, he had demanded that Jews wear yellow badges to distinguish them from Gentiles. This order is thought to have been taken from Moslem decrees that were first documented in 1121 in Baghdad, which

[decreed that they should wear] two yellow badges, one on the headgear and one on the neck. Furthermore each Jew should have hanging on his neck a piece of lead weighing one dirhem [3.125 grams approximately], on which the word *dhimmi* ["non-Muslim"] was engraved. He also should wear a belt around his waist. On the women two distinctive signs were imposed. They should wear one red and one black shoe and have a small brass bell on their necks or shoes in order to distinguish them from Muslim women. (Goitein 1971: 287)

From these Moslem and Christian decrees, the Nazis adopted the special badges used to classify Jews, homosexuals, and other marginalized groups.

Another pope, Gregory IX, condemned the Talmud, the collection of Jewish rabbinical texts. He sent a letter to European rulers in 1239 asking them to seize all Talmuds on the first Saturday of Lent, "while the Jews are gathered in the synagogue," and place them "in [the] custody of our dear sons, the Dominican and Franciscan Friars" (Grayzel 1966: 243). Louis IX was the only monarch to comply with Gregory's request. Though the Franciscans outwardly preached love, this did not apply to Jews. According to the Franciscan friar Bernardino of Sienna, "In respect of abstract and general love, we are permitted to love [Jews]. However there can be no concrete love towards them" (Ben-Sasson 1976: 579).

Protestant leaders like Martin Luther were also extremely hostile toward Jews. Luther published a pamphlet entitled "On the Jews and Their Lies" in 1526, which some have called "the first work of modern anti-Semitism." He recommended: "First, their synagogues should be set on fire, and whatever is left should be buried in dirt so that no one may ever be able to see a stone or cinder of it." Jewish prayer books, he advised, should be destroyed and rabbis forbidden to preach. The homes of Jews should likewise be "smashed and destroyed" and their residents "put under one roof or in a stable like gypsies, to teach them they are not master in our land." He also suggested that Jews be banned from the roads and markets and their property seized. Then these "poisonous envenomed worms should be drafted into forced labor. The young and strong Jews and Jewesses should be given the flail, the ax, the hoe, the spade, the distaff, and the spindle and let them earn their bread by the sweat of their noses." As a last resort, they should simply be kicked out "for all time." Luther concentrated his scorn against Jews for their role as moneylenders and insisted that their wealth did not belong to them, since it had been "extorted usuriously from us." The usurer, he asserted, "is a double-dyed thief and murderer. . . . [T]herefore is there on earth no greater enemy of man, after the devil, than a gripe-money and usurer, for he wants to be God over all men" (Luther [1526] 1936).

Immature Developmental Stage

Many past and present-day religious leaders consider Judaism to be merely an intermediate or immature stage on the way to Christianity, the advanced, mature faith, and view the Hebrew Bible as only a prelude to the coming of Christ. For example, the Missouri Synod of the Lutheran church has published a booklet entitled *How to Respond to Judaism*, in which the authors characterize the Jewish faith as "*inadequate* because it does not have Jesus, *the* Messiah, as the object of faith" (Kolb 1984: 24; my emphasis) and suggest strategies to convince Jews to accept Jesus as their savior. Similarly, followers of the so-called "Jews for Jesus" movement refer to themselves as "Completed Jews," "Fulfilled Jews," or "Messianic Jews," because, for them, the Messiah *has* come in the form of Jesus Christ. It is this image of the infantilized Jew that underlies the contemporary representation of the young Jewish woman (derogatorily referred to as the "Jewish American Princess" or "JAP") as a perpetual child, dependent on her father.

With the development of the field of psychology in the late nineteenth century, medical practitioners were likewise professing that homosexuality was merely an intermediate or immature developmental stage leading to the highest or mature stage of heterosexuality.[2] Inspired largely by Charles Darwin's theory of evolution, two American physicians, James Kiernan and Frank Lydston, posited homosexuality and homosexuals as congenital throwbacks to an earlier stage of human evolution, a kind of remnant of the primitive organisms from which humans developed. Another physician, Sigmund Freud, advanced a four-stage model of psychosexual development in which newborn infants were "polymorphously perverse," deriving pleasure from tactile sensations anywhere on the body, before developing a sexual drive in the mouth, then the anus, and ultimately, the genitals. He concluded that homosexuality was a developmental disorder, a fixation at one of the intermediate "pregenital" stages, which he believed to be caused at least in part by an incomplete resolution of the Oedipal complex. In this way, Freud saw gay men as perpetual children. It is this image of the rather silly, childish gay man which has adorned movies and other popular media in the twentieth century.

Immutable Biological Types

By the late nineteenth century, Judaism and homosexuality had come to be viewed by the scientific community as immutable biological characteristics — a trend that increased markedly in the twentieth century.[3] Once seen as largely a religious, ethnic, or political group, Jews were increasingly considered members of a "mixed race" (a "mongrel" or "bastard" race), a people who crossed racial barriers by interbreeding with black Africans in the Diaspora. The "racial" characteristics of Jews were thought to be evident in their physiognomy. Although in actuality Jews are members of every "race," scientist Robert Knox argued, for example, that Jews as a group had "African" features:

> [H]is muzzle-shaped mouth and face remov[e] him from certain other races . . . the [body] contour is convex, the eyes long and fine, the outer angles running towards the temples; the brow and nose apt to form a single convex line; the nose comparatively narrow at the base, the eyes consequently approaching each other; lips very full, mouth projecting, chin small, and the whole physiognomy, when swarthy, as it often is, has an African look. (Knox 1850: 133–34)

By the end of the century, the popular image of the "Jewish type" (portrayed invariably as the Jewish male) consisted of a "hooked nose, curling nasal folds, thick prominent lips, receding forehead and chin, large ears, curly black hair, dark skin, stooped shoulders, and piercing, cunning eyes" (Isaacs 1940: 119).

Both the Jewish male and the homosexual male were, and continue to be, represented as feminized men. During the Middle Ages, for example, Jewish men were said to menstruate. For many non-Jews, the Jewish practice of circumcision also made them the "feminized" other. In the nineteenth century, the diagnosis of "hysteria," which had been considered primarily a "feminine affliction," was increasingly thought of as a neurological impairment associated with Jewish males. Their supposed racial differences — the stereotypical "weak Jewish foot" (flat foot) and their purported narrow chest measurements — disqualified Jewish men from military service, which, in the late nineteenth century, was an essential marker of social acceptance and acculturation in many European societies. In Russia, for example, in the 1880s Jews were banned from the military guards, the navy, the gendarmerie, and the commissariat and were prevented from entering military schools and from taking army examinations, thereby effectively excluding them from becoming army officers.

Lesbians, gays, and bisexuals have likewise been excluded from the military. In 1943, psychiatrists at U.S. induction centers were instructed by government officials to bar "persons habitually or occasionally engaged in homosexual or other perverse sexual practices" (Bérubé 1990: 19). In 1982, during Ronald Reagan's presidency, the Department of Defense issued Directive 1332.14, which legally prevented lesbian, gay, and bisexual people from serving in the armed forces. The current so-called "Don't ask, Don't tell, Don't pursue" policy continues to support the idea that these groups are unsuited for military service. Since World War II, literally thousands of women and men have been prevented from enlisting, have been discharged, or have even been incarcerated for alleged homosexuality.

Although records dating back to antiquity have documented the universal existence of homosexual acts, it wasn't until the nineteenth century that science, particularly the medical profession, constructed categories of sexual orientation. No longer were there merely homosexual acts; now people who pursued same-sex sexual relationships were labeled "inverts," "Urnings," and especially, "homosexuals." While physicians and sexologists did not entirely reject environmental factors, they suggested a largely somatic or biological basis for same-sex eroticism, thereby leading to the "medicalization" of homosexuality in the late nineteenth century.

Austrian sex researcher Richard von Krafft-Ebing, one of the most influential sexologists, described homosexuality in his massive *Psychopathia Sexualis* as a fundamental sign of "degeneration" and a product of vice (Krafft-Ebing 1886: 339–40). French physician Ambroise Tardieu claimed that this "degeneracy" was evidenced in men who engaged in same-sex eroticism by their underdeveloped, tapered penis, resembling that of a dog, and a naturally smooth anus lacking in radial folds (Tardieu 1857: 236). Lesbians were likewise subjected to the biological determinism of sexologists. For example, Allan McLane Hamilton, an American physician, wrote in 1896 that the lesbian is "usually of a masculine type, or if she presented none of the 'characteristics' of the male, was a subject of pelvic disorders, with scanty menstruation, and was more or less hysterical or insane" (Hamilton 1896: 505). Lesbians were also thought to have enlarged clitorises, which some writers believed made sexual intercourse with other women possible. Writing about lesbians, Auguste Forel, a Swiss psychiatrist, claimed that "the [sexual] excesses of female inverts exceed those of the male," and that "this is their one thought, night and day, almost without interruption" (Forel [1906] 1924: 252). He also concluded that male homosexuals "feel the need for passive submission" and "occupy themselves with feminine pursuits," while "nearly all [female and male] inverts are in a more or less marked degree psychopaths or neurotics" (243, 244). Other writers, such as Karl Heinrich Ulrichs, considered homosexuals (whom he called "Urnings") as members of one sex trapped in the body of the other, a sort of "Third Sex" (Ulrichs 1864).

The medicalization of homosexuality and the construction of Judaism as a separate and distinct racial type have contributed to the notion that members of these groups are somehow inferior and less than completely human. Such representations of Jews and people sexually attracted to members of their own sex served as the cornerstone of Nazi philosophy, which considered both groups to have sprung from "racially inferior" strands. Jews, for example, were portrayed with misshapen heads, crooked noses, drooping lower lips, bent legs, and other demeaning characteristics that denoted a dangerous and disease-laden enemy. Even before his rise to power, Adolph Hitler's official newspaper, *Volkischer Beobachter*, had stated:

> [A]mong the many evil instincts that characterize the Jewish race, one that is especially pernicious has to do with sexual relations. The Jews are forever trying to propagandize sexual relations between siblings, men and animals, and men and men. We National Socialists [Nazis] will soon unmask and condemn them by law. (Rosenberg 1930: 13)

Heinrich Himmler, the chief of the Gestapo (the German secret police) and architect of its anti-homosexual campaign, stated in a speech in 1936:

> As National Socialists we are not afraid to fight against this plague within our own ranks. Just as we have readopted the ancient Germanic approach to the question of marriage between alien races, so too, in our judgment of homosexuality — a symptom of racial degeneracy destructive to our race — we have returned to the guiding Nordic principle that degenerates would be exterminated. Germany stands or falls with the purity of its race. (Wilde 1969: 36)

Himmler felt that male homosexuals corrupted what he termed "normal" men. He also warned that homosexuals, whom he considered to be effeminate, lacked the strength and will to be good soldiers: "All homosexuals are cowards; they lie just like Jesuits. Homosexuality leads to a state of mind that doesn't know what it does" (Plant 1986: 89). Benito Mussolini, the Fascist premier of Italy, reportedly told Himmler that there were no homosexuals in Italy, because "Italian men are too masculine." Between 1943 and 1945, however, men who were alleged to be homosexuals were incarcerated in Italian penal colonies. An explicit connection between Jews and homosexuals was made by Hitler, who theorized that homosexuality was caused by having "Jewish blood," meaning that somewhere on the homosexual's family tree one would find a Jewish ancestor.

Abuse and "Recruitment" of Children

A crucial point in the psychology of scapegoating is the representation of minorities as, in John Boswell's words, "animals bent on the destruction of the children of the majority" (Boswell 1980: 16), and, accordingly, both Jews and LGBTs have long been accused of being dangerous to children. Jews, in the so-called "blood libel" of the Middle Ages, were accused of killing Christian children and using their blood to make matzos, and lesbians, gays, and bisexuals are seen today as child abusers, who molest and recruit youths into their so-called "deviant lifestyle" (Johnson 1987: 208–10).

The "blood libel" originated in Norwich, England in the year 1144, when a priest and the mother of a young boy accused Jews of stabbing the boy to death. Christian maidservants who worked in a Jewish household embellished the myth, stating that just before Passover, they had witnessed Jews abducting the boy, gagging him, tying him with cords, piercing his head with thorns, and finally binding him as if on a cross (Ben-Sasson 1976: 482). This supposed ritual murder of a Christ-substitute at Easter was explained by the premise that Jews knew the truth of Christianity but rejected it. Stories spread that Jews killed Christian children, draining their blood to make the sacred matzos that cured them of bodily maladies, such as hemorrhoids, and to restore the blood that Jewish men supposedly lost in menstruation. Jews were also accused of inflicting circumcision on Christian infants as a means of involuntarily converting them to Judaism (Johnson 1987: 209–11). The blood libel and other allegations of ritual murder continued into the twentieth century. Jews have also been accused of "promoting" unhealthy sexuality in their own children by encouraging, at various points in their history, marriages between people in their middle teen years, and by supposedly maintaining a closed society, which allegedly led to incest.

Although, in the overwhelming majority of cases, child abuse and molestation is committed by heterosexual men — a recent study found that a child is one hundred times more likely to be molested by a heterosexual than by a homosexual (Jenny, Roesler, and Poyer 1994) — the cultural perception persists that primarily gay men — and, by association, lesbians and bisexuals — attack young children. For example, Lou Sheldon of the Traditional Values Coalition was able to foment hostility toward LGBTs by writing: "Gays and lesbians live perverted, twisted lives that feed upon the unsuspecting and the innocent, like our children." And in an April 1991 fundraising letter, he wrote: "[Homosexuals] want your children" (Cantor 1994: 110). According to this myth, since gays purportedly cannot reproduce, they need to recruit "innocent victims" into their "lifestyle." This stereotype has been validated institutionally. Several states explicitly ban lesbians, gays, and bisexuals from adopting children or serving as foster parents, while all but three states discriminate against lesbians, gays, and bisexuals through policies that deny jointly same-sex couples the right to adopt. The 1992 Republican Party platform openly endorsed this form of oppression, stating that the party "oppose[s] any legislation or law which legally recognizes same-sex marriages and allows such couples to adopt children or provide foster care." The repercussions of such prejudice are readily apparent: a poll conducted by *Newsweek* magazine in 1992 found that 46 percent of those surveyed believed that gays and lesbians should not be hired as high school teachers, and 49 percent felt that they should not be hired as elementary school teachers (Turque, Cohn, and Clift 1994). Thus the belief still remains widespread that LGBTs must be kept away from young, "impressionable" children and youths.

Domination and Destruction of "Civilized" Society

While the dominant society has frequently been concerned that Jews and people attracted to others of the same sex can "pass" without detection into the mainstream, they have also historically portrayed these groups as destroyers of society. During the Middle Ages, for example, Jews were characterized as having tails concealed beneath their garments and a peculiar smell. This led to reports that they were in the service of the Devil. The "Judensau," an anti-Jewish motif that was used in medieval texts and even carved on a number of churches in Central Europe, depicted a Jew sexually entwined with a pig, sucking the sow's utter and eating and drinking its excrement. Furthermore, a thirteenth-century law endorsed the idea that Jews were less than human by explicitly stating that Christians who had sex with Jews were the same as Christians who had sex with animals. The ravages of the Black Death throughout Europe, which wiped out an estimated one-fourth to one-half of the population in the twelfth and thirteenth centuries, were also blamed on Jews, who were accused of poisoning drinking wells (Johnson 1987: 216–17).

Jews have been charged with transmitting other diseases as well, most notably syphilis, which was called "the Jewish disease" throughout Europe in the nineteenth century, even though the incidence of syphilis within the Jewish community had been no higher than in the larger population. Medical literature of the time alleged that syphilis was spread to newly circumcised Jewish infants through the practice of *metsitsah*, the sucking on the penis by the *mohel* (the ritual circumciser) to stop the bleeding. Fellatio thus became not only a marker of "perversion" but also a sign of the Jewish transmission of disease (Gilman 1991: 93–94).

Those engaging in same-sex eroticism were likewise viewed as working in league with the Devil and were accused of bringing evils into the world. In 538, for example, the Roman emperor Justinian issued a law which declared that, due to the crime of men having sex with other men, "there are famines, earthquakes, and pestilences; wherefore we admonish men to abstain from the aforesaid unlawful acts, that they may not lose their souls" (Bailey 1955: 73). Six years later, following a devastating plague in Constantinople, Justinian demanded that his citizenry resist evil temptation, particularly same-sex acts, "that abominable and impious conduct deservedly hated by God" and warned, "If, with eyes as it were blinded, we overlook such impious and forbidden conduct, we may provoke the good God to anger and bring ruin upon all — a fate which would be but deserved" (Bailey 1955: 74–75).

In more contemporary times, the 1940 Nazi propaganda film *The Eternal Jew* and the 1992 U.S. Radical Right propaganda film *The Gay Agenda* portray Jews and LGBTs, respectively, as spreading infection and degeneracy, which, if allowed to continue, would result in the eventual collapse of civilization and its institutions. In *The Eternal Jew*, Jews are said to commit 47 percent of all robberies and to make up 98 percent of those involved in prostitution. "The Jews," according to the film's narrator, "are only 1 percent of the population," but they know how to "terrorize a great, tolerant nation" by controlling finance, the arts, education, and the media. In *The Gay Agenda*, 17 percent of gays are said to consume human feces for erotic thrills, and 28 are said to engage in sodomy with more than one thousand partners, thereby spreading diseases that imperil the entire society (Solomon 1993: 29). Although AIDS existed in epidemic proportions among *heterosexual* populations in parts of the African continent prior to its entry into many Western countries, the blame for it has come to rest on gay and bisexual men. In fact, medical researchers in the United States initially gave it the name Gay-Related Immune Deficiency (GRID) but soon changed it to Acquired Immune Deficiency

Syndrome following objections from activists, who argued against naming a syndrome of unknown origins after an already stigmatized group.

On the one hand, Jews and LGBTs have been characterized as "super capitalists" whose inordinate wealth enables them to manipulate banking systems and to control politicians and the media through well-financed lobbying campaigns. Both are perceived as a "privileged class," highly educated and disproportionately represented in the "cultural elite" (Solomon 1993: 29). On the other hand, though, they are seen as radicals attempting to overthrow the capitalist system and the dominant culture. During the "McCarthy Era," for example, a number of Congressional legislators declared that Communists (associated in the public mind at the time with Jews) corrupted the minds, and homosexuals corrupted the bodies, of good, "upstanding Americans," and therefore both had to be purged from the government (D'Emilio 1983: 48).

Jews, who were excluded from land owning and from most professions during the Middle Ages, increasingly became moneylenders, especially since the Catholic Church forbade Christians from practicing usury. Functioning at times as royal moneylenders and tax collectors, Jews began to be scapegoated by local princes as alien "bloodsuckers" and to be despised by the populace. Even the yellow badges that were used to mark Jews in the Middle Ages and in Hitler's Germany represented the Jews' alleged relationship with wealth (gold), and for Christians recalled Judas's betrayal of Christ for money. By the fourteenth century, usury and sodomy incurred severe penalties in canon (church) law, and both were excoriated in exactly the same terms, equated explicitly with sins against nature's law and "unnatural" deviant sexuality. The sexual aspect of sodomy is clear, but usury was also framed in sexual terms, because it was seen as making money unnaturally. "They do not plough, harrow, or sow," wrote an Italian physician in 1700, "but they always reap" (Ramazzini 1964: 287). Jews taking money was likened to prostitution, a degradation of the higher values of love and beauty. According to Sander Gilman, in his book *The Jews' Body*, "the Jew becomes the representative of the deviant genitalia, the genitalia not under the control of the moral, rational conscience" (Gilman 1991: 124).

The stereotype of Jews as obsessed with money and power persisted into the modern era. First appearing around 1895 in Europe, the infamous *Protocols of the Elders of Zion*, a pamphlet attributed to members of the czarist secret police, was circulated to convince the Russian people that those who favored a revolution were actually plotting to impose a Jewish government, on their way toward eventual worldwide domination. At the other end of the political spectrum, Karl Marx, a Jewish anti-Semite, wrote of Jews:

> What is the worldly cult of the Jew? *Huckstering*. What is his worldly God? *Money* . . . Money is the universal and self-sufficient *value* of all things. It has, therefore, deprived the whole world, both the human world and nature, of their own proper value. (1963: 34, 37)

In the 1920s, automotive pioneer Henry Ford, Sr. encouraged the notion that Jews controlled finance and introduced *The Protocols* to a large American audience through his newspaper, *The Dearborn Independent*, and through a series of pamphlets, which together formed his book *The International Jew: The World's Foremost Problem*. In 1938, Hitler presented Ford with the highest award given to a non-German, and at the

Nuremberg tribunal following World War II, Baldur von Shirach, Hitler's youth leader, asserted that he had become "Jew-wise" through reading Ford's writings (Dinnerstein 1994: 82–83).

The theocratic Right in this country today is similarly portraying lesbians, gays, and bisexuals as a privileged, controlling class, making it the cornerstone of their vicious assault on the civil rights of LGBT people. For example, Beverly LaHaye of the right-wing group Concerned Women for America argues that "[homosexuals] are aided in the implementation of their hidden agenda by powerful allies in government, education, entertainment, and the media," while the film *Gay Rights/Special Rights* misrepresents gays as having average incomes of $55,000 — far in excess of the national average. Likewise, Lou Sheldon states that gays have an average income which is $23,000 *higher* than that of heterosexuals and that this fact serves as clear proof that they do not suffer from discrimination but are, instead, a highly powerful group in a position to undermine the moral fiber of the country (Solomon 1993: 29). These income figures are taken from surveys conducted by Simmons Market Research Bureau and Overlooked Opinions, both of whom polled unrepresentative samples of LGBT people. The apparent economic advantage evaporates when we look at data from a nationally representative sample developed by the National Opinion Research Center at the University of Chicago, which concluded that, after differences in education, age, and other factors were taken into account, "behaviorally gay/bisexual men earned 11 percent to 27 percent less than similar heterosexual men. Behaviorally lesbian/bisexual women earned 5 percent to 14 percent less than similar heterosexual women." This study aside, even if LGBTs *did* earn more on average than heterosexuals, Sheldon, LaHaye, and other right-wing ideologues would be ignoring the magnitude of oppression, for the denial of equality and dignity are not simply matters of economics. Moreover, it is no coincidence that the Right is using its "No Special Rights for Gays and Lesbians" campaign as a scapegoating tactic at a time of economic uncertainty.

In "Common Ground and Strategies," the keynote address at the Colorado for Family Values Conference in 1994, John Eldridge, the director of Seminar Research and Public Policy for the right-wing group Focus on the Family, depicted LGBTs as a faceless enemy who would eventually, if not stopped, bring about the destruction of civilized society:

> I think the gay agenda has all the elements of that which is truly evil. . . . It presents an extraordinarily deceptive face to the public at large. This is one of the primary marks of something which is truly evil, because while it is offering all of the pleasures and liberties of happiness and autonomy and personal fulfillment, it is destroying the souls and the lives of those who embrace it, and it has a corrosive effect on the society which endorses it, either explicitly or even implicitly. (Eldridge 1994)

Pat Robertson, founder of the Christian Coalition and the ironically named American Center for Law and Justice, added feminists to this conspiratorial plot. In a letter sent to Iowa Republicans urging them to oppose the state's proposed Equal Rights Amendment in 1992, he stated: "The Feminist agenda is not about equal rights for women. It is about a socialist, anti-family political movement that encourages women to leave their husbands, kill their children, practice witchcraft, destroy capitalism, and become lesbians." Largely due to such rhetoric, Iowa's Equal Rights Amendment failed to pass. A number of theocratic right-wing groups have also succeeded in placing on the ballot in state and local elections initiatives that restrict the rights of LGBT people, including the infamous "Amendment 2," which was passed by 53 percent of Colorado voters in 1992.

Jews have likewise been targeted legislatively. During the nineteenth century, for example, lawmakers in the U.S. House of Representatives attempted to pass a constitutional amendment acknowledging the supremacy of Christianity. Though eventually killed in the 1870s, the proposed amendment was a reaction against perceived Jewish social and economic gains up to that time (Dinnerstein 1994: 38).

Currently, the theocratic Right is attempting to drive a deep wedge between traditionally disenfranchised groups in the U.S., pitting one group against another in order to build its power base and undermine past gains in *all* areas of civil rights. Using anti-gay rhetoric as its centerpiece, the far Right has launched massive *recruitment* efforts in communities of color and even in Jewish communities — an outreach effort that is insidiously ironic given that these same right-wing organizations have consistently opposed virtually every civil rights initiative in this country. A recent attempt to impair alliances between Jews and LGBTs was made by Scott Lively, the membership director of the Oregon Citizens' Alliance, a theocratic right-wing group that is attempting to restrict LGBT rights in that state. In his video, *The Homosexual and the Nazi Party*, Lively reconstructs history:

> It wasn't just that homosexuals were involved in the Nazi party. Homosexuals created the Nazi party, and everything that we think about when we think of Nazis is actually comes [sic] from the minds and the perverted idea of homosexuals. . . . When you think about the Nazi party . . . you cannot help but to understand that this organization was a machine that was constructed by militant, sadomasochistic, pedophilic homosexuals.

Lively even alleges that Hitler was bisexual, supposedly having sex in prison with Rudolph Hess, who, according to Lively, was "a known homosexual."

The victims of Nazi persecution thus become the perpetrators in Lively's libelous scenario. For example, according to Lively, books and records of the Institute for Sexual Science were burned by *homosexual* Nazi storm troopers, who feared that their own case studies would be discovered. He also argues that Hitler placed "militant, sadomasochistic, pedophilic homosexuals" in charge of the concentration camps. Without providing any real evidence, he states that some of the most vicious offenses against women inmates were perpetrated by lesbian guards, and that the supposedly few male homosexuals who were put into the camps were the feminized ones, who were sexually tortured to death by butch homosexual guards.

Lively then makes direct links between these allegedly homosexual Nazis and the United States gay rights movement. Henry Gerber, a German-American who served in the U.S. army in Germany after World War I, and who was one of the founders of the first homosexual emancipation organization in the U.S., was influenced, according to

Lively, by his association with Nazi homosexuals. Lively also alleges that another of the group's co-founders, Champ Simmons, sexually seduced a seventeen-year-old, Harry Hay, who would later found the Mattachine Society, an organization which helped establish the modern gay rights movement. Lively's representations are quite clear: lesbians and gays were the Nazis then, and we are the Nazis now; and if we were to have our civil rights — if we were to achieve institutional and societal equality — the United States would become like Nazi Germany.[4]

Conclusion

So, now that the links between the hatred of Jews and LGBTs have been identified, where do we go from here? As the theocratic Right spreads its lies and dehumanizing representations of LGBT people, we can expose these clear connections for all to see and can relate homophobia to anti-Semitism, thus potentially defusing both. And we can continue to show the links between seemingly disparate forms of oppression as a way of bringing people of various social identities together.

A central tenet of Jewish tradition is *tikkun olam*: the transformation, healing, and repairing of the world so that it becomes a more just, peaceful, and nurturing place. In the final analysis, we are most certainly all in this together. We cannot allow the theocratic Right to revise history and to frame the terms of the debate. I say, then, let us go out and work together for tikkun. Let us transform the world.

NOTES

1. All scriptural quotations are from the *New English Bible* (1976).

2. My thanks to Paul B. Franklin for suggesting to me the idea of an immature developmental stage as one of the disparaging characterizations used to belittle Judaism.

3. In fact, the term "homosexual" was coined by Károly Mária Benkert (under the pseudonym Karl Maria Kertbeny) in 1869, just ten years before another German, Wilhelm Marr, introduced the term "anti-Semitism."

4. To further tarnish homosexuality, Lively attempts to discredit the word "Urning," a term coined by Karl Heinrich Ulrichs in 1862 to describe those sexually attracted to their own sex. Noting that it was taken from Plato's *Symposium*, Lively argues that "Plato was also a homosexual pedophile." Here, Lively tips his hand and exposes the true "agenda" of the Right. In attacking Plato, he criticizes ancient Greek culture by implication, the same culture which introduced the Western world to the concept of "democracy" — a political philosophy which is in direct opposition to the theocratic Right's aim of ultimately instituting their own religious form of government.

REFERENCES

Bailey, Derrick Sherwin. 1955. *Homosexuality and the Western Christian Tradition*. London: Longmans, Green.

Ben-Sasson, H. H., ed. 1976. *A History of the Jewish People*. Cambridge: Harvard University Press.

Bérubé, Allan. 1990. *Coming Out under Fire: The History of Gay Men and Women in World War Two*. New York: Plume.

Blumenfeld, Warren J. 1992. A Letter to My Great-Grandfather on Being Jewish and Gay. *Empathy* 3(1): 83–86.

Boswell, John. 1980. *Christianity, Social Tolerance, and Homosexuality: Gay People in Western Europe from the Beginning of the Christian Era to the Fourteenth Century.* Chicago: University of Chicago Press.

Cantor, David. 1994. *The Religious Right: The Assault on Tolerance and Pluralism in America.* New York: Anti-Defamation League.

D'Emilio, John. 1983. *Sexual Politics, Sexual Communities: The Making of a Homosexual Minority in the United States, 1940–1970.* Chicago: University of Chicago Press.

Dinnerstein, Leonard. 1994. *Anti-Semitism in America.* New York: Oxford University Press.

Eldridge, John. 1994. Common Ground and Strategies. Keynote address presented at the Colorado for Family Values Conference, Colorado Springs, Colorado. Transcribed from recorded tape.

Forel, Auguste. [1906] 1924. *The Sexual Question: A Scientific, Psychological, Hygienic, and Sociological Study.* New York: Physicians and Surgeons Book Company.

Gilman, Sander L. 1991. *The Jew's Body.* New York: Routledge.

Goitein, S. D. 1971. *A Mediterranean Society: The Jewish Communities of the Arab World as Portrayed in the Documents of the Cairo Geniza.* Vol. 2, *The Community.* Berkeley: University of California Press.

Grayzel, Solomon. 1966. *The Church and the Jews in the Thirteenth Century.* Trans. Constantine Fitzgibbon and James Oliver. New York: Hermon Press.

Hamilton, Allan McLane. 1896. The Civil Responsibility of Sexual Perverts. *American Journal of Insanity* 52 (April): 503–9.

Isaacs, Raphael. 1940. The So-Called Jewish Type. *Medical Leaves* 3: 119.

Jenny, Carole, Thomas A. Roesler, and Kimberly L. Poyer. 1994. Are Children at Risk for Sexual Abuse by Homosexuals? *Pediatrics* 94 (July): 41–46.

Johnson, Paul. 1987. *A History of the Jews.* New York: Harper and Row.

Kersten, Felix. 1957. *The Kersten Memoirs, 1940–1945.* New York: Macmillan.

Knox, Robert. 1850. *The Races of Men: A Fragment.* Philadelphia: Lea and Blanchard.

Kolb, Erwin J. 1984. *How to Respond to Judaism.* St. Louis: Concordia Publishing House.

Krafft-Ebing, Richard von. 1886. *Psychopathia Sexualis: Eine klinisch-forensische Studie.* Stuttgart: Ferdinand Enke.

Luther, Martin. [1526] 1936. Von den Juden und Ihren Lugen (On the Jews and Their Lies). In *Luthers Kampfschriften gegen das Judentum.* Ed. Walther Linden. Berlin: Klinkhardt and Biermann.

Marx, Karl. 1963. *Karl Marx: Early Writings.* Ed. and trans. T. B. Bottomore. London: C. A. Watts.

Meeks, Wayne A., and Robert L. Wilken. 1978. *Jews and Christians in Antioch in the First Four Centuries of the Common Era.* Missoula, MT: Scholars Press.

New English Bible. 1976. Oxford Study Edition. New York: Oxford University Press.

Plant, Richard. 1986. *The Pink Triangle: The Nazi War against Homosexuals.* New York: Henry Holt and Company.

Ramazzini, Bernardino. 1964. *The Diseases of Workers.* Trans. Wilmer Cave Wright. New York: Hafner.

Roehr, Bob. 1994. Hope, Fear, and Loathing: Landmark ENDA Hearings in U.S. Senate. *Newsweekly* (August 7): 10.

Rosenberg, Alfred. 1930. *Volkischer Beobachter* (August 2): 13.

Solomon, Alisa. 1993. The Eternal Queer: In the Symbolic Landscape of Homophobia, We Are the Jews. *Village Voice* (April 27): 29, 34.

Tardieu, Ambroise. 1857. *Étude médico-legale sur les attentats aux moeurs*. Paris: J.B. Baillière.

Turque, Bill, Bob Cohn, and Eleanor Clift. 1992. Gays under Fire. *Newsweek* 120 (September 14): 34–40.

Ulrichs, Karl Heinrich. 1864. *Vindex* and *Inclusa*. Offenbach am Main.

Wilde, Harry. 1969. *Das Schicksal der Verfamten*. Tübingen: Katzmann.

QUEER THEORY IN PRACTICE

In editing this anthology, we have tried to select essays which can facilitate a better understanding of theory and make it accessible to a wider audience. Too much of what passes for queer theory today, like other types of academic theory, gets mired in academic jargon that largely prevents it from being read or discussed by people without several advanced degrees. Even more damaging is the fact that such highly theoretical material alienates some lesbian, gay, bisexual, and transgendered people from queer theory, even though they could potentially benefit from a better understanding of this theory and the ways in which it challenges dominant heterosexist paradigms. Although it is true that obtaining university positions and tenure may rely upon producing jargonistic, inaccessible prose, we nonetheless believe that those of us privileged to work in higher education have a responsibility to the communities that support and nurture us. This includes translating our work for general consumption; texts in queer theory, and in queer studies in general, should not be reserved for a few theorists but made available to a wide range of queer people and queer communities.

Queer theorists have to remember that many readers or potential readers are puzzled over what constitutes queer theory and how it differs from queer studies or lesbian, gay, and bisexual studies. This fact should not be surprising, since work that is labeled queer theory comes from a variety of academic disciplines, such as history, sociology, and literature, and there are no clear boundaries between queer theory, queer studies, and lesbian, gay, and bisexual studies. One of the earliest uses of the term "queer theory" was in a special issue of the journal *differences*, edited by Teresa de Lauretis, which was entitled "Queer Theory: Lesbian and Gay Sexualities." In the introduction, de Lauretis discusses the history of queer scholarship, tracing the different paths that theory took in the 1970s and 1980s when women experienced sexism in the male-dominated gay movement and people of color experienced racism in predominantly white lesbian and gay communities. She proposes that the term "queer theory" is a way to repair such rifts and to "transgress and transcend" the fine lines of distinction within these communities.[1] Although never clearly defining queer theory, she does characterize its boundaries and social locations as follows:

> Thus, rather than marking the limits of the social space by designating a place at the edge of culture, gay sexuality in its specific female and male cultural (or subcultural) forms acts as an agency of social process whose mode of functioning is both interactive and yet resistant, both participatory and yet distinct, claiming at once equality and difference, demanding political representation while insisting on its material and historical specificity.[2]

Interestingly enough, this definition is built on the very dualisms that much of queer theory purports to disrupt or dismantle (female and male, equality and difference), and de Lauretis never provides evidence to prove that queer theory actually does transcend lines of difference. For instance, how does queer theory address issues of racial and gender oppression?

In his anthology *Fear of a Queer Planet: Queer Politics and Social Theory*, Michael Warner simply defines queer theory as "elaborating, in ways that cannot be predicted in advance, this question: What do queers want?"[3] It appears from this definition that queer theory is almost anything and everything that the author wants it to be. How, for example, does it differ from lesbian, gay, and bisexual studies?

Henry Abelove, Michèle Aina Barale, and David Halperin choose to title their anthology The *Lesbian and Gay Studies Reader* (emphasis in the original), rather than calling it A *Queer Studies Reader*, because

> The forms of study whose institutionalization we seek to further have tended, so far at least, to go by the names of "lesbian" and "gay." The field designated by them has become a site for inquiry into many kinds of sexual non-conformity, including, for instance, bisexuality, trans-sexualism [sic], and sadomasochism. Moreover, the names "lesbian" and "gay" are probably more widely preferred than is the name "queer." And the names "lesbian" and "gay" are not assimilationist. Just as the project of seeking legitimate institutional and intellectual space for lesbian/gay studies need not render less forceful its challenge to the scholarly and critical *status quo*, so our choice of "lesbian/gay" indicates no wish on our part to make lesbian/gay studies look less assertive, less unsettling, and less queer than it already does.[4]

Many people who identify as bisexual or transgendered or who practice s/m may feel marginalized or excluded by this branding of their identities as "sexual non-conformity," in contrast to the "legitimate" identities of lesbians and gays. Others would argue that the terms "lesbian" and "gay" have indeed become assimilated into the academy, if not into the larger society, so that they have lost their critical edge.

This anthology explores some of the conflicting definitions of "queer theory." But whatever we choose to call the body of work that critiques and expands our knowledge about sexuality, there are some inherent dangers in this theory-making process. First, what passes for queer theory has often been formulated by a largely white, male-dominated academy, resulting in the reproduction of some of the same flaws that have undermined previous forms of academic theory. For example, in spite of its claims to be radical thought, queer theory often accepts a binary gender system, thereby treating bisexual and transgender identities as irrelevant or nonexistent, and frequently assumes a "white" racial norm. Moreover, Sheila Jeffreys notes that queer theory "disappears" lesbians by its emphasis on gay male sexual and cultural practices like drag, camp, and leather sexuality. She is particularly concerned with queer theory's "feminist-free" attitude, which disregards lesbian feminist work of the past twenty years.[5]

Another danger lies in the rooting of much of queer theory in postmodernism, which has the power to deny the real-life experiences of people who are already largely excluded, marginalized, or ignored by contemporary theorizing.[6] Steven Seidman sees postmodernism as "a broad cultural and intellectual standpoint that views science, and all claims to knowledge, as moral and social forces and that is suspicious of systematizing, theory-building projects" — a definition which has much in common with lesbian feminism and the beliefs of early gay liberationists. However, Seidman goes on to say:

> I view postmodernism as speaking of multiple, local, intersecting struggles whose aim is less "the end [of] domination" or "human liberation" than the creation of social spaces that encourage the proliferation of pleasures, desires, voices, interests, modes of individuation and democratization.[7]

At this point, the definition departs significantly from lesbian feminism and radical gay politics, as it replaces the struggle for liberation with the pursuit of pleasure. Lesbian feminists in particular have often resisted the emergence of this kind of theory in the academy. As Susan Wolfe and Julia Penelope argue, "In one hundred short years, German sexologists have 'appeared' Lesbians in order to pathologize us and French poststructuralists have 'disappeared' us in order to deconstruct sex and gender categories and to 'interrogate' 'the' subject."[8]

Postmodern theory does take the important step of considering identity as a social construction, but, as Ki Namaste discusses in reference to transgendered people, it still often shows very little concern for real-life experiences, including the harassment and discrimination faced by queer people. It is perhaps no coincidence that postmodern theory, which denies the reality of identity markers like gender, race, and sexuality, should emerge at the historic moment when the voices of previously marginalized groups are beginning to have some impact on the academy.[9] Could postmodernism simply be a backlash against the rising tide of scholarship by people of color, feminists, and LesBiGayTrans people?

If queer theory has so many problems, is it even worth our time and energy to understand it? Can it have any possible benefits? One important aspect of queer theory is that it allows us to view the world from perspectives other than those which are generally validated by the dominant society; we can put a queer slant, for example, on literature, movies, television news reports, and current events. Such queer(ed) positions can challenge the dominance of heterosexist discourses. In addition, queer theory has the *potential* to be inclusive of race, gender, sexuality, and other areas of identity by calling attention to the distinctions between identities, communities, and cultures, rather than ignoring these differences or pretending that they don't exist, as it often does now.

Queer theory, for instance, could be used to address the links between different forms of oppression and to develop coalition-building strategies. By including the voices of people whose lived experiences involve non-normative race, gender, and sexual identities/ practices, queer theory can stretch the limits of current thought and possibly revolutionize it.

The works in this section of the anthology all apply, expand, or critique queer theory. In the first essay, Ruth Goldman searches for her queer self within existing queer theory and discovers that this theory often ignores or marginalizes her experiences and the complexities of being queer. She concludes that queer theory must develop a framework that challenges not only heterosexism and homophobia but also racism, misogyny, and other oppressive discourses/norms. Analyzing a performance by Madonna, Goldman shows how queer theory can be used more inclusively and effectively by addressing the intersections of race, gender, and sexuality within a text.

Ki Namaste considers the treatment of the transgendered subject within queer theory and finds that transgendered people are objects of study rather than voices of authority. For example, theories of "gender play" trivialize the lives of people who are not playing with gender, who experience it, rather, as a fundamental aspect of their identities. Namaste suggests that transgendered people are accepted in queer communities only at the level of entertainment; they are not seen as possessing legitimate social identities.

Amber Ault shows how lesbian feminist theorizing has often erased and denigrated bisexual women in the same ways that the dominant discourse has marginalized and condemned lesbians. Because bisexuality is perceived as a challenge to separatist theories and movement politics, some lesbian feminists employ what Ault calls "techniques of neutralization" against bisexual women, including suppression, incorporation, marginalization, and delegitimation.

Christopher James discusses how bisexuality frequently serves as a "structuring silence" within existing forms of queer theory and argues that this omission must be rectified if we are to begin to develop more viable theories of sexuality. Conceptualizing bisexuality as a valid sexual category could allow theorists to understand the role of compulsory monosexuality in heterosexism, to move beyond dichotomous thinking, and to avoid appropriating historical figures or texts that may be better understood from bisexual perspectives.

Siobhan Somerville examines medical and psychological literature to pinpoint the emergence of racism and heterosexism within "science" — prejudices which continue to undermine studies of lesbian, gay, bisexual, and transgendered people. Specifically, she surveys racial and sexual classification systems, asking the question "Is it merely a historical coincidence that the classification of bodies as either 'homosexual' or 'heterosexual' emerged at the same time that the United States was aggressively policing the imaginary boundary between 'black' and 'white' bodies?" Her analysis suggests that it was not by chance that the medical discourses on race and sexuality have continually overlapped and intersected throughout history.

Lynda Goldstein focuses on the contradictory nature of MTV for queer subjectivity. She argues that MTV's eclectic programming, particularly its dance music videos and participatory non-musical shows, enables viewers to perform different gender/race/class/ sexual identities. The use of various forms of drag in music videos, for example, provides audiences with the means to question categories of sexuality and to vicariously experience the embodiment of queerness. Yet Goldstein demonstrates that MTV ultimately contains the queer(ed) subject within the "video closet" by recirculating "queer" as simply a style to be tried on and discarded, like this year's fashions.

Tracy Morgan examines one particular aspect of queer history: the publication of male physique magazines, the first gay print medium to develop in the U.S. She critiques the lack of attention paid to African American queer identities in these magazines, where the bodies of men of color were often nonexistent or appeared in ways that perpetuated racial stereotypes. Such instances of racism need to be acknowledged and discussed if we are to create theories that are inclusive and non-oppressive.

Finally, Lee Badgett sets a very different tone for queer theory. In her essay, she explores the decision-making process by which lesbians, gays, and bisexuals come out or remain closeted in the workplace. Her economically based model considers the factors that lead to disclosure, offering a practical application of queer theory to everyday life. Thus far, queer theory has had little impact upon disciplines outside of the arts and humanities; Badgett's work is an example of how it can be applied to economics.

Despite their different approaches and topics, all of the authors contribute to queer theory by stretching it, remolding it, or pointing out its weaknesses, in order to make it more applicable to their academic disciplines and/or lived experiences. They demonstrate both the problems within current queer theory and its potentials for further devlopment.

NOTES

1. Teresa de Lauretis, "Queer Theory: Lesbian and Gay Sexualities. An Introduction," *differences: A Journal of Feminist Cultural Studies* 3 (Summer 1991): v.

2. Ibid., iii.

3. Michael Warner, ed., *Fear of a Queer Planet: Queer Politics and Social Theory* (Minneapolis: University of Minnesota Press, 1993), vii.

4. Henry Abelove, Michèle Aina Barale, and David M. Halperin, eds., The *Lesbian and Gay Studies Reader* (New York: Routledge, 1993), xvii.

5. Sheila Jeffreys, "The Queer Disappearance of Lesbians: Sexuality in the Academy," *Women's Studies International Forum* 17 (1994): 459.

6. Somer Brodribb, *Nothing Mat(t)ers: A Feminist Critique of Postmodernism* (New York: New York University Press, 1992).

7. Steven Seidman, "Identity and Politics in a 'Postmodern' Gay Culture: Some Historical and Conceptual Notes," *Fear of a Queer Planet*, 106.

8. Susan J. Wolfe and Julia Penelope, "Sexual Identity/Textual Politics: Lesbian {De/Com}positions," *Sexual Practice, Textual Theory: Lesbian Cultural Criticism*, ed. Susan J. Wolfe and Julia Penelope (Cambridge, MA: Blackwell, 1993), 1.

9. Ibid., 5. bell hooks and Barbara Christian have also criticized academic theory for its elitist, white, male-dominated perspective, although hooks sees potentials in postmodernism for

theorizing multiple, diverse African American identities. See bell hooks, "Postmodern Blackness," *Yearning: Race, Gender, and Cultural Politics* (Boston: South End Press, 1990), 23–31; and Barbara Christian, "The Race for Theory," *Making Face, Making Soul/Haciendo Caras: Creative and Critical Perspectives by Women of Color,* ed. Gloria Anzaldúa (San Francisco: Aunt Lute, 1990), 335–45.

Who Is That *Queer* Queer?

Exploring Norms around

Sexuality, Race, and Class

in Queer Theory

Ruth Goldman

Several years ago, when I came across the term "queer theory," I thought I had finally found my academic home, a theoretical space in which my voice would be welcome. Because I understood the term "queer" to represent any number of intersecting anti-normative identities, I expected queer theory to provide an appropriate framework in which to continue my explorations of the intersections between representations of race, sexuality, and gender (with an emphasis on bisexuality) in popular culture. However, I found that it was very difficult to apply existing queer theory to popular culture without collapsing some of the very nuances that I was trying to highlight. This led me to begin to consider some of the existing tensions and contradictions within and without queer theory, and in this article, I intend to explore the roots of some of these tensions and contradictions as well as to suggest some possible resolutions.[1] I am particularly interested in examining the ways in which rhetoric operates to produce a normative discourse within queer theory, which in turn serves to limit, in the words of Gloria Anzaldúa, "the ways in which we think about being queer."[2]

Although queer theory scholars have taken great pains to differentiate their work from lesbian and gay studies, lesbian and gay studies is now often referred to as queer studies (in order, theoretically, to make space for diversity), and both of these fields are frequently conflated with queer theory. But, while lesbian and gay studies and queer studies are primarily concerned with documenting past and current manifestations and implications of same-sex attractions, queer theory operates from the perspective that heterosexuality, or "normative" sexuality, could not exist without queer, or "anti-normative," sexualities. That is, that which is not normal works to define the normal. The fact that such very different approaches to scholarship are often lumped into the same category indicates that queer theory has many, sometimes conflicting, interpretations. To some people, queer theory represents simply another nebulous, abstract form of academic discourse, understood only through the signifier of "queer": a complex term which itself allows for many, sometimes contradictory, interpretations. Thus, depending on one's position and knowledge, queer theory lends itself to a variety of definitions, including: a theoretical perspective from which to challenge the normative; another term for lesbian and gay studies; another term for queer studies; a theory about queerness and queers (intentionally vague); another way that queer academics waste their time and taxpayers' money; or, at worst, judging simply from article titles like Eve Sedgwick's, "How to Bring Your Kids Up Gay," a plot by sexually perverted academics to recruit and indoctrinate unsuspecting young undergraduates.

In order to explore and clarify some of the conflicting ideas associated with queer theory, I decided to turn to the theory itself. I chose to examine a number of articles that address the subject of queer theory, as well as several articles and books that claim to be applying queer theory to various topics. I was interested in looking at both early and ongoing goals of queer theory, which include a strong commitment to creating/maintaining a theoretical space for polyphonic and diverse discourses that challenge heteronormativity.

At the core of any discussion of queer theory lies the question of rhetoric: the significance of the term "queer." Although queer theorists distanced themselves from the queer power movement, specifically Queer Nation, from the start,[3] I will be considering the evolution of the term "queer" along with the evolution of the field of queer theory, because of the way in which the two are inextricably linked in so many people's minds.

The term "queer" emphasizes the blurring of identities, and as a young bisexual activist who had encountered a great deal of resistance to the concept of bisexuality within lesbian and gay communities, it didn't take me long to embrace all that I perceived "queer" as representing. In fact, the queer movement/community was founded on principles of inclusivity and flexibility, summed up quite nicely by Elisabeth Daümer: "In the queer universe, to be queer implies that not everybody is queer in the same way. It implies a willingness to articulate their own queerness."[4]

As Daümer indicates, the signifier "queer" goes further than simply signaling an alternative sexuality; it offers a way in which to express many intersecting queer selves — in my case, to name just a few, as a bisexual,[5] a Jew, a feminist, an anti-capitalist, an anti-racist — all of which stand in opposition to powerful societal norms. And finally, as a strident reminder of difference, perversity, and a willingness to position oneself outside of the norm, the term "queer" simply makes many people uncomfortable. It is something most often uttered behind people's backs or yelled out of car windows, and thus its recuperative powers cannot be underestimated.

According to Jeffrey Escoffier, "Queer politics offers a way of cutting across race and gender lines. It implies the rejection of a minoritarian logic of toleration or simple interest-representation. Instead, queer politics represents an expansive impulse of inclusion; specifically, it requires a resistance to regimes of the normal."[6] However, we all must be aware of the risks inherent in embracing the term "queer" as a signifier of community, identity, politics, or theory. Gloria Anzaldúa argues that "queer" can be used/understood to disappear the very diversity which we are trying to highlight: "Queer is used as a false unifying umbrella which all 'queers' of all races, ethnicities and classes are shoved under. At times we need this umbrella to solidify our ranks against outsiders. But even when we seek shelter under it we must not forget that it homogenizes, erases our differences."[7] Although many people employ the term "queer" in part because it blurs — and some would argue erases — boundaries, Anzaldúa's point must be carefully considered. She herself chooses to identify as queer rather than as lesbian because of lesbian's Anglo-European roots and associations, but as "queer" gains currency, it is increasingly being appropriated and commodified, and thus increasingly risks collapsing into another term for white lesbians and gays, and ultimately white gay men. This is due to the fact that we live in a society in which the hegemonic discourses center around whites, men, and monosexuals, and so as "queer" becomes more popular *amongst* these "dominant" groups, it will increasingly come to *represent* these "dominant" groups.

Thus many lesbian feminists resist the term because they feel that it threatens to collapse gender and, in doing so, risks erasing awareness of gender-based oppression.[8] However, we are left with the fact that for many individuals like Anzaldúa and myself, who claim any number of anti-normative identities, the term "queer" best encompasses these identities. Additionally, "queer" provides an acceptable alternative for the many people who wish to try to avoid essentializing identities.

Contemporary queer theory embodies similar contradictions/tensions in relation to the term "queer." In his introduction to *Fear of a Queer Planet: Queer Politics and Social Theory*, Michael Warner gives queer theory the potential to engage in a radical polyphonic discourse: "For both academics and activists, 'queer' gets a critical edge by defining itself against the normal rather than the heterosexual and normal includes normal business in the academy."[9] However, as I shall illustrate, in many ways queer theory does tend to support the normal business of the academy.

In 1990, Jeffrey Escoffier wrote an article for *OUT/LOOK* that warned of a growing gap in lesbian and gay studies between "the field's 'new historicists' and the lesbians and gays of communities." According to Escoffier, these "new historicists" "emphasize[d] sophisticated interpretation of texts rather than the social history or the sociology of gay life." Additionally, Escoffier pointed out that this new field had thus far failed "to incorporate women and people of color into its ranks and analyses" and warned that the utilization of theoretical concepts from French postmodernists like Michel Foucault and Jacques Derrida "make the work of the new generation difficult and obscure to those outside of the academy."[10]

In 1991, Teresa de Lauretis introduced the term "queer theory" to encompass the work of these "new historicists" in the introduction to a special issue of *differences* entitled "Queer Theory: Lesbian and Gay Sexualities." Escoffier's criticisms are especially interesting in light of the fact that de Lauretis chose to differentiate queer theory from Queer Nation by stating in an endnote to the issue's introduction that: "My 'queer,' had no relation to the Queer Nation group of whose existence I was ignorant at the time."[11] This serves to distance *her* "queer" — and thus queer theory — from the version of "queer" widely circulating in lesbian, gay, bisexual, and transgender non-academic communities. However, the fact that the term "queer" was chosen at a time when Queer

Nation was active and getting frequent coverage in the lesbian, gay, and bisexual media, as well as in the mainstream media, has served to link queer theory in many people's minds with a growing queer power movement.

De Lauretis explains that the term "queer" was suggested to her by a 1989 conference whose proceedings were subsequently published in the book *How Do I Look? Queer Film and Video*. Interestingly enough, in the introduction to this book, the editorial collective freely exchange the term "queer film theory" with the term "lesbian and gay film theory." And nowhere is there an explanation as to why they chose the word "queer" for the title, implying that by then it had become an accepted and convenient terminology that allowed space for differences among lesbians and gays, while still maintaining the exclusivity of those identities.

How Do I Look? Queer Film and Video does contain several articles by and about "queer" people of color, but Gloria Anzaldúa argues that from the field's inception, it has been white middle-class lesbians and gay men "who have produced queer theory and for the most part their theories make abstractions of us colored queers. They control the production of queer knowledge in the academy and in the activist communities. . . . They police the queer person of color with theory. . . . Their theories limit the ways we think about being queer."[12] Part of the problem here lies in the fact that, as Anzaldúa herself points out, "queer" can serve as a term that erases difference. So that unless we strive to elaborate its meaning whenever we use it in our theories, it becomes like theoretical tofu: it will simply absorb the meaning of whatever particular aspect or aspects of queerness we are addressing. However, Oscar Montero, in his article "Latino Queers and National Identity" considers this characteristic of queer theory to be a positive one:

> "Queer" (from the German quer: oblique) puts the spectacle back in "theory" (theorema = spectacle); in other words, it puts a number of slants into any reading, and these slants are not always clearly defined. . . . Queer theory skirts identity, sometimes literally and brings other identities, ethnic, racial, and national into play.[13]

I would argue that while queer theory certainly has the potential for such an impact, it fails to do so at present, because it is being generated mainly by white academics. Just as the academy has been structured around heterosexuality in such a way as to limit discourses on other sexualities, it has been similarly structured around whiteness. Thus scholars of color, by virtue of the fact that they are not white, find themselves in an oppositional stance to the academy itself. And, as a result, many lesbian, bisexual, queer, and gay scholars of color choose to focus on issues of race and not issues of gender and sexuality. All the anthologies on queer theory include work by lesbians and gays of color, but we rarely find white lesbian or gay theorists discussing how intersections between anti-normative identities inform or affect one's queer perspective. If queer theory were to promote these types of discourses, it might then provide a more welcoming space for lesbian, gay, bisexual, and queer scholars of color.

Teresa de Lauretis calls for contributions to queer theory by other than white lesbians and gays:

The difference made by race in self-representation and identity argue for the necessity to examine, question, or contest the usefulness and/or the limitations of current discourses on lesbian and gay sexualities. . . . These differences urge the reframing of the question of queer theory from different perspectives, histories, experiences, and in different terms.[14]

The fundamental problem with this line of reasoning is that it leaves the burden of dealing with difference on the people who are themselves different, while simultaneously allowing white academics to continue to construct a discourse of silence around race and other queer perspectives. Thus those of us who write from such "other" queer perspectives must set ourselves up in opposition to the norm within queer theory. We are forced to essentialize our identities by drawing attention to the ways in which certain parts of ourselves are consistently being left out of the discourse.

As I have indicated, one of the major problems lies in the use of rhetoric. The term "queer" has now been so wholeheartedly embraced by lesbian and gay academic and non-academic communities alike that, in many cases, it has simply become an abbreviated way of saying "lesbian and gay" or, less often, "lesbian, gay, and bisexual." However, as Montero, Escoffier, and de Lauretis all point out, queer theory is theoretically structured around the concept of intersecting identities. And, in fact, as Judith Butler explains, all of us take-on or "perform" many different identities in any given day.[15]

Relying heavily on postmodernist theorists such as Foucault and Derrida, queer theory aims to transform power structures by altering discourses about sexuality and gender or, in Butler's terms, "disrupting" "performances" of heterosexuality,[16] and thus disrupting the hegemony of heteropatriarchy. For example, when we choose to view (or "queer") an advertisement with two women as representing a lesbian couple, we disrupt the flow of the notoriously heterosexist world of advertising. However, these disruptions also have the potential to be significantly undermined or even collapsed when undertaken from a queer perspective that brings into play notions of more than just gender and sexuality. In Gloria Anzaldúa's words, "Identity is not a bunch of little cubbyholes stuffed respectively with intellect, race, sex, class, vocation, gender. Identity flows between, over, aspects of a person. Identity is a river — a process."[17] Even though the concept might get lost in individual queer theory scholarship, definitions of queer theory do consider identity to be multivalent.

Thus we must ask ourselves why, in a theory that intends to problematize identity and challenge the normative, we often foreground sexuality and gender (and the latter only as a theoretical concept — the experiences of transgendered people are rarely discussed) to the exclusion of all other notions of identity. For example, those of us who are white tend not to dwell on our race, perhaps because this would only serve to normalize us — reduce our queerness, if you will. However, by failing to consider the ways in which such aspects of our identity inform our queer perspectives, we also fail to disrupt the hegemonic discourses around race and other anti-normative categories/identities. And, despite claims to the contrary, this is one of the ways in which queer theory continues to practice normal business in the academy.

At present, queer theory is sufficiently narrow to almost prohibit a discourse that

allows for considerations of the multiplicity of identities possible within the term "queer."
Alexander Doty's work *Making Things Perfectly Queer: Interpreting Mass Culture* provides an excellent example of this phenomenon. Doty's book serves as a ground-breaking
text in its convincing use of queer theory to destabilize — or queer — texts produced
within the very heterosexist medium of television. However, in his introduction, Doty
states that "[u]ltimately, queerness should challenge and confuse our understanding and
uses of sexual and gender categories."[18] By defining the progressive potential of
queerness as such, he participates in imposing the type of limitations on queerness that,
as Anzaldúa points out, characterize most of the work of white queer theorists. In fact,
when Doty does examine television shows like *The Jack Benny Show* or *Peewee's Play-
house*, he mentions their racist and/or misogynist aspects without undertaking a truly
critical analysis of them.[19] He does this because these aspects of television are neither on
his main agenda in writing this book, nor on the main agenda of queer theory in
general.

One book cannot, of course, cover everything, and Doty's book does provide some
excellent groundwork, but if queer theory is to truly challenge the "normal," it must
provide a framework in which to challenge racist, misogynist, and other oppressive
discourses/norms, as well as those that are heterosexist and homophobic. We must not
simply challenge heteronormativity but must instead question the very system that
sustains heteronormativity.

By examining a performance by Madonna which took place at the 1993 MTV Music
Video awards, I intend to provide an example which illuminates the complexity that
queer theory allows when the queer discourse is broadened. Madonna performed a piece
entitled "This Is Not a Love Song," which featured Madonna and two other women
wearing top hats and tails performing opposite three women wearing only bathing suits.
In casting women opposite one another in such "traditional" male/female garb, Madonna was obviously playing with lesbian butch/femme roles. And if we were to apply a
queer reading which centered only around gender and sexuality to this performance, we
would certainly find it a queer performance, in the sense of being positively oppositional.

We could then argue, as Doty does, that such a performance would have the effect of
queering the audience, however temporarily. We could also argue that, as queers, the
portrayal of same-sex couples is important for our own well-being; that is, any kind of
visibility provides us with reassurance that there are others out there like us. And finally,
we might argue that watching such queer couplings would provide pleasure to many
lesbians and bisexual women. In all of these ways, Madonna's performance would be
operating to disrupt the heteronormative discourse within popular culture.

However, when we examine the performance from a more complex queer perspective
that includes issues of race and class, we get entirely different readings. The butches are
played by Madonna, another white woman, and an African-American woman, and all of
the femmes are played by Asian-American women. In addition, the actions and lyrics
within the performance consistently set the Asian-American women up as bad and
deserving of punishment. The refrain is: "You're never going to see me cry again . . .
Bye-bye, baby, bye-bye" and includes Madonna chanting, "This is not a love song." At
one point, Madonna and the other butches grab the femmes' faces and at another,

simulate rough sexual penetration. The butches physically control the femmes, and, since Madonna sings the lyrics, they control the language and the story as well. The fact that Madonna chose Asian-American women as the femmes reinforces stereotypes of Asian women as the passive, exotic, and feminine "other." It also mocks the fact that Asian women have been economically exploited as "comfort girls" for American servicemen for many years now.

That Madonna would "do" lesbian butch/femme in this nationally televised performance at a time when "lesbian chic" was all the rage — around the same time that lesbians appeared on the cover of *Newsweek* and k.d. lang and Cindy Crawford did the famous *Vanity Fair* spread — might seem a victory to anyone who champions visibility and the idea of queering popular culture (and having pop culture queer society). However, since Madonna has insisted on labeling herself as heterosexual, it can also be viewed as another of Madonna's cultural commodification efforts — what bell hooks refers to as "eating the other."[20] This same type of commodification would apply to the use of Asian-American women in her performance. Thus, were we to claim this performance as queer without qualifying it, we would be complicit in allowing racist, classist, and misogynistic discourses to continue uninterrupted. This performance may be queer in its use of same-sex couples and female- to-male cross-dressing, but it is normalized in its use of classism, sexual racism, and commodification, and any disruption of the heteronormative discourse would be mitigated by these factors. As Donald Morton argues:

> The emancipation of the word "queer" cannot be achieved without a radical transformation of the regimes of labor, family, . . . and other social structures that produce homophobia in the first place. . . . [H]omophobia is . . . a structure of exploitation linked — not eccentrically, locally, or contingently, but systemically — to other social practices.[21]

If we truly want to create theories that will enable us to eradicate homophobia and heterosexism, we must understand the ways in which they are linked to all systems of oppression and undertake discourses that seek to undermine/expose that entire system.

Another way in which existing queer theory serves to limit the ways in which we conceptualize queerness is in its preservation of binary notions of sexuality. In the introduction to the special issue of *differences* referred to above, de Lauretis calls for queer theory to undertake "the necessary critical work of deconstructing our own discourses and their constructed silences."[22] However, bisexuality, along with race, continues to be one of the "constructed silences" within queer theory, as it is within lesbian and gay studies. Although queer theory indicates a significant ideological shift from lesbian and gay studies, it has carried with it the essentializing categories of "lesbian" and "gay," and although queer theory scholarship sometimes includes superficial mentions of bisexuality, it is often disappeared at best and disarticulated at worst. Thus, in some ways, bisexuality has become the contemporary version of "the love that dare not speak its name."

Michael Warner's anthology, *Fear of a Queer Planet*, is notable for its emphasis on community politics and social theory, but for the most part, it fails to incorporate understandings of diversity. There are articles written by and about lesbians and gays of color, but bisexuality is mentioned in only one essay. For example, in his introduction, Warner states that "queers live as queers, as lesbians, as gays, as homosexuals, in contexts other than sex."[23] Although some might argue that "queer" could include bisexual and, as I will illustrate, there are many bisexuals who identify as queer, the fact that Warner uses other essentializing categories, such as "lesbian" and "gay," renders bisexuality noticeably absent from his equation. This exclusion of bisexuality from discussions concerning issues of sexuality and gender has been typical of queer theory, unless the theory is being written by bisexuals themselves.

This is especially disturbing in light of the fact that early queer theorists like Teresa de Lauretis claimed that queer theory intended "to both transgress and transcend . . . or at the very least problematize" monolithic categories like "lesbian" and "gay."[24] In pointing out the necessity of finding new ways to conceptualize our alternative sexualities, de Lauretis was primarily referring to the fact that the terms "lesbian" and "gay" (because of their Anglo-European roots) are considered to be white terms, but in employing the term "queer," she was also bringing into question the whole notion of identity. Interestingly enough, bisexuals, especially feminist bisexuals, have been using the concept of bisexuality to pose similar questions and challenges for a number of years now. For instance, Elisabeth Daümer argues that bisexuality offers a unique "epistemological as well as ethical vantage point from which we can examine and deconstruct the bipolar framework of gender and sexuality."[25] She goes on to argue that the "ambiguous position" of bisexuals "can also lead to a deep appreciation of the differences among people — whether cultural, sexual, gendered — since any attempt to construct a coherent identity in opposition to another would flounder on the multiplicity of at times conflicting identifications generated by the bisexual point of view."[26]

Compare Daümer's comments about the concept of bisexuality to Rosemary Hennessy's definition of queer theory:

> Queer theory calls into question obvious categories (man, woman, latina, jew, butch, femme), oppositions (man vs. woman, heterosexual vs. homosexual), or equations (gender = sex) upon which conventional notions of sexuality and identity rely.[27]

Theoretically then, queer theory and bisexual feminist theory seem to have much in common. Thus I was surprised to find that queer theory — except that written by bisexuals themselves — consistently ignored bisexuality and rarely quoted bisexual theorists.

The notable exception is Alexander Doty, who includes a lengthy endnote on bisexuality in *Making Things Perfectly Queer*.

> Looking through this book, I realize I have given rather cursory attention to specifically bisexual positions. Since examining bisexuality seems crucial in many ways to theorizing nongay and nonlesbian queerness — indeed, some see bisexuality as queerness — I consider the absence of any extended discussion of bisexuality and mass culture a major omission.[28]

He goes on to quite provocatively suggest that we might consider texts that contain both opposite-sex and same-sex narratives as bisexual texts. When I questioned him as to why he initially ignored bisexuality, he explained that, because there was so little existing scholarly work on bisexuality, he wasn't quite sure how to theorize about it in relation to popular culture.[29] The fact that Doty's discussion of bisexuality is contained in an endnote further emphasizes the fact that bisexuality has not been a central part of discourses within queer theory. However, the fact that Doty does choose to broaden his own discourse on queerness to include bisexuality can serve as an example/foundation for other queer theorists to build upon.

Bisexuality is sometimes mentioned as an identity within queer theory, but it remains relatively invisible, in part because of resistance to viewing bisexuality as an identity on its own, separate from both heterosexuality and homosexuality. In fact, in a discussion on lesbian and gay spectatorship, Judith Mayne, one of the contributors to *How Do I Look? Queer Film and Video*, characterizes bisexuality as " 'wishy-washy' in the sense that such a subject-object position carries very little political impact in our present society."[30] In contrast, bisexual sociologist Paula Rust proclaims that bisexuals have the potential "to radically alter the way we think about not only gender and sexuality, but also the nature of power itself."[31] In other words, since a belief in monosexuality and binary notions of gender are built into the very foundations of this society, the concept of bisexuality threatens the very structure of heteropatriarchy. Thus I would argue that bisexuality actually carries a phenomenal amount of political impact, and this is one reason why it encounters so much resistance as a concept and an identity.

One of the few discussions that I came across which actually considered bisexuality as a political concept was an exchange that took place on the e-mail list "Queer Studies." In the course of this discussion, Eve Sedgwick claimed that bisexuality as a political concept, while providing a place for "the many people who are not fixed or exclusive in gender-of-object choice," ultimately fails to adequately challenge existing models of sexuality, because these paradigms are structured around gender-of-object choice.[32] Sedgwick argued that using bisexuality, as currently conceived, would simply function as an addition to, or completion of, the existing paradigm, so that what is now a dichotomy would become a trichotomy. What Sedgwick fails to consider, though, is that the concept of bisexuality could function to disrupt and further open a paradigm that depends on binary oppositions. Indeed, Gilbert Herdt argues that "the third is emblematic of other possible combinations that transcend dimorphism."[33] Thus, in the case of bisexuality, the third becomes significant, not in and of itself, but as a reminder that there are more than just two ways to conceptualize sexuality.

Sedgwick goes on to argue that, in posing the questions of "the relation of bisexual to gay/lesbian" and "the relation of bisexual to queer, . . . bisexuality as a political concept could function to break boundaries in the first context and yet to preserve them in the second." This is based on the premise that the meaning behind the utilization of "queer" as a political concept is to challenge "the decisiveness of gender-of-object choice as a way of understanding sexuality."[34] Certainly part of this argument revolves around the question of terminology — that is, the "bi" in "bisexuality" points us directly to binary notions of gender and sexuality. Rebecca Kaplan explains that:

> The very existence of the word "bisexual" is based on a false belief in sexual dichotomy. . . .
> The word implies that there are two (and only two) groups, groups that are discrete,

discontinuous and mutually exclusive. . . . It also indicates that this particular method of grouping people is the single most important form of categorization.[35]

Many bisexuals and bisexual theorists have expressed discomfort with the term for these very reasons. Paula Rust suggests that "what we need to do . . . is to remove the characteristic of partner sex from its privileged position altogether so that we are free to choose our own ways of defining ourselves and choosing our partners." She goes on to suggest that bisexuals rename themselves "pansensuals," in order to avoid emphasizing "biological sex as the basis for sexual identification," as well as to avoid the term "bi," which suggests binary attraction and returns us to the notion that we need to be either/ or or both. The term "pansensuals" also allows us to conceptualize a broader notion of sexuality and creates a category exclusively for those of us who reject binary notions of gender and sexuality.[36]

Many of Rust's arguments for the use of the term "pansensual" could be made for the term "queer," but, as with any group, self-identified queers encompass a wide range of people, who do not necessarily share the same ideological beliefs. And, as I have been arguing, the term "queer" has its own set of limitations, most significantly the power to collapse difference, compounded by its current interchangeability with the categories of lesbian and gay, or lesbian, gay, and bisexual. In my own experience, I have found that to argue from a queer perspective, as opposed to a bisexual perspective, lends added weight by eliminating the troublesome word "bisexual," while also enabling me to argue from a perspective that does not carry the kind of negative stereotypes and misunderstandings that bisexuality does.[37] Additionally, many bisexuals believe that bisexuality and queerness are fundamentally linked. As Carol Queen observes, "It is the queer in me that . . . lets me question the lies we were all told about who women are, who men are. . . . The queer in all of us clamors for pleasure or change, will not be tamed or regulated, wants a say in the creation of a new reality."[38]

Since many bisexuals, like myself, are attracted to people in spite of their gender and not because of it,[39] and the gender of object choice (based on binary notions of gender and sexuality) is what informs the sexual identity of lesbians, gays, and heterosexuals, then bisexuality is nothing *but* queer, odd, different — *existing in opposition to and challenging the norm.* And, if we understand "queer" to represent an identity/community/theoretical space that is fluid and specifically defined only through its opposition/ resistance to heteronormativity, then bisexuals and bisexuality would certainly be included within such a framework. However, if we understand "queer" to mean only lesbian and gay, then bisexuals become *queer* queers, standing outside the norms of queerness. Similarly, if we simply define queerness as anti-normative modes of gender and sexuality, then claiming other anti-normative identities besides sexual preference, such as race, ethnicity, or class — to name a few — would also render one a *queer* queer. This is not to fall into reductive arguments about the hierarchy of oppression, but simply to point out the ways in which we manage to establish norms even when we are struggling to resist and challenge them.

The focus on lesbian and gay sexualities and a constructed silence around race operate to establish part of the norm within queer theory. Another part of the norm that needs to be addressed involves class. Here I mean class to encompass those of us who position ourselves within the academy, thus occupying a certain intellectual, if not economic, class. In a discussion about queer theory as it is presented in *Fear of a Queer Planet*, Jeffrey Escoffier points out that: "[t]o identify the problem of queer politics as *normalization* rather than *intolerance* suggests that, overwhelmingly, the power of homophobia resides not in the power of repression and physical violence, but in normalizing moral and scientific discourses."[40]

And this is where queer theory has consistently failed to make its case outside of a rather narrow academic community — largely because the "norm" in queer theory is also about privilege. As academics, we often write theories onto the bodies of "others," and while we are certainly at risk of suffering discrimination and violence based on our sexual orientation, the academy is in many ways a protected and insular environment. A large number of academic institutions have anti-discrimination clauses that include sexual orientation, and more and more are instituting domestic partnership benefits for same-sex couples. Unfortunately, such basic rights are not found within many other working environments. Because of the relative safety of our surroundings, some of us are able to direct our energies to theorizing our sexualities and in doing so, many of us focus on texts, and not actual lived experience.[41]

The threat of violence combined with the fact that anti-lesbian, -gay, and -bisexual legislation is appearing all over the country leads many queer community activists to resent academicians' persistence in working on theories that have no obvious practical applications. While extremely important, our efforts to "counteract dominant discourses"[42] are centered within the academy and seem at odds with the political activism that takes place outside it. As Jeffrey Escoffier notes, "Queer theory and the cultural studies paradigm are mapping the discursive regimes of power/knowledge that constitute the queer, the homosexual and the sexual pervert. These regimes of cultural hegemony are immensely powerful, but the performative character of discourse does not exhaust the forms of domination that shape the lives of homosexuals and other sexual perverts."[43] In order to be a truly progressive field, to be what Rosemary Hennessy calls "an in-your-face rejection of the proper response to heteronormativity, a version of acting up,"[44] queer theory has to include theories that we queers, in our multiplicity of identities, can use in more than just our academic lives.

By expanding the ways that we think about queerness, we will also be opening up our theories to a wider audience. If one of the inherent goals of queer theory is to undermine heteronormative hegemonic discourses — to reconceptualize the ways that we think about the relationships between power and the heteropatriarchal norm — then it behooves us to create and utilize theories that will pass through the doors of the ivory tower and spill into the streets and minds of queers everywhere.

As I have illustrated in this essay, existing queer theory, despite attempts to avoid normativity, harbors a normative discourse around race, sexuality, and class. Those of us who fall outside of this normativity are thus rendered *queer* queers and must position ourselves and our work in opposition to it. However, I want to make clear that I believe that the work that is being done within queer theory is quite significant, and I am by no means suggesting that it should be dismissed because of its limitations. What I am

suggesting is that we strive to continuously problematize that which we have created —
that we identify the constructed silences within our work and transform them into
meaningful discourses.

NOTES

1. This chapter was supported in part by a grant from the Student Research Allocations
Committee of the Graduate Student Association at the University of New Mexico.

2. Gloria Anzaldúa, "To(o) Queer the Writer: Loca, escrita y chicana," *InVersions: Writing by
Dykes, Queers and Lesbians*, ed. Betsy Warland (Vancouver: Press Gang, 1991), 251.

3. See Teresa de Lauretis, Introduction to *differences* 3 (Summer 1991): xvii.

4. Elisabeth Daümer, "Queer Ethics, or the Challenge of Bisexuality to Lesbian Ethics,"
Hypatia 7 (Fall 1992): 100.

5. I use "bisexuality" because, as an identity, it best represents my dissatisfaction with the
narrow confines of binary notions of sexuality and gender. Throughout this chapter, I find myself
falling back into essentialist notions of identity in order to make my points clear, but because of
the language currently available with which to discuss sexuality, I felt that I had no choice.

6. Jeffrey Escoffier, "Under the Sign of the Queer," *Found Object* (Fall 1994): 135.

7. Anzaldúa, "To(o) Queer the Writer," 250.

8. The term "queer" is intended by many to challenge binary notions of gender. But because
women as a socially constructed category are still subject to both sexism and misogyny, many
lesbian feminists quite understandably feel that it is important to recognize that gender categories
remain an enforced reality.

9. Michael Warner, Introduction to *Fear of a Queer Planet: Queer Politics and Social Theory*
(Minneapolis: University of Minnesota Press, 1993), xxvi.

10. Jeffrey Escoffier, "Inside the Ivory Closet: The Challenges Facing Lesbian and Gay Studies," *OUT/LOOK* 3 (Fall 1990): 40–48.

11. de Lauretis, Introduction, xvii.

12. Anzaldúa, "To(o) Queer the Writer," 251.

13. Oscar Montero, "Latino Queers and National Identity," *Radical America* 24, no. 4 (April
1993): 16–17.

14. de Lauretis, Introduction, x.

15. Judith Butler, "Imitation and Gender Insubordination," *The Lesbian and Gay Studies
Reader*, ed. Henry Abelove, Michèle Aina Barale, and David M. Halperin (New York: Routledge,
1993), 308.

16. Ibid., 315.

17. Anzaldúa, "To(o) Queer the Writer," 252–53.

18. Alexander Doty, *Making Things Perfectly Queer: Interpreting Mass Culture* (Minneapolis:
University of Minnesota Press, 1993), xvii.

19. Doty does condemn misogyny and includes a lengthy endnote in which he asserts the
importance of differentiating between straight male misogyny and gay male misogyny, but he does
not consider just how misogyny (in any form) might affect the transformative powers of a queer(ed)
text.

20. bell hooks, "Eating the Other," *Black Looks: Race and Representation* (Boston: South End
Press, 1992), 21.

21. Donald Morton, "The Politics of Queer Theory in the (Post)Modern Moment," *Genders* 17
(Fall 1993): 122.

22. de Lauretis, Introduction, iv.

23. Warner, *Fear of a Queer Planet*, vii.

24. de Lauretis, Introduction, v. De Lauretis uses words like "transgress" and "transcend" as part of an ongoing debate about the usefulness and truthfulness of identities, but it seems ridiculous to suggest that we can transcend/transgress terms that inform our identities, as well as endanger our lives/families/careers, in that they are foisted upon us by a heterosexist society whenever we act queerly. Despite arguments that we should do away with identities/labels, the fact remains that many of us structure our lives around these concepts and will continue to use them, whatever theorists say. This is not intended as an argument against the term "queer" (which is itself understood/claimed by some as an identity), but simply a cautionary note that we need to continuously problematize it.

25. Daümer, "Queer Ethics," 98.

26. Ibid., 98.

27. Rosemary Hennessy, "Queer Theory: A Review of the *differences* Special Issue and Wittig's *The Straight Mind*," *Signs* 18 (Summer 1993): 964.

28. Doty, *Making Things Perfectly Queer*, 105.

29. I spoke with Doty about this in April 1994 at the "Console-ing Passions" conference in Tucson, Arizona. Interestingly enough, at the same conference, Maria Pramaggiore presented a paper entitled "Double Crossing Identities: Constructing Queerness in Contemporary Television and Film," in which she used Doty's idea of bisexuality as the mediating force in homoerotic "straight" texts to analyze *Singing in the Rain* and other movies. The only published work that I'm aware of that deals with bisexuality and popular culture is Robin Wood's *Hollywood from Vietnam to Reagan* (1986), which considers bisexuality more as a concept (derived from Freud) than as a viable identity.

30. Judith Mayne, discussion following "Dorothy Azner and Female Authorship," *How Do I Look? Queer Film and Video*, ed. Bad Object Choices (Seattle: Bay Press, 1992), 137.

31. Paula Rust, "Who Are We and Where Do We Go from Here? Conceptualizing Bisexuality," *Closer to Home: Bisexuality and Feminism*, ed. Elizabeth Reba Weise (Seattle: Seal Press, 1992), 306.

32. Eve Sedgwick, "Queer Studies List," August 17, 1994.

33. Gilbert Herdt, *Third Sex, Third Gender: Beyond Sexual Dimorphism in Culture and History* (New York: Zone, 1994), 20. Thanks to Rebecca Kaplan for bringing my attention to Herdt's ideas by starting a discussion on the topic on the "Bisexual Theory" e-mail list.

34. Ibid., 20, emphasis in original text.

35. Rebecca Kaplan, "Compulsory Heterosexuality and the Bisexual Existence: Toward a Bisexual Feminist Understanding of Heterosexism," *Closer to Home*, 274.

36. Rust, "Who Are We and Where Do We Go from Here?," 299–304.

37. However, I realize that the term "queer" is rapidly losing such a status, for as it gains a wider circulation, it becomes more problematic, especially as it is increasingly being understood as a "male" term.

38. Carol Queen, "The Queer in Me," *Bi Any Other Name: Bisexual People Speak Out*, ed. Loraine Hutchins and Lani Kaahumanu (Boston: Alyson, 1991), 20–21.

39. I realize that I am once again encountering a terminology problem. To say that one is attracted to someone in spite of, but not because of, their gender is infinitely problematic in a society that organizes itself around gender. However, what I am trying to express here is that for many bisexuals, gender is not the primary organizational concept in their attractions to people.

40. Escoffier, "Under the Sign of the Queer," 135.

41. I realize that the academy is in fact structured in such a way as to promote these types of scholarship: it is what many of us are paid to do, and to shift our focus away from such "traditional" scholarship could mean jeopardizing one's career. That notwithstanding, we must consider why it is that the academy promotes such scholarship; our exclusive language alone often serves to effectively limit the message that we are trying to disseminate.

42. de Lauretis, Introduction, iii.

43. Escoffier, "Under the Sign of the Queer," 141.

44. Hennessy, "Queer Theory," 967.

"Tragic Misreadings": Queer Theory's Erasure of Transgender Subjectivity

Ki Namaste

> They cannot represent themselves, they must be represented.
>
> — Karl Marx, *The Eighteenth Brumaire of Louis Bonaparte*

> And we do have something else to say, if you will but listen to the monsters: the possibility of meaningful agency and action exists.
>
> — Susan Stryker, "My Words to Victor Frankenstein above the Village of Chamounix: Performing Transgender Rage"

In recent years, the field known as queer theory has witnessed a veritable explosion of essays, presentations, and books on the subjects of drag, gender, performance, and transsexuality.[1] Yet these works have shown very little concern for those who identify and live as drag queens, transsexuals, and/or transgenders. The violation of compulsory sex/gender relations is one of the topics most frequently addressed by critics in queer theory. These discussions, however, rarely consider the implications of an enforced sex/gender system for people who live outside it. Critics in queer theory are fond of writing about the ways in which specific acts of gender transgression can help dismantle binary gender relations and hegemonic heterosexuality. While such an intellectual program is important, it is equally imperative that we reflect on which aspects of transgender lives are presented and how this discussion is framed. For example, critics in queer theory write page after page on the inherent liberation in the transgression of gender codes, but they have nothing to say about the precarious position of the transsexual woman who is battered, and who is unable to access a woman's shelter because she was not born a biological woman.

My essay reflects on this paradox: why is it that transgendered people are the chosen objects of the field of queer theory, and why does the presentation of these issues ignore the daily realities of transgendered people? Before turning to the field of queer theory, I want to consider some of the historical, disciplinary, and national questions which figure in the study of culture. Attention to these issues is important in order to locate the emergence of queer theory and to appreciate how its disciplinary and national locations inform both its designation of an "object" of study (transgendered people), as well as the theoretical approaches used to examine that object. Once we understand where queer theory came from, and once we acknowledge its methodological approach as an effect of that position, we can contemplate different ways to address the same issues as those taken up by critics in queer theory.

Historically, the field of cultural studies emerged within departments of sociology in Britain.[2] Research projects associated with the Birmingham Centre for Cultural Studies reflected on how culture is shaped by social and historical practices, as well as the ways in which it constitutes (and can challenge) these relations. The specific "objects" of study in this area were quite diverse — everything from biker gangs, to racism in late-1970s Britain, to punk rock culture.[3] Methodological approaches to these issues were equally eclectic: Paul Willis relied on ethnographic interviews in his survey of bikers,[4] Pratibha Parmar examined the location of South Asian women workers in relation to a global political economy,[5] and Dick Hebdige offered a semiotic analysis of the signs produced and consumed within a punk rock milieu.[6] Despite their methodological differences, though, these studies were all committed to thinking about the relations between lived experience and representation. This emphasis on specific cultural forms and practices was, at the same time, an institutional intervention. As Stuart Hall points out, cultural studies emerged within departments of sociology, but it was often professed by critics who were not trained in the discipline of sociology itself.[7] The entire project involved critical reflection not only on what but how to study. In Hall's words: "It was never a question of which disciplines would contribute to the development of this field, but of how one could decenter or destabilize a series of interdisciplinary fields."[8]

While the history of cultural studies involves such methodological and institutional reflection, the field is very different today, particularly within the context of American, humanities-based research. Susan Willis notes that the project of the Birmingham school centered around the dialectical relations between culture and capital.[9] Most cultural critics in the United States today, however, direct their attention to textual meanings, without connecting these significations to the material relations in which they are embedded.

The concerns raised by Willis have also been articulated by other scholars in the field. Angela McRobbie makes a programmatic call for an ethnographic conception of identity, while Tony Bennett envisions a kind of cultural studies which has application at the level of social policy.[10] Similarly, Hazel Carby wonders why the heated debates about the "inclusion" of people of color on course syllabi occur with no consideration of the current economic realities for black communities.[11] Gayatri Spivak addresses these issues from a related perspective. She cautions against a simplistic framework which posits novels created in post-colonial contexts "as direct expressions of cultural consciousness, with no sense of the neo-colonial traffic in cultural identity and the slow and agonizing triumph of the migrant voice."[12] Like Willis and Carby, Spivak forces scholars to think about the material conditions in which culture is created. She also demands an acknowledgment of the ways in which "post-colonial" novels as commodities can be used in the economic interests of the (American) university. Such a perspective articulates a global analysis concerned with the geopolitical divisions of the world, divisions which can be perpetuated by Euro-American intellectual practices.

These recent writings in the field of cultural studies have emphasized methodological issues. The question at hand, however, is much broader than the objects that academics choose to study or which theories they will draw on for an explanation. The impetus behind this criticism is one concerned with institutional politics. Willis, Carby, and Spivak all demand that intellectuals locate themselves within the university, and that they account for the role their theory plays in legitimating certain conceptions of the social world (i.e., one in which capital is absent).

Reflection on these matters is particularly useful in a consideration of queer theory, since this area of inquiry emerged within American departments of film, literature, and cultural studies.[13] These disciplinary and national locations have marked the objects to be examined (literary and cultural texts), as well as the theoretical approaches employed (semiotics, deconstruction). In this essay, I focus on these methodological issues, with an emphasis on the ways in which critics in queer theory represent transgendered individuals, communities, and social realities. By locating the field of queer theory within its disciplinary and national contexts, we can begin to imagine different ways of thinking about transgender issues. To that end, this essay presents some of the social scientific research on transgendered people. I hope to demonstrate the radically different manner in which social scientists address many of the same questions that recent queer theorists do, but without undermining the lives and experiences of the transgendered people they study.

"Transsexuals Are Not Your Entertainment!"

It is useful to begin this discussion with the work of Judith Butler, since the publication of *Gender Trouble* played a tremendous role in the development of queer theory. Butler argues that drag exposes the imaginary relations of compulsory heterosexuality. Drag queens are not miming "real" women but demonstrating the ways in which categories such as "women" can only be secured through a process of metalepsis, where the effects of meaning are taken to be the cause of its articulation. In her words, "*drag implicitly reveals the imitative structure of gender itself — as well as its contingency.*"[14] In this manner, Butler exposes the appeal to origin for the ideological myth that it is.

This proposition is surely an important one, and Butler's work has been instrumental in the advancement of queer theory and gender studies. But it fails to account for the context in which these gender performances occur. The drag queens Butler discusses perform in spaces created and defined by gay male culture. Although Butler locates these spaces in relation to heterosexual hegemony, she refuses to examine this territory's own complicated relations to gender and gender performance. Consider the paradox which drag queens live: while many gay male bars have drag queens on stage, some of them deny entry to women. In the late 1980s in Montréal, for example, the leather bar K.O.X. banned genetic women, males in "women's" clothes, males in lipstick, and all transsexuals. At the time, other gay bars in the Montréal area were almost exclusively segregated along sex/gender lines. As a result, "Ladies' Nights" became popular venues for men and women — "fag hags," lesbians, gay and bisexual men, bisexual women, transsexuals — who wished to socialize together in the same space. Here was the ultimate irony: gay male bars would refuse genetic women admittance, and would then turn around and capitalize on this discrimination at a later time (only once a year, in the case of K.O.X.) by allowing them entry. Elements of femininity and femaleness are highly regulated within gay male consumer culture.

Even when genetic women, transsexual women, and males in drag are permitted entry into gay male establishments, they remain peripheral to the activities at hand. Drag queens, for example, are tolerated as long as they remain in a space clearly designated for performance: the stage. Listen to the voice of transgender Michelle de Ville, interviewed in the fanzine *Fuzzbox*:

> [deVille]: The drag queen in the gay world is meant to be on stage or "walking" the streets. Don't get off the stage, baby! It's like the bird in the gilded cage.
> [Fuzzbox]: K.O.X. says that on their "Ladies' Night" they won't accept women wearing make-up, high heel shoes, dresses, loud clothing, etc. Yet they had a woman perform tarted up to the hilt, wearing all these things. Because she was on stage, they could handle her.[15]

De Ville raises a crucial point: drag queens can move freely within gay male settings as long as they abide by the implicit rules of such circulation. What would happen if a drag queen was not on the stage, but rather cruised one of the many dark corridors of K.O.X. in search of a sexual partner? That gay men can accommodate the presence of drag queens on stage does not mean that gender liberation has arrived. Indeed, relegating such gender performance to the stage implies that gay men do not "perform" their identities; they just *are*.[16] This containment of gender transgression can, in turn, work against gender outlaws in a variety of ways. Drag queens are reduced to entertainment, coiffed bodies whose only purpose is to titillate the gay male viewer. Framed as pure spectacle, this negates a variety of reasons why people might choose to cross-dress in a club: an exploration of one's gender identity, a gesture of political intervention, a creative solution to boredom, and/or a way to pay the rent.

The limiting of drag queens to the stage also suggests that drag is something you do; it is not someone you are. Eve Sedgwick disavows drag subject-positions in precisely this way when she establishes a relation "between drag performance and homoerotic identity formation and display."[17] Note the ways in which categories of sexuality and gender work against each other, even as they are syntagmatically aligned. Drag is about performance, while the homoerotic is about identity. Moreover, Sedgwick claims that the performance of drag secures a homoerotic identity. She does not stipulate why a *drag* performance cannot articulate a *drag* subject-position.

In Montréal, the organizers of the 1992 Lesbian and Gay Pride Parade attempted to ban drag queens from participating.[18] They believed that drag queens and people in leather exceeded "respectable" community standards. When challenged on their drag-phobia, organizers pointed to the presence of L'Entrepeau (a drag queen bar) in the parade as evidence of their inclusive politics. The relegation of drag to the stage is a supplementary move which excludes transgenders even as it includes us. Appropriate objects to look at, we are not subjects to march alongside.

In 1993, a new Pride committee emerged in Montréal under the rubric of "Divers/cité." As the name suggests, this organization seeks to be as inclusive as possible, and the banner at the front of the parade is subtitled "La fierté lesbienne, gaie, bisexuelle, travestie, et transsexuelle" (lesbian, gay, bisexual, and transgender pride). Notwithstanding this comprehensive semantic field, parade organizers have yet to include any bisexual and/or transgender activists among the political speakers at the event.[19] It goes without saying that drag queens provided entertainment for the activities on the day of the march. Despite their rhetorical strategies, the organizers of Divers/cité staged transgender identities in exactly the same manner as the organizers of previous Pride parades in Montréal.

The relegation of drag queens to the stage has profound implications when it comes to the politics of HIV and AIDS. Sandra LaFramboise, executive director of High Risk Project, a drop-in center for transgender sex trade workers in Vancouver, points out that there are no AIDS education materials for transgenders. She remarks on the irony of this situation:

> [HIV/AIDS is] a condition of living, and a teacher. And people have not learned yet. Because if I look around, there's nothing for transgendered people. All over again! Then I'm going, "Geesh! Guys, this is chicken shit!" You know? Like, fuck. We were in the forefront for gay community activists. We raised thousands of dollars for your projects, transvestites on the stages. And now we're here, and you're putting us aside again. . . . And that's the bottom line. What I've found [from gay-dominated AIDS service organizations] is a lot of patronizing.[20]

If drag queens are forced to remain within a space clearly designated for performance, transsexuals experience a similar staging within lesbian and gay male communities. Recent events in Toronto's lesbian and gay arts organizations bear this out. The program for the Third Annual Inside Out Lesbian and Gay Film and Video Festival (May 6–16, 1993) included a night entitled "gender-bending." The event was described as follows:

> Bearded ladies, chicks with dicks and drag queens, are among the queer sightings in Gender Bender, an evening of gender-bending film and video. Throwing open the question of sex and its relation to gender identification and sexual orientation, this programme explores cross-dressing, transsexualism, transvestism, androgyny, and other sexual anomalies [sic].

The classification of transsexuals, drag queens, and other gender outlaws as "sexual anomalies" incensed many of Toronto's transgender activists. From their perspective, this description represents one of the many ways in which lesbian and gay identities stabilize themselves as natural, while simultaneously relegating other positions to that of "anomaly." The publication of this program gave birth to a new activist group: TAC, Transsexual Activist Committee. TAC produced a flyer which reprinted the above description and also proclaimed "NO TO THE GERALDO APPROACH! TRANSSEXUALS ARE NOT YOUR ENTERTAINMENT!!" This strategy interrogates the staging of transgender subjects within a lesbian and gay setting.

TAC's intervention offers a useful starting point for thinking about how critics in queer theory represent transgendered people. Butler's presentation of drag queens, like the description of "gender-bending" in the Inside Out Film Festival program, ignores the specificity of the milieu in which drag practices are situated. Given the overwhelmingly gendered nature of such a setting, it seems problematic to merely cite drag practices as an exposition of the constructed nature of all gender. While Butler reads drag as a means of exposing the contingent nature of gender and identity, I suggest that we point to the essential paradox of drag within gay male communities: at the precise moment that it underlines the constructed nature of gendered performances, drag is contained as a performance in itself.[21] Gay male identity, in contrast, establishes itself as something prior to performance.

Butler's most recent work continues this distortion of transgender realities. In *Bodies That Matter*, Butler provides a reading of transsexual Venus Extravaganza from the film *Paris Is Burning*. Butler argues that Extravaganza enacts an imaginary relation to the category "woman" in an effort to escape the cruel realities of her class and ethnicity (Latina) in New York City. Gender is thus a vehicle which functions to displace the material and symbolic conditions of race and class. When Venus Extravaganza is murdered, presumably by one of her clients (she is a sex trade worker), Butler writes that her death represents "a tragic misreading of the social map of power."[22] For Butler, Extravaganza does not escape her situation; rather, she is treated as women are treated — especially women of color.

In this interpretation, Butler elides Extravaganza's transsexual status. Here is the point: Venus Extravaganza was killed because she was a transsexual. An acknowledgment of violence against gender outlaws is explicit in *Paris Is Burning*, although Butler chooses to ignore it. After the murder of Extravaganza, her best friend, Angie, makes the insightful comment "That's part of being a transsexual and surviving in New York City." Since Butler has reduced Extravaganza's transsexuality to an allegorical state, she cannot conceptualize the specificity of violence with which transsexuals, especially transsexual sex trade workers, are faced. This, to my mind, is the most tragic misreading of all.

Clearly, as scholars and as activists, we need to challenge Butler's negation of transgender identity. Moreover, we must account for the boundaries which are implicitly drawn by her research: drag queens expose compulsory sex/gender relations, while transsexuals can only offer an "uncritical miming of the hegemonic [sex/gender system]."[23] This framework is questionable for three overlapping reasons: (1) it can be deployed in a violently *anti-transsexual* manner, (2) it forces a separation of drag queens from transsexuals (a division which is already quite strong within transgender communities), and (3) it prevents the elaboration of a broad-based transgender politics. Moreover, by lauding drag practices over transsexual ontological positions, Butler ignores political activism within transsexual communities, particularly efforts to repeal cross-dressing ordinances.[24] Once we acknowledge the energies transsexuals have invested in repealing legislation which enforces a compulsory sex/gender system, it is impossible to reduce transsexual identities to those which enact an "uncritical miming of the hegemonic."

Is There a Transvestite in This Text?[25]

While Butler ignores the context in which drag performances occur, critics such as Marjorie Garber undermine transgender identity in a different manner. Garber contends that most academic analyses of the transvestite appropriate it into a binary framework, looking *through* the transvestite in order to understand the constructed nature of gender. Against the grain of this approach, Garber proposes that we look *at* the transvestite. From this stance, we can observe a destabilization of the categories "male" and "female." In Garber's words, "*transvestite is a space of possibly structuring and confounding culture: the descriptive element that intervenes not just as a category crisis of male and female, but the crisis of category itself.*"[26] This formulation allows Garber to observe that transvestites locate a crisis which is often elsewhere — in relations of class or race, for example. Yet I want to suggest that as interesting as Garber's claims may be, they remain politically suspect. While I share her concern with theorizing the transvestite, we part ways when it comes to methodology.

As a literary critic, Garber is interested in the representation of cross-dressing. Her analysis spans a wide variety of cultural texts, from the Kabuki theatre to the Renaissance stage to the performances of David Bowie. But what is missing from her research is a conceptualization of transvestite identity as a real, lived, viable experience. Naming the second section of her book "Transvestite Effects," Garber implies that the transvestite is an effect of performance and nothing else. Insofar as she reduces the transvestite to a mere tropological figure, a textual and rhetorical device which points to the crisis of category and the category of crisis, she has effectively undermined the possibility of "transvestite" as a viable identity in and of itself. In this light, I want to turn Garber back upon herself and suggest that the real "crisis of elsewhere" to which she refers is the very possibility of a transvestite identity. In other words, the "crisis of elsewhere" is always-already a crisis of *here*.

Like Butler, Garber engages in a superficial reading of transgender culture which distorts the diversity within transgender communities. She moves from a discussion of Hollywood films like *The Silence of the Lambs* to magazines produced by and for transgendered people, such as *Tapestries*. Garber never distinguishes between the conditions of possibility for these representations, implying that academics can "look at" transvestites in these texts without accounting for their material, discursive, and institutional locations. Since she ignores the context of production for the images she examines, it is little wonder that she makes a rather dubious statement like "*The Silence of the*

Lambs is in one sense, determinedly politically correct — Buffalo Bill is *not* a transsexual, and both transsexuals and gender clinics are exonerated from even associative blame." [27] When Garber proclaims this, she makes no reference to how the film was received within transgender communities. Although the narrative explains that Buffalo Bill is not a transsexual, it is clear that this person is gender dysphoric. Transgender activists know that transsexuality, transvestism, and gender dysphoria are linked within the psychiatric establishment — it is more than mere coincidence that they are grouped in the same section of the American Psychiatric Association's *Diagnostic and Statistical Manual*. To merely accept psychiatric categories of gender identity, as Garber does, is to unwittingly legitimate this institution's control in both regulating and defining transsexuality.

Garber's paradigm of "looking at" is limited insofar as it ignores the intertextual relations in which meaning is situated. This framework also enacts familiar binary oppositions between academics and "our" objects of inquiry. Transvestites are those figures "we" look at; they are not those people with whom "we" speak. And "they" are certainly not "us."

Sociological Research and Transgendered People

It should be clear by now that critics in queer theory only ask certain questions when it comes to the representation of transgendered people. As such, this field of knowledge repeats many of the limitations of recent American, humanities-based scholarship. While it is useful to situate the disciplinary and national locations of queer theory, an investigation of different disciplinary approaches to studies of sexuality and gender is also valuable. To that end, I will present some of the historical contributions of sociology to a (trans)gender research agenda.

The most obvious place to begin this discussion is with Harold Garfinkel's ethnomethodology. [28] Ethnomethodology is the name given to the sociological framework which helps uncover the unwritten rules by which all social actors guide their lives. Garfinkel studied the case of Agnes, a male-to-female transsexual who presented herself to the gender identity clinic in Los Angeles in 1958. When she sought the clinic's assistance in obtaining sex reassignment surgery, Agnes had already been living as a woman for years. What was interesting about this case for Garfinkel was how Agnes's behavior revealed the unspoken rules of gender which we all follow. For instance, Agnes spoke in a soft voice, waited to hear the opinions of others (especially men) before voicing her own, and worked in the kitchen. According to Garfinkel, Agnes demonstrates how gender is managed on a daily basis.

Other ethnomethodologists continue the project initiated by Garfinkel. Suzanne Kessler and Wendy McKenna, for instance, examine how gender is coded in Western cultures. [29] They presented undergraduate students with a variety of visual images and asked them to indicate whether the picture was of a man or a woman. Some of the pictures had an individual with long hair, breasts, and a vagina, while others had a person with a vagina, short hair, and no visible breasts. Kessler and McKenna discovered that if a penis was present, the photograph would be classified as "male" approximately 95 per cent of the time. In contrast, an image with a vagina needed to have at least two other secondary sex characteristics indicating femininity in order to be classified as "female" with a similar frequency. Kessler and McKenna conclude that the cultural interpretation of gender is overwhelmingly skewed in favor of masculine referents.

More recently, Suzanne Kessler has researched the case of intersexed infants, those individuals with "ambiguous" genitalia at birth.[30] That these individuals are surgically altered to have a sex which can be "recognized" illustrates the priority placed upon genitals in this culture. Kessler also notes that the criterion of chromosomes is less relevant in determining an intersexed child's gender than the length and appearance of the phallus. Like Garfinkel, Kessler exposes some of the underlying assumptions which govern our most taken-for-granted conceptions of gender. She shows us that sexed bodies (male or female) are not the basis of gender identities (men and women); rather, our binary conception of gender produces these sexed bodies through surgery.

There are many obvious parallels between Judith Butler's work and the ethnomethodological tradition within sociology. Like ethnomethodologists, Butler is interested in thinking about the unwritten rules of a compulsory sex/gender system. Given the fact that Garfinkel's work was published in 1967, it is rather curious that he is not cited by Butler. Such an omission points to one of the most regrettable aspects of queer theory: its refusal   ead across disciplines.[31] As Steven Epstein remarks, "to some recent students of sexuality working outside sociology, the concept of social construction is assumed to have sprung, like Athena, fully formed from the head of Michel Foucault."[32] Butler's ideas in *Gender Trouble* came as no surprise to people with even a cursory familiarity with ethnomethodology.[33] Yet it would be a serious mistake to merely equate ethnomethodological analyses of gender with Butler's project. Ethnomethodology, like all social theories, is a framework which emerges from the everyday social world.[34] Garfinkel focuses on Agnes's speech and communication style in order to understand how gendered norms govern verbal and nonverbal interactions for all social actors. Kessler and McKenna's research on the coding of gender extends this analysis, in an illustration of how the meanings of gender are applied to sexed bodies. Kessler also investigates the medical and surgical interventions which literally construct two mutually exclusive sexes in the case of intersexed infants. All of these studies examine the everyday reproduction of gender. They begin with a consideration of the daily practices through which gender is repeated and secured.

While Butler seems to offer a framework which is also premised on the everyday, she does not provide a theoretical analysis of gender which is situated within the banality of people's day to day experiences. As I demonstrated above, Butler pays very little attention to the context of gay male consumer culture in which the drag practices she cites occur. This neglect obscures the containment of gender transgressions within gay male communities. The end result is a "theory" of gender which cannot account for the nuances and contradictions of social context. Butler's work requires an ambiguous extrapolation from drag queens on stage in a gay bar to a compulsory sex/gender system in the social world. So while ethnomethodologists and Butler may share an interest in thinking about the daily reproduction of gender, there are significant differences in how they conduct their research. Butler offers a cursory discussion of drag performances within gay male consumer culture and fails to account for the containment of gender transgression on the stage. Furthermore, she extends this analysis of drag performance on the stage to a compulsory sex/gender system — an extension which, once again, ignores the nuances and contradictions of social context. The work of ethnomethodologists, in contrast, is rooted in the everyday social world and offers a detailed examination of the social relations and practices of gender.

I do not want to suggest that research on drag queens cannot be part of critical work on gender. I do want to emphasize, however, that scholarship which addresses this issue must provide a social, historical, and cultural background on the setting in which drag performances are enacted. Esther Newton's anthropological study of drag queens realizes this research program.[35] Newton gives an ethnographic account of the work environments, identities, and lives of female impersonators. In her study, she notes that people can adopt a variety of drag identities, such as the "street fairy," who flaunts femininity in public, the "glamour queen," who adopts an air of sophistication and aristocracy, and the impressionist, who mimics Hollywood stars such as Mae West and Bette Davis.[36] Newton also examines the different kinds of shows that can be created by female impersonators. Drag queens stripping in front of a predominantly heterosexual audience, she claims, must always remove their bras to reveal their flat chests. The same performers in front of a gay crowd, in contrast, do not remove their bras.[37] While heterosexual patrons need the biological status of the female impersonator confirmed (through the removal of the bra), gay patrons do not.

This attention to social context proves particularly useful for thinking about the politics of gender. Newton's research reveals that, even within the world of female impersonators, gender is highly regulated. For example, while all female impersonators wear "women's" clothes for their acts, within the communities studied by Newton those individuals who wore "women's" clothes in their everyday lives were viewed with disdain: " '[T]ransy drag' is either some item of feminine apparel which is not related to the necessities of performance, or feminine clothing which is worn in everyday circumstances. . . . Transy drag is wrong [within the subculture of female impersonators] because it violates the glamour standard."[38] Newton's scholarship certainly reveals that gender is socially constructed. Yet it is especially valuable, I suggest, because it illustrates that this construction varies in different social, historical, political, and regional locations. Throughout her work, Newton remains faithful to the project of ethnography: she presents the ways in which female impersonators perceive their social world, rather than how she as a researcher sees it.[39] Moreover, Newton explains the meanings of particular cultural symbols and signs (such as clothing which could be classified as "transy drag") in terms of the worldview of female impersonators.

Recent scholarship in the social sciences builds on the writings of Garfinkel and Newton, with an emphasis on studying transgender issues in a manner which is relevant to transgender communities. Vern Bullough and Bonnie Bullough, for instance, document individuals who cross-dressed throughout history, and discuss cross-dressing in different cultures. The strength of their work is an historical, contextualized interpretation of what cross-dressing means and how these meanings can change across time and cultures. In addition to providing historical data, Bullough and Bullough examine the development of a medical model of transvestism and transsexualism. Tracing the emergence of these categories through the writings of nineteenth-century sexologists, they demonstrate a collapse of gender and sexuality in the definition of transvestism, such that effeminacy was equated with homosexuality.[40] The authors subsequently explore how gender and sexuality can be juxtaposed, as they were in the writings of Magnus Hirschfeld,[41] in an explicit rejection of this collapse. This *historical* approach encourages critical reflection on the *contemporary* definitions of transvestism and transsexualism.

Anne Bolin's study of transgendered people in the United States reflects a similar commitment to social scientific inquiry.[42] She interrogates the uniform nature of psychiatric categories of transsexualism and transvestism. In particular, Bolin examines the ways in which psychiatric discourses assume that all transsexuals are heterosexually identified, an assumption which was not validated by her field research.[43] She also remarks on the diversity of gender identities among transsexuals and transvestites, noting that a fluid articulation of gender has been marked at the semantic level: "*Transgenderist* is a community term denoting kinship among those with gender-variant identities. It supplants the dichotomy of transsexual and transvestite with a concept of continuity. Additionally, it highlights a growing acceptance of nonsurgical options for physical males who wish to live as women."[44] By attending to the particular ways in which transgenderists conceive their gender identities, Bolin exposes the regulatory functions of psychiatric practices.[45] This perspective also acknowledges the manner in which transgenderists expand gender identities, rather than reify a binary gender system.[46] Like Bullough and Bullough, Bolin is careful to situate the practices she cites within their proper historical contexts. For instance, she maintains that a specifically *transgender* identity is a relatively recent phenomenon, which can be understood with reference to three factors: "(1) the closing of university-affiliated gender clinics, (2) the grass-roots organizational adoption of a political agenda and (3) social alternatives to embodiments of femininity as somatic frailty."[47] Bolin does more than state that we are presently witnessing a variety of transgender identities. She situates the fluidity of these positions with regard to broader social processes, such as the decreased regulation of transgender and transsexual identities with the closing of university-based gender clinics. In this context of an emerging transgender identity and politics, seemingly contradictory subject-positions, such as male-to-female transsexual body builders, are possible.[48]

Historically, the disciplines of sociology and anthropology have produced some of the most insightful work on transgender issues; in certain cases (such as with Garfinkel's research), this scholarship has attained canonical status. It is thus curious that the recent field of queer theory neglects these contributions. While social scientific research privileges questions of methodology, critics like Butler and Garber devote very little attention to how they actually go about doing research.

Race, Class, Gender: Facts or Figures?

It should be quite clear by now that social scientific investigations of transgender issues are markedly different from the analyses offered by critics in queer theory. While I have devoted considerable attention to the erasure of transgender subjectivity within the field of queer theory, it is also useful to reflect on how critics in queer theory conceptualize race, especially since they use transgendered individuals to speak about processes of racialization.

Recall Butler's discussion of Venus Extravaganza. Butler maintains that Extravaganza adopts the identity of "woman" in an attempt to escape her position as a poor Latina in New York City. I have already suggested that this argument is premised on a denial of Extravaganza's transsexual status. Butler does more than simply negate Extravaganza's transsexuality, however; she uses it in order to speak about race and class. While Butler makes a vague gesture toward the economic and racial realities of Latinas in New York City, she only arrives at these "realities" through the tropological use of Extravaganza's gender.

Butler is hardly the sole critic in queer theory to reduce transgender identities to the figural dimensions and functions of discourse. Garber's emphasis on a "category crisis" also uses the *figure* of the transvestite to speak about race and class.[49] Not only does this position prevent any possible analysis of transgendered lives; it begins with the somewhat naive assumption that questions of race and class can be separated from those of gender. In a similar way, Carole-Anne Tyler berates gay male camp and drag practices for their implicit misogyny and racism:

> If boys will be girls they had better be ladies. A real woman is a real lady; otherwise, she is a female impersonator, a camp or mimic whose "unnaturally" bad taste — like that of the working-class, ethnic, or racially "other" woman — marks the impersonation as such. Miming the feminine means impersonating a white, middle-class impersonation of an "other" ideal of femininity.[50]

Tyler's intervention is remarkable for its contradictions. While some gay male camp and drag practices can be interpreted as misogynist and racist, it is curious that Tyler overlooks African-American and working-class forms of drag, as for instance in the performances and representations of Joan Jett Blakk, Vaginal Creme Davis, and DeAundra Peek.[51] In this light, Tyler's argument is tautological: she looks at drag practices within white, middle-class, gay male communities in order to claim that drag *per se* reflects white, middle-class, masculine values.[52]

A figural use of transgender identities and practices is obviously deficient when it comes to accounting for transgender realities. This perspective is also not the best model, I suggest, for thinking about race, ethnicity, and class. There are significant parallels between the presentation of transgender issues in queer theory and its discussions of race, class, and ethnicity. Queer theorists, for instance, often make a gesture toward a social context in which racialized, sexualized, and gendered bodies are produced. Yet they do not begin their research with a discussion of these social practices and relations.[53] Queer theory demands that readers infer the entire Western sex/gender system from specific examples of drag. Likewise, we are supposed to make sense of the history of racism and colonialism in the United States from a few brief remarks on "poor black women who are single mothers without the support of men."[54] This framework, I submit, is not a productive one for understanding the dialectical relations between micrological and macrological social processes.

I have already mentioned that sociologists and anthropologists begin their inquiries from the lived daily conditions of their subjects. By maintaining this focus on everyday social relations, we can think about what it would mean to address questions of race, class, and ethnicity with respect to transgendered identities and communities. What kinds of things could be included in such a research program? One pressing need would be an examination of the relations between urban police departments and black transgender communities. When New York police raided the black transvestite/ transsexual bar Blue's on September 29, 1982, they locked the doors, pulled out their weapons, and beat the patrons for nearly an hour.[55] When the body of black transgender sex trade worker Marsha Johnson was found floating in the Hudson River, the New York Police Department declared her death to be a suicide — a declaration which was amended to "drowning of an unknown cause" only after intense lobbying efforts.[56]

Or, perhaps a study of race, class, and transgendered issues could focus on questions of health care. Access to hormones, for example, remains a severe problem for many transsexuals, especially those who are young, poor, and/or of color. The lack of safe and affordable access to hormones creates a situation in which poor transsexuals are at increased risk of harming their bodies. The sharing of needles to shoot hormones has been identified as one way in which HIV is transmitted in American inner-city transsexual communities.[57] Likewise, some transsexuals inject themselves with low-quality silicone obtained on the black market. Sophia Pastel, a black transsexual in Atlanta, Georgia, died after being injected with silicone from an auto parts store.[58]

Perhaps an examination of race and class in a transgender framework would study the situation of transsexuals in prison — individuals who are incarcerated according to their biological sex, and who are often denied their hormones once imprisoned.[59] A study of transsexuals in prison would be directly relevant to transgenders of color, given the overrepresentation of black and native peoples in prison institutions.[60] The transmission of HIV in transgender communities could be an additional area of inquiry. A recent study in Atlanta, Georgia indicates a seropositive rate of 68 percent among transgender sex trade workers; more than 80 percent of the individuals in the sample were black.[61]

While these subject areas concentrate on transgenders who are of color and/or poor, one could also imagine a critical research program which investigates the relations of class and race implicit in normative definitions of transsexualism and transvestism. Why does a middle-class, white transsexual identity (sometimes evidenced in the magazine *Tapestries*) emphasize the "professional" status of transsexual women and men? How are categories of class and race deployed to "normalize" one's transgender status? How is this discourse on transsexualism complicit with the practices of gender identity clinics, which require that transsexuals live full-time in their chosen gender in order to receive hormones and sex reassignment surgery? (This practice is referred to as the "real-life test"; note the assumption that individuals who do not live full-time in their chosen gender are not living a "real life"). What does this normalization of transsexualism mean for transgenders of color, for those who are poor, for artists, or for sex trade workers?

These areas of inquiry are useful starting points for a research agenda which accounts for the intersections of race, class, and gender in the context of the lived social relations of transgendered people. I do not wish to suggest that we must retreat into positivist, quantitative analysis in order to engage in any kind of *meaningful* research. And given a general dismissal of discourse analysis within the Anglo-American social sciences,[62] allow me to clarify that I do not seek to valorize sociology over literature, Marxism over deconstruction, practice over theory. Indeed, much of the social science scholarship I have cited is explicitly concerned with questions of language. Bolin places the emergence of the term "transgender" within the context of broader social processes, such as the closing of university-affiliated gender clinics, while Newton provides the cultural background necessary to understand what is meant by the phrase "transy drag." Just as this attention to language can illuminate macrological social relations, so too can one apply specific literary interpretive devices in order to make sense of the social construction of transgender identities. A reading of *The Silence of the Lambs*, for instance, could focus on the metonymic relations between the categories "transvestism," "transsexualism," and "gender dysphoria" in psychiatric discourse. A recognition of how these identities are contiguously related would prove valuable in developing an appropriate political response to the film. By studying the substitution of gender dysphoria for transsexualism in the narrative, we can offer a response more complex than Garber's declaration that the film is "politically correct" because Buffalo Bill is not a transsexual.[63]

Thus, while I do not wish to reject humanities-based interpretive methodologies outright, I do want to force a consideration of how these methodologies are used and the conceptions of the social world they legitimate.[64] The main difficulty in Garber's and Butler's figural use of transgendered people is that it elides the everyday realities of individuals who live outside normative sex/gender relations.[65] Violence against transsexuals, lack of access to health care and social services, police harassment of transgender sex trade workers, the rape of transsexuals in prison, the staggering incidence of HIV within transgender communities, the difficulties transgendered individuals have in finding employment:[66] these are the day-to-day realities of transgendered people which Butler and Garber consistently ignore.

Conclusion

This essay has explored the violence implicit in queer theory's representation of transgendered people. Within queer theory, transgendered people are only looked at, observed, scrutinized, and spoken about. While it is important to criticize these methodologies (or perhaps more accurately, this lack of methodology), and while we must emphasize the need for an analysis located in the social world, we must also attend to the ways in which this kind of theory is complicit with hegemonic definitions, interpretations, and elisions of transgender identity.

On April 10, 1990, a male-to-female transsexual sex trade worker was hit and killed by a police car in Montréal. The *Montréal Gazette* reported the incident that day, noting that the police had originally identified the person as a woman, since there was a high-heeled shoe at the accident scene. Three days later, the newspaper coverage made an important shift: "M[ontréal] U[rban] C[ommunity] police have yet to identify a man who was killed when hit on St. Denis St. by a police car. . . . The man carried no identification."[67] In a mere three days, the accident victim went from some kind of gender outlaw — a genetic male who lived and worked as a woman — to a "man."

Although I know that the birth name of this person was Robert Turpin, I do not know the name she chose for herself when she began to live full-time as a woman. Newspaper coverage of the incident stated that she was a man, and her legal identification remained in her masculine name. For these reasons, we will never know what this transsexual woman called herself. The state and the mainstream media, like critics in queer theory, do not allow for the articulation of transgender voices.

Queer theory's fascination with drag, transvestism, and transsexualism is mirrored in contemporary popular culture. Over the past few years, numerous mainstream films have been produced with transgender protagonists. *The Silence of the Lambs; The Crying Game; The Adventures of Priscilla, Queen of the Desert; Le sexe des étoiles; Lipgloss;* and *Draghoula* are only some of the more recent cinematic representations of drag and transsexuality. Like queer theory, these films are more interested in titillating the viewer with transgressions of gender norms than with a sustained examination of what it means to live as a gender outlaw.

At gender-identity clinics, transsexuals are encouraged to lie about their transsexual status. They are to define themselves as men or women, not transsexual men and women. Individuals are encouraged to invent personal histories in their chosen genders; female-to-male transsexuals, for example, should speak about their lives as little boys. Furthermore, they are to conceive of themselves as heterosexuals, since psychiatry cannot even begin to acknowledge male-to-female transsexual lesbians and female-to-male transsexual gay men. This elision of transsexual specificity has profound political implications. As Sandy Stone asserts, "it is difficult to generate a counter-discourse if one is programmed to disappear."[68] The practitioners of queer theory who are most interested in looking at the transvestite are also those most heavily influenced by psychoanalytic theory.[69] That these scholars cannot recognize the institutional psychiatric location in which transgendered people find themselves (gender-identity clinics) is surely ironic. Expanding on Stone's remark, we can state that "it is difficult to generate a counter-discourse if one is programmed to disappear," and even more difficult when the theory that purports to make you visible ignores the institutional operations which underlie such programming.

Call me old-fashioned, but I believe in the elaboration of organic intellectual practices, in which academics create knowledge useful to activist communities and provide a productive translation of civil and political societies.[70] Theory is a practice in itself — not just an interpretation of the social world, but a way in which it is legitimated. The reciprocal relations between theory and practice are perhaps best illustrated in our methodologies. That American, humanities-based queer theory expresses little angst over methodology is reason enough to interrogate its project.

Sadly, queer theory represents an uncritical citation of its disciplinary and national locations: a repetition of American, humanities-based scholarship which actively ignores the history of ethnographic cultural studies, as well as the historical contributions of sociology and anthropology to investigations of sexuality and gender. Given queer theory's declared interest in Derrida's notion of iterability — repetition with alteration — this lack of reflection on the intersections of methodology, institutions, and nationalism is both unfortunate and ironic.

Allow me to conclude on a happier note: while queer theory has undermined the very possibility of a transgender identity, and while this elision sustains a social world in which transgendered people cannot represent themselves, the field has nevertheless provided an occasion to contemplate how we can best study culture. As students and as teachers, then, let us read queer theory with an attention to questions of methodology. A critical analysis of representation must do more than specify the social, historical, and political contexts of the subject under investigation (although this is a useful starting point); this work must also acknowledge the disciplinary and national locations of the theoretical frameworks called upon to explain a particular phenomenon.

Were critics in queer theory to address these methodological issues, the field as we know it would be radically displaced. Scholars would be forced to negotiate sites other than those endorsed by the American humanities; intellectuals could no longer represent transgender realities in such a myopic and distorted manner; categories of race and class would be examined in terms of everyday social practices; and the relations between ethics and methodology would be foregrounded. If scholars *really* did their homework, the voices of people like Marsha Johnson, Sophia Pastel, and Michelle de Ville would be loud and clear. Is this a utopian dream, or an agenda for the future of queer studies?

NOTES

Acknowledgments: This essay benefited from conversations and exchanges with many people. For reflection on the political and methodological issues in queer theory, I thank Gary Kinsman, Lorna Weir, Jessica Piper, Steven Seidman, Ellen Jacobs, Elspeth Probyn, Susan Stryker, and Michael du Plessis. Additional thanks to Brett Beemyn for his editorial suggestions and comments.

1. For an incomplete list, see Judith Butler, *Gender Trouble: Feminism and the Subversion of Identity* (New York: Routledge, 1990); Butler, "Performative Acts and Gender Constitution: An Essay in Phenomenology and Feminist Theory," *Performing Feminisms: Feminist Critical Theory and Practice*, ed. Sue Ellen Case (Baltimore: Johns Hopkins University Press, 1991), 270–82; Butler, *Bodies That Matter: On the Discursive Limits of "Sex"* (New York: Routledge, 1993); Marjorie Garber, *Vested Interests: Cross-Dressing and Cultural Anxiety* (New York: Routledge, 1992); Carole-Anne Tyler, "Boys Will Be Girls: The Politics of Gay Drag," *Inside/Out: Lesbian Theories, Gay Theories*, ed. Diana Fuss (New York: Routledge, 1991), 32–70; Michael Moon and Eve Sedgwick, "Divinity: A Performance Piece. A Dossier. A Little-Understood Emotion," *Discourse* 13, no. 1 (Fall–Winter 1990–91): 12–39.

2. For a useful historical overview of cultural studies, see Patrick Brantlinger, *Crusoe's Footprints: Cultural Studies in Britain and America* (New York: Routledge, 1990).

3. Paul Willis, *Profane Culture* (London: Routledge and Kegan Paul, 1978); Centre for Contemporary Cultural Studies [CCCS], *The Empire Strikes Back: Race and Racism in 70s Britain* (London: Hutchinson, 1982); Dick Hebdige, *Subculture: The Meaning of Style* (London: Methuen, 1979).

4. Willis, *Profane Culture*.

5. Pratibha Parmar, "Gender, Race and Class: Asian Women in Resistance," *The Empire Strikes Back*, 236–75.

6. Hebdige, *Subculture*.

7. Stuart Hall, "The Emergence of Cultural Studies and the Crisis of the Humanities," *October* 53 (1990): 16.

8. Ibid., 16.

9. Susan Willis, "Hardcore: Subculture American Style," *Critical Inquiry* 19 (Winter 1993): 365–83.

10. Angela McRobbie, "Post-Marxism and Cultural Studies: A Post-Script," *Cultural Studies*, ed. Lawrence Grossberg, Cary Nelson, and Paula Treichler (New York: Routledge, 1992), 719–30; Tony Bennett, "Putting Policy into Cultural Studies," *Cultural Studies*, 23–37.

11. Hazel Carby, "The Multicultural Wars," *Black Popular Culture*, ed. Gina Dent (Seattle: Bay Press, 1992), 187–99.

12. Gayatri Spivak, "Feminism in Decolonization," *differences* 3, no. 3 (1991): 142.

13. For more on the historical emergence of queer theory, see Jeffrey Escoffier, "Inside the Ivory Closet: The Challenges Facing Lesbian and Gay Studies," *OUT/LOOK* 10 (Fall 1990): 40–48; Michael Warner, "Introduction: Fear of a Queer Planet," *Social Text* 29 (1991): 3–19; Steven Seidman, "Symposium: Queer Theory/Sociology: A Dialogue," *Sociological Theory* 12, no. 2 (July 1994): 166–77.

14. Butler, *Gender Trouble*, 130, emphasis in original.

15. Interview with Michelle de Ville, *Fuzzbox*, circa 1990, no page.

16. An investigation of the gendered construction of gay male sexuality is available in Seymour Kleinberg, "The New Masculinity of Gay Men, and Beyond," *Beyond Patriarchy: Essays by Men on Pleasure, Power and Change*, ed. Michael Kaufman (Toronto: Oxford University Press, 1987), 120–38.

17. Moon and Sedgwick, "Divinity," 19.

18. I discuss these events in more detail in Ki Namaste, "Fighting Back with Fashion: Pride Day Perversions and the Tyranny of the Homogeneous," *Fuse* 16, no. 2 (Fall 1992): 7–9.

19. One bisexual transgendered political speaker was scheduled to talk at Divers/cité in 1994, but this person was eliminated due to "time constraints." Numerous lesbian and gay political speakers, however, addressed the crowd that day.

20. Interview with Sandra LaFramboise, October 12, 1994.

21. Historical research on these questions reveals that while gender transgressions on stage were often tolerated, this acceptance rarely extended to individuals who cross-dressed in everyday public space. See, for instance, George Chauncey, Jr.'s discussion of a straight-identified navy man who was arrested for being involved with a female impersonator, in George Chauncey, Jr., "Christian Brotherhood or Sexual Perversion? Homosexual Identities and the Construction of Sexual Boundaries in the World War I Era," *Hidden from History: Reclaiming the Gay and Lesbian Past*, ed. Martin Duberman, Martha Vicinus, and George Chauncey, Jr. (New York: New American Library Books, 1989), 294–317. As his defense, the man claimed that he did not find his male partner to be "peculiar" (i.e., queer) since his partner wore "women's" clothes for his stage role. Chauncey points out that, in some instances, the impersonation of femininity on the stage was permissible, even to the extent that some of these female impersonators wore "women's" clothes in their everyday lives. Also see Chauncey's discussion of drag cultures in pre–World War I New York, in which he demonstrates that drag balls provided an occasion to cross-dress which was socially acceptable. Chauncey, *Gay New York: Gender, Urban Culture and the Making of the Gay Male World, 1890–1940* (New York: Basic Books, 1994), 298. Vern Bullough and Bonnie Bullough demonstrate that cross-dressing was sanctioned and even encouraged during certain seasonal

celebrations and festivities — an acceptance which can be witnessed in the contemporary celebration of Halloween. Bullough and Bullough, *Cross Dressing, Sex and Gender* (Philadelphia: University of Pennsylvania Press, 1993), 66, 75. For an examination of performance drag, see Sara Maitland, *Vesta Tilley* (London: Virago Press, 1986). For a more detailed study of cross-dressing on stage in the British context, see J.S. Bratton, "Irrational Dress," *The New Woman and Her Sisters: Feminism and Theatre 1850–1914*, ed. Vivien Gardner and Susan Rutherford (Ann Arbor: University of Michigan Press, 1992), 77–91. The legal restrictions on transvestism are also discussed in Rudolf Dekker and Lotte van de Pol, *The Tradition of Female Transvestism in Early Modern Europe* (New York: St. Martin's Press, 1989).

22. Butler, *Bodies That Matter*, 131.

23. Ibid., 131.

24. For a discussion of how the city of Houston's cross-dressing ordinance was revoked, see Phyllis Frye, "Repeal of the Houston Crossdressing Ordinance," *Proceedings from the First International Conference on Transgender Law and Employment Policy* (Houston, TX: International Conference on Transgender Law and Employment Policy, 1992), 104–7. Readers interested in this question may also wish to consult Mary Dunlap, "The Constitutional Rights of Sexual Minorities: A Crisis of the Male/Female Dichotomy," *Hastings Law Journal* 30 (March 1979): 1132–49. My thanks to Judith Marshall for the latter reference.

25. In one of our many conversations about queer theory and cultural studies, Michael du Plessis asked this question with regard to Garber's book.

26. Garber, *Vested Interests*, 17.

27. Ibid., 116.

28. Harold Garfinkel, *Studies in Ethnomethodology* (Englewood Cliffs, NJ: Prentice-Hall, 1967).

29. Suzanne Kessler and Wendy McKenna, *Gender: An Ethnomethodological Approach* (New York: John Wiley, 1978).

30. Suzanne Kessler, "The Medical Construction of Gender: Case Management of Inter-Sexed Infants," *Signs* 16, no. 1 (1990): 3–26. Also see Deborah Findlay, "Discovering Sex: Medical Science, Feminism and Intersexuality," *Canadian Review of Sociology and Anthropology* 32, no. 1 (February 1995): 25–52.

31. Steven Epstein, "A Queer Encounter: Sociology and the Study of Sexuality," *Sociological Theory* 12, no. 2 (July 1994): 188–202.

32. Ibid., 189.

33. Here, I take issue with the conditions of reception for Butler's work, and not her work per se.

34. For an excellent introduction to the project of social theory, see Brian Fay, *Social Theory and Political Practice* (London: George Allen and Unwin, 1975).

35. Esther Newton, *Mother Camp: Female Impersonators in America* (Englewood Cliffs, NJ: Prentice-Hall, 1972). Also see Colette Piat, *Elles . . . "les Travestis": La vérité sur les transsexuels* (Paris: Presses de la Cité, 1978).

36. Newton, *Mother Camp*, 41–58.

37. Ibid., 45.

38. Ibid., 51.

39. For an introduction to ethnography, see David Fetterman, *Ethnography: Step by Step* (London: Sage, 1989); and James Spradley, *The Ethnographic Interview* (New York: Holt, Rinehart, and Winston, 1979). For contemporary debates on ethnography, consult Margery Wolf, *A Thrice-Told Tale: Feminism, Postmodernism, and Ethnographic Responsibility* (Stanford, CA: Stanford

University Press, 1992); and Martin Hammersley, *What's Wrong with Ethnography? Methodological Explorations* (New York: Routledge, 1992).

40. Bullough and Bullough, "The Development of the Medical Model," *Cross Dressing, Sex and Gender*, 203–25. Also see Gert Hekma, " 'A Female Soul in a Male Body': Sexual Inversion as Gender Inversion in Nineteenth-Century Sexology," *Third Sex, Third Gender: Beyond Sexual Dimorphism in Culture and History*, ed. Gilbert Herdt (New York: Zone Books, 1994), 213–39.

41. Magnus Hirschfeld, *The Transvestite: An Investigation of the Erotic Desire to Cross-Dress*, trans. Michael Lombardi (Buffalo, NY: Prometheus Books, 1991 [1910]).

42. Anne Bolin, "Transcending and Transgendering: Male-to-Female Transsexuals, Dichotomy, and Diversity," *Third Sex, Third Gender*, 447–85. Also see Bolin, *In Search of Eve: Transsexual Rites of Passage* (South Hadley, MA: Bergin and Garvey, 1988).

43. Bolin, "Transcending and Transgendering," 460. For a similar argument, consult Deborah Feinbloom, Michael Fleming, Valerie Kijewski, and Margo Schulter, "Lesbian/Feminist Orientation among Male-to-Female Transsexuals," *Journal of Homosexuality* 2, no. 1 (Fall 1976): 59–71. Also note the work of Eli Coleman, Walter Bockting, and Louis Gooren, "Homosexual and Bisexual Identity in Sex-Reassigned Female-to-Male Transsexuals," *Archives of Sexual Behavior* 22, no. 1 (1993): 37–50.

44. Bolin, "Transcending and Transgendering," 461.

45. Although Bolin is writing as an anthropologist, one can imagine similar critical work located outside this discipline. For instance, Sandy Stone elaborates a politics of "posttranssexuality" which displaces traditional definitions of transsexualism. Stone, "The *Empire* Strikes Back: A Posttranssexual Manifesto," *Body Guards: The Cultural Politics of Gender Ambiguity*, ed. Julia Epstein and Kristina Straub (New York: Routledge, 1991), 280–304.

46. One of the most common oppositions to transsexualism (usually put forward under the banner of "feminism") is the assumption that it reinforces sexist stereotypes. Examples of this argument can be found in Dwight Billings and Thomas Urban, "The Socio-Medical Construction of Transsexualism: An Interpretation and Critique," *Social Problems* 29, no. 3 (1982): 266–82. The most extreme example of this position is Janice Raymond, *The Transsexual Empire: The Making of the She-Male* (Boston: Beacon, 1979).

47. Bolin, "Transcending and Transgendering," 462.

48. Ibid., 478–82.

49. Garber, *Vested Interests*, 17.

50. Tyler, "Boys Will Be Girls," 57.

51. A discussion of DeAundra Peek is available in Gabriel Gomez, "DQTV: Public Access Queers," *Fuse* 17, no. 1 (Fall 1993): 8–11. The video work of Vaginal Creme Davis is presented in Matias Viegener, " 'The Only Haircut That Makes Sense Anymore': Queer Subculture and Gay Resistance," *Queer Looks: Lesbian and Gay Perspectives on Film and Video*, ed. Martha Gever, John Greyson, and Pratibha Parmar (New York: Routledge, 1993), 116–33. For a useful summary of Joan Jett Blakk's activities, consult Joe Jeffreys, "Joan Jett Blakk for President: Cross-Dressing at the Democratic National Convention," *Drama Review* 37, no. 3 (Fall 1993): 186–95.

52. For a more elaborate critique of Tyler's essay, see Michael du Plessis, "Queer Pasts Now: Historical Fiction in Lesbian, Bisexual, Transgender and Gay Film," Ph.D. dissertation, Department of Comparative Literature, University of Southern California, 1993. Du Plessis emphasizes the ways in which Tyler's analysis lacks historical and cultural specificity.

53. Steven Seidman writes that an absence of sociologists in queer theory "is somewhat ironic in light of the gesturing of queer theory towards a general social analysis." Seidman, "Symposium," 174.

54. Butler, *Bodies That Matter*, 132.

55. See the news item "Cops Trash New York Gay *[sic]* Bar," *Body Politic* 88 (November 1982): 21.

56. Randy Wicker, "Marsha P. Johnson: Police Stonewall Murder," *The New York Pride Guide: Official Guide to Lesbian and Gay Pride and History Month 1993*, 51. My thanks to Ellen Jacobs for providing me with this documentation.

57. Walter Bockting, B. R. Simon Rosser, and Eli Coleman, *Transgender HIV/AIDS Prevention Program* (Minneapolis: Program in Human Sexuality, 1993); S. Goihman with A. Ferreira, S. Santos, and J.L. Grandi, "Silicone Application as a Risk Factor for HIV Infection," presentation at the International Conference on AIDS, August 7–12, 1994, Yokohama, Japan.

58. See the news item "Back Alley Transsexual Injections?" *San Francisco Bay Times* 14, no. 11 (February 25, 1993): 11.

59. Laura Masters, *The Imprisoned Transgenderist* (St. Catharine's, Ontario: TransEqual, 1993). This document can be obtained by writing TransEqual at 165 Ontario Street, Unit 609, St. Catharine's, Ontario L2R 5K4 Canada.

60. For statistical documentation on aboriginal peoples in Canadian prisons, see *Task Force on Aboriginal Peoples in Federal Corrections: Final Report* (Ottawa: Solicitor-General, Correctional Services of Canada, 1989).

61. Kirk Elifson, Jacqueline Boles, Ellen Posey, Mike Sweat, William Darrow, and William Elsea, "Male Transvestite Prostitutes and HIV Risk," *American Journal of Public Health* 83, no. 2 (1993): 260–62.

62. See, for instance, Bryan Palmer, *Descent into Discourse: The Reification of Language and the Writing of Social History* (Philadelphia: Temple University Press, 1990). A more balanced overview of these debates can be found in Pauline Rosenau, *Insights, Inroads, Intrusions: Postmodernism and the Social Sciences* (Princeton, NJ: Princeton University Press, 1992).

63. Garber, *Vested Interests*, 116.

64. For an examination of how queer theory uses semiotics, and the need for a specifically social semiotic analysis, see Ki Namaste, "From Performativity to Interpretation: Towards a Social Semiotic Account of Bisexuality," *RePresenting Bisexualities: Subjects and Cultures of Fluid Desire*, ed. Maria Pramaggiore and Donald E. Hall (New York: New York University Press, forthcoming).

65. This is not to argue that an investigation of the figure of transgendered people has no import. See, for instance, Susan Stryker's review of *The Crying Game*, *Transsexual News Telegraph* 1 (Summer 1993): 10–11. Stryker contends that the transgender protagonist Dil is conceived in relation to the concept of home, as evidenced by Fergus's remark to her that she should have just "stayed home." This policing of national and gender borders, for Stryker, locates transgendered people as those who always betray themselves and the very idea of nationhood.

This interpretation is useful because it theorizes the cinematic representation of transgendered people in relation to common myths and stereotypes about who we are and the impossibilities of our identities. While Garber and Butler examine the transgender figure to look elsewhere (i.e., at relations of class and race), Stryker develops an analysis which appreciates the ways in which gender, race, and nation intersect. For sociological perspectives on these methodological issues, see G. Lakoff and M. Johnson, *Metaphors We Live By* (Chicago: University of Chicago Press, 1980); and Norman Fairclough, *Discourse and Social Change* (Cambridge, UK: Polity Press, 1992).

66. See Christine Burnham, in consultation with Patricia Diewold, *Gender Change: Employability Issues* (Vancouver: Perceptions Press, 1994).

67. *Montréal Gazette* (April 13, 1990): A3.

68. Stone, "The *Empire* Strikes Back," 295.

69. Butler, *Bodies That Matter*, *Gender Trouble*, "Performative Acts"; Tyler, "Boys Will Be Girls"; Garber, *Vested Interests*.

70. The reference here, of course, is to Antonio Gramsci, *Selections from the Prison Notebooks*, ed. and trans. Quintin Hoare and Geoffrey Nowell Smith (New York: International Publishers, 1971). See especially "The Formation of the Intellectuals," 5–14; "The Different Position of Urban and Rural-Type Intellectuals," 14–23; and "Critical Notes on an Attempt at Popular Sociology," 419–72.

chapter 11

Hegemonic Discourse in an Oppositional Community:

Lesbian Feminist Stigmatization of Bisexual Women

Amber Ault

Negative sentiment toward bisexuality and bisexual women finds expression in a wide variety of forms of discrimination, erasure, invalidation, and prejudice in lesbian feminist communities and discourse. Ranging from blatant personal bigotry to political exclusion, such practices silence bisexuals as individuals, disrupt the formation of a politicized bisexual identity, and prevent substantive debate over the implications of the emergence of a bisexual identity marker for feminist and gay critiques of dominant culture. The intense and personal objections of many lesbian feminists to bisexuality among women, particularly as it is signified by the use of "bisexual" as a label for sexual subjectivity, and the silence of feminist academics on the politics of bisexuality, suggest that many lesbian feminists perceive bisexuality as a deep and formidable challenge to both personal identity and movement politics. In this essay, I define and deconstruct some of the bases of lesbian feminist resistance to bisexuality as a legitimate sexual identity category.

Recent sociological work on bisexuality has documented lesbian antipathy toward bisexual women (Silber 1990; Rust 1992, 1993; George 1993; Weinberg, Williams, and Pryor 1994), and a growing number of personal accounts by bisexual women have reported and theorized lesbian resistance to acknowledging the bisexual category as socially legitimate (Clausen 1990; Blasingame 1992; Eridani 1992; McKeon 1992; Young 1992). This essay extends these analyses by focusing on the meaning which a lesbian discourse that is hostile to bisexual women has for our understandings of the production of lesbian subjectivity. Because I write as a lesbian feminist sociologist, the critique offered here is an internal one, interested in examining how lesbian antipathy toward bisexual women recirculates a larger cultural discourse that lesbian feminists have theorized as misogynist when it has been deployed against them. I am particularly interested in examining the reification in lesbian discourse on bisexual women of binary constructions that have been widely problematized in feminist theory as being central to Western patriarchal discourse and as underwriting multiple systems of social domination. While my stance toward the current common bases of lesbian enmity toward bisexual women is a critical one, I do not intend this essay as a defense of bisexual women or the propriety of any particular location of bisexual women within lesbian communities or politics. I offer instead a critique of particular social practices that seem to originate not in feminist theory but in heteropatriarchal systems of domination. Having begun to excavate the relationship between a lesbian discourse that is unfriendly to bisexual women and a dominant discourse that is hostile toward lesbians, I suggest, not an end to this debate, but, instead, a shifting of its terms.

The Problem/The Effects

Before I proceed to identify the techniques through which lesbian feminist discourse negates bisexuality and the standpoints from which lesbians object to bisexuality, I offer three examples that demonstrate the effects of such discursive practices. The first example focuses on personal relationships, the second on lesbian/gay and bisexual politics, and the last on academic life. Although the responses in the following examples come from thirty-five bisexual women who participated in my qualitative study of the social relations between bisexual women and lesbians, my intention here is not to describe bisexuality or bisexuals, nor to identify a bisexual speaking position. I hope, however, to substantiate my claim that some lesbian discourse marginalizes bisexuals and to begin to theorize the trouble therein.

First, an example from the realm of personal relationships, in which a bisexual woman recounts her partnership with a lesbian who is negatively disposed toward bisexuality:

> My "ex" used to say she couldn't trust me because I'm bi. I have seen this in other relationships too. As much as we, the bisexuals, try to convince the people we love that there is a difference between being bisexual and being unfaithful, promiscuous, or disloyal, we can't seem to convince the people we love. I would never leave someone for anyone else. I'm an extremely loyal and honest person, and it hurt not to have my girlfriend trust me, especially when she became the one to have an extra-partnership affair.

Second, an example from public politics:

> I used to be very out, as the founder of the local bisexual women's group. My name was posted on the bulletin board at the Lesbian and Gay Center. Sometimes I would get harassing phone calls, telling me to "get the hell out of our community." One lesbian called to say that she "wasn't sure of our right to exist." She yelled at me for twenty minutes, until I hung up. We are accused of neurosis, disloyalty, and immorality. This kind of reaction from separatist lesbians caused me to leave the lesbian/gay community for several years.

Finally, an example from academia, one with clear ramifications for the treatment of bisexual women in academic projects and research:

S—, a bisexual woman of color who centers her academic attention on post-colonial theory, reports attending a work group on diversity issues at a lesbian-dominated feminist conference. Reviewing the axes of diversity to which the group will attend, S— notices the absence of sexuality issues and raises this. The group's moderator responds with an acknowledgment of a need to include gay and lesbian issues in theorizing by Third World women. "And bisexual issues too," S— interjects. "No," responds the moderator, "bisexuals don't exist." (Taken from field notes)

This example from the academic world indicates that considerations of bisexual participation in lesbian and gay community life and the theoretical and political implications of bisexuality are frequently ignored in academic lesbian feminist writing. On those occasions where such writing acknowledges bisexual existence, it often reinscribes bisexuality as apolitical and as merely a substratum of either lesbianism or heterosexuality. Even Judith Butler's (1990) strenuous deconstruction of the relationship between institutionalized heterosexuality and the binary sex-gender system is guilty of this. Butler rescues lesbianism from Julia Kristeva's "prediscursive, psychotic," apolitical abyss but leaves female bisexuality mired there.

The issues raised by the examples cited above are recurrent ones in bisexual women's accounts of how they are situated by lesbians within lesbian feminist communities. I postulate that a recursive relationship exists between the treatment of bisexual women in academic lesbian feminist circles, feminist texts, and both personal and political life in lesbian feminist communities. Under this formulation, personal hostility becomes political censure and theoretical invisibility, which supports some lesbians' sense that a bisexual identity is not legitimate in a lesbian feminist culture in which the credo that "the personal is political" has somehow come to signify that the sexual is the intellectual as well.

The Participants

In the following section, I identify four practices through which some lesbian discourse constructs and "neutralizes" or, alternately, refuses to construct, bisexual women. It is important to note here that not all lesbians treat bisexuality this way and to remind the reader that this research explicitly focuses on lesbian discourse that is hostile to bisexual women, which exists within wider lesbian discourses on sexuality, community, relationships, and politics. The data upon which this conceptualization rests come from a set of in-depth interviews with lesbian feminists.

The thirteen lesbian feminists interviewed for this research are white, middle class, well educated, twenty-eight to fifty-three years old, and employed in feminist organizations, gay and lesbian organizations, or academia. The discursive practices I identify here, and the attitudes underlying them, may only be common among members of this particular socioeconomic and ethnic segment of what many casually call "the" lesbian community. While I object both politically and theoretically to allowing privileged white women to stand for a more diverse community and to define its culture, it is important to limit the data this way, because it allows for a mapping of the meaning-making processes of these women, a group often criticized for its social influence over lesbian feminist culture and, more generally, the broader social and discursive space referred to as "the women's community." My interest here is not in documenting all lesbian feminist discourse on bisexual women, but, instead, on exploring the anti-bisexual discourse that is deployed by those lesbian feminists who arguably enjoy the greatest "power to define" within lesbian culture. I would like to suggest that readers attend to the submerged dynamics of race in the narratives that follow. Although I will not be exploring this issue here, it appears that the category "bisexual" may be working as a proxy for the category "Black" in a white lesbian feminist discourse that has been purged of overt expressions of racism.

Interviewees were recruited through a snowball sampling technique known as purposive sampling; I used professional and social opportunities to describe my work and interviewed women who, upon hearing of my research, volunteered to participate. The phrase "representative sample," used in the conventional sense, is irrelevant to a study of discourse, but I am comfortable regarding the in-depth interviews with this project's lesbian participants as a "representation sample" that effectively allows access to a lesbian discourse that is hostile to bisexual women: I interviewed volunteers until the refrains of the discourse had become so familiar that they were predictable. Although the focus of this project is on the discourse itself, and not the frequency of its deployment by lesbian feminists, Paula Rust's (1992) large quantitative study of lesbians and bisexual women is suggestive in this area, for more than a third of the lesbians participating in Rust's research held negative attitudes toward bisexual women. These attitudes are more closely examined here, in the hope of understanding them in a broader social context.

Lesbian Discursive Techniques of Bisexual Neutralization

The sociologists Gresham Sykes and David Matza (1957) called the practices that male juvenile delinquents used to discount the harm they inflicted on their victims "techniques of neutralization." I borrow the phrase here as an umbrella term to describe the ultimate effects of the practices deployed in this strain of lesbian discourse on bisexuality: to discount, negate, erase, and depoliticize it. In short, these techniques of neutralization serve as an index of the political and personal threat that bisexuality poses to lesbian identity and culture.

When it turns its attention toward neutralizing bisexuality, lesbian discourse employs four identifiable strategies: suppression, incorporation, marginalization, and delegitimation. While I have described these strategies as analytically distinctive, they are, in practice, interconnected and often interpermeable. All four strategies reside within a larger narrative on sex, gender, and sexuality that is centered on a system of dualistic categories in which one category's coherence depends upon the definition and stigmatization of an identifiable "other." I will define these techniques of neutralization, offer examples of them, and problematize them by deconstructing the positions which promote them.

Suppression.   Anti-bisexual discourse among lesbians suppresses bisexuality both passively and actively. Passive suppression elides the existence of bisexuality by refusing to acknowledge it. This refusal promotes the construction of a unitary community and culture composed exclusively of women who identify as lesbians and whose sexual and emotional conduct meets the performative requirements of lesbian discourse. This universalization of lesbianism among women who are in relationships with other women rests on the following assumption: lesbians are women who sleep with women; women who sleep with women are, therefore, lesbians. Discursively, then, bisexuals in relationships with women do not exist. One woman I interviewed summarized this position with the simple pronouncement, "I know that they are not part of the lesbian community." Another woman elaborated on the common refrain that "bisexuals do not exist":

> It just strikes me as — I just don't think bisexuality exists. There! As a *legitimate* category. You want me to say that again, loudly and clearly? I think it doesn't matter what people are saying, and this is not a polite conversation — these are the impolite thoughts, right? — It's not a thing. Can't be a category because it's not complete yet; it's not there.

Active suppression takes a variety of forms. One lesbian's statement that "if a woman wants to date a lesbian, the last thing she should do is say that she's bisexual" indicates the intimate stakes of successful suppression, as does the following account:

> At the point where she said, "I think I'm bisexual; how would you feel if I slept with men?" I had to address that in an immediate way, and I just said, "Well, I'd say, 'It's been real fun, and you're out of my life, in terms of a sexual relationship.' "

This sentiment enjoys currency beyond the domain of romantic encounters. For example, in a recent study of a lesbian feminist community, Verta Taylor and Nancy Whittier (1992) reported that "the significance of lesbian identity for feminist activists is well summarized by the name of a feminist support group at a major university, Lesbians Who Just Happen to Be Dating Politically Correct Men" (115). For these "lesbians dating men" and others within lesbian discourse, the valorization of a lesbian identity depends on the active suppression of a bisexual one.

The discursive production of a unitary lesbian culture and community also depends upon the suppression of bisexuality. This "boundary work" maintains lesbian culture as a unitary whole that is opposed to the presumably unitary dominant heterosexual culture. By insisting on an internal monosexual culture, lesbian feminists reproduce the gay/straight and male/female binary systems, dichotomies which lesbian feminist politics conventionally theorizes as promoting male dominance. Thus, by refusing to acknowledge bisexuality, the lesbian feminist discourse that is hostile toward bisexual women *perpetuates* the very cultural dualisms that feminist thinking usually analyzes as fundamentally oppressive.

Incorporation.   I use the term "incorporation" to designate the practices through which lesbian discourse claims bisexuals as lesbians. Unlike discursive suppression, incorporation acknowledges bisexual existence but denies its integrity by constructing bisexuals as "really either heterosexual or homosexual." This creates the presumption that those bisexuals who are "really lesbians" will eventually experience enlightenment and thereby become legitimate. Bisexuals are incorporated through the construction of their status as "lesbian gonnabes." A lesbian colleague reported that she'd heard this referred to as the "Bi-Now-Gay-Later Plan." One of my interviewees used this discourse of incorporation as she recounted her new lover's process of identity formation:

> When I got involved with my current partner, this is her first experience with a woman. When she first came out, she was saying, "Gee, I don't know who I am." That was fine; we all go through that. Then she was saying, "I think I'm bisexual." And I kind of said, "Yeah, right, you go through that stage for a while, and we'll see what happens."

In the following two interview excerpts, incorporation hinges on an essentialist and binary construction of sexual identity. In this discourse, sexual identity is constructed as bifurcated; subjects "are" either heterosexual or homosexual, and once a woman who claims to be bisexual recognizes her "true identity," she can be incorporated into lesbian culture, if, of course, she is "not straight":

> [F]or whatever reason that I don't think I can defend, anyway, the way I feel is that you're straight or you're gay. You may not know, but it seems to me if you're sleeping with men and women at the same time, or in the same time frame, you might as well just call yourself straight, until you become a *real* lesbian and cut that shit out.

> I probably believe equally that they're heterosexual or they're homosexual. They're lesbians who can't say they're lesbians, or they're heterosexuals who can't admit they're heterosexual, because it means they're missing out on something.

Another example of the tendency toward incorporation appeared in a lesbian feminist interviewee's assertion that bisexual women in relationships with lesbians "should call themselves lesbian." One woman seemed to realize during the course of our interview that the pressure on bisexual women to define themselves as lesbian may account for some of the "suddenness" with which long-time participants in lesbian feminist culture sometimes become involved with men. A further example of the tendency toward incorporation is apparent in the use of the phrase, "lesbians, whether bisexual or homosexual," by lesbian feminist researchers Liz Stanley and Sue Wise (1991: 275). For Stanley and Wise, bisexuality is an overt category, but it only exists with reference to its homosexual component.

While "incorporation" acknowledges bisexuality at a nominal level, its certainty that bisexuality exists only as a mask for an ambivalent heterosexuality or lesbianism reconstructs the dominant culture's bifurcated sexual systems. This technique of neutralization refuses to treat bisexuality as an identity that has the potential to disrupt binary oppositions. Further, incorporation commonly serves as a strategy through which a hegemonic culture neutralizes its challengers; when lesbian feminist discourse incorporates bisexual identity as a way of neutralizing its threat to the binary system upon which lesbian feminist discourse ultimately depends, it employs the very strategies that are used against lesbians by the dominant culture. Heteropatriarchal discourse has long maintained, for example, that lesbians merely need the oxymoronic "good screw" before we "come to our senses" and acknowledge our "true" heterosexuality. Lesbians themselves deploy this discursive neutralization technique by claiming that bisexuals should "come to their senses" and realize that they, too, are lesbian.

Marginalization.   The techniques of neutralization that lesbian discourse often use to construct bisexuals as marginal involves, not surprisingly, many metaphors of location. I have identified two general categories of "marginalization" in the lesbian discourse that is critical of bisexual women: the common idea of being "on the edge" and the nearly ubiquitous one of being "on the fence." Some social movement theorists describe the construction of boundaries as necessary for the production and maintenance of cultures of resistance (Taylor and Whittier 1992); in this discourse, bisexuals become territory markers.

The women I interviewed used a number of phrases to marginalize bisexuals. They referred to bisexual women variously as culturally "on the edge," "on the fringe," "marginal," "trendy," and "dabbling" or "experimenting." The suggestion that they are trying to be "avant garde" also surfaces repeatedly in lesbian discourse that is hostile to bisexual women. One interviewee summarized this sentiment with the statement that "the whole thing smacks of hippy-ness to me."

This discourse also writes bisexuals as opportunists who are taking advantage of lesbian political progress, riding on the tails of the proverbial flannel shirt. In efforts to reinforce the marginality of bisexuals to lesbian culture, community, and politics, several lesbians suggested that bisexuals "get their own movement" or "form their own centers." The political common ground between lesbians and bisexual women resides, according to this discourse, in what is constructed as the "lesbian part" of bisexual women, a construction that marginalizes bisexual women by depicting them as only partially interested in lesbian concerns. Alternatively, several interviewees reported "tolerating" bisexual women's participation in political efforts, while "drawing the line" at social interactions with them beyond activist contexts. One woman reported that she would accept a bisexual woman working on lesbian issues in a political organization, "but you're not coming home to dinner, honey. When we're all engaged in some sort of political something-or-other, we have to get along, I suppose. But other than that, bisexual women can just go to hell." While there is some variation on this theme, this technique of neutralization positions bisexual women as either politically or socially marginal.

From an insider's perspective, the metaphor of "the fence" in lesbian discourse represents a line of demarcation between lesbian territory and the heterosexual world, and it is upon this fence that lesbian discourse accuses bisexual women of sitting. Ironically, this discourse invokes essentialism to press constructionist choices: lesbians deploying this logic argue that because "we are all heterosexual or homosexual, bisexuals should decide what they are." For example, one woman stated, "You're either for us, or you're against us" — thereby demonstrating how this common sentiment is contingent on the assumption of a unitary lesbian subject. This metaphor is nearly universal in lesbian discourse resistant to bisexuality. Moreover, one interviewee reported that she had been taught that "bisexual" in American Sign Language consisted of an elaborate version of the sign for "indecision," a sign built upon the sign for "fence." Thus, in sign language, according to this account, indecision about the side of the fence on which one belongs is embedded in the term "bisexual."

In addition to the binary structures that are again apparent in the marginalization of bisexuals, there is also a subtext about gender. In particular, this lesbian discourse constructs bisexual women as not only on the sexual fringe but also on a gender fence: though perhaps moving in a lesbian world, bisexual women are seen as "more feminine than the average dyke." Even femme lesbians disparage the traditional feminine gender presentation that they assign to bisexual women. One lesbian, who noted that she probably unintentionally passes as heterosexual, offered the following analysis:

> Women who are bisexual and call themselves bisexual usually look heterosexual. They still want to hang on to looking pretty and feminine and wearing feminine clothes, and wanting men to like them. Especially, or including, heterosexual men.

Another woman explicated the difference between traditionally feminine lesbians and bisexual women by making reference to a hypothetical bipolar Butch-Femme Scale:

> On the Butch-Femme Scale, I'd probably give the [bisexual] women a seven, with ten being femme and one being butch. They feel more safe with the heterosexual side than the lesbian side. Or they want to appear more heterosexual than not. And I don't think that a lesbian who would put herself at a seven on the scale is doing it to fit into the patriarchy. . . . Joan, for instance, I put her at, like, an eight, maybe an eight and a half. But I think that's just how she is. Maybe that's how she was socialized, and that's how she's comfortable. I'm very comfortable putting pantyhose on every day. It doesn't bother me. I feel very comfortable in my business attire. I just feel like me. But I think that these bisexuals, they're gonna be a seven on the scale because they've got to put themselves on the edge.

A third woman reported that, on the same scale, bisexual women would be ranked "ten plus," with their "long, flowing skirts, long hair, and pasty faces." The difference between such a bisexual woman and a similarly situated lesbian was defined as something discernable but indescribable. In all of their constructions of bisexual women's gender presentations, the lesbians interviewed for this research situated heterosexual women at one end of the "Butch-Femme" Scale, thereby collapsing the gender category "femme" with the sexual category "heterosexual." Such constructions indicate the imbrication of the dominant sex/gender system into lesbian feminist discourse and offer an explanation for both the lesbian description of the bisexual woman's femme excesses and the lesbian construction of the femme as heterosexual. Marginalization thus deploys sexism, double standards for both gender and sexual identity, and the fracturing of the bisexual subject into component "lesbian parts" and "straight parts" to construct bisexual identity and bisexual women as outside the concern of lesbian politics and culture, and appropriately peripheral to lesbian community life.

Delegitimation.   I use "delegitimation" to describe the moral content of lesbian discourse hostile to bisexual women. Perhaps most fundamentally, lesbian discourse often delegitimizes bisexual identity by constructing bisexuals as untrustworthy. Explanations for bisexual "fence sitting," for example, are based on the belief that bisexuals are either "confused" or unwilling to "just make a choice," and therefore cannot be trusted.

A second focus for lesbian mistrust of bisexuals involves their purported sexuality and its supposed difference from lesbian sexual practices. One woman, for instance, said:

> When I think of "bisexual" I think of bedhopping. . . . They not only can't commit to being one or the other, but probably can't commit to whoever they're with, be it male or female. How could someone who wants to be in a long-term committed relationship still call themselves bisexual, without some infidelity coming into the picture?

The following statement, from another interviewee, echoes a core theme in this discourse:

> You get the sense they don't have a political commitment to women, to being involved with women to destroy patriarchy and its linchpin of heterosexuality. You get the sense they would leave you for a man, if they fell in love with a man, because they still want to retain their heterosexual privilege, and because deep down they still feel that being involved with a man is as good as, or better than, even, being involved with a woman.

For both of these speakers, the prospect of being left for a man constituted a nearly unbearable threat. The first reasoned that "lesbian love is the highest form; it's pure, it's more emotional, it's the closest thing, to have two women together. Being left for a man, it would be devastating." The second speaker asserted that being left for a man would be a "slap in the face," because "it would be like someone leaving you for a dog! Woof! 'My wife left me for a poodle.' " Such a construction moves the lesbian into a subject position similar to the cuckolded heterosexual husband and the bisexual woman into the subject position of the adulterous, hyper-femme wife.

In this process of delegitimation, lesbian discourse deploys against bisexuals the same discursive techniques used by the dominant culture to discredit lesbians. For example, just as lesbians are sexualized by the dominant discourse, lesbian discourse sexualizes bisexuals. And just as the dominant discourse challenges the capacity of lesbians to form coherent, stable family units, lesbian discourse constructs bisexuals as unable to maintain long-term, committed relationships with same-sex partners and, in the process, valorizes the idea of the nuclear family centered on a monogamous pair. This discourse insists on ignoring a feminist ideology of sexual liberation that centers on women's desires, if that desire is for the forbidden: in this case, for heterosexual sex.

The sense that bisexual women eventually always choose men reflects not bisexual phallocentrism but the phallocentrism of this lesbian discourse, which attributes to the phallus the power to define the bisexual woman's life. The despair that lesbians anticipate feeling in the wake of "being left for a man" demonstrates both internalized sexism and internalized homophobia. By saying that a lesbian "could not compete with a man," this discourse reflects broader patterns of female socialization that promote women's deference to males. At the same time, the sense that the prospect of a heterosexual relationship would be irresistibly alluring to a bisexual woman already involved in a same-sex partnership reproduces the primacy of heterosexuality.

Finally, lesbian distrust of bisexuals is further amplified in the construction of bisexual women as "foreign bodies," sources of literal and metaphoric pollution to the lesbian body. My interviewees variously described bisexual women as "carriers of AIDS into the lesbian community," as "bringing male energy" into the community, and as "infiltrators" from the dominant culture. Just as biological systems protect themselves from disease through various strategies that distinguish "the self" from "the other," the lesbian body attempts to maintain its integrity by employing discursive techniques of neutralization that construct and control "the bisexual other." Biological bodies, however, do not always accurately identify threats to their well-being and sometimes destroy themselves in an effort to destroy a mistaken threat. Some feminist theory has argued that the contemporary language around infection and immunity has served as a trope for justifying political imperialism (Haraway 1991), and this seems to be its function here too, as lesbian discourse constructs bisexual women as invading, polluting carriers of male energy and disease.

Techniques of Neutralization: A Metaphorical Summary

In contemplating the effects of these techniques of neutralization, I am reminded of a story involving other bodies and other boundaries. The primatologist Dian Fossey, a white U.S. citizen, marked out a sanctuary in an African country, Rwanda, in order to protect, preserve, and study one species, the mountain gorilla. According to a story that circulates among anthropologists, one afternoon a cow wandered into the compound that Fossey had established in the forest reserve. Incensed that the Rwandan citizens who lived outside the reserve territory had failed to keep their property under control, Fossey spray-painted "FUCK YOU" on the animal's side and sent it toward home at a clip.

Together, the strands of lesbian discourse on bisexuality that I have identified here define the bisexual woman as male-identified and as male property. In this lesbian discourse, bisexual women represent the phallus itself, and the lesbian response to a bisexual woman wandering into the lesbian sanctuary is, oddly enough, to return her to the patriarchal world, after scrawling upon her body a message to the men on the other side of the fence. In this instance, however, the "FUCK YOU" functions both to reject male dominance over women and to perpetuate it; the bisexual body becomes not only a vehicle for the rejection of male definition and male invasion but also a lesbian-produced object for male domination. The metaphorical expletive becomes a message to the men banned from lesbian territory; this lesbian discourse returns the bisexual body to heteropatriarchy, a woman upon whom lesbians have written "FUCK ME."

Points, Counterpoints, and Concluding Musings

I have identified and illustrated the techniques that lesbian discourse employs to neutralize bisexuality in order to reveal how these techniques are extensions of the conceptual practices of power that dominant discourses turn against lesbians. Specifically, I argue that the dualism, sexism, and homophobia of male-dominated dynamics of sexual social control pervade the resistance of lesbians to the idea of bisexuality and to self-identified bisexual women. By moving beyond these more narrow considerations of sex and gender to incorporate considerations of race, this analysis would allow us to begin to understand what Shane Phelan (1993) has argued is the privilege of whiteness embedded in constructions of a unitary and essential lesbian self, constructions which are supported by their juxtaposition to the confused, fence-sitting bisexual.

Given the fact that most white lesbian feminists in Western societies are socialized through the practices of the dominant culture — practices that reinscribe compulsory heterosexuality (Rich 1992) in a restrictively gendered order — the reproduction of that order in some lesbian feminist discourse is not surprising. Much feminist criticism has analyzed how race marks lesbian feminist discourse; less attention has been paid to analyzing the phallocentrism of this discourse. Decoding the lesbian discourse that is hostile to bisexual women begins to raise new questions and furthers our understanding of how systems of domination built along lines of social demarcation reinforce one another. Is lesbian discourse inherently and irremediably phallocentric? Are bisexuals in lesbian discourse "the new femmes," providing a dualistic resolution to the androgynous ambiguity of the 1980s? Can the lesbian subject — and can lesbian discourse — move beyond the terms set by the dominant discursive system? Is it possible for a lesbian discourse predicated upon the privileges of white subjectivity to survive its critique? Should it be possible? And when it comes to the degrading construction of the bisexual other, what are the stakes?

A politicized bisexuality might pose a distinct challenge to the system that produces a world of pairs, in which one member always dominates the other. Beyond this, a feminist bisexuality might represent a challenge to male dominance that is distinct from, but related to, that presented by lesbian feminism. A bisexual feminism, as seen in the deployment of politicized bisexual identities in everyday life, might produce a unique set of radical meanings. For instance, a bisexual woman who chooses to make her life with women and refuses to make her life with men sends a clear message; as does the bisexual woman who makes her life with men and refuses to deny her affinity for women and the bisexual woman who consciously, politically, refuses to choose.

I do not argue, however, that lesbians should conceive of bisexuality as an original, prediscursive, universal sexuality. Indeed, to argue for bisexual originality reproduces the foundational binary code to which I object throughout this essay. While I argue that women's use of the bisexual label in both a political and practical sense does not represent the threat to lesbian feminism that is articulated by the current discourse, and that to recirculate these terms constitutes lesbian participation in hegemonic systems of domination, neither of these criticisms negates the possibility that the dissemination of a third category for marking sexual subjectivity could be politically damaging to lesbian, feminist, and other oppositional projects, despite the radical political intentions of many bi activists. Indeed, what is at stake is not so much whether a woman will leave her woman lover for a man as whether the dissemination and institutionalization of a bisexual identity category during the present period constitutes a hegemonic move that could incorporate lesbians into dominant cultural systems.

The bisexual identity category is as worthy of critique as the lesbian discourse that is hostile to it. Unconvinced that more categories of oppression produce more liberation, I believe that it is important for feminists to examine the political, social, and sexual expediency of creating, promoting, and supporting a proliferation of sexual identity categories that mark subjects who need to be mobilized into movements for their respective rights. Perhaps the bisexual category carries with it the prospect of disrupting the sex/gender/sexuality system; however, it assumes for the sake of its existence the stability of a binary system, and those moving steadily toward solidifying it as a third category support the retrenchment of a dualistic sex/gender/sexuality system. From my lesbian feminist position, it is in this particular binary construction that the real trouble always begins, and it is from this perspective that we might legitimately begin to theoretically interrogate bisexuality.

NOTE

Acknowledgments: I wish to thank Laurel Richardson, Gary Fine, Jude Preissle, Linda Grant, Marlene Longenecker, Jennifer Terry, Gisela Hinkle, Carla Corroto, Steph Brzuzy, Kim Davies, Joseph Hopper, Stefan Timmermans, Mindy Stombler, Stacy Copenhaver, Kathrin Zippel, Julia Wallace, Brett Beemyn, and the three anonymous *Critical Sociology* reviewers for their support of this work and for specific suggestions for its improvement. The research reported here was funded in part by a 1993 National Science Foundation fellowship to the University of Georgia's Summer Field Work Workshop and a 1993 Ohio State University Department of Sociology summer dissertation fellowship.

REFERENCES

Blasingame, Brenda Marie. 1992. The Roots of Biphobia: Racism and Internalized Heterosexism. In *Closer to Home: Bisexuality and Feminism*, ed. Elizabeth Reba Weise, 47–53. Seattle: Seal Press.

Butler, Judith. 1990. *Gender Trouble*. New York: Routledge.

———. 1991. Imitation and Gender Insubordination. In *Inside/Out: Lesbian Theories, Gay Theories*, ed. Diana Fuss, 13–31. New York: Routledge.

Clausen, Jan. 1990. My Interesting Condition. *Journal of Sex Research* 27 (3): 445–59.

Eridani. 1992. Is Sexual Orientation a Secondary Sex Characteristic? In *Closer to Home: Bisexuality and Feminism*, ed. Elizabeth Reba Weise, 173–81. Seattle: Seal Press.

George, Sue. 1993. *Women and Bisexuality*. London: Scarlet Press.

Haraway, Donna. 1991. The Biopolitics of Postmodern Bodies: Constitutions of Self in Immune System Discourse. In *Simians, Cyborgs, and Women: The Reinvention of Nature*, 203–30. New York: Routledge.

McKeon, Elizabeth. 1992. To Be Bisexual and Underclass. In *Closer to Home: Bisexuality and Feminism*, ed. Elizabeth Reba Weise, 27–34. Seattle: Seal Press.

Phelan, Shane. 1993. (Be)Coming Out: Lesbian Identity and Politics. *Signs: Journal of Women in Culture and Society* 18 (4): 765–89.

Rich, Adrienne. 1992. Compulsory Heterosexuality and Lesbian Existence. In *Feminist Frontiers III*, ed. Laurel Richardson and Verta Taylor, 158–79. New York: McGraw-Hill.

Rust, Paula C. 1992. Who Are We and Where Do We Go From Here? Conceptualizing Bisexuality. In *Closer to Home: Bisexuality and Feminism*, ed. Elizabeth Reba Weise, 281–310. Seattle: Seal Press.

———. 1993. Neutralizing the Political Threat of the Marginal Woman: Lesbians' Beliefs about Bisexual Women. *Journal of Sex Research* 30 (3): 214–28.

Silber, Linda. 1990. Negotiating Sexual Identity: Non-Lesbians in a Lesbian Feminist Community. *Journal of Sex Research* 27 (1): 131–40.

Stanley, Liz, and Sue Wise. 1991. Feminist Research, Feminist Consciousness, and Experiences of Sexism. In *Beyond Methodology: Feminist Scholarship as Lived Research*, ed. Mary Margaret

Fonow and Judith A. Cook, 265–83. Bloomington: Indiana University Press.

Sykes, Gresham, and David Matza. 1957. Techniques of Neutralization. *American Sociological Review* 22: 664–70.

Taylor, Verta, and Nancy E. Whittier. 1992. Collective Identity in Social Movement Communities: Lesbian Feminist Mobilization. In *Frontiers in Social Movement Theory*, ed. Aldon D. Morris and Carol McClurg Mueller, 104–28. New Haven: Yale University Press.

Weinberg, Martin, Colin Williams, and Douglas Pryor. 1994. *Dual Attraction: Understanding Bisexuality.* New York: Oxford University Press.

Young, Stacey. 1992. Breaking Silence about the "B-Word": Bisexual Identity and Lesbian-Feminist Discourse. In *Closer to Home: Bisexuality and Feminism*, ed. Elizabeth Reba Weise, 75–87. Seattle: Seal Press.

Denying Complexity: The Dismissal and Appropriation of Bisexuality in Queer, Lesbian, and Gay Theory

Christopher James

— *for Jonas, Jage, Nils, and Stephanie*

Vivaldo is thinking it, but he's trying not to. He is on the edge of discovery, the limit before he falls into himself . . . into Ida . . . into Eric. Sitting alone in a smoky working-class bar, he claims that "love is a country he knows nothing about," but that's not quite true.[1] Vivaldo, one of the behaviorally bisexual protagonists of James Baldwin's *Another Country*, is in the midst of unraveling a portion of love's mystery at the moment that he's telling himself he's not. Denial has a power, and discovery has its own deception. Similarly, contemporary queer, lesbian, and gay theorists are on the edge of theorizing bisexuality as a significant component of modern sexuality, with some theorists already falling toward it at full speed. Yet, like Vivaldo, through much textual maneuvering, selective silencing, and conceptual sleight of hand, they have convinced themselves and many readers that bisexuality is a country they know nothing about, or that they know enough of it that no mention need be made.

Current theories of mutual interiority are emblematic of this denial. Now almost a given in queer theory, this social and psychological theorization of the "queer" within the "straight" and vice versa comes dangerously close to once again collapsing bisexuality beneath the weight of the old false dichotomy of straight and gay. Thus this scholarship on permeable sexual binarism falls well within the acceptable realm of "gay and lesbian studies" as proclaimed on the dust jacket, in the course catalogue, and in the hearts and minds of queer-aware America. We have seen the future — queer is now and the queen is dead, boys — but why does the silence rage now as loudly as ever? Why, if there's so much permeability, must bisexuality remain a footnote (if that), an absence in the index, a vacuum, drawing us closer, but at the same time rendering us unable to name it for what it is?

Once deemed universal by sexologists and early gay and lesbian activists,[2] bisexuality is currently used in queer, lesbian, and gay theory as a misfit third category of sexual identity, generally reserved for ambiguous historical figures, indiscriminate lovers, fence sitters, or closet cases. This denial of bisexuality as a category of worth functions as a structuring silence within queer, lesbian, and gay theory.[3] Serving as the contested middle ground between heterosexuality and homosexuality, bisexuality must ultimately disappear in order to prop up theories of hetero/homosexual difference. Although bisexuality's omission is central to current queer, lesbian, and gay theories, it is a silence that must be broken to begin production of a more viable academic and political theory of sexuality. Theorizing bisexuality as a valid epistemological site allows theorists to understand compulsory monosexuality's role as an essential component of heterosexism, to move beyond dichotomized theories of mutual interiority, to strengthen theories attenuated through the denial of bisexuality, and to avoid queer, lesbian, and gay appropriation of historical figures or texts that may be better understood with or from a bisexual interpretation. Although bisexuality is no less heterogeneous than either homosexuality or heterosexuality on axes of race, class, gender, ability, and other categories of difference, the theorization of bisexuality as a subject position must nonetheless begin in order for emerging bisexual epistemologies to contribute to a fuller, more accurate theorization of sexuality.[4]

In order to explicate both the necessity and the utility of bisexual epistemology, bisexuality must be more concretely defined. It can be a slippery notion, depending on who is using it and how it is being used. While I am less concerned with a rigid definition of bisexuality than with the role of sexual identity in Western societies, I nonetheless must define what I mean when I use the term. Bisexuality is defined here as the sexual or intensely emotional, although not necessarily concurrent or equal, attraction of an individual to members of more than one gender. This definition comes from current articulations within the bisexual rights movement and, out of respect for contemporary transgender activists, is an attempt to avoid dichotomized understandings of gender, despite the implied duality of the word "bisexuality."[5] The cornerstone of this definition of bisexuality is attraction, although behavior and performative identity can also be implicated. As behavior is often an indicator of bisexual attraction, persons who act upon these multiple attractions will be referred to here as behaviorally bisexual. Performative self-identification can be another important indicator of attraction, increasingly central to contemporary theories of sexual identity and an essential component of bisexual politics' emphasis on self-definition.[6] Although Eve Kosofsky Sedgwick and others rightly expose the "incoherence" of all identities based on sexual object choice, as well as the "overlap" and "permeability" of sexual categorization,[7] most theorists nonetheless find value in theorizing the persistent social categories of "heterosexuality" and "homosexuality." While "latent homosexuality" and "bisexuality" have been theorized alongside the hetero/homosexual dichotomy, dating as far back as Richard von Krafft-Ebing's *Psychopathia Sexualis*, there has not always been much interest in extensively theorizing the category of bisexuality. However, in light of the recent growth of the international bisexual rights movement and increasing societal awareness of bisexuality as a viable sexual identity,[8] bisexuality must begin to be respectfully included, substantially examined, and coherently addressed within any theory of sexual identities and in discourses reliant on those identities.

A recognition of bisexuality's value as an epistemological site sheds new light on components of compulsory heterosexuality by illustrating the extent to which that system of oppression is defined, not only by its opposition to homosexuality, but also by its denial of bisexuality as a possible sexual identity. Rereading Adrienne Rich's 1980 essay on lesbian existence, one is struck by how closely the denial of lesbian existence that Rich outlines parallels the denial of bisexual existence. Although lesbianism often differentiates itself from bisexuality on the basis of exclusive sexual object choice, Rich's assertion that sexual and cultural theorists have an obligation to respectfully recognize lesbian existence could just as easily be applied to bisexual existence: "Any theory or cultural/political creation that treats lesbian existence as a marginal or less 'natural' phenomenon, as mere 'sexual preference,' or as the mirror image of either heterosexual or male homosexual relations is profoundly weakened thereby, whatever its other contributions."[9] Rich's statement, cogent and precise, is still the standard by which much of contemporary Western society fails lesbians and women-loving women. As a bisexual scholar, however, I would similarly assert that theories treating *bisexual existence* as marginal or as equally composed of heterosexuality and homosexuality are no less profoundly weakened and no less harmful, whatever the theories' other contributions. Although queer theory seeks to move beyond the identity politics of any bisexual or lesbian "existence," the persistent institutional denial of these existences, though they may be tenable only as self-chosen identities, nonetheless forces the queer movement and queer theorists to return to questions of identity as a matter of political necessity.[10] As queer theorists return to questions of sexual identity as a means of integrating theory with political action, however, inclusion of bisexuality within their theories becomes a more pressing issue. If, as Sedgwick argues in *Tendencies*, "the specification of any distinct 'sexual' identity magnetizes and reorients in new ways the heterogeneous erotic and epistemological energies of everyone in its social vicinity,"[11] then the emergence of bisexuality as a sexual identity, and more specifically the strain of out, queer-identified bisexuality developing in the U.S. and the U.K., has a significant impact upon theories of Western sexual identity, especially upon queer, lesbian, and gay theory.

To consider the impact of a bisexual positionality upon concepts of compulsory heterosexuality, one must examine the origin of the bisexual subject position. Although bisexuality was born of the same nineteenth-century sexology texts which begot homosexuality in Western societies, the histories of those terms are significantly different. Krafft-Ebing is considered the first to use the word "bisexuality" to denote "the state or condition of being sexually attracted to members of both sexes."[12] Bisexual theorist Clare Hemmings has argued that beginning with sexology, bisexuality became "endlessly displaced," always defined as mere potential or behavior.[13] Thus the anomalies and ambiguities within the more recognized heterosexual or homosexual identities were conveniently "dumped" on bisexuality.[14] Additionally, Freud, "the Founding Father of bisexual theory," claimed that everyone "goes through a period of bisexuality," but that well-adjusted adults make, and thus set, their mature, singular "sexual object choice." [15] Freud's theories of bisexuality, developed to explain the origins of homosexuality, likewise normalize mature heterosexual and homosexual orientations to the exclusion of bisexuality. Theorist Marcia Ian, in a bi-positive reconception of Freud, posits that "Freud was evidently uncomfortable with the idea of bisexuality, partly, it now appears, because he got the idea from [his associate Wilhelm] Fliess, with whom he had a complicated love/like relationship." [16] Though Freud's theorization of bisexuality can be read as reinforcing dichotomized notions of sexual identity, it nonetheless appears that the Viennese psychoanalyst knew more about mature bisexuality than he let on.

Despite Freud's early theorizations of original bisexuality, a binarized landscape of sexual identity soon developed. The widespread emergence of the dichotomized "homosexual" and "heterosexual" categories of sexual identity is intricately tied in with the "chronic, now endemic crisis of homo/heterosexual definition" that Sedgwick identifies as a structuring silence within Western epistemology dating from the end of the nineteenth century. [17] Manifestations of this definitional crisis include what Rich has named "compulsory heterosexuality," the social ideology that demands the heterosexuality of women. Similarly, Sedgwick identifies "a secularized and psychologized homophobia" that viciously structures the Western "continuum of male homosocial bonds." [18]

While compulsory heterosexuality, heterosexism, and homophobia can be viewed as roughly parallel terms referring to related and inseparable forms of institutional oppression, I wish to look more closely at one particular manifestation of heterosexism which Joseph Bristow calls "the precarious break between 'homo' and 'hetero' that dominant culture strives to keep as distinct as possible." [19] This brutal Western opposition between what is "heterosexual" and what is "homosexual" demands that all within its scope choose a side, select a single object choice (heterosexuality being most strongly encouraged), and fall out in clear ranks on the battlefield of sexual identity. For more exclusively same- or opposite-sex oriented individuals, the social implications of that "choice" have often been qualitatively different from those experienced by people who don't fall as obviously into one camp or the other. While oppression based on sexual identity is always painful, limiting, and endangering, this particular differentiation has been named as a key means of oppressing bisexuals.

This differentiation between heterosexuality and homosexuality, a component of heterosexism whose effects are unique enough to warrant another name, is what bisexual activists often refer to as monosexism or compulsory monosexuality: the social ideology that demands of individuals a singular sexual object choice. Similar to what Gloria Anzaldúa names as the "absolute despot duality" of gender that allows people "to be only one or the other," [20] compulsory monosexuality is the instrument by which the false, but nonetheless pervasive, dichotomy of homo/heterosexual definition is enforced. Structuring power relations between dichotomized hetero/homosexual identity categories, as well as those outside of or straddling that dichotomy, compulsory monosexuality affects people in these categories in unequal and complicated ways. The result of compulsory monosexuality within the heterosexual-identified community is an affirmation of heterosexuality as monolithic, self-contained, and, by definition, opposed to homosexuality. Heterosexual-identified people who might otherwise approach sexual identity as more fluid and make the reflective moves that Rich seeks are encouraged not to do so through this belief in strict sexual dichotomization.[21] Rigid sexual dichotomy also keeps many youths from seeking answers to questions they have about sexual identity from people in gay and lesbian communities.

To the extent that gay- and lesbian-identified people affirm dichotomous understandings of sexuality, they are encouraged to believe in the distinct nature of their sexual orientation, in the inherent naturalness of their desire for only one gender, and in the homogeneity of queer, lesbian, and gay communities. Although many gay- and lesbian-identified individuals believe that they have nothing to learn from different-sex desire or relations with people of the other gender, many of the same individuals nevertheless believe, conversely, that the life of many heterosexuals "would be richer if [they] could only respond sexually and emotionally to others of their own gender."[22] Heterosexuals are encouraged to reflect upon their suppressed desires, but not gay men and lesbians. For example, the opening of Dvora Zipkin's essay in *Closer to Home: Bisexuality and Feminism* describes a lesbian-identified woman who falls in love with a man but ultimately rejects him because he wouldn't "fit into" her life.[23] Thus the moves that Rich requests of heterosexual women are ones that many gay- and lesbian-identified people refuse to make themselves. Any resistance to compulsory heterosexuality certainly requires reflection on societal channeling of desire toward heterosexuality, but doesn't necessitate resistance to different-sex attraction in and of itself. Resisting compulsory monosexuality, however, does require additional reflection upon the dichotomized nature of channeled desire, no matter which community's institutions use their power to direct that desire.

Compulsory heterosexuality does indeed operate differently than compulsory monosexuality within the gay and lesbian community, but often the results of institutional silencing are surprisingly similar. Bisexual people are erased and devalued through compulsory monosexuality just as gay- and lesbian-identified people are through compulsory heterosexuality. While power is necessary for the exercise of any institutional oppression, gay- and lesbian-identified people who believe that, because they have no institutional power, they could never oppress bisexuals rely on an overly simplistic zero-sum, dichotomized understanding of oppression. They also fail to recognize the power of their own community organizations and resources to define for many people, especially those exploring new feelings of same-sex attraction, the norms of same-sex sexuality, regardless of whether that same-sex sexuality is gay or bisexual.[24] This act of speaking over bisexuality, whether from a straight or gay perspective, typifies and is constitutive of compulsory monosexuality. Bisexual-identified people may be more or less accepted, depending upon a specific context, but much of their reception depends upon how *others* perceive them and bisexuality, factors over which bisexual-identified people do not always have control. Uniquely, the erasure of bisexuality occurs in *both* ostensibly straight and queer communities. In both contexts, erasure and exclusion of bisexuals occurs, depending on whether they are perceived as "truly" gay, "truly" straight, or in a "safe" or "dangerous" limbo between the two. Acceptance or opprobrium thus becomes a matter of perception and performativity for bisexual-identified individuals, in much the same way that it is for gay- or lesbian-identified individuals. Unlike most gay- or lesbian-identified people, however, out bisexuals risk rejection not only from heterosexist straight communities but from many exclusively defined queer, lesbian, and gay communities as well.[25]

This Western push toward compulsory monosexuality, enforcing the split between the "truly" gay and the "truly" straight, has been adopted in the past thirty years by both heterosexual-identified individuals motivated by "homosexual panic" and by gay-or lesbian-identified individuals who define themselves in opposition or resistance to, not only heterosexism, but heterosexuality itself. While it is not clear when compulsory monosexuality first made its appearance in the emerging gay and lesbian communities of the twentieth century, it nonetheless began reaching critical mass with the emergence of a strong gay rights movement in the U.S. and the development of lesbian separatism in the late 1970s.[26] Liz Highleyman attributes this development to the popularity of the conservative "identity-based model of sexual orientation" and a general redefinition of the term "lesbian."[27] She writes, "Previously a woman was defined as a lesbian if she loved and was committed to women; during the 1980s, lesbianism came to be defined more in terms of not loving or having sexual relationships with men."[28] Such a definition, though, is not equally applicable to all U.S. cultures. Brenda Marie Blasingame notes that "older people of color who are queer" indicate that much same-sex sexual activity took place within their communities in previous decades, but that this activity wasn't always labeled lesbian, gay, or bisexual: "People knew who was in a relationship with whom, that was how it was, and life went on."[29] Nonetheless, Blasingame notes that many gay- or lesbian-identified people of color have, as of late, taken up what she refers to as a monosexist and "white" project of excluding "their bisexual brothers and sisters."[30]

Maintenance of compulsory monosexuality assists in the policing of the "border" between homosexuality and heterosexuality to the detriment of border-crossers and those who seek to live outside of this overpowering sexual dichotomy or to resist it from within. As a social phenomenon, compulsory monosexuality does the most damage to bisexual-identified individuals. This ideology, which can never fully deny the existence of bisexuality (or why would its policing be necessary?), nonetheless serves as bisexuality's negator. It attempts to erase, diminish, and deny bisexuality's validity as a sexual identity and seeks to limit bisexuality to a fence, a border zone, and/or an unrealizable potential. Though it is staunchly policed, bisexuality manifests itself variously in "slippages" between sexual identities and desires, bridging in surprising ways the long slide from one end of the homosocial continuum to the other.[31] In queer, lesbian, and gay theory, however, slippages between sexual identities and desires are mentioned almost exclusively as the purview of straight- or bisexual-identified individuals who do not know their "true" gay or lesbian selves. Individuals whose sexual practices seem out of line with their self-proclaimed sexual orientation are often assumed to be "truly" gay or lesbian, but are seldom assumed to be "truly" bisexual.

Compulsory heterosexuality is, of course, the acknowledged force precipitating any such slippage into false consciousness. This simplistic analysis, lacking further consideration of compulsory monosexuality's ability to constrain the desires of gay-, lesbian-, or queer-identified people, suggests that all slippages between identity and desire are unidirectional, that people can only "truly" be gay or lesbian, and that gay- and lesbian-identified people have some privileged position of lucidity regarding their desires that people of any other sexual identity do not. All these untenable suggestions are the result of theories that deny the validity of bisexuality and underestimate compulsory monosexuality's role in the policing of desire. For example, in her discussion of Henry James and male homosexual panic, Sedgwick identifies how heterosexism affects those whom she sees as gay and straight, but she does not theorize heterosexism's impact upon bisexuals. Instead, she theorizes the "arbitrarily mapped, self-contradictory, and anathema-riddled quicksands of the middle distance of male homosocial desire" as a threat to male privilege that only a small group of self-accepting homosexual men ever escape.[32] Without invoking bisexuality or compulsory monosexuality, Sedgwick simply hasn't the tools to theorize this middle ground as anything but "anathema-riddled," even though it can be just as effectively negotiated by self-accepting bisexual men as by self-accepting homosexual men. Thus, without an understanding of compulsory monosexuality, current queer, lesbian, and gay theories oversimplify compulsory heterosexuality and misrepresent the intricate power relations among asymmetrical bi, homo, and heterosexual identities. A recognized bisexual epistemology, however, would enable theorists to understand compulsory monosexuality's role within compulsory heterosexuality and allow for a more comprehensive theorization of sexual identity.

While there have been few theories which consider a triad of sexual identity and little discussion of the limits of such theories, there are theorists currently attempting to account for more than the traditional binary of sexual identity. Yet bisexuality's complication of binary theories of sexuality still undermines the latest attempts by queer theorists like Diana Fuss to represent relations among sexualities. Current theories of mutual interiority are an effort to both deconstruct sexual binarism and theorize the permeable social and psychological dialectic of heterosexuality and homosexuality.[33] An admirable attempt to deconstruct the false dichotomy of sexuality, these conceptions of mutual interiority still fail to deconstruct fully the hetero/homosexual dichotomy. In particular, mutual interiority, as it is currently conceived, insufficiently represents slippages between sexual identities and desires, defines interiority in a limited manner, and theorizes a permeable border no less problematic than its more rigidly conceived predecessor. As such, the concept must be reexamined in light of bisexual epistemology and rendered responsive to the concerns found therein.

Mutual interiority — the theorization of the social and psychological interconnectedness of heterosexuality and homosexuality that appears to encompass slippages between sexual identities and desires — does not currently include bisexuality in its scope. While Diana Fuss, for example, raises the question of how bisexuality affects theories of mutual interiority, she is unable to provide an answer within her own dichotomized language, which erases bisexuality as a valid sexual identity through consistent reference to a "hetero/homo binary."[34] Within Fuss's theory, slippages between sexual identities and desires become a matter of permeability.

Yet slippages that create "passages" between, outside, or alongside other sexual identities are more than simple examples of permeability between falsely dichotomized categories. Bisexual-identified people have been forced to construct such passageways and have begun politicizing these contested locations of desire and theorizing from them. As such, bisexuality can be viewed as a destabilizing third category, both within and outside the hetero/homosexual dichotomy. Such a destabilizing subject position redefines categories, creates new understandings, and challenges the rigidity of all sexual subject positions. The result is similar to Hemming's theory of bisexuals as "revolutionary double agents" or Jo Eadie's comparison of bisexuality with cultural hybridity.[35] It is possible, though, to theorize not only bisexuality but also transgenderism as a destabilizing third category. While neither bisexuality nor transgenderism is fully reducible to the position of a third category, tentative theoretical constructs like "destabilizing third categories" assist in the reconception of sexual and gender identity as more consistently varied and fluid than previously thought. Although bisexuality is more than mere slippage between dichotomous poles, mutual interiority, as conceived by Fuss and, to a lesser extent, by Sedgwick, seems to limit bisexuality to just such a fragmentary position.[36]

Without a more complete theorization of bisexuality, it is impossible for mutual interiority to represent the complex social and psychological phenomenon that is interiority. Fuss's conception of interiority is itself heavily binarized. To explain mutual interiority, she writes, "Heterosexuality can never fully ignore the close psychical proximity of its terrifying (homo)sexual other, any more than homosexuality can entirely escape the equally insistent social pressures of (hetero)sexual conformity."[37] While the varying qualities attributed by Fuss to the interiorities of heterosexuality and homosexuality are reasonable given a heterosexist social context, Fuss does not see that monosexist privileging of "pure" homosexuality (meaning exclusive of different-sex desire) similarly creates its own terrifying *hetero- or bi*sexual other. To the extent that renunciation of different-sex desire is the yardstick for membership in many gay and lesbian communities, manifested in what June Jordan identifies as "gay or lesbian contempt for bisexual modes of human relationship,"[38] social pressure toward sexual conformity can no longer be simplistically understood as an exclusively heterosexist phenomenon. While many gay- and lesbian-identified people assume that fear of the "terrifying (homo)sexual other" keeps many bisexual-identified people from coming out as gay or lesbian, it is perhaps equally the fear of the *hetero- or bi*sexual other in exclusive "gay and lesbian" contexts that keeps many gay- or lesbian-identified individuals from coming out as bisexual or as any identity that is less than exclusively same-sex oriented.[39] It is by no means the exclusive purview of any particular sexual identity group to try to assume or retain certain privileges by deliberately identifying outside the sexual identity category that seems closest to one's attractions.

Therefore, we must not only reconceptualize interiority but also theorize a more complex multiple interiority. Fuss's theory recognizes the dichotomy of sexual identity as false, but the unstable border between those identities in her theory is nonetheless built upon dichotomy. While she recognizes the problem that bisexuality poses to her theory, Fuss still theorizes homosexuality as the border between her primary categories.[40] Her border, however, is a particularly heterosexist construct, as it relies on the conceptualization of homosexuality as "specter."[41] Fuss's theorization of homosexuality as the "contaminated and expurgated insides of the heterosexual subject" allows heterosexuals to define homosexuality. Thus bisexuality is conflated with either homosexuality or heterosexuality through Fuss's dichotomizing conception of the "heterosexual subject."[42] Nevertheless, Fuss's particular method of examining the projection of heterosexuality onto homosexuality does rightly highlight the fact that perversion can *never* be wholly displaced onto homosexuality. Differences in sexual behavior and gender presentation, like s/m and crossdressing, both exist within the categories of heterosexuality and homosexuality (as well as bisexuality) and allow for no such easy projection.[43] Unfortunately, in Fuss's theory, heterosexist projection is allowed to define the border between heterosexuality and homosexuality to the exclusion of bisexuality. As such, her theory requires a new metaphor, a reconception of the relations among sexual identities that is truly inclusive of bisexuality.

Although it is not sufficiently represented within mutual interiority's present form, bisexuality does provide some of its own metaphors for sexual identity. In fact, it perhaps has too many. The pervasive homo/heterosexual binarism can be replaced by a continuum, but preferably one that is not reducible to its ends. A more inclusive sexual map might be represented by a Venn diagram of three overlapping circles marked "gay" "straight," and "bisexual" in a triangular formation, but questions of symmetry and placement crop up. Bisexuality can also be considered as a crossroads — a space of sexual convergence — and as its own distinct category. Within theories of mutual interiority, bisexuality can be viewed as an open and growing site of contact within an otherwise permeable binarism, a disruptive third category significantly problematizing the others. Fuss's representation would then be informed by a bisexual locality, a "borderland" perhaps, but one that allows for what Ruth Gibian has named "a bisexuality of wholeness," a unity despite polar opposition.[44] Gloria Anzaldúa, probably the most bi-affirming queer theorist who does not herself identify as bisexual, writes of a powerful "new *mestiza* consciousness" that performs many of the functions Gibian outlines as necessary to affirm such a wholeness.[45] Anzaldúa's mestiza crosses borders, tolerates ambiguity, reinterprets the world, recognizes oppression, and serves as a mediator of conflicts.[46] The new mestiza is whole, "the split between the two mortal combatants somehow healed."[47] Standing on both shores, she sees multiple perspectives and "can't hold concepts or ideas in rigid boundaries."[48] Fuss's theory lacks such a locale, a borderland that is inclusive of bisexual modes of sexual expression and identity. Like Anzaldúa, June Jordan sees bisexuality's closest analogy as an "interracial or multiracial identity" and argues that existing paradigms must be reconceived to make room for "a multicultural, multiethnic, multiracial world view" that transcends simple binarisms, even permeable ones.[49]

Most of bisexuality's metaphors, however, like the origin of the word itself, are heavily invested in dichotomized ideas about gender. Although transgender and feminist theorists have identified the gender dichotomy as oppressive, it is a difficult concept to avoid within theories of sexual identity that are based on gender. Even my descriptors "same-sex" and "different-sex" still rely upon the idea of distinguishable genders, although the ambiguity of these words lacks the gender rigidity of the phrase "opposite-sex." Creating descriptors of sexual behavior that are more responsive to issues of gender flux and gender transition can change the way we understand sexual identity, but it is not enough by itself to help us reimagine gender and sexuality. Despite the addition of disruptive third categories to sexual or gender dichotomies, there is obviously no way to tidily wrap up either bisexual or transgender theory as it relates to queer, lesbian, and gay theory. Questions remain, and perhaps that is the point: theorizing bisexuality as an epistemological site does not cleanly divide up the areas of sexual identity into thirds. Bisexuality's theorization, as a third category or as anything else, is not a panacea; however, to dismiss its validity, to ignore it, or to leave it undertheorized is even more problematic, given heterosexist scholars' attempts to divvy up the world of theory along a straight and gay divide. In the eyes of some queer, lesbian, and gay theorists, the dismissal of bisexuality within their own theories helps to build gay and lesbian solidarity by not addressing the grey areas of sexuality. In the long term, though, this particular move will diminish the ability of many queers to resist heterosexism and, eventually, the denial of the validity and relevance of bisexuality as a sexual identity will be seen as a fatal weakness in the work of these theorists.

Yet this denial remains common. Bisexuality is in a state of undertheorization, dismissal, and exclusion within most significant texts in queer, lesbian, and gay theory today. Eve Sedgwick, Michael Warner, Diana Fuss, Jeffrey Weeks, and Bonnie Zimmerman all dismiss or devalue bisexuality in their theories, rendering it a structuring silence in their work. The omission is necessary in much current queer, lesbian, and gay theory because, despite all of the talk of deconstructing binarism, many theorists are still fully reliant upon the hetero/homosexual dichotomy as a means of distinguishing the two communities. Although some sexual theory resists attempts to remove completely the (often necessary) third category "bisexual," many theorists maintain their silences by referring to bisexuality only when unavoidable and subsequently dismiss the concept as devoid of significant meaning.[50] These textual and theoretical maneuvers to deny bisexuality undermine these authors' otherwise significant contributions and result in a variety of scholarly inaccuracies. For example, in a 1992 essay, Zimmerman dispenses with the complications of theorizing bisexuality by identifying it as "politically controversial" (as if homosexuality no longer was) and by otherwise ignoring the subject.[51] As a result, Zimmerman's problematic assertion that "sexual difference may not exist between or among lesbians" fails to recognize how certain lesbians define their sexuality through the exclusion of men, while others, like Pat Califia, for example, do not.[52] Similarly, Weeks dispenses with serious consideration of bisexuals by embedding them within lists of other, dissimilar groups — "transvestites, transsexuals, paedophiles, sado-masochists, fetishists, bisexuals, prostitutes and others" — and by referencing bisexuality only four times in his ironically titled *Sexuality and Its Discontents*.[53] In a different manner, Fuss, although she mentions bisexuality in her introduction to *Inside/Out: Lesbian Theories, Gay Theories*, allows it to remain untheorized in the face of what she calls the "binary structure of sexual orientation."[54]

Dismissal or exclusion of material that is interpreted as bisexual or that seriously complicates exclusive queer, lesbian, or gay interpretations is too often a norm within the field. Some queer, lesbian, and gay theorists overtly exclude bisexuality from their work but make exceptions for well-known, behaviorally bisexual historical or literary figures. Some scholars even suppress textual evidence of historical figures' different-sex attractions in the same manner that many straight scholars suppress evidence of same-sex attractions or affairs.[55] The end result is the same: heterosexual and homosexual scholars argue past each other in instances where a historically grounded, bisexually informed interpretation may be most fitting.[56] Bisexual theorist Frann Michel notes that queer academics have been "rightly skeptical" of heterosexist interpretations of all same-sex affection as "bisexual."[57] Yet the homophobia of many straight biographers and their inappropriate use of the bisexual label have contributed to queer, lesbian, or gay readings that go to the opposite extreme. Historical dismissal of gay or lesbian experience should not result in a similar dismissal of bisexuality by queer, lesbian, and gay scholars. I would assert that without compelling reasons grounded in scholarly methodology, labeling same-sex affection wholly bisexual or wholly gay or lesbian constitutes poor scholarship and calls for a challenge from responsible academics.

The denial of bisexuality and the resulting inaccuracies, though, take a variety of forms. Although current understandings of bisexuality are not reducible to Freud's notion of original bisexuality, nor to universalizing utopian theories of bisexuality, many contemporary queer, lesbian, and gay scholars dismiss either the concept of bisexuality itself or bisexual-identified people on the basis of these selective and biased definitions. The conflation of these manifestly different understandings of bisexuality allows theorists to appear as if they have engaged with the subject when, in fact, they've simply dismissed its historical shadow. For example, in his introduction to *Fear of a Queer Planet: Queer Politics and Social Theory*, Warner criticizes Freud's theory of "innate bisexuality" as not "very subtle" in its recognition of historical or cultural differences.[58] While I agree with Warner's critique, this singular reference to bisexuality in his twenty-two-page introduction serves as a dismissal of the subject and is emblematic of many queer, lesbian, and gay scholars' handling of bisexuality.

While Sedgwick more openly contemplates the territory of modern bisexual definition, she also falls into the dismissal-through-antecedent trap. Because bisexuality is a necessary component of most theories of sexuality, if only as a dumping ground, it is not long into a text on the subject that one encounters oblique references to it. Page 1 of Sedgwick's *Between Men* hypothesizes "the potential unbrokenness of a continuum between the homosocial and the homosexual,"[59] a continuum which serves as the beginning of Sedgwick's deconstruction of the Western homo/heterosexual dichotomy and would seemingly include bisexuality. In *Epistemology of the Closet*, she goes even further, acknowledging bisexuals by name underneath her first axiom, that "people are different from each other."[60]

Despite her own analysis of the fallacy of the homo/heterosexual distinction, however, and her view of sexuality and homosociality as a continuum, Sedgwick's critique of Paula Bennett's work on Emily Dickinson congratulates Bennett for her highly dichotomized treatment of Dickinson's poetics of same- and different-sex affection. Specifically, Sedgwick commends Bennett's avoidance of the "all-too-available rhetoric of the polymorphous, of a utopian bisexual erotic pluralism."[61] In this passage, however, Sedgwick dismisses *not only* polymorphous or utopian readings of erotic pluralism but the idea of *any* holistic reading of erotic pluralism that is not dichotomized. Like Louis Crompton's analyses of the "sides" of Lord Byron,[62] Sedgwick attempts to make clear distinctions between Dickinson's "heteroerotic" and "homoerotic" poetics, as if Dickinson's sexual poetics were not already pluralized through proximity to each other.

What *is* bisexuality if it is not what Sedgwick describes in Dickinson's case as a recognition of both "intense female homosocial bonds, including genitally figured ones," and the "salience and power of the male-directed eros" without mitigation of "tensions acted out between the two"?[63] I would argue that Sedgwick keeps different- and same-sex erotics separate because, despite her theorization of a continuum of homosocial/homosexual bonds, her theory is deeply invested in sexual binarism. Sedgwick reinscribes the oppressive power of the homo/heterosexual dichotomy by not theorizing the particularly pluralistic ground on which Dickinson's "dual" poetics lie. Sedgwick's dichotomization is also accomplished through her use of the terms "heteroerotic" and "homoerotic" and "gay" and "non-gay" in *Epistemology of the Closet*, as well as her use of "heterosexual" and "non-heterosexual" in *Tendencies*, all phrasings which collapse and negate the concept of bisexuality.[64] Thus, despite Sedgwick's intent to deconstruct sexual binarisms, they persist in her language.

In response to Sedgwick's analysis of Bennett's work, one might ask why theories of bisexual erotic pluralism are "all too available" in the poetics of Emily Dickinson. What about the life or the works of Henry James? H. D.? Virginia Woolf? Colette? Langston Hughes? Richard Bruce Nugent? Djuna Barnes? Lorraine Hansberry? James Baldwin? Paul and Jane Bowles? Is it because textual evidence that supports such interpretations is itself "all too available," either in the biographies of these authors or in the texts which they produced? In many of these cases, a theorization of bisexual erotic pluralism is more than appropriate: it is the most accurate historical or textual interpretation available. For example, if I were to eschew theories of bisexual erotic pluralism while analyzing "Free Flight," by June Jordan, an out bisexual poet and feminist theorist, I would be reduced to talking about the sides of her displaced or misdirected desire, outlining the extremes to which heterosexism drove her, citing some false consciousness she manifested, or ignoring either the different- or same-sex content of her work.[65] All such bi-hostile interpretations miss the point of this bi-identified poet's most obviously bisexual poem. Sadly, such approaches are common within queer theory and will remain so as long as bisexuality itself remains untheorized within that theory. Yet, if theorists do allow themselves the extravagance of theorizing a bisexual erotic pluralism, must they then avoid any bi-positive portrayals, for fear of being dismissed as utopian? And are bi theorists to speak only of contemporary, out bisexual authors like Jordan? Many writers in recent years have produced texts which explore bisexual identities and which examine issues relevant to bisexuals, but historic works by authors who, by contemporary definitions, would be considered bisexual predate those writers and texts. Thus theories of sexuality must begin to address bisexuality in the past, as well as today and in the future.

Another, particularly lamentable, way in which bisexuality is dismissed in much contemporary queer, lesbian, and gay scholarship is through a phenomenon I call appropriation without representation. Such appropriation often occurs when a theorist excludes bisexuality as a relevant category of sexual identity, yet claims behaviorally bisexual people or texts with bisexual characters or content as "queer," "gay," or "lesbian." While some theorists surely believe that "queer," "gay," or "lesbian" are terms that encompass bisexuality, for many others these words most certainly denote exclusive homosexuality.[66] Thus the burden upon theorists who use these terms either inclusively or exclusively is to justify their particular usage and to explicate how emerging understandings of bisexuality fit or do not fit into their specific theories of sexuality. For example, it is no longer sufficient (if it ever was) to speak of a kiss between any two men as a "gay kiss." It may be a same-sex kiss or a male/male kiss, but to call a kiss between two bisexual men a "gay kiss" moves well beyond the situation of the kiss and begins to do the work of (inaccurate) sexual categorization of those men. It would be misleading to name their kiss a "gay kiss" or to call their relationship a "gay relationship" without further indicators that the participants considered it so or that they are indeed gay-identified men. For theorists who define the terms "queer," "gay," or "lesbian" *exclusive* of bisexuality and who then use those terms to identify the actions of bisexual-identified or behaviorally bisexual individuals, these appropriating maneuvers become especially problematic.

Particular scholarly examples of this appropriation would include David Bergman's *Gaiety Transfigured*, in which he claims Herman Melville, Henry David Thoreau, and Henry James as "gay" or "homosexual."[67] An interpretation of these figures as behaviorally bisexual would probably be more accurate. A bisexual interpretation is unequivocally demanded in the case of Paul, a character from Wallace Thurman's *Infants of the Spring*, whom even gay scholar Eric Garber feels compelled to identify as "unapologetically bisexual."[68] Yet Bergman claims Paul as gay, in the face of Thurman's portrayal of Paul, the character's description of his own sexual attractions, and the fact that the character is modeled after Richard Bruce Nugent, a behaviorally bisexual writer of the Harlem Renaissance.[69] Even though Thurman's character refers to Oscar Wilde in the passage Bergman cites, that reference does not serve as sufficient authority to define the character as exclusively gay.[70] Bergman makes a point to distinguish among what he labels "gay," "straight," and "intramale," the latter category apparently encompassing bisexuality. According to Bergman's own distinctions, however, Paul would more likely fit into Bergman's "intramale," rather than "gay," category. Furthermore, Bergman defines gayness on the basis of four criteria: gay men's sense of otherness, their experience of gayness as a lifelong condition, their inherently equitable (non–role-differentiated) relations with their partners, and their genuineness of experience.[71] The model is simplistic at best and not particularly useful, since many men who exclusively pursue same-sex sexual relationships would not be defined as "gay" on the basis of these criteria and many gay and bisexual men would be nearly indistinguishable. Furthermore, a bisexual positionality does not inherently deny one a sense of otherness, a lifelong condition, equitable relations, or genuineness of experience. Even though Bergman attempts to use a bi-exclusive definition of gayness by creating the intermediate category of intramale against which to define gayness, he nonetheless appropriates behaviorally bisexual figures in support of his theories of "gay self-representation" and fails to recognize bisexuality as a genuine experience.

In a different manner, Karla Jay and Joanne Glaskow's *Lesbian Texts and Contexts: Radical Revisions* also excludes bisexuality. In their introduction, not only do the authors fail to mention bisexuality, but they clearly dichotomize sexual identity along the axes of "lesbian" and "straight," or "lesbian" and "non-lesbian," erasing a bisexual positionality through a reliance on false dichotomies.[72] However, it is only a few pages after these references that Jay and Glaskow begin their readings of Emily Dickinson, Virginia Woolf, H. D., and Djuna Barnes as lesbian authors.[73] I do not mean to suggest that reading these authors as lesbian is not a valid pursuit, but I would argue that doing so within an oversimplified monosexist framework is highly problematic, both intellectually and politically, as it facilitates and encourages the appropriation of behaviorally bisexual authors who may be better understood using theories that are inclusive and respectful of a bisexual positionality.[74]

Obviously, more is at stake here than simple category definition. The issue of constructing a usable past and a literary tradition for people who identify as gay, lesbian, bisexual, and/or transgender[75] is of extreme political and personal importance to many people. Yet this construction does not have to create unnecessary antagonisms between these communities. For example, there is at least one text that could be claimed by all four groups. Given the fact that "overlap" is inherent in the project of sexual and literary categorization, it should come as no surprise that a novel like Virginia Woolf's gender-bending *Orlando* can be claimed as meaningful by all four of these groups and as speaking to particular concerns within each of them. Gay men may interpret *Orlando*'s early relations with the Archduchess (a man who crossdresses to win Orlando's affections) as gay;[76] lesbians may read *Orlando* as coding both Orlando's affection for Sasha and Woolf's affection for Vita Sackville-West; bisexual people may read *Orlando*'s relations with both men and women as representative of similar experiences in the lives of either Woolf or Sackville-West; and transgender people may view Orlando's change in gender as the author's fictive imagining of gender transition.

Yet how is it that we come to understand these various readings as constituting exclusive claims on the text? Shouldn't multiple claims, especially for ambiguous texts, be more the norm than the exception within queer, lesbian, and gay theory? What difference does it make, for example, whether Jack Kerouac's protagonist in *The Subterraneans* is a closeted gay man or a closeted bisexual man? The text is open to either interpretation. While Kerouac foregrounds the protagonist's different-sex sexual experiences, the character's closeted same-sex ones are nonetheless centrally located within the text. In such a case, I believe it is preferable to state that both interpretations may be effectively argued, rather than to insist on the validity of only one. Through scholarship recognizing a variety of positionalities, it will be possible for bi theorists to demonstrate, not only that sexualities other than heterosexuality have a literary history, but that sexualities other than homosexuality do as well. Thus queer, lesbian, gay, and bisexual scholars have the ability to break the silences surrounding bisexuality and homosexuality to build a stronger, more viable theory of sexuality in general.

As queer-identified bisexual scholars begin asking their own questions and examining literary representations of same- and different-sex attraction (as well as other complex sexualities),[77] new understandings of sexuality, new sexual theories, and more nuanced historical reclamation of sexual identities will be possible. Because it brings unique epistemologies to the project of queer, lesbian, and gay theory, bisexual and transgender scholarship will likely become more critical to theories of sexuality and gender. Just as straight-identified scholars learn much about sexuality by understanding contemporary queer, lesbian, and gay theories, so too do queer, lesbian, and gay scholars learn much about their own theories by understanding emerging bisexual and transgender theories. To posit a queer universe, as one bisexual theorist has put it, "is to imply that not everybody is queer in the same way."[78] Understanding issues of bisexuality, transgenderism, race, class, gender, ability, or other differences within and outside queerness can help us understand more clearly the intricate relations and intersections between these various identities and axes.

"The positive, politicizing significance of bisexual affirmation," writes June Jordan, "[is] to insist upon complexity . . . to insist upon the equal validity of all of the components of social/sexual complexity."[79] Currently, some sophisticated bisexual theories are beginning to emerge. Bisexual scholarship is responding to bi appropriation, erasure, and dismissal, seeking to make room for transgender theorists, and theorizing its own subject in surprising ways. Bisexual theory shows signs of continual growth and development, especially as an academic project. While a few core texts helped to articulate the experiences of bisexual individuals and communities in the U.S. and the U.K., the impact of these texts in academia, especially in cultural and literary studies, has been limited.[80] Scholars coming out of the bi community, however, have recently begun to publish strong academic works on bisexuality, including bisexuality in literature.[81] Others, who have no connection to the bisexual rights movement, have been working for some time on the subject, either as allies or as academics who refuse wholly dichotomous thinking about sexuality.[82] The recent literary works of June Jordan, Hanif Kureishi, and others,[83] the emergence of texts showcasing bisexual and lesbian writing together,[84] and the development of bi academic theory are signs that both bisexual literature and its theorization are blossoming. A number of bisexual and bi-inclusive scholarly projects are also in the works, including Warren Blumenfeld's new, inclusive *Journal of Gay, Lesbian, and Bisexual Identity* and a book with the working title *Epistemology of the Fence.*[85] A variety of bisexual viewpoints are now emerging, despite the extent to which bisexuality has been an underlying, silenced component of queer, lesbian, and gay theory.

As bisexuals across the globe organize and claim a voice in discussions of sexuality, bisexual epistemology will significantly impact many aspects of queer, lesbian, and gay theory and theories on sexuality in the years to come. This emerging bisexual epistemology allows for recognition of compulsory monosexuality's role as an essential component of heterosexism, encourages movement beyond inherently dichotomized theories of mutual interiority, strengthens theories attenuated through structural denial of bisexuality, and seeks an end to the appropriation by gays, lesbians, and straights of many bisexual and behaviorally bisexual historical figures and texts. The ongoing production of a scholarly and political theory of sexuality that is more inclusive of bisexuality should come as no surprise to queer, lesbian, and gay scholars. Just like Vivaldo in *Another Country*, queer, lesbian, and gay scholars know a great deal about bisexuality, despite their denial; they will likely know more in years to come. As Adrienne Rich reminds us, "Truthfulness anywhere means a heightened complexity."[86] The field of queer, lesbian, gay, bisexual, and transgender studies is obviously no exception.

NOTES

Acknowledgments: I am indebted to Gloria Anzaldúa, Eve Kosofsky Sedgwick, Adrienne Rich, Audre Lorde, Michel Foucault, Hélène Cixous, Judith Butler, Diana Fuss, Steven Seidman, Kate Bornstein, Clare Hemmings, Frann Michel, Jo Eadie, and many other exceptional theorists. I also owe much to Lani Ka'ahumanu, Loraine Hutchins, Elias Farajajé-Jones, Elise Matthesen, and others for creating safe spaces for outlaws and outcasts everywhere. Throughout my writing and editing process, the encouragement and guidance of Nina Miller, Kathy Hickok, Mary Helen Dunlap, Brett Beemyn, and Stephanie Kuduk have been indispensable.

1. James Baldwin, *Another Country* (New York: Random House, 1993), 296.

2. For a discussion of early gay and lesbian "liberationism" and its bisexual rhetoric, see Steven Seidman, "Identity and Politics in a 'Postmodern' Gay Culture: Some Historical and Conceptual Notes," *Fear of a Queer Planet: Queer Politics and Social Theory*, ed. Michael Warner (Minneapolis: University of Minnesota Press), 105–42.

3. Other bisexual scholars have also noted the exclusion of bisexuality as a structuring silence within much queer, lesbian, and gay theory. See also Clare Hemmings, "Resituating the Bisexual Body," *Activating Theory: Lesbian, Gay, Bisexual Politics*, ed. Joseph Bristow and Angelia R. Wilson (London: Lawrence and Wishart, 1993), 125; and, in the same volume, Jo Eadie, "Activating Bisexuality: Towards a Bi/Sexual Politics," 144.

4. In preparing this essay, I have been well aware of the limitations of current bisexual theory. Not enough has been published by bisexual-identified people of color, working-class bisexuals, bisexuals with disabilities, and other bisexual people. I have included available materials from these groups and sought not to "speak over" different people's experiences of bisexuality. I hope to encourage dialogue, not to limit discussion of these matters to any supposedly "definitive" understanding of bisexuality.

5. For an introduction to the ever-present issue of defining bisexuality, see Loraine Hutchins and Lani Kaahumanu, eds., *Bi Any Other Name: Bisexual People Speak Out* (Boston: Alyson, 1991), 2–5. For an introduction to transgender issues, see Kate Bornstein, *Gender Outlaw: On Men, Women, and the Rest of Us* (New York: Routledge, 1994). For an exploration of the limits of dichotomized constructions of both sex and gender, see Judith Butler, *Gender Trouble: Feminism and the Subversion of Identity* (New York: Routledge, 1990).

6. Performative sexual identities, the process of self-definition, and resistance to categorization based on sexual identity are all phenomena that are only now being examined for their contributions to sexual theory. While norms regarding sexual identification have existed for years in most queer, lesbian, gay, and bisexual communities, they have yet to be fully considered. For example, within the bisexual communities I first came out to, there was always great tolerance for people who identified ambiguously or who eschewed identification, not out of deference to heterosexism, but in resistance to it. Such tolerance for ambiguity has yet to be sufficiently theorized outside of bisexual contexts or outside of the mixed-race context of Gloria Anzaldúa's work.

7. Eve Kosofsky Sedgwick, *Epistemology of the Closet* (Berkeley: University of California Press, 1990), 85; Sedgwick, *Tendencies* (Durham, NC: Duke University Press, 1993), 6–9; Diana Fuss, ed., *Inside/Out: Lesbian Theories, Gay Theories* (New York: Routledge, 1991), 1–10.

8. Elizabeth Reba Weise, ed., *Closer to Home: Bisexuality and Feminism* (Seattle: Seal Press, 1992), xii–xiv; Robyn Ochs, ed., *International Directory of Bisexual Groups*, 11th ed. (Cambridge, MA: Bisexual Resource Center, 1994).

9. Adrienne Rich, "Compulsory Heterosexuality and Lesbian Existence," *Adrienne Rich's Poetry and Prose*, ed. Barbara Charlesworth Gelpi and Albert Gelpi (New York: Norton, 1993), 206.

10. Frann Michel, " 'I Just Loved Thelma': Djuna Barnes and the Construction of Bisexuality," *Review of Contemporary Fiction* 13, no. 3 (Fall 1993): 55–56.

11. Sedgwick, *Tendencies*, 116.

12. The cited use is from Richard von Krafft-Ebing's *Psychopathia Sexualis* (1892). See J. A. Simpson et al., eds., *Oxford English Dictionary*, 2d ed., vol. 2 of 20 (Oxford: Clarendon Press, 1989), 222.

13. Clare Hemmings, "Becoming a Desiring Subject: Bisexuality and Foucault," unpublished essay, 6–7. This paper, presented at the Five College Women's Studies Research Center at Mount Holyoke College, on October 4, 1994, is part of Hemming's Ph.D. thesis, "A Feminist Genealogy of Bisexuality," Women's Studies, York University, England.

14. Hemmings, "Becoming a Desiring Subject," 7.

15. Martin Bauml Duberman, "Bisexuality," *About Time: Exploring the Gay Past* (New York: Gay Presses of New York, 1986), 250; David Bergman, *Gaiety Transfigured: Gay Self-Representation in American Literature* (Madison: University of Wisconsin Press, 1991), 37.

16. Marcia Ian, *Remembering the Phallic Mother: Psychoanalysis, Modernism, and the Fetish* (Ithaca, NY: Cornell University Press, 1993), 3.

17. Sedgwick, *Epistemology of the Closet*, 1.

18. Ibid., 185.

19. Joseph Bristow, ed., *Sexual Sameness: Textual Differences in Lesbian and Gay Writing* (London: Routledge, 1992), 5.

20. Gloria Anzaldúa, *Borderlands/La Frontera: The New Mestiza* (San Francisco: Aunt Lute Books, 1987), 19.

21. For a discussion of Rich's essay from a bisexual feminist perspective and an interpretation of Rich's intended and actual audiences, see Rebecca Kaplan, "Compulsory Heterosexuality and the Bisexual Existence: Toward a Bisexual Feminist Understanding of Heterosexism," *Closer to Home*, 269–80.

22. Duberman, "Bisexuality," 249.

23. Dvora Zipkin, "Why Bi?" *Closer to Home*, 55.

24. This zero-sum understanding of oppression does not take into account the multiple axes and intersections of oppression and assumes that if two people are linked by oppression, one person will be the oppressor and the other will be the oppressed. Yet, depending on the context, a white lesbian may have power to oppress a straight Latina woman, or vice versa, or neither might have the power to oppress the other. As a bisexual, I would assert that I am oppressed not simply as a pseudo-gay person but as a bisexual, on the basis of my non-singular sexual object choice. As such, within contexts where bisexuality itself is suspect and where singular sexual object choice is the criterion by which people are judged, straight, lesbian, and gay people do easily have the power to oppress bisexuals by devaluing their sexual identities.

25. Bisexual exclusion from "gay and lesbian" communities is still prevalent in the West today. In the spring of 1990, lesbian-and gay-identified people in Northampton, Massachusetts, voted to keep the word "bisexual" out of the title of their annual pride march, despite long-standing participation and planning by bisexual-identified community activists. Citing heterosexual privilege, some lesbians expressed chagrin at bisexual women's efforts to "attach themselves" to the lesbian community and to the event. While in certain contexts out bisexuals do, in fact, receive limited acceptance from the straight community, this "privilege" is one that many gay-and lesbian-identified people take advantage of themselves to varying degrees in attempting to pass as straight in a heterosexist society. For example, no one can out themselves in every single context they find themselves in, and many "straight-acting" gays and lesbians surely pass for straight more effectively

than many out bisexuals do. People truly concerned about ending compulsory heterosexuality should differentiate allies and enemies on the basis of the individual's willingness to confront heterosexism rather than on his or her sexual identity. For more on Northampton and the treatment of bisexual women in the lesbian press, see Stacey Young, "Breaking Silence about the 'B-word': Bisexual Identity and Lesbian-Feminist Discourse," *Closer to Home*, 75–87.

26. Ibid., 82–86.

27. Liz A. Highleyman, "The Evolution of the Bisexual Movement," *Anything That Moves: Beyond the Myths of Bisexuality* 8 (Summer 1994): 24.

28. Ibid., 24.

29. Brenda Marie Blasingame, "The Roots of Biphobia: Racism and Internalized Heterosexism," *Closer to Home*, 51.

30. Ibid., 52.

31. Sedgwick posits that a slippage exists between men's identification with each other and their desire for women, an example of the "queer" within the "hetero." However, she does not theorize any similar slippage that would demonstrate the "hetero" within the "queer," apart from the obvious issue of internalized oppression. Such slippages of identity and desire certainly occur, for example, through the juxtaposition of certain gay men's identification with and desire for women and through the slippages mentioned by Pat Califia in "Gay Men, Lesbians, and Sex: Doing It Together" (from *Public Sex: The Culture of Radical Sex* [San Francisco: Cleis Press, 1994], 183–89) and by Jo Eadie in "Activating Bisexuality: Towards a Bi/Sexual Politics." Yet Sedgwick finds only the first slippage, the one that she herself names, to be significant. Additionally, Sedgwick fails to theorize bisexuality's position within her own dichotomized framework of mutual interiority. This omission and her one-sided application of the concept of slippage suggest larger problems within Sedgwick's overall theory; specifically, that bisexuality is reduced to a slippage between poles, one that she is uncertain how to address. See Sedgwick, *Epistemology of the Closet*, 62; *Tendencies*, 73–103.

32. Sedgwick, *Epistemology of the Closet*, 186.

33. Fuss, *Inside/Out*, 1–10.

34. Ibid., 2.

35. Hemmings, "Resituating the Bisexual Body," 130–31; and Eadie, "Activating Bisexuality," 158–62.

36. Sedgwick's work on mutual interiority begins in earnest in her aptly titled *Tendencies* chapter "Is the Rectum Straight? Identification and Identity in *The Wings of the Dove*." She builds upon Kaja Silverman's analysis of the "Jamesian phantasmatic" as an enclosure of "homosexuality within heterosexuality, and heterosexuality within homosexuality." See Kaja Silverman, "Too Early/Too Late: Subjectivity and the Primal Scene in Henry James," *Novel* 21 (Winter/Spring 1988): 165; and Sedgwick, *Tendencies*, 73.

37. Fuss, *Inside/Out*, 3.

38. June Jordan, "The New Politics of Sexuality," *Technical Difficulties: African-American Notes on the State of the Union* (New York: Pantheon, 1992), 188.

39. Examples of less exclusively same-sex–oriented identifiers would include, among others, "a lesbian who sleeps with queer men," "a gay man who makes exceptions," "a lesbian-identified bisexual," and possibly any queer or queer-friendly individuals who vocally and publicly refuse to define their sexualities at all. Social resistance to ambiguous identities is often high in many gay and lesbian communities, despite the preponderance of queer and queer-friendly performers of some renown who, either in their work or in interviews, publicly identify in such a manner. Examples include Holly Near, Sandra Bernhardt, Michael Feinstein, and Holly Hughes.

Social resistance to ambiguous identities is common in many communities and even found its way into the introduction of Tim Miller's keynote speech at InQueery, InTheory, InDeed: The Sixth North American Lesbian, Gay, and Bisexual Studies Conference in Iowa City, Iowa, on November 17, 1994. His introducer opened the conference by displaying a poster she'd created that read "100% Lesbian: Accept no Substitutes." Such a declaration, similar to buttons that read "Perfect Kinsey Six," takes its affirmative power not only from its statement of pride but also from its exclusion of different-sex affection and, by extension, bisexuality.

40. Fuss, *Inside/Out*, 3.

41. Ibid., 3.

42. Ibid., 3.

43. In her speech at Iowa State University on October 3, 1994, entitled "Sexualities and Communities," Twin Cities bisexual writer and activist Elise Matthesen spoke at great length about the overly simplistic heterosexist assumptions that many anti-gay activists have about the supposedly moral and monolithic straight community.

44. Ruth Gibian, "Refusing Certainty: Toward a Bisexuality of Wholeness," *Closer to Home*, 3, 14.

45. Anzaldúa, *Borderlands/La Frontera*, 77.

46. Ibid., 77–91.

47. While some of these references contain particularly binarized language like "two" and "both," Anzaldúa's theory would nonetheless seem responsive to "mestizas" with more than two allegiances. Anzaldúa, *Borderlands/La Frontera*, 78.

48. Ibid., 78–79.

49. In her keynote speech at the InQueery conference, Gloria Anzaldúa indicated her sympathy for bisexuals organizing within the queer community by suggesting that there are indeed similarities between multiracial and bisexual identities. Jordan, "The New Politics of Sexuality," 192.

50. Eadie notes that presently, "it is becoming harder to ignore the fact of bisexuality, but still lesbian- and gay-identified researchers do not really understand how to theorize it." Ironically, the introduction to the anthology in which Eadie's essay appears even suffers from this problem. Engaging with the concept of bisexuality only in reference to the two contributions on the subject, Joseph Bristow and Angelia R. Wilson write an otherwise insightful history of the lesbian and gay rights movement that skips from lesbian organizing to the emergence of the queer, as if the bisexual rights movement didn't have its own history and similar struggles for legitimacy. Bisexuality made it into the title of Bristow and Wilson's anthology and even into the book itself, but a true understanding of bisexual issues did not follow. Put simply, Eadie's critique of other queer, lesbian, and gay scholars' work is more applicable to Bristow and Wilson's introduction than it should be. Apparently, the reference to "lesbian, gay, and bisexual politics" in the book's subtitle was not intended to give equal consideration to each group named. Sadly, this treatment of bisexuality is more the norm in queer, lesbian, and gay theory than the exception. See Bristow and Wilson, *Activating Theory*, 1–15; and Eadie, "Activating Bisexuality," 147.

51. Bonnie Zimmerman, "Lesbians Like This and That: Some Notes on Lesbian Criticism for the Nineties," *New Lesbian Criticism: Literary and Cultural Readings*, ed. Sally Munt (New York: Columbia University Press, 1992), 7, 11.

52. Ibid., 12; and Califia, *Public Sex*, 183–89.

53. Jeffrey Weeks, *Sexuality and Its Discontents: Meanings, Myths, and Modern Sexualities* (London: Routledge and Kegan Paul, 1985), 186–87.

54. Fuss, *Inside/Out*, 3.

55. While researching same-sex thematics in the work of the now obscure nineteenth-century American poet, novelist, and travel writer Bayard Taylor, I found his latest biographer's heterosexist analysis of Taylor's work and life severely lacking. At the same time, Robert K. Martin's treatment of the same material from a gay perspective was perhaps more lacking, never mentioning either of Taylor's two wives or his daughter. While marriage and children are no inherent indicator of sexuality, and the circumstances of Taylor's marriages are, in fact, rather curious, Martin withholds from his readers any information that might lead to an interpretation of Taylor as anything but gay or create a more complicated picture of Taylor's same-sex expression. Whether by contemporary standards Taylor would be considered gay or bisexual is a matter which only more careful and complete scholarship can help to determine. See Marie Hansen-Taylor and Horace E. Scudder, eds., *Life and Letters of Bayard Taylor*, 4th ed. (Boston: Houghton Mifflin, 1885); Robert K. Martin, *The Homosexual Tradition in American Poetry* (Austin: University of Texas Press, 1979); Paul C. Weremuth, *Bayard Taylor* (New York: Twayne, 1973); and Christopher James, " 'The Truth and Tenderness of Man's Love for Man, as of Man's Love for Woman': Straight, Gay, and Bisexual Readings of Bayard Taylor and *Joseph and His Friend*," unpublished paper, 1994.

56. For a brief summary of just such a gay/straight debate over Langston Hughes's sexuality, see Hutchins and Kaahumanu, *Bi Any Other Name*, 128–29.

57. For more on how bisexuality as a concept has been used in particularly heterosexist ways, see Michel, " 'I Just Loved Thelma'," 55.

58. Warner, *Fear of a Queer Planet*, xii.

59. Eve Kosofsky Sedgwick, *Between Men: English Literature and Male Homosocial Desire* (New York: Columbia University Press, 1985), 1.

60. Sedgwick, *Epistemology of the Closet*, 22–26.

61. Sedgwick, *Tendencies*, 115.

62. See Louis Crompton, *Byron and Greek Love: Homophobia in Nineteenth-Century England* (Berkeley: University of California Press, 1985), 8, 109–11, 241–44; and Christopher James, " 'All Will Forgive Who Feel the Same': Byron's Bisexuality and Reconciliation with Georgian Homophobia in Three Early Poems," unpublished paper, 1992, 2–4.

63. Sedgwick, *Tendencies*, 115.

64. See also Sedgwick's similar dichotomized interpretation of Jane Austen's *Sense and Sensibility* in *Tendencies*, 80, 113–16; and Sedgwick, *Epistemology of the Closet*, 159.

65. June Jordan, *Haruko/Love Poems: New and Selected Love Poems* (New York: Pantheon, 1992), 97–101.

66. See Susan J. Wolfe and Julia Penelope, *Sexual Practice/Textual Theory* (Cambridge, MA: Blackwell, 1993); and Bergman, *Gaiety Transfigured*.

67. Bergman, *Gaiety Transfigured*, 11.

68. Ibid., 11, 23; and Eric Garber, "Richard Bruce Nugent," *Dictionary of Literary Biography: Afro-American Writers from the Harlem Renaissance to 1940*, vol. 51, ed. Trudier Harris (Detroit: Bruccoli Clark Layman, 1987), 216.

69. Bergman, *Gaiety Transfigured*, 23; Garber, "Richard Bruce Nugent," 213–21; Eric Garber, "T'ain't Nobody's Business," *Advocate*, May 13, 1982, 39–43, 53; Wallace Thurman, *Infants of the Spring* (Boston: Northeastern University Press, 1992).

70. Bergman, *Gaiety Transfigured*, 23.

71. Ibid., 27–43.

72. Karla Jay and Joanne Glasgow, eds., *Lesbian Texts and Contexts: Radical Revisions* (New York: New York University Press, 1990), 3, 5.

73. Ibid., 7.

74. Recent work by Bonnie Zimmerman appears to give queer, lesbian, and gay theorists another tool which could be applied in particularly appropriating ways, the "metaphorical lesbian." Such a move toward the lesbian-as-sign, a response to issues of essentialism, may unfortunately both encourage further bisexual erasure within lesbian theory and foster further appropriation of the images and works of bisexual-identified or behaviorally bisexual women authors. Sally Munt even refers to the metaphorical lesbian as a means by which lesbians can read Madonna "as one of us." Such moves, within contexts where "lesbian" is as exclusively defined as it appears to be in Zimmerman's theories, are dangerous in their potential to erase bisexual women and bisexuality as a category. See Zimmerman, "Lesbians Like This and That," 3–4; Munt, *New Lesbian Criticism*, xviii.

75. Some people identify *both* on axes of sexual identity and gender identity; thus, "and/or" would seem appropriate.

76. While I simply had faith that a gay male reading could be done (given all the gender high jinks in *Orlando*), Bonnie Zimmerman actually suggested this particular analysis of the text at the InQueery conference.

77. I should also include here "indiscriminate-" and "ambiguous-sex" attractions, terms I use to help describe bisexual attractions. Despite the availability of the terms "same-" and "different-sex attraction," corresponding to gay and straight sexual identities, bisexuality has no such single parallel term. Avoiding the dichotomized language of "dual-sex" attraction, there are not many descriptors that encompass all that is bisexuality. While "indiscriminate-sex" attraction may have a negative connotation to many people, it is a possible descriptor of bisexuality, one that is inclusive of those who say they are attracted to someone not *because* of their gender but in spite of it. This is a point that Ruth Goldman raised in her paper "Who Is That *Queer* Queer? Exploring Bisexuality and the 'Norm' in Queer Theory," presented at the InQueery conference. The term "ambiguous-sex" attraction describes attraction to gender ambiguity, a kind of attraction that may be found in both bisexual and transgender, as well as other, communities.

78. Elisabeth D. Däumer, "Queer Ethics; or, The Challenge of Bisexuality to Lesbian Ethics," *Hypatia* 7 (Fall 1992): 100.

79. Jordan, "The New Politics of Sexuality," 193.

80. For example, Hutchins and Kaahumanu, *Bi Any Other Name*; Weise, *Closer to Home*; and Sue George, *Women and Bisexuality* (London: Scarlet Press, 1993).

81. June Jordan, Amanda Udis-Kessler, Paula Rust, Rebecca Kaplan, Clare Hemmings, Frann Michel, and Jo Eadie, among many others, have been publishing bisexual theory of enormous potential within the field of sexual theory. However, this list is by no means exhaustive.

82. Ian, *Remembering the Phallic Mother*; Crompton, *Byron and Greek Love*; Claire Buck, *H. D. and Freud: Bisexuality and a Feminine Discourse* (New York: Harvester Wheatsheaf, 1991); Seidman, "Identity and Politics in a 'Postmodern' Gay Culture"; Anne Boyman, "Dora or the Case of *l'écriture féminine*," *Qui Parle: A Journal of Literary and Critical Studies* 3, no. 1 (Spring 1989): 180–88.

83. See Jordan, *Haruko/Love Poems*; Hanif Kureishi, *The Buddha of Suburbia* (New York: Viking, 1990).

84. See Sharon Lim-Hing, ed., *The Very Inside: An Anthology of Writing by Asian and Pacific-Islander Lesbian and Bisexual Women* (Toronto: Sister Vision Press, 1994); and Mona Oikawa, Dionne Falconer, Rosamund Elwin, and Ann Decter, eds., *Outrage: Dykes and Bis Resist Homophobia* (Toronto: Women's Press, 1993).

85. Maria Pramaggiore and Donald E. Hall's book now bears the less allusive title *RePresenting Bisexualities: Subjects and Cultures of Fluid Desire* (New York: New York University Press, forthcoming).

86. Many thanks to Lani Ka'ahumanu, who made this reference to Adrienne Rich in her keynote speech at the InQueery conference. Rich, "Women and Honor: Some Notes on Lying," *Adrienne Rich's Poetry and Prose*, 202.

BIBLIOGRAPHY

Anzaldúa, Gloria. *Borderlands/La Frontera: The New Mestiza*. San Francisco: Aunt Lute Books, 1987.

Baldwin, James. *Another Country*. New York: Random House, 1993.

Bergman, David. *Gaiety Transfigured: Gay Self-Representation in American Literature*. Madison: University of Wisconsin Press, 1991.

Blasingame, Brenda Marie. "The Roots of Biphobia: Racism and Internalized Heterosexism." *Closer to Home: Bisexuality and Feminism*. Ed. Elizabeth Reba Weise. Seattle: Seal Press, 1992. 47–53.

Bornstein, Kate. *Gender Outlaw: On Men, Women, and the Rest of Us*. New York: Routledge, 1994.

Boyman, Anne. "Dora or the Case of *l'écriture féminine*." *Qui Parle: A Journal of Literary and Critical Studies* 3, no. 1 (Spring 1989): 180–88.

Bristow, Joseph, ed. *Sexual Sameness: Textual Differences in Lesbian and Gay Writing*. London: Routledge, 1992.

Bristow, Joseph, and Angelia R. Wilson, eds. *Activating Theory: Lesbian, Gay, Bisexual Politics*. London: Lawrence and Wishart, 1993.

Buck, Claire. *H. D. and Freud: Bisexuality and a Feminine Discourse*. New York: Harvester Wheatsheaf, 1991.

Butler, Judith. *Gender Trouble: Feminism and the Subversion of Identity*. New York: Routledge, 1990.

Califia, Pat. *Public Sex: The Culture of Radical Sex*. San Francisco: Cleis Press, 1994.

Crompton, Louis. *Byron and Greek Love: Homophobia in Nineteenth-Century England*. Berkeley: University of California Press, 1985.

Däumer, Elisabeth D. "Queer Ethics; or, The Challenge of Bisexuality to Lesbian Ethics." *Hypatia* 7 (Fall 1992): 91–105.

Duberman, Martin Bauml. "Bisexuality." *About Time: Exploring the Gay Past*. New York: Gay Presses of New York, 1986. 249–64.

Eadie, Jo. "Activating Bisexuality: Towards a Bi/Sexual Politics." *Activating Theory: Lesbian, Gay, Bisexual Politics*. Ed. Joseph Bristow and Angelia R. Wilson. London: Lawrence and Wishart, 1993.

Fuss, Diana, ed. *Inside/Out: Lesbian Theories, Gay Theories*. New York: Routledge, 1991.

Garber, Eric. "Richard Bruce Nugent." *Dictionary of Literary Biography: Afro-American Writers from the Harlem Renaissance to 1940*. Ed. Trudier Harris. Vol. 51. Detroit: Bruccoli Clark Layman, 1987.

———. "T'ain't Nobody's Business." *Advocate*, May 13, 1982, 39–43, 53.

George, Sue. *Women and Bisexuality*. London: Scarlet Press, 1993.

Gibian, Ruth. "Refusing Certainty: Toward a Bisexuality of Wholeness." *Closer to Home: Bisexuality and Feminism*. Ed. Elizabeth Reba Weise. Seattle: Seal Press, 1992. 3–16.

Goldman, Ruth. "Who Is That *Queer* Queer? Exploring Bisexuality and the 'Norm' in Queer Theory." Paper presented at InQueery, InTheory, InDeed: The Sixth North American Lesbian, Gay, and Bisexual Studies Conference, Iowa City, Iowa, November 17–20, 1994.

Hansen-Taylor, Marie, and Horace E. Scudder, eds. *Life and Letters of Bayard Taylor.* 4th ed. 2 vols. Boston: Houghton Mifflin, 1885.

Hemmings, Clare. "Becoming a Desiring Subject: Bisexuality and Foucault." Paper presented at the Five College Women's Studies Research Center at Mount Holyoke College, October 4, 1994.

———. "Resituating the Bisexual Body." *Activating Theory: Lesbian, Gay, Bisexual Politics.* Ed. Joseph Bristow and Angelia R. Wilson. London: Lawrence and Wishart, 1993.

Highleyman, Liz A. "The Evolution of the Bisexual Movement." *Anything That Moves: Beyond the Myths of Bisexuality* 8 (Summer 1994): 24–25.

Hutchins, Loraine, and Lani Kaahumanu, eds. *Bi Any Other Name: Bisexual People Speak Out.* Boston: Alyson, 1991.

Ian, Marcia. *Remembering the Phallic Mother: Psychoanalysis, Modernism, and the Fetish.* Ithaca, NY: Cornell University Press, 1993.

James, Christopher. " 'All Will Forgive Who Feel the Same': Byron's Bisexuality and Reconciliation with Georgian Homophobia in Three Early Poems." Unpublished paper, 1992.

———. " 'The Truth and Tenderness of Man's Love for Man, as of Man's Love for Woman': Straight, Gay, and Bisexual Readings of Bayard Taylor and *Joseph and His Friend.*" Unpublished paper, 1994.

Jay, Karla, and Joanne Glasgow, eds. *Lesbian Texts and Contexts: Radical Revisions.* New York: New York University Press, 1990.

Jordan, June. "Free Flight." *Haruko/Love Poems: New and Selected Love Poems.* New York: Pantheon, 1992. 97–101.

———. "A New Politics of Sexuality." *Technical Difficulties: African-American Notes on the State of the Union.* New York: Pantheon, 1992. 187–93.

Kaplan, Rebecca. "Compulsory Heterosexuality and the Bisexual Existence: Toward a Bisexual Feminist Understanding of Heterosexism." *Closer to Home: Bisexuality and Feminism.* Ed. Elizabeth Reba Weise. Seattle: Seal Press, 1992. 269–80.

Kerouac, Jack. *The Subterraneans.* New York: Grove Weidenfeld, 1981.

Kureishi, Hanif. *The Buddha of Suburbia.* New York: Viking, 1990.

Lim-Hing, Sharon, ed. *The Very Inside: An Anthology of Writing by Asian and Pacific-Islander Lesbian and Bisexual Women.* Toronto: Sister Vision Press, 1994.

Martin, Robert K. *The Homosexual Tradition in American Poetry.* Austin: University of Texas Press, 1979.

Matthesen, Elise. "Sexualities and Communities." Presentation given at Iowa State University, Ames, Iowa, on October 3, 1994.

Michel, Frann. " 'I Just Loved Thelma': Djuna Barnes and the Construction of Bisexuality." *Review of Contemporary Fiction* 13, no. 3 (Fall 1993): 55–56.

Munt, Sally, ed. *New Lesbian Criticism: Literary and Cultural Readings.* New York: Columbia University Press, 1992.

Ochs, Robyn, ed. *International Directory of Bisexual Groups.* 11th ed. Cambridge, MA: Bisexual Resource Center, 1994.

Oikawa, Mona, Dionne Falconer, Rosamund Elwin, and Ann Decter, eds. *Outrage: Dykes and Bis Resist Homophobia.* Toronto: Women's Press, 1993.

Rich, Adrienne. "Compulsory Heterosexuality and Lesbian Existence." *Adrienne Rich's Poetry and Prose*. Ed. Barbara Charlesworth Gelpi and Albert Gelpi. New York: Norton, 1993. 203–24.

———. "Women and Honor: Some Notes on Lying." *Adrienne Rich's Poetry and Prose*. Ed. Barbara Charlesworth Gelpi and Albert Gelpi. New York: Norton, 1993. 195–203.

Sedgwick, Eve Kosofsky. *Between Men: English Literature and Male Homosocial Desire*. New York: Columbia University Press, 1985.

———. *Epistemology of the Closet*. Berkeley: University of California Press, 1990.

———. *Tendencies*. Durham, NC: Duke University Press, 1993.

Seidman, Steven. "Identity and Politics in a 'Postmodern' Gay Culture: Some Historical and Conceptual Notes." *Fear of a Queer Planet: Queer Politics and Social Theory*. Ed. Michael Warner. Minneapolis: University of Minnesota Press, 1993. 105–42.

Silverman, Kaja. "Too Early/Too Late: Subjectivity and the Primal Scene in Henry James." *Novel* 21 (Winter/Spring 1988): 147–73.

Simpson, J. A. et al., eds. *Oxford English Dictionary*. 2d ed. Vol. 2 of 20. Oxford: Clarendon Press, 1989.

Thurman, Wallace. *Infants of the Spring*. Boston: Northeastern University Press, 1992.

Warner, Michael, ed. *Fear of a Queer Planet: Queer Politics and Social Theory*. Minneapolis: University of Minnesota Press, 1993.

Weeks, Jeffrey. *Sexuality and Its Discontents: Meanings, Myths, and Modern Sexualities*. London: Routledge and Kegan Paul, 1985.

Weise, Elizabeth Reba, ed. *Closer to Home: Bisexuality and Feminism*. Seattle: Seal Press, 1992.

Weremuth, Paul C. *Bayard Taylor*. New York: Twayne, 1973.

Wolfe, Susan J., and Julia Penelope. *Sexual Practice/Textual Theory*. Cambridge, MA: Blackwell, 1993.

Young, Stacey. "Breaking Silence about the 'B-Word': Bisexual Identity and Lesbian-Feminist Discourse." *Closer to Home: Bisexuality and Feminism*. Ed. Elizabeth Reba Weise. Seattle: Seal Press, 1992. 75–87.

Zimmerman, Bonnie. "Lesbians Like This and That: Some Notes on Lesbian Criticism for the Nineties." *New Lesbian Criticism: Literary and Cultural Readings*. Ed. Sally Munt. New York: Columbia University Press, 1992. 1–15.

Zipkin, Dvora. "Why Bi?" *Closer to Home: Bisexuality and Feminism*. Ed. Elizabeth Reba Weise. Seattle: Seal Press, 1992. 55–73.

Scientific Racism and the

Invention of the

Homosexual Body

Siobhan Somerville

One of the most important insights developed in the fields of lesbian and gay history and the history of sexuality is the notion that homosexuality and, by extension, heterosexuality are relatively recent inventions in Western culture, rather than transhistorical or "natural" categories. As Michel Foucault and other historians of sexuality have argued, sexual acts between two people of the same sex had been punishable through legal and religious sanctions well before the late nineteenth century, but they did not necessarily define individuals as homosexual per se.[1] Only in the late nineteenth century did a new understanding of sexuality emerge in which sexual acts and desires became constitutive of identity. Homosexuality as the condition, and therefore identity, of particular bodies is thus a production of that historical moment.

Medical literature, broadly defined to include the writings of physicians, sexologists, and psychiatrists, has been integral to this historical argument. Although medical discourse was by no means the only — nor necessarily the most powerful — site of the emergence of new sexual identities, it does nevertheless offer rich sources for at least partially understanding the complex development of these categories in the late nineteenth and early twentieth centuries. Medical and sexological literature not only became one of the few sites of explicit engagement with questions of sexuality during this period but also held substantial definitional power within a culture that sanctioned science to discover and tell the truth about bodies.

As historians and theorists of sexuality have refined a notion of the late nineteenth-century "invention" of the homosexual, their discussions have drawn primarily upon theories and histories of gender. George Chauncey, in particular, has provided an invaluable discussion of the ways in which paradigms of sexuality shifted according to changing ideologies of gender during this period.[2] He notes a gradual change in medical models of sexual deviance, from a notion of sexual inversion, understood as a reversal of one's sex role, to a model of homosexuality, defined as deviant sexual object choice. These categories and their transformations, argues Chauncey, reflected concurrent shifts in the cultural organization of sex/gender roles and participated in prescribing acceptable behavior, especially within a context of white middle-class gender ideologies.

While gender insubordination offers a powerful explanatory model for the "invention" of homosexuality, ideologies of gender also, of course, shaped and were shaped by dominant constructions of race. Indeed, although it has received little acknowledgment, it is striking that the "invention" of the homosexual occurred at roughly the same time that racial questions were being reformulated, particularly in the United States. This was the moment, for instance, of *Plessy v. Ferguson*, the 1896 U.S. Supreme Court ruling that insisted that "black" and "white" races were "separate but equal." Both a product of and a stimulus to a nationwide and brutal era of racial segregation, this ruling had profound and lasting effects in legitimating an apartheid structure that remained legally sanctioned for more than half of the twentieth century. The *Plessy* case distilled in legal form many fears about race and racial difference that were prevalent at the time. A deluge of "Jim Crow" and anti-miscegenation laws, combined with unprecedented levels of racial violence, most visibly manifested in widespread lynching, reflected an aggressive attempt to classify and separate bodies as either "black" or "white."

Is it merely a historical coincidence that the classification of bodies as either "homosexual" or "heterosexual" emerged at the same time that the United States was aggressively policing the imaginary boundary between "black" and "white" bodies? Although some historians of sexuality have included brief acknowledgments of nineteenth-century discourses of racial difference, the particular relationship and potentially mutual effects of discourses of homosexuality and race remain unexplored.[3] This silence around race may be due in part to the relative lack of explicit attention to race in medical and sexological literature of the period. These writers did not self-consciously interrogate race, nor were those whose gender insubordination and/or sexual transgression brought them under the medical gaze generally identified by race in these accounts.[4] Yet the lack of explicit attention to race in these texts does not mean that it was irrelevant to sexologists' endeavors. Given the upheavals surrounding racial definition during this period, it is reasonable to assume that these texts were as embedded within contemporary racial ideologies as they were within contemporary ideologies of gender.

Take, for instance, the words of Havelock Ellis, whose massive *Studies in the Psychology of Sex* was one of the most important texts of the late nineteenth-century medical and scientific discourse on sexuality. "I regard sex as the central problem of life," began the general preface to the first volume. Justifying such unprecedented boldness regarding the study of sex, Ellis said the following:

> And now that the problem of religion has practically been settled, and that the problem of labour has at least been placed on a practical foundation, the question of sex — *with the racial questions that rest on it* — stands before the coming generations as the chief problem for solution.[5]

Despite Ellis's oddly breezy dismissal of the problems of labor and religion, which were far from settled at the time, this passage points suggestively to a link between sexual and racial anxieties. Yet what exactly did Ellis mean by "racial questions"? More significantly, what was his sense of the relationship between racial questions and the "question of sex"? Although Ellis himself left these issues unresolved, his elliptical declaration nevertheless suggested that a discourse of race — however elusively — somehow hovered around or within the study of sexuality.

In this article, I offer speculations on how late nineteenth- and early twentieth-century discourses of race and sexuality might be, not merely juxtaposed, but brought together in ways that illuminate both. I suggest that the concurrent bifurcations of categories of race and sexuality were not only historically coincident but in fact structurally interdependent and perhaps mutually productive. My goal, however, is not to garner and display unequivocal evidence of the direct influence of racial categories on those who were developing scientific models of homosexuality. Nor am I interested in identifying whether or not individual writers and thinkers are racist. Rather, my focus here is on racial ideologies, the systems of representation and cultural assumptions about race through which individuals understood their relationships within the world.[6] My emphasis is on understanding the relationships between the medical/scientific discourse around sexuality and the dominant scientific discourse around race during this period, that is, scientific racism.

My approach combines literary and historical methods of reading, particularly that which has been so crucial to lesbian, gay, and bisexual studies: the technique of reading to hear "the inexplicable presence of the thing not named,"[7] of being attuned to the queer presences and implications in texts that do not otherwise name them. Without this collective and multidisciplinary project to see, hear, and confirm queer inflections where others would deny their existence, it is arguable that the field of lesbian, gay, and bisexual studies itself, and particularly our knowledge and understanding of the histories, writing, and cultures of lesbians, gay men, and bisexuals, would be impoverished, if not impossible. In a similar way, I propose to use the techniques of queer reading, but to modulate my analysis from a focus on sexuality and gender to one alert to racial resonances as well.

My attention, then, is focused on the racial pressure points in exemplary texts from the late nineteenth-century discourse on sexuality, including those written by Ellis and other writers of the period who made explicit references to homosexuality. I suggest that the structures and methodologies that drove dominant ideologies of race also fueled the pursuit of scientific knowledge about the homosexual body: both sympathetic and hostile accounts of homosexuality were steeped in assumptions that had driven previous scientific studies of race.[8] My aim is not to replace a focus on gender and sexuality with one on race but rather to understand how discourses of race and gender buttressed one another, often competing, often overlapping, to shape emerging models of homosexuality.

I suggest three broadly defined ways in which discourses of sexuality seem to have been particularly engaged — sometimes overtly, but largely implicitly — with the discourse of scientific racism. All of these models pathologized to some degree both the non-white body and the non-heterosexual body. Although I discuss these models in separate sections here, they often coexisted, despite their contradictions. These models are speculative and are intended as a first step toward understanding the myriad and historically specific ways in which racial and sexual discourses shaped each other at the moment in which homosexuality entered scientific discourse.

Visible Differences: Sexology and Comparative Anatomy

Ellis's *Sexual Inversion*, the first volume of *Studies in the Psychology of Sex* to be published, became a definitive text in late nineteenth-century investigations of homosexuality.[9] Despite the series' titular focus on the psychology of sex, *Sexual Inversion* was a hybrid text, poised in methodology between the earlier field of comparative anatomy, with its procedures of bodily measurement, and the nascent techniques of psychology, with its focus on mental development.[10] In *Sexual Inversion*, Ellis hoped to provide scientific authority for the position that homosexuality should be considered not a crime but rather a congenital (and thus involuntary) physiological abnormality. Writing *Sexual Inversion* in the wake of England's 1885 Labouchère Amendment, which prohibited "any act of gross indecency" between men, Ellis intended in large part to defend homosexuality from "law and public opinion," which, in his view, combined "to place a heavy penal burden and a severe social stigma on the manifestations of an instinct which to those persons who possess it frequently appears natural and normal."[11] In doing so, Ellis attempted to drape himself in the cultural authority of a naturalist, eager to exert his powers of observation in an attempt to classify and codify understandings of homosexuality.[12]

Like other sexologists, Ellis assumed that the "invert" might be visually distinguishable from the "normal" body through anatomical markers, just as the differences between the sexes had traditionally been mapped upon the body. Yet the study of sexual difference was not the only methodological precedent for the study of the homosexual body. In its assumptions about somatic differences, *Sexual Inversion*, I suggest, also drew upon and participated in a history of the scientific investigation of race.

Race, in fact, became an explicit, though ambiguous, structural element in Ellis's *Sexual Inversion*. In chapter 5, titled "The Nature of Sexual Inversion," Ellis attempted to collate the evidence from case studies, dividing his general conclusions into various analytic categories. Significantly, "Race" was the first category he listed, under which he wrote, "All my cases, 80 in number, are British and American, 20 living in the United States and the rest being British. Ancestry, from the point of view of race, was not made a matter of special investigation" (264). He then listed the ancestries of the individuals whose case studies he included, which he identified as "English . . . Scotch . . . Irish . . . German . . . French . . . Portuguese . . . [and] more or less Jewish" (264). He concluded that "except in the apparently frequent presence of the German element, there is nothing remarkable in this ancestry" (264). Ellis used the term "race" in this passage interchangeably with national origin, with the possible exception of Jewish ancestry. These national identities were perceived to be at least partially biological and certainly hereditary in Ellis's account, though subordinate to the categories "British" and "American." Although he dismissed "ancestry, from the point of view of race" as a significant category, its place as the first topic within the chapter suggested its importance to the structure of Ellis's analysis.[13]

Ellis's ambiguous use of the term "race" was not unusual for scientific discourse in this period, during which it might refer to groupings based variously on geography, religion, class, or color.[14] The use of the term to mean a division of people based on physical (rather than genealogical or national) differences had originated in the late eighteenth century, when Johann Friedrich Blumenbach first classified human beings into five distinct groups in *On the Natural Variety of Mankind*. This work in turn became a model for the nineteenth-century fascination with anthropometry, the measurement of the human body.[15] Behind these anatomical measurements lay the assumption that the body was a legible text, with various keys or languages available for reading its symbolic codes. In the logic of biological determinism, the surface and interior of the individual body, rather than its social characteristics, such as language, behavior, or clothing, became the primary sites of its meaning. "Every peculiarity of the body has probably some corresponding significance in the mind, and the cause of the former are the remoter causes of the latter," wrote Edward Drinker Cope, a well-known American paleontologist, summarizing the assumptions that fueled the science of comparative anatomy.[16] Although scientists debated which particular anatomical features carried racial meanings — skin, facial angle, pelvis, skull, brain mass, genitalia — the theory that anatomy predicted intelligence and behavior nevertheless remained remarkably constant. As Nancy Stepan and Sander Gilman have noted, "The concepts within racial science were so congruent with social and political life (with power relations, that is) as to be virtually uncontested from inside the mainstream of science."[17]

Supported by the cultural authority of an ostensibly objective scientific method, these readings of the body became a powerful instrument for those seeking to justify the economic and political disenfranchisement of various racial groups within systems of slavery and colonialism. As Barbara Fields has noted, however, "Try as they would, the scientific racists of the past failed to discover any objective criterion upon which to classify people; to their chagrin, every criterion they tried varied more within so-called races than between them."[18] Although the methods of science were considered to be outside the political and economic realm, in fact, as we know, these anatomical investigations, however professedly innocent their intentions, were driven by racial ideologies already firmly in place.[19]

Ideologies of race, of course, shaped and reflected both popular and scientific understandings of gender. As Gilman has argued, "Any attempt to establish that the races were inherently different rested to no little extent on the sexual difference of the black."[20] Although popular racist mythology in the U.S. in the nineteenth century focused on the supposed difference between the size of African-American and white men's genitalia, the male body was not necessarily the primary site of medical inquiry into racial difference.[21] Instead, as a number of medical journals from this period demonstrate, comparative anatomists repeatedly located racial difference through the sexual characteristics of the female body.[22]

In exploring the influence of scientific studies of race on the emerging discourse of sexuality, it is useful to look closely at a study from the genre of comparative anatomy. In 1867, W. H. Flower and James Murie published their "Account of the Dissection of a Bushwoman," which carefully catalogued the "more perishable soft structures of the body" of a young Bushwoman.[23] They placed their study in a line of inquiry concerning the African woman's body that had begun at least a half-century earlier with French naturalist Georges Cuvier's description of the woman popularly known as the "Hottentot Venus," or Saartje Baartman, who was displayed to European audiences fascinated by her "steatopygia" (protruding buttocks).[24] Significantly, starting with Cuvier, this tradition of comparative anatomy located the boundaries of race through the sexual and reproductive anatomy of the African female body, ignoring altogether the problematic absence of male bodies from their studies.

Flower and Murie's account lingered on two specific sites of difference: the "protuberance of the buttocks, so peculiar to the Bushman race" and "the remarkable development of the labia minora," which were "sufficiently well marked to distinguish these parts from those of any ordinary varieties of the human species" (208). The racial difference of the African body, implied Flower and Murie, was located in its literal excess, a specifically sexual excess that placed her body outside the boundaries of the "normal" female. To support their conclusion, Flower and Murie included corroborating "evidence" in the final part of their account. They quoted a secondhand report, "received from a scientific friend residing at the Cape of Good Hope," describing the anatomy of "two pure bred Hottentots, mother and daughter" (208). This account also focused on the women's genitalia, which they referred to as "appendages" (208). Although their account ostensibly foregrounded boundaries of race, their portrayal of the sexual characteristics of the Bushwoman betrayed Flower and Murie's anxieties about gender boundaries. The characteristics singled out as "peculiar" to this race, the (double) "appendages," fluttered between genders, at one moment masculine, at the next moment exaggeratedly feminine. Flower and Murie constructed the site of *racial* difference by marking the sexual and reproductive anatomy of the African woman as "peculiar." In their characterization, sexual ambiguity delineated the boundaries of race.

The techniques and logic of late nineteenth-century sexologists, who also routinely included physical examinations in their accounts, reproduced the methodologies employed by comparative anatomists like Flower and Murie. Many of the case histories in Krafft-Ebing's *Psychopathia Sexualis*, for instance, included a paragraph detailing any anatomical peculiarities of the body in question.[25] Although Krafft-Ebing could not draw any conclusions about somatic indicators of "abnormal" sexuality, physical examinations remained a staple of the genre. In Ellis's *Sexual Inversion*, case studies often focused more intensely on the bodies of female "inverts" than those of their male counterparts.[26] Although the specific sites of anatomical inspection (hymen, clitoris, labia, vagina) differed, the underlying theory remained constant: women's genitalia and reproductive anatomy held a valuable and presumably visual key to ranking bodies according to norms of sexuality.

Sexologists reproduced not only the methodologies of the comparative anatomy of races but also its iconography. One of the most consistent medical characterizations of

the anatomy of both African-American women and lesbians was the myth of an unusu-
ally large clitoris.[27] As late as 1921, medical journals contained articles declaring that "a
physical examination of [female homosexuals] will in practically every instance disclose
an abnormally prominent clitoris." Significantly, this author added, "This is particularly
so in colored women."[28] In an earlier account of racial differences between white and
African-American women, one gynecologist had also focused on the size and visibility of
the clitoris; in his examinations, he had perceived a distinction between the "free"
clitoris of "negresses" and the "imprisonment" of the clitoris of the "Aryan American
woman."[29] In constructing these oppositions, such characterizations literalized the sexual and racial ideologies of the nineteenth-century "Cult of True Womanhood," which
explicitly privileged white women's sexual "purity," while implicitly suggesting African-
American women's sexual accessibility.[30]

It is evident from the case histories in *Sexual Inversion* that Ellis gave much more
attention to the presumed anatomical peculiarities of the women than to those of the
men. "As regards the sexual organs it seems possible," Ellis wrote, "so far as my
observations go, to speak more definitely of inverted women than of inverted men" (256).
Ellis justified his greater scrutiny of women's bodies in part by invoking the ambiguity
surrounding women's sexuality in general: "we are accustomed to a much greater
familiarity and intimacy between women than between men, and we are less apt to
suspect the existence of any abnormal passion" (204). To Ellis, the seemingly impercepti-
ble differences between "normal" and "abnormal" intimacies between women called for
closer scrutiny of the subtleties of their anatomy. He included the following detailed
account as potential evidence for distinguishing the fine line between the lesbian and
the "normal" woman:

> *Sexual Organs.* — (a) Internal: Uterus and ovaries appear normal. (b) External: Small
> clitoris, with this irregularity, that the lower folds of the labia minora, instead of uniting one
> with the other and forming the frenum, are extended upward along the sides of the clitoris,
> while the upper folds are poorly developed, furnishing the clitoris with a scant hood. The
> labia majora depart from normal conformation in being fuller in their posterior half than in
> their anterior part, so that when the subject is in the supine position they sag, as it were,
> presenting a slight resemblance to fleshy sacs, but in substance and structure they feel
> normal (136).

This extraordinary taxonomy, performed for Ellis by an unnamed "obstetric physician of
high standing," echoed earlier anatomical catalogues of African women. The exacting
eye (and hand) of the investigating physician highlighted every possible detail as meaningful evidence. Through the triple repetition of "normal" and the use of evaluative
language like "irregularity" and "poorly developed," the physician reinforced his position
of judgment. Although he did not provide criteria for what constituted "normal" anatomy, the physician assumed abnormality and simply corroborated that assumption
through sight and touch. Moreover, his characterization of what he perceived as abnormal echoed the anxious account by Flower and Murie. Although the description of the
clitoris is a notable exception to the tendency to exaggerate its size, the account

nevertheless scrutinized another site of genital excess. The "fleshy sacs" of this woman, like the "appendages" fetishized in the earlier account, invoked the anatomy of a phantom male body inhabiting the lesbian's anatomical features.[31]

Clearly, anxieties about gender shaped both Ellis's and Flower and Murie's taxonomies of the lesbian and the African woman. Yet their preoccupation with gender cannot be understood as separate from the larger context of scientific assumptions during this period, which one historian has characterized as "the full triumph of Darwinism in American thought."[32] Gender, in fact, was crucial to Darwinist ideas. One of the basic assumptions within the Darwinian model was the belief that, as organisms evolved through a process of natural selection, they also showed greater signs of differentiation between the (two) sexes. Following this logic, various writers used sexual characteristics as indicators of evolutionary progress toward civilization. In *Man and Woman*, for instance, Ellis himself cautiously suggested that since the "beginnings of industrialism," "more marked sexual differences in physical development seem (we cannot speak definitely) to have developed than are usually to be found in savage societies."[33] In this passage, Ellis drew from theories developed by biologists like Patrick Geddes and J. Arthur Thomson. In their important work *The Evolution of Sex*, which traced the role of sexual difference in evolution, Geddes and Thomson stated that "hermaphroditism is primitive; the unisexual state is a subsequent differentiation. The present cases of normal hermaphroditism imply either persistence or reversion."[34] In characterizing the bodies of lesbians or African-American women as less sexually differentiated than the norm (always posited as white heterosexual women's bodies), anatomists and sexologists drew upon notions of natural selection to dismiss these bodies as anomalous "throwbacks" within a scheme of cultural and anatomical progress.

The Mixed Body

The emergence of evolutionary theory in the late nineteenth century foregrounded a view of continuity between the "savage" and "civilized" races, in contrast to earlier scientific thinking about race, which had focused on debates about the origins of different racial groups. Proponents of monogeny argued that all races derived from a single origin. Those who argued for polygeny believed that each race descended from its own biological and geographical source, a view, not coincidentally, that supported segregationist impulses.[35] With Darwin's publication of *The Origin of Species* in 1859, the debate between polygeny and monogeny was superseded by evolutionary theory, which was appropriated as a powerful scientific model for understanding race. Its controversial innovation was its emphasis on the continuity between animals and human beings. Evolutionary theory held out the possibility that the physical, mental, and moral characteristics of human beings had evolved gradually over time from ape-like ancestors.[36] Although the idea of continuity depended logically on the blurring of boundaries within hierarchies, it did not necessarily invalidate the methods or assumptions of comparative anatomy. On the contrary, notions of visible differences and racial hierarchies were deployed to corroborate Darwinian theory.

The concept of continuity was harnessed to the growing attention to miscegenation, or "amalgamation," in social science writing in the first decades of the twentieth century. Edward Byron Reuter's *The Mulatto in the United States,* for instance, pursued an exhaustive quantitative and comparative study of the "mulatto" population and its achievements in relation to those of "pure" white or African ancestry. Reuter traced the presence of a distinct group of mixed-race people back to early American history: "Their physical appearance, though markedly different from that of the pure blooded race, was sufficiently marked to set them off as a peculiar people." [37] Reuter, of course, was willing to admit the viability of "mulattoes" only within a framework that emphasized the separation of races. Far from using the notion of the biracial body to refute the belief in discrete markers of racial difference, Reuter perpetuated the notion by focusing on the distinctiveness of this "peculiar people."

Miscegenation was, of course, not only a question of race, but also one of sex and sexuality. Ellis recognized this intersection implicitly, if not explicitly. His sense of the "racial questions" implicit in sex was surely informed by his involvement with eugenics, the movement in Europe and the United States that, to greater or lesser degrees, advocated selective reproduction and "race hygiene." [38] In the United States, eugenics was both a political and scientific response to the growth of a population beginning to challenge the dominance of white political interests. The widespread scientific and social interest in eugenics was fueled by anxieties expressed through the popular notion of (white) "race suicide." This phrase, invoked most notably by Theodore Roosevelt, summed up nativist fears about a perceived decline in reproduction among white Americans. The new field of eugenics worked hand in hand with growing anti-miscegenation sentiment and policy, provoked not only by the attempts of African-Americans to gain political representation but also by the influx of large populations of immigrants. [39] As Mark Haller has pointed out, "Racists and [immigration] restrictionists . . . found in eugenics the scientific reassurances they needed that heredity shaped man's personality and that their assumptions rested on biological facts." [40] Ellis saw himself as an advocate for eugenics policies. As an active member of the British National Council for Public Morals, he wrote several essays on eugenics, including *The Problem of Race Regeneration,* a pamphlet advocating "voluntary" sterilization of the unfit as a policy in the best interest of "the race." [41] Further, in a letter to Francis Galton in 1907, Ellis wrote, "In the concluding volume of my Sex 'Studies' I shall do what I can to insinuate the eugenic attitude." [42]

The beginnings of sexology, then, were related to, and perhaps even dependent on, a pervasive climate of eugenic and anti-miscegenation sentiment and legislation. Even at the level of nomenclature, anxieties about miscegenation shaped sexologists' attempts to find an appropriate and scientific name for the newly visible object of their study. Introduced into English in 1892 through the translation of Krafft-Ebing's *Psychopathia Sexualis,* the term "homosexuality" itself stimulated a great deal of uneasiness. In 1915, Ellis reported that "most investigators have been much puzzled in coming to a conclusion as to the best, most exact, and at the same time most colorless names [for same-sex desire]." [43] Giving an account of the various names proposed, such as Karl Heinrich Ulrichs's "Uranian" and Carl von Westphal's "contrary sexual feeling," Ellis admitted that "homosexuality" was the most widely used term. Far from the ideal "colorless" term,

however, "homosexuality" evoked Ellis's distaste because of its mixed origins: in a
regretful aside, he noted that "it has, philologically, the awkward disadvantage of being a
bastard term compounded of Greek and Latin elements" (2). In the first edition of
Sexual Inversion, Ellis stated his alarm more directly: " 'Homosexual' is a barbarously
hybrid word."[44] A similar view was expressed by Edward Carpenter, an important
socialist organizer in England and an outspoken advocate of homosexual and women's
emancipation. Like Ellis, Carpenter winced at the connotations of illegitimacy in the
word: " '[H]omosexual,' generally used in scientific works, is of course a bastard word.
'Homogenic' has been suggested, as being from two roots, both Greek, i.e., 'homos,'
same, and 'genos,' sex."[45] Carpenter's suggestion, "homogenic," of course, resonated both
against and within the vocabularies of eugenics and miscegenation. Performing these
etymological gyrations with almost comic literalism, Ellis and Carpenter expressed
pervasive cultural anxieties around questions of racial origins and purity. Concerned
above all else with legitimacy, they attempted to remove and rewrite the mixed origins
of "homosexuality." Ironically, despite their suggestions for alternatives, the "bastard"
term took hold among sexologists, thus yoking together, at least rhetorically, two kinds of
mixed bodies: the racial "hybrid" and the invert.

Although Ellis exhibited anxieties about biracial bodies, for others who sought to
naturalize and recuperate homosexuality, the evolutionary emphasis on continuity offered potentially useful analogies. Xavier Mayne, for example, one of the earliest American advocates of homosexual rights, wrote, "Between [the] whitest of men and the
blackest negro stretches out a vast line of intermediary races as to their colours: brown,
olive, red tawny, yellow."[46] He then invoked this model of race to envision a continuous
spectrum of gender and sexuality: "Nature abhors the absolute, delights in the fractional.
. . . Intersexes express the half-steps, the between-beings."[47] In this analogy, Mayne
reversed dominant cultural hierarchies that privileged purity over mixture. Drawing
upon irrefutable evidence of the "natural" existence of biracial people, Mayne posited a
direct analogy to a similarly mixed body, the intersex, which he positioned as a necessary
presence within the natural order.

Despite Carpenter's complaint about "bastard" terminology, he, like Mayne, also
occasionally appropriated the scientific language of racial mixing in order to resist
the association between homosexuality and degeneration. In *The Intermediate Sex*, he
attempted to theorize homosexuality outside of the discourse of pathology or abnormality; he too suggested a continuum of genders, with "intermediate types" occupying a
place between the poles of exclusively heterosexual male and exclusively heterosexual
female. In an appendix to *The Intermediate Sex*, Carpenter offered a series of quotations
supporting his ideas, some of which drew upon racial analogies:

Anatomically and mentally we find all shades existing from the pure genus man to the pure
genus woman. Thus there has been constituted what is well named by an illustrious
exponent of the science "The Third Sex". . . . As we are continually meeting in cities
women who are one-quarter, or one-eighth, or so on, *male* . . . so there are in the Inner Self
similar half-breeds, all adapting themselves to circumstances with perfect ease.[48]

Through notions of "shades" of gender and sexual "half-breeds," Carpenter appropriated dominant scientific models of race to construct and embody what he called the intermediate sex. These racial paradigms, along with models of gender, offered Carpenter a coherent vocabulary for understanding and expressing a new vision of sexual bodies.

Sexual "Perversion" and Racialized Desire

By the early twentieth century, medical models of sexuality had begun to shift in emphasis, moving away from a focus on the body and toward psychological theories of desire. It seems significant that this shift took place within a period that also saw a transformation of scientific notions about race. As historians have suggested, in the early twentieth century, scientific claims for exclusively biological models of racial difference were beginning to be undermined, although, of course, these models have persisted in popular understandings of race.[49]

In what ways were these shifts away from biologized notions of sexuality and race related in scientific literature? One area in which they overlapped and perhaps shaped one another was through models of interracial and homosexual desire. Specifically, two tabooed sexualities — miscegenation and homosexuality — became linked in sexological and psychological discourse through the model of "abnormal" sexual object choice.

The convergence of theories of "perverse" racial and sexual desire shaped the assumptions of psychologists like Margaret Otis, whose "A Perversion Not Commonly Noted" appeared in a medical journal in 1913. In all-girl institutions, including reform schools and boarding schools, Otis had observed widespread "love-making between the white and colored girls."[50] Both fascinated and alarmed, Otis remarked that this perversion was "well known in reform schools and institutions for delinquent girls," but that "this particular form of the homosexual relation has perhaps not been brought to the attention of scientists" (113). Performing her ostensible duty to science, Otis carefully described these rituals of interracial romance and the girls' "peculiar moral code." In particular, she noted that the girls incorporated racial difference into courtship rituals self-consciously patterned on traditional gender roles: "One white girl ... admitted that the colored girl she loved seemed the man, and thought it was so in the case of the others" (114). In Otis's account, the actions of the girls clearly threatened the keepers of the institutions, who responded to the perceived danger with efforts to racially segregate their charges (who were, of course, already segregated by gender). Otis, however, did not specify the motivation for segregation: Did the girls' intimacy trouble the authorities because it was homosexual or because it was interracial? Otis avoided exploring this question and offered a succinct theory instead: "The difference in color, in this case, takes the place of difference in sex" (113).

Otis's explicit discussion of racial difference and homosexuality was extremely unusual in the burgeoning social science literature on sexuality in the early twentieth century.[51] Significantly, Otis characterized this phenomenon as a type of "the homosexual relation" and not as a particular form of interracial sexuality. Despite Otis's focus on desire rather than physiology, her characterization of the schoolgirls' "system" of romance drew upon stereotypes established by the earlier anatomical models. She used a simple analogy between race and gender in order to understand their desire: black was to white as masculine was to feminine.

Recent historical work on the lesbian subject at the turn of the century in the United States offers a useful context for considering the implications of Otis's account. In a compelling analysis of the highly publicized 1892 murder of Freda Ward by her lover, Alice Mitchell, Lisa Duggan has argued that what initially pushed the women's relationship beyond what their peers accepted as normal was Mitchell's decision to pass as a man.[52] Passing, according to Duggan, was "a strategy so rare among bourgeois white women that their plan was perceived as so radically inappropriate as to be insane."[53] Duggan characterizes passing as a kind of red flag that visually marked Mitchell and Ward's relationship. Suddenly, with the prospect of Mitchell's visible transformation from "woman" to "man," the sexual nature of their relationship also came into view — abnormal and dangerous to the eyes of their surveyors.

Following Duggan's line of analysis, I suggest that racial difference performed a similar function in Otis's account. In turn-of-the-century American culture, where Jim Crow segregation erected a structure of taboos against any kind of public (non–work-related) interracial relationship, racial difference visually marked the alliances between the schoolgirls as already suspicious. In a culture in which Ellis could remark that he was accustomed to women being on intimate terms, race became a visible marker for the sexual nature of that liaison. In effect, the institution of racial segregation and its cultural fiction of "black" and "white" produced the girls' interracial romances as "perverse."[54]

It is possible that the discourse of sexual pathology, in turn, began to inform scientific understandings of race. By 1903, a southern physician drew upon the language of sexology to legitimate a particularly racist fear: "A perversion from which most races are exempt, prompts the negro's inclinations towards the white woman, whereas other races incline toward the females of their own."[55] Using the medical language of perversion to naturalize and legitimate the dominant cultural myth of the black rapist, this account characterized interracial desire as a type of congenital abnormal sexual object choice. In the writer's terms, the desire of African-American men for white women (though not the desire of white men for African-American women) could be understood and pathologized by drawing upon emergent models of sexual orientation.[56]

Divergences in Racial and Sexual Science

The "invention" of homosexuality and heterosexuality was inextricable from the extraordinary pressures attached to racial definition at this particular historical moment in the late nineteenth century. Although sexologists' search for physical signs of sexual orientation mirrored the methods of comparative racial anatomists, the modern case study marked a significant departure from comparative anatomy by attaching a self-generated narrative to the body in question. As Jeffrey Weeks has written, Krafft-Ebing's *Psychopathia Sexualis* was a decisive moment in the "invention" of the homosexual because "it was the eruption into print of the speaking pervert, the individual marked, or marred, by his (or her) sexual impulses."[57]

The case study challenged the tendency of scientific writers to position the homosexual individual as a mute body whose surface was to be interpreted by those with professional authority. Whether to grant a voice, however limited, to the homosexual body was a heavily contested methodological question among sexologists. The increasingly central position of the case study in the literature on homosexuality elicited concern from contemporary professionals, who perceived an unbridgeable conflict between autobiography and scientific objectivity. Invested in maintaining authority in medical writing, Morton Prince, a psychologist who advocated searching for a "cure" to homosexuality, described in exasperation his basic distrust of the case history as a source of medical evidence, especially in the case of "perverts":

> Even in taking an ordinary medical history, we should hesitate to accept such testimony as final, and I think we should be even more cautious in our examination of autobiographies which attempt to give an analysis, founded on introspection, of the feelings, passions and tastes of degenerate individuals who attempt to explain their first beginnings in early childhood.[58]

For Prince, the "speaking pervert" was a challenge to the "truth" of medical examination and threatened to contradict the traditional source of medical evidence, the patient's mute physical body as interpreted by the physician. In Prince's view, the case history also blurred the boundaries between the legal and medical spheres:

> Very few of these autobiographies will stand analysis. Probably there is no class of people whose statements will less stand the test of a scorching cross-examination than the moral pervert. One cannot help feeling that if the pervert was thus examined by an independent observer, instead of being allowed to tell his own story without interruption, a different tale would be told, or great gaps would be found, which are now nicely bridged, or many asserted facts would be resolved into pure inferences.[59]

A "different tale" indeed. Prince's focus on "testimony" and "cross-examination" illustrated the overlapping interests and methods of the medical and the legal spheres. His tableau of litigation placed the homosexual individual within an already guilty body, one that defied the assumption that it was a readable text; its anatomical markers did not necessarily correspond to predictable sexual behaviors. The sure duplicity of this body demanded investigation by the prosecutor/physician, whose professional expertise somehow guaranteed his access to the truth.

Ellis, who sought legitimacy both for himself as a scientist and for the nascent field of sexology, also worried about the association between autobiographical accounts and fraud. In *Sexual Inversion*, he stated that "it may be proper, at this point, to say a few words as to the reliability of the statements furnished by homosexual persons. This has sometimes been called in[to] question" (89). Although he also associated the homosexual voice with duplicity, Ellis differed from Prince by placing this unreliability within a larger social context. He located the causes of insincerity not in the homosexual individual but in the legal system that barred homosexuality: "[W]e cannot be surprised at this [potential insincerity] so long as inversion is counted a crime. The most normal persons, under similar conditions, would be similarly insincere" (89).

With the movement toward the case study and psychoanalytic models of sexuality, sexologists relied less and less upon the methodologies of comparative anatomy and implicitly acknowledged that physical characteristics were inadequate evidence for the "truth" of the body in question. Yet the assumptions of comparative anatomy did not completely disappear. Although they seemed to contradict more psychological understandings of sexuality, notions of biological difference continued to shape cultural understandings of sexuality, particularly in popular representations of lesbians, gay men, and bisexuals.

Troubling Science

My efforts here have focused on the various ways in which late nineteenth- and early twentieth-century scientific discourses around race became available to sexologists and physicians as a way to articulate emerging models of homosexuality. Methodologies and iconographies of comparative anatomy attempted to locate discrete physiological markers of difference through which to classify and separate types of human beings. Sexologists drew upon these techniques to try to position the "homosexual" body as anatomically distinguishable from the "normal" body. Likewise, medical discourses around sexuality appear to have been steeped in pervasive cultural anxieties about "mixed" bodies, particularly the "mulatto," whose literal position as a mixture of black and white bodies acquires a symbolic position in scientific accounts. Sexologists and others writing about homosexuality borrowed the model of the mixed body as a way to make sense of the "invert." Finally, racial and sexual discourses converged in psychological models that understood "unnatural" desire as a marker of perversion: in these cases, interracial and same-sex sexuality became analogous.

Although scientific and medical models of both race and sexuality held enormous definitional power at the turn of the century, they were variously and complexly incorporated, revised, resisted, or ignored both by the individuals they sought to categorize and within the larger cultural imagination. My speculations are intended to raise questions and to point toward possibilities for further historical and theoretical work. How, for instance, were analogies between race and sexual orientation deployed or not within popular cultural discourses? In religious discourses? In legal discourses? What were the material effects of their convergence or divergence? How have these analogies been used to organize bodies in other historical moments, and, most urgently, in our own?

In the last few years alone, for example, there has been a proliferation of "speaking perverts" in a range of cultural contexts, including political demonstrations, television, magazines, courts, newspapers, and classrooms. Despite the unprecedented opportunities for lesbian, gay, bisexual, and queer speech, however, recent scientific research into sexuality has reflected a determination to discover a biological key to the origins of homosexuality. Highly publicized new studies have purported to locate indicators of sexual orientation in discrete niches of the human body, ranging from a particular gene on the X chromosome to the hypothalamus, a structure of the brain.[60] In an updated and more technologically sophisticated form, comparative anatomy is being granted a peculiar cultural authority in the study of sexuality.

These studies, of course, have not gone uncontested, arriving as they have within a moment characterized not only by the development of social constructionist theories of sexuality but also, in the face of AIDS, by a profound and aching skepticism about prevailing scientific methods and institutions. At the same time, some see political efficacy in these new scientific studies, arguing that lesbians, gay men, and bisexuals might gain access to greater rights if sexual orientation could be proven an immutable biological difference. Such arguments make an analogy, whether explicit or unspoken, to the previous understanding of race as immutable difference. Reverberating through these arguments are echoes of late nineteenth- and early twentieth-century medical models of sexuality and race, whose earlier interdependence suggests a need to understand the complex relationships between constructions of race and sexuality during our own very different historical moment. How does the current effort to re-biologize sexual orientation and to invoke the vocabulary of immutable difference reflect or influence existing cultural anxieties and desires about racialized bodies? To what extent does the political deployment of these new scientific "facts" about sexuality depend upon reinscribing biologized racial categories? These questions, as I have tried to show for an earlier period, require a shift in the attention and practices of queer reading and lesbian, gay, and bisexual studies. We must begin to see questions of race as inextricable from the study of sexuality. To date, these connections have only been a part of our peripheral vision; we must make them a central focus.

NOTES

Acknowledgments: I would like to thank the following people who generously read and commented on earlier versions of this article: Hazel Carby, Lisa Cohen, Susan Edmunds, Heather Hendershot, David Rodowick, Michael Rogin, the anonymous referees for the *Journal of the History of Sexuality*, and especially Regina Kunzel.

1. See, for example, Michel Foucault, *The History of Sexuality*, vol. 1, *An Introduction* (New York: Vintage, 1980); George Chauncey, "From Sexual Inversion to Homosexuality: Medicine and the Changing Conceptualization of Female Deviance," *Salmagundi*, nos. 58–59 (Fall 1982–Winter 1983): 114–46; Jeffrey Weeks, *Sex, Politics, and Society: The Regulation of Sexuality since 1800* (New York: Longmans, 1981); and David Halperin, "Is There a History of Sexuality?" in *The Lesbian and Gay Studies Reader*, ed. Henry Abelove, Michèle Aina Barale, and David M. Halperin (New York: Routledge, 1993), 416–31. On the invention of the classification "heterosexual," see Jonathan Katz, "The Invention of Heterosexuality," *Socialist Review* 20 (1990): 17–34. For a related and intriguing argument that locates the earlier emergence of hierarchies of reproductive over non-reproductive sexual activity, see Henry Abelove, "Some Speculations on the History of 'Sexual Intercourse' during the 'Long Eighteenth Century' in England," *Genders* 6 (1989): 125–30.

2. Chauncey, "From Sexual Inversion to Homosexuality."

3. In "Homosexuality: A Cultural Construct," from his *One Hundred Years of Homosexuality; and Other Essays on Greek Love* (New York: Routledge, 1990), David Halperin has briefly and provocatively suggested that

all scientific inquiries into the aetiology of sexual orientation, after all, spring from a more or less implicit theory of sexual races, from the notion that there exist broad general divisions between types of human beings corresponding, respectively, to those who make a homosexual and those who make a heterosexual object-choice. When the sexual racism underlying such inquiries is more plainly exposed, their rationale will suffer proportionately — or so one may hope. (50)

In a recent article, Abdul R. JanMohamed offers a useful analysis and critique of Foucault's failure to examine the intersection of the discourses of sexuality and race. See his "Sexuality on/of the Racial Border: Foucault, Wright, and the Articulation of 'Racialized Sexuality,' " in *Discourses of Sexuality: From Aristotle to AIDS*, ed. Domna C. Stanton (Ann Arbor: University of Michigan Press, 1992), 94–116. I explore a different (though related) set of questions in this essay.

4. In *Disorders of Desire: Sex and Gender in Modern American Sexology* (Philadelphia: Temple University Press, 1990), Janice Irvine notes that, for example, "the invisibility of Black people in sexology as subjects or researchers has undermined our understanding of the sexuality of Black Americans and continues to be a major problem in modern sexology." She adds that Kinsey, the other major sexologist of the twentieth century, planned to include a significant proportion of African-American case histories in his *Sexual Behavior in the Human Male* (1948) and *Sexual Behavior in the Human Female* (1953) but failed to gather a sufficient number of them and so "unwittingly colluded in the racial exclusion so pervasive in sex research" (43).

5. Havelock Ellis, *Studies in the Psychology of Sex*, vol. 1, *Sexual Inversion* (1897; London, 1900), x, emphasis added.

6. My use of the concept of ideology draws upon Barbara Fields, "Slavery, Race, and Ideology in the United States of America," *New Left Review* 181 (1990): 95–118; Louis Althusser, "Ideology and Ideological State Apparatuses (Notes towards an Investigation)," in his *Lenin and Philosophy and Other Essays*, trans. Ben Brewster (New York: Monthly Review Press, 1971), 121–73; and Teresa de Lauretis, "The Technology of Gender," in her *Technologies of Gender: Essays on Theory, Film, and Fiction* (Bloomington: Indiana University Press, 1987), 1–30.

7. I borrow this phrase from Willa Cather's essay "The Novel Démeublé," in her *Not under Forty* (New York, 1922), 50.

8. I am not implying, however, that racial anxieties caused the invention of the homosexual, or that the invention of the homosexual caused increased racial anxieties. Both of these causal arguments seem simplistic and, further, depend upon separating the discourses of race and sexuality, whose convergence, in fact, I am eager to foreground.

9. Havelock Ellis, *Studies in the Psychology of Sex*, vol. 2, *Sexual Inversion*, 3d ed. (Philadelphia, 1915). Further references to this edition will be noted parenthetically unless otherwise stated. Although *Sexual Inversion* was published originally as volume 1, Ellis changed its position to volume 2 in the second and third editions, published in the United States in 1901 and 1915, respectively. In the later editions, volume 1 became *The Evolution of Modesty*.

Ellis originally coauthored *Sexual Inversion* with John Addington Symonds. For a discussion of their collaboration and the eventual erasure of Symonds from the text, see Wayne Koestenbaum, *Double Talk: The Erotics of Male Literary Collaboration* (New York: Routledge, 1989), 43–67.

10. In "Sex and the Emergence of Sexuality," *Critical Inquiry* 14 (Autumn 1987): 16–48, Arnold I. Davidson characterizes Ellis's method as "psychiatric" (as opposed to "anatomical") reasoning. Arguing that "sexuality itself is a product of the psychiatric style of reasoning" (23), Davidson explains that "the iconographical representation of sex proceeds by depiction of the body, more specifically by depiction of the genitalia. The iconographical representation of sexuality is given

by depiction of the personality, and it most usually takes the form of depiction of the face and its expressions" (27). The case studies in *Sexual Inversion*, and especially those of women, however, tend to contradict this broad characterization. My understanding of Ellis differs from that of Davidson, who readily places Ellis in a psychiatric model. Instead, Ellis might be characterized as a transitional figure, poised at the crossroads between the fields of comparative anatomy and psychiatry. To borrow Davidson's terms, anatomical reasoning does not disappear; it stays in place, supporting psychiatric reasoning.

11. Ellis, *Sexual Inversion* (1900), xi. Ironically, upon publication in 1897, *Sexual Inversion* was judged to be not a scientific work but "a certain lewd, wicked, bawdy, scandalous libel." Effectively banned in England, subsequent copies were published only in the United States. See Jeffrey Weeks, "Havelock Ellis and the Politics of Sex Reform," in *Socialism and the New Life: The Personal and Sexual Politics of Edward Carpenter and Havelock Ellis*, ed. Sheila Rowbotham and Jeffrey Weeks (London: Pluto Press, 1977), 154; and Phyllis Grosskurth, *Havelock Ellis: A Biography* (New York: Knopf, 1980), 191–204.

12. For further discussion of Ellis's similarity to Charles Darwin as a naturalist and their mutual interest in "natural" modesty, see Ruth Bernard Yeazell, "Nature's Courtship Plot in Darwin and Ellis," *Yale Journal of Criticism* 2 (1989): 33–53.

13. Elsewhere in *Sexual Inversion*, Ellis entertained the idea that certain races or nationalities had a "special proclivity" to homosexuality (4), but he seemed to recognize the nationalistic impulse behind this argument and chided those who wielded it: "The people of every country have always been eager to associate sexual perversions with some other country than their own" (57–58).

14. Classic discussions of the term's history include Peter I. Rose, *The Subject Is Race: Traditional Ideologies and the Teaching of Race Relations* (New York: Oxford University Press, 1968), 30–43; and Thomas F. Gossett, *Race: The History of an Idea in America* (Dallas: Southern Methodist University Press, 1963). For a history of various forms and theories of biological determinism, see Stephen Jay Gould, *The Mismeasure of Man* (New York: Norton, 1981).

15. John S. Haller, Jr., *Outcasts from Evolution: Scientific Attitudes of Racial Inferiority, 1859–1900* (Urbana: University of Illinois Press, 1971), 4.

16. Ibid., 196. On Cope, see also Gould, *The Mismeasure of Man*, 115–18.

17. Nancy Leys Stepan and Sander Gilman, "Appropriating the Idioms of Science: The Rejection of Scientific Racism," in *The Bounds of Race: Perspectives on Hegemony and Resistance*, ed. Dominick LaCapra (Ithaca, NY: Cornell University Press, 1991), 74.

18. Fields, "Slavery, Race, and Ideology in the United States of America," 97, n. 3.

19. Haller, "Outcasts from Evolution," 48.

20. Sander Gilman, *Difference and Pathology: Stereotypes of Sexuality, Race, and Madness* (Ithaca, NY: Cornell University Press, 1985), 112.

21. According to Gilman, "When one turns to autopsies of black males from [the late nineteenth century], what is striking is the absence of any discussion of the male genitalia" (ibid., 89).

The specific absence of male physiology as a focus of nineteenth-century scientific texts, however, should not minimize the central location of the African-American male body in popular cultural notions of racial difference, especially in the spectacle of lynching, which had far-reaching effects on both African-American and white attitudes toward the African-American male body. One might also consider the position of the racialized male body in one of the most popular forms of nineteenth-century entertainment, the minstrel show. See Eric Lott, *Love and Theft: Blackface Minstrelsy and the American Working Class* (New York: Oxford University Press, 1993).

22. The *American Journal of Obstetrics (AJO)* was a frequent forum for these debates. On the

position of the hymen, for example, see C. H. Fort, "Some Corroborative Facts in Regard to the Anatomical Difference between the Negro and White Races," *AJO* 10 (1877): 258–59; H. Otis Hyatt, "Note on the Normal Anatomy of the Vulvo-Vaginal Orifice," *AJO* 10 (1877): 253–58; A. G. Smythe, "The Position of the Hymen in the Negro Race," *AJO* 10 (1877): 638–39; Edward Turnipseed, "Some Facts in Regard to the Anatomical Differences between the Negro and White Races," *AJO* 10 (1877): 32–33. On the birth canal, see Joseph Taber Johnson, "On Some of the Apparent Peculiarities of Parturition in the Negro Race, with Remarks on Race Pelves in General," *AJO* 8 (1875): 88–123.

This focus on women's bodies apparently differed from earlier studies. In her recent work on gender and natural history, Londa Schiebinger discusses how eighteenth-century comparative anatomists and anthropologists developed their theories by examining male bodies. See *Nature's Body: Gender in the Making of Modern Science* (Boston: Beacon, 1993), especially 143–83.

23. W. H. Flower and James Murie, "Account of the Dissection of a Bushwoman," *Journal of Anatomy and Physiology* 1 (1867): 208. Subsequent references will be noted parenthetically within the text.

Flower was the conservator of the Museum of the Royal College of Surgeons of England; Murie was prosector to the Zoological Society of London. For brief discussions of this account, see Gilman, *Difference and Pathology*, 88–89; and Anita Levy, *Other Women: The Writing of Class, Race, and Gender, 1832–1898* (Princeton, NJ: Princeton University Press, 1991), 70–72. Although she does not consider questions surrounding the lesbian body, Levy offers an astute reading of this case and its connection to scientific representations of the body of the prostitute.

24. Georges Cuvier, "Extraits d'observations faites sur le cadavre d'une femme connue à Paris et à Londres sous le nom de Vénus Hottentote," *Mémoires du Musée d'histoire naturelle* 3 (1817): 259–74. After her death in 1815 at the age of twenty-five, Baartman's genitalia were preserved and re-displayed within the scientific space of the Musée de l'Homme in Paris.

On Baartman, see Schiebinger, *Nature's Body*, 160–72; and Stephen Jay Gould, *The Flamingo's Smile: Reflections in Natural History* (New York: Norton 1985), 291–305.

25. Richard von Krafft-Ebing, *Psychopathia Sexualis*, 12th ed., trans. Franklin S. Klaf (1902; reprint, New York: Putnam, 1965).

26. This practice continued well into the twentieth century. See, for example, Jennifer Terry's discussion of the anatomical measurement of lesbians by the Committee for the Study of Sex Variants in the 1930s, in "Lesbians under the Medical Gaze: Scientists Search for Remarkable Differences," *Journal of Sex Research* 27 (August 1990): 317–39; and "Theorizing Deviant Historiography," *differences* 3 (Summer 1991): 55–74.

27. In the first edition of *Sexual Inversion*, Ellis, who did search the lesbian body for masculine characteristics, nevertheless refuted this claim about the clitoris: "there is no connection, as was once supposed, between sexual inversion and an enlarged clitoris" (98).

28. Perry M. Lichtenstein, "The 'Fairy' and the Lady Lover," *Medical Review of Reviews* 27 (1921): 372. In "Lesbians under the Medical Gaze," Terry discusses sexologists' conjectures about the size of lesbians' genitalia in a report published in 1941. Researchers were somewhat uncertain whether perceived excesses were congenital or the result of particular sex practices. On the history of scientific claims about the sexual function of the clitoris, see Thomas Laqueur, *Making Sex: Body and Gender from the Greeks to Freud* (Cambridge: Harvard University Press, 1990), 233–37.

29. Morris, "Is Evolution Trying to Do Away with the Clitoris?" (paper presented at the meeting of the American Association of Obstetricians and Gynecologists, St. Louis, September 21, 1892), Yale University Medical Library, New Haven, CT.

30. See Hazel Carby, *Reconstructing Womanhood: The Emergence of the Afro-American Woman*

Novelist (New York: Oxford University Press, 1987), 20–39; and Barbara Welter, "The Cult of True Womanhood, 1820–1860," in her *Dimity Convictions: The American Woman in the Nineteenth Century* (Columbus: Ohio University Press, 1976), 21–41.

31. Characterizing this passage as "punitively complete," Koestenbaum in *Double Talk* has suggested that Ellis also had personal motivations for focusing so intently on the lesbian body: "Ellis, by taking part in this over-description of a lesbian, studied and subjugated the preference of his own wife; marrying a lesbian, choosing to discontinue sexual relations with her, writing *Sexual Inversion* with a homosexual [Symonds], Ellis might well have felt his own heterosexuality questioned" (54, 55).

32. George Fredrickson, *The Black Image in the White Mind: The Debate on Afro-American Character and Destiny, 1817–1914* (New York: Harper and Row, 1971), 246.

33. Havelock Ellis, *Man and Woman: A Study of Human Secondary Sexual Characters* (1894; New York, 1911), 13. Of course, the "beginnings of industrialism" coincided with the late eighteenth century, the period during which, as Schiebinger has shown, anatomists began looking for more subtle marks of differentiation. See Londa Schiebinger, *The Mind Has No Sex? Women in the Origins of Modern Science* (Cambridge: Harvard University Press, 1989), 189–212.

34. Patrick Geddes and J. Arthur Thomson, *The Evolution of Sex* (London, 1889; New York, 1890), 80. Ellis no doubt read this volume closely, for he had chosen it to inaugurate a series of popular scientific books (the Contemporary Science Series) that he edited for the Walter Scott Company. For more on this series, see Grosskurth, *Havelock Ellis*, 114–17.

35. For a full account of the debates concerning monogeny and polygeny, see Gould, *The Mismeasure of Man*, 30–72. Polygeny was a predominantly American theoretical development and was widely referred to as the "American school" of anthropology.

36. See Nancy Stepan, *The Idea of Race in Science: Great Britain, 1800–1960* (Hamden, CT: Archon Books, 1982), 53.

37. Edward Byron Reuter, *The Mulatto in the United States: Including a Study of the Role of Mixed-Blood Races throughout the World* (Boston, 1918), 338. Interestingly, in a paper delivered to the Eugenics Society of Britain in 1911, Edith Ellis (who had at least one long-term lesbian relationship while she was married to Havelock Ellis) had also used the phrase "peculiar people" to describe homosexual men and women. See Grosskurth, *Havelock Ellis*, 237–38.

38. Francis Galton (a cousin of Charles Darwin) introduced and defined the term "eugenics" in his *Inquiries into Human Faculty and Its Development* (1883; reprint, New York: AMS Press, 1973) as "the cultivation of the race" and "the science of improving stock, which . . . takes cognisance [sic] of all influences that tend in however remote a degree to give to the more suitable races or strains of blood a better chance of prevailing speedily over the less suitable than they otherwise would have had" (17).

39. For a discussion of Roosevelt's place within the racial ideology of the period, see Thomas G. Dyer, *Theodore Roosevelt and the Idea of Race* (Baton Rouge: Louisiana State University Press, 1980). See also John Higham, *Strangers in the Land: Patterns of American Nativism, 1860–1925* (New Brunswick, NJ: Rutgers University Press, 1955; reprint, New York: Atheneum, 1963), 146–57.

40. Mark H. Haller, *Eugenics: Hereditarian Attitudes in American Thought* (New Brunswick, NJ: Rutgers University Press, 1963), 144.

41. Jeffrey Weeks, *Sexuality and Its Discontents: Meanings, Myths, and Modern Sexualities* (Boston: Routledge and Kegan Paul, 1985), 76; Grosskurth, *Havelock Ellis*, 410. See also Havelock Ellis, "The Sterilization of the Unfit," *Eugenics Review* (October 1909): 203–6.

42. Quoted by Grosskurth, *Havelock Ellis*, 410.

43. Ellis, *Sexual Inversion* (1915), 2.

44. Ellis, *Sexual Inversion* (1900), 1n.

45. Edward Carpenter, "The Homogenic Attachment," in his *The Intermediate Sex: A Study of Some Transitional Types of Men and Women*, 5th ed. (London, 1918), 40n.

46. Xavier Mayne [Edward Irenaeus Prime Stevenson], *The Intersexes: A History of Similisexualism as a Problem in Social Life* ([Naples?], ca. 1908]; reprint, New York: Arno Press, 1975), 14.

47. Ibid., 15, 17.

48. Quoted in Carpenter, *The Intermediate Sex*, 133, 170. Carpenter gives the following citations for these quotations: Dr. James Burnet, *Medical Times and Hospital Gazette* 34, no. 1497 (November 10, 1906); and Charles G. Leland, "The Alternate Sex" (London, 1904), 41, 57.

49. In *New People: Miscegenation and Mulattoes in the United States* (New York: Free Press, 1980), Joel Williamson suggests that a similar psychologization of race was underway: "By about 1900 it was possible in the South for one who was biologically purely white to become behaviorally black. Blackness had become not a matter of visibility, not even, ironically, of the one-drop rule. It had passed on to become a matter of inner morality and outward behavior" (108). See also Elazar Barkan, *The Retreat of Scientific Racism: Changing Concepts of Race in Britain and the United States between the World Wars* (New York: Cambridge University Press, 1992).

Legal scholars have begun to explore the analogies between sodomy laws and anti-miscegenation statutes. See, for example, Andrew Koppelman, "The Miscegenation Analogy: Sodomy Law as Sex Discrimination," *Yale Law Journal* 98 (November 1988): 145–64. See also Janet Halley, "The Politics of the Closet: Towards Equal Protection for Gay, Lesbian, and Bisexual Identity," *UCLA Law Review* 36 (1989): 915–76. I am grateful to Julia Friedlander for bringing this legal scholarship to my attention.

50. Margaret Otis, "A Perversion Not Commonly Noted," *Journal of Abnormal Psychology* 8 (June–July 1913): 113–16. Subsequent references will be noted parenthetically within the text.

51. In "From Sexual Inversion to Homosexuality," Chauncey notes that "by the early teens the number of articles of abstracts concerning homosexuality regularly available to the American medical profession had grown enormously" (115, n. 3).

52. Lisa Duggan, "The Trials of Alice Mitchell: Sensationalism, Sexology, and the Lesbian Subject in Turn-of-the-Century America," *Signs: Journal of Women in Culture and Society* 18 (Summer 1993): 791–814.

53. Ibid., 798.

54. In a useful discussion of recent feminist analyses of identity, Lisa Walker suggests that a similar trope of visibility is prevalent in white critics' attempts to theorize race and sexuality. See her "How to Recognize a Lesbian: The Cultural Politics of Looking like What You Are," *Signs* 18 (Summer 1993): 866–90.

55. W. T. English, "The Negro Problem from the Physician's Point of View," *Atlanta Journal-Record of Medicine* 5 (October 1903): 468.

56. On the other hand, anti-lynching campaigns could also invoke the language of sexology. Although the analogy invoked sadism, rather than homosexuality, in 1935 a psychologist characterized lynching as a kind of "Dixie sex perversion. . . [m]uch that is commonly stigmatized as cruelty is a perversion of the sex instinct." Quoted in Phyllis Klotman, " 'Tearing a Hole in History': Lynching as Theme and Motif," *Black American Literature Forum* 19 (1985): 57. The original quote appeared in the *Baltimore Afro-American*, March 16, 1935.

57. Weeks, *Sexuality and Its Discontents*, 67. Weeks points out that beginning with Krafft-Ebing's *Psychopathia Sexualis*, the case study became the standard in sexological writing. The dynamic between medical literature and a growing self-identified gay (male) subculture is exemplified by the growth of different editions of this single work. The first edition of *Psychopathia*

Sexualis, published in 1886, contained 45 case histories and 110 pages; the twelfth edition, published in 1903, contained 238 case histories and 437 pages. Many of the subsequent case histories were supplied by readers who responded to the book with letters detailing their own sexual histories. This information suggests that, to at least some extent, an emerging gay male subculture was able to appropriate the space of "professional" medicolegal writing for its own uses, thus blurring the boundaries between professional medical and popular literature.

58. Morton Prince, "Sexual Perversion or Vice? A Pathological and Therapeutic Inquiry," *Journal of Nervous and Mental Disease* 25 (April 1898): 237–56; reprinted in *Psychotherapy and Multiple Personality: Selected Essays*, ed. Nathan G. Hale (Cambridge: Harvard University Press, 1975), 91.

59. Prince, *Psychotherapy and Multiple Personality*, 92.

60. See Simon LeVay, *The Sexual Brain* (Cambridge: MIT Press, 1993); and Dean Hamer, *The Science of Desire: The Search for the Gay Gene and the Biology of Behavior* (New York: Simon and Schuster, 1994).

chapter 14

Revamping MTV: Passing for

Queer Culture in the

Video Closet

Lynda Goldstein

[T]ransvestism is a space of possibility structuring and confounding culture: the disruptive element that intervenes, not just a category crisis of male and female but the crisis of category itself.

— Marjorie Garber, *Vested Interests: Cross-Dressing and Cultural Anxiety* (1993)

[Simulation] is the map that precedes the territory — *precession of simulacra* — it is the map that engenders the territory.

— Jean Baudrillard, "Simulacra and Simulations" (1988)

Possessing the means of recording allows one to monitor noises, to maintain them, and to control their repetition within a determined code.

— Jacques Attali, *Noise: The Political Economy of Music* (1985)

Like its privileged stars, Madonna and Michael Jackson, MTV has a history of revamping itself. By aggressively changing its roster of VJs who introduce music videos, incorporating new kinds of non-music video programming, shifting music video block slots and non-music programming schedules, introducing "buzz clips" of the newest "alternative" music, and killing shows regardless of popularity, MTV has perpetually refashioned itself to maintain its corporate position as the cutting-edge popular culture form for its consumer youth market. Concomitant with its increased status as arbiter of popular youth culture, MTV has gained an increased viewership largely through revamping its programming schedule to accommodate discrete audiences. Rather than simply moving from narrowcasting to broadcasting (from the heavy metal videos of the early 1980s, for example, to a mélange of more broadly popular videos), MTV shifted in 1986 to an increasingly eclectic mix of music and non-music programming with crossover appeal.[1] Through its highly fragmented proliferation of narrowcast programming ("MTV Jams," "Alternative Nation," "Headbanger's Ball," "The Grind"), each slot could assert a coherent identity with appeal to specific audience populations (rap, alternative, post-punk/metal, dance). Yet music videos shown during each slot are often far less categorically containable than program titles might suggest. And it is precisely the uncontainable crossover quality of many of the music videos themselves, as well as MTV's mix of music videos and non-music programming within each marketing slot, that establishes MTV's aesthetics and politics of eclecticism. Indeed, MTV has defined itself as "eclectic" since 1993 in heavily advertised promotional spots. It is this eclecticism which operates as the foundation for queer interactions with MTV's programming.[2]

Instead of simply running individual music videos or other shows with readable (and more threatening) "queer" content, MTV's eclectic programming could promote a less threatening, crossover queer style to its audiences. Particularly through dance music videos and participatory non-music programming, viewers could try on different identity styles, because crossover enlarges our repertoires of performative possibilities. It allows us to perform sexual, gender, or racial differences, often in (problematic) intersections with one another, while still inhabiting our "selves." Consider the crossover appeal of hip-hop fashion. We might note the proliferation of baggy jeans and baseball caps — first worn by inner-city Black and Latino youths — among suburban white kids (with some variation when adopted by young women). Or we might think of crossover in terms of the musical styles of some artists' work; say, the blending of rock, funk, and rap by the Red Hot Chili Peppers or the post-punk soul of Luscious Jackson. In each of these cases, the "performers" (whether suburban white kids in jeans and caps or white musicians) perform simultaneously as their essential (white) selves *and* as (Black, Latino, male) Other selves that are so associated with a style of clothing or music that we culturally conflate hip hop with Black/Latino or punk music with male.

Crossover enables us to shuttle so quickly between "real" and "fantasy" identities that we seem to occupy them all at the same time. For this reason, we must pay attention to how it organizes complex, multilayered cultural meanings. Because of MTV's enormous resources in offering nonstop access to all kinds of styles, its perpetual crossing-over is especially dense in the ways that it references life outside of itself.[3] Consider, for instance, the resonances of Queer Nation (an in-your-face, grass-roots queer organization) and *Alien Nation* (a paranoid 1988 sci-fi film) in MTV's program title "Alternative Nation," which offers at once the illusory coherence of a nationalized identity and the incoherences of "alternative," non-mainstream, non-corporate, punk-influenced music culture. These jumbled references to "alternative" politics, sci-fi realities, and music are held together by Kennedy, the "Alternative Nation" VJ. Yet her sarcasm, neo-conservative politics, and appropriation of "granola culture" granny dresses seem to contradict the more radical politics, realities, and aesthetics of Queer Nation, *Alien Nation*, and Seattle post-punk music culture. These contradictions are precisely what crossover is about.

This chapter will consider some of the ways in which MTV as a hyperkinetic postmodern culture vulture specifically privileges its trope of eclectic crossover as a means of fostering what passes for queer style. By queer style, I mean that which celebrates performative and perpetually unstable gender/race/class/sexual identities.[4] In MTV's rendition, this is most often coded as various forms of drag performance. Insofar as MTV gives its consumers access to this style, it provides them with the space and time to envision and rehearse sexuality as performative, as an unstable, potentially campy transvestism underlying the regime of heterosexuality. It provides them with the means to question the categories of sexuality and to pass for queer. Ultimately, however, I'd like to suggest that this passing as an embodied queer (often in rapid and dizzying succession from program to program, even image to image) is contained by and within the "video closet" of MTV, with dire ramifications for the "real" body politics of queer identity.

Passing for Queer

By the 1992–93 seasons, MTV viewers could participate in a kind of queerness that relied heavily on the paradoxically aligned tropes of authenticity and performativity. As unlikely as it seems, the politics and styles of Queer Nation, haute couture, and drag performance converged in dance music videos privileging the "realness" of voguing, runway fashion, makeup, and drag (especially RuPaul's).[5] Passing as the Other, with all of its instabilities, miscues, and misreadings, became one way of expressing progressive sentiments that raised questions about closets, passing, and identity politics *as* style. Dance music videos were not alone here. Transforming the self into an Other was evident in the techno-morphing body slippages of Michael Jackson's "Black or White" and in numerous advertisements urging viewers to refashion their bodies (such as Top Secret's Pump-Up Bikini Top, Bugle Boy jeans, and Soloflex).[6] By incorporating and promoting these dance video and commercial tropes of passing, MTV clearly revamped its own corporate identity to become the popular culture site for numerous performative cultural differences, queer among them.[7]

Indeed, MTV offered a number of opportunities for audiences to pass for queer by participating in the *production* of its programming. In addition to singing and dancing along with music videos that incorporated drag, audiences were directly invited to participate in programs such as "The Grind" (a dance show), "Lip Service" (a lip-synching game show), and "Spring Break '93." At the same time, the "Free Your Mind" campaign, which combined an hour-long town meeting forum with slick public service announcements against sexism, racism, and homophobia, openly appealed to viewers' social consciences. And audiences could retain their cutting edge style — "you heard it first" — by watching numerous queer-friendly reports produced by MTV News for "Week in Rock." As part of MTV's eclectic, crossover programming, all of these queer-friendly sites allowed their participants to temporarily pass for queer, although within the chic safety zone of MTV-approved youth culture.

To Be Real . . .

As representational strategies, the tropes of runway vamping and (super)modeling are particularly useful for articulating the performativity of identity categories, relying as they do on the repeated and stylized enactments of the body to perform readable identities. As models vamp onto a runway or take on a series of identities in a photo shoot, they repeatedly foreground the fashioning and refashioning of identity. Change your clothes, change your "look," change your "self." But, of course, each repetition, each stylized enactment of an(other) identity, is subject to differences in performance. Even as we "perform" ourselves in our everyday lives, we never do so in precisely the same fashion. These differences, according to theorist Judith Butler, problematize or "trouble" the cultural standards regulating our performances, especially our gender identities.[8] The "performativity" of gender is a kind of citation that re-enacts or re-cites the cultural norms governing one's body. But if each performance is always slightly different from the last, then one's ability to perform the gender norm is "troubled." Consequently, the culture persistently reminds us of the codes governing our gender performances so that they adjust to an ever-shifting norm.[9]

Just as runway (super)modeling indicates how style can provide viewers with a way to participate in crossover identities, Butler argues that crossdressing performances indicate how *all* gender performances are a kind of drag. Following Esther Newton's ground-breaking work on the topic,[10] she examines how camp/drag performances "enact the very structure of impersonation by which *any gender* is assumed."[11] Drag performances display the signifiers of gender identity as visible and interchangeable, as "vested interests," not as "natural" attributes. Dance music videos that incorporate drag and runway modeling demonstrate that identities work as style, as "put on" or improvisation. So too does "House of Style," an "insider" look at the world of haute couture hosted by supermodel Cindy Crawford and featuring gay fashion designer Todd Oldham.[12] But such programming also indicates the extent to which identities as style are available to others through consumer culture. Through them, consumers gain access to a kind of transgendering "queerness," in which they too can put on a queered style, if not a queer identity.

Seduced by Drag

> *I am not trying to seduce you.*
> *Would you like me to seduce you?*

Is that what you're trying to tell me?
3, 2, 1 kick. 3, 2, 1 kick . . .

Kicking off George Michael's 1992 hit "Too Funky" on *Red Hot + Dance*, a compilation album to benefit AIDS programs, these lines initiate a fairly standard representation of the vamp as a dangerous, dominating seductress.[13] Spoken as a refrain by a female voice, the question asked repeatedly near the end of the song — "Would you like me to seduce you?" — is counterpointed by Michael's ambivalent response — "Everybody wants a lover like that. Yeah, yeah" — on both the *Red Hot + Dance* recording and its video version. The gendered positions of power in these lyrics of sexual exchange shift repeatedly between receptive and active sexual positioning.[14] The video version, however, revises these shifting relations by initiating the song with Michael's reply to an already spoken, but now implicit, seductive message:

> Hey, just too funky for me.
> I gotta get inside of you,
> and I'll show you heaven if you let me.

By beginning with Michael's reply rather than the vamp's question, the fluidity of exchange in the recorded version is altered, establishing instead the primacy and fixity of *his* masculine, and presumably heterosexual, position in the video's sexual exchange.[15]

Such differences between recorded and videotaped versions are highly unusual since the purpose of the video is to sell the music. Indeed, Jody Berland argues that "music videos, almost without exception, do not make so much as a single incision in the sound or structure of the song."[16] Clearly, the dance music video of "Too Funky" is such an exception, not only "positing itself in the place of what it represents," video for song, but also positing a part of itself — the opening shots of supermodel Linda Evangelista — in place of its opening speech.[17] What is especially interesting about the video's erasure of the initial vamping dialogue is that it replaces the sequence of seduction and response ("too funky") with a simultaneous match between Michael's sung lyrics and the visual image of a runway model (inscribed "Linda"), sheathed in a Jayne Mansfield slinky white evening dress and fur stole, mouth agape in a smile under her platinum blonde Jane Jetson wig. The explicitly enunciated seduction in the album's lyrics is made implicit in light of Michael's answer to an unsung question, while the visual coding of a series of models beginning with "Linda," each of whom are inscribed as the "too funky" objects of desire, dominate the aural coding. As Berland has argued, "the visual plane tends to dominate our attention right away, simply by arresting our eyes, by being (on) television. Television seems to absorb the musical matrix effortlessly and irrevocably into its visual field."[18] In other words, the images of "Linda," the high-glam Jane/Jayne clone, substitute for "Would you like me to seduce you?": her image, rather than her voice, becomes the point of seduction. These kinds of substitutions demonstrate the constantly changing power relations between seducer and object of seduction throughout the video. For example, Michael agrees to verbal seduction while trying to control the seductress's images through his role as camera operator. Exceeding filmic containment, they remain "too funky": the Jane/Jayne clone, the dominatrix (wearing black vinyl and a metallic breastplate with rearview mirrors attached), and, implicitly, the Black woman.

But perhaps none of the models challenges her inscription into the text of Michael's vamping film narrative as much as one unnamed and anxious model, a white drag queen who flings herself onto the runway after a fit of temper in the stage wings, disrupting the "natural" order of the other models.[19] Two other drag models are seen in brief shots: an extreme close-up shows a model with campy, batting eyelashes and a cigarette holder, while another shot frames a model expressing exaggerated distress at a broken fingernail. These two images are presented in quick succession, accompanied by the refrain, "Would you like me to seduce you? Is that what you're trying to tell me?" The significance of the close-ups here both articulates "realness" — because we associate realness with proximity — and its simulation of gender identity. In other words, the images become more readable as camp drag performances because of their enlarged detailing.

What's "too funky" here? While the drag queens are contained by the video's story, their disruptions onto the runway and mugging at the camera are an excessive revamping of gendered identities. While the drag queen who storms the stage is narratively incorporated, "passing" for just another bizarrely costumed, diva-tempered model, the two very short takes of the campily made-up drag performers visually underline the seduction refrain in a more disturbing way. The seduction question and camp drag shots are so disruptive of the soundtrack and visual imagery that Michael can only answer with "Everybody wants a lover like that" over a series of shots in which all of the models vamp one after another onto the runway.[20] This effectively names each model, including the drag queen, as "a lover like that."

But his answer here also suggests the ways in which the disruptions revamp heterosexual desire. Situated between the two drag instances, a dance/modeling sequence with a man and woman is repeatedly marked by the soundtrack as "too funky." If this image of heterosexual desire is "too funky," it is because the drag queens problematize the "normality" and non-performativity of gender and sexuality. In other words, the drag performances are not only a synecdoche for "queer," but they serve as evidence that all gender and sexual identities are performative.

Of course, a textual reading of a single dance music video with campy drag scenes is not enough to show how MTV plays with queer style, though dance music videos have offered some of the most consistently playful ways of remapping gender performativity.[21] And reading this text within the context of other videos in the "televisual flow," as Raymond Williams termed it, does indicate how MTV discursively commodifies and recirculates "queer" identity as drag or crossover style. Take, for instance, Whitney Houston's cover of Chaka Khan's "I'm Every Woman," which uses the movement of dance performance, instead of crossdressing, as its visual signifier of identity fluidity. Houston is always her "authentic self," though the lyrics celebrate plural gender identifications, all of which reference heterosexuality.[22] Yet, despite the lyrics' persistent reinforcement of Houston's gender identity as every heterosexual woman (perhaps in response to the rumors that she is a lesbian), that identity is far from stable when juxtaposed with, say, Annie Lennox's angry camp performance in the video version of "Why" from her *Diva* album and RuPaul's dance video hit "Supermodel (You Better Work It Girl)."

In Lennox's video, the initial and fragmentary quick-cut images of her "becoming" a woman through the application of "feminine" signifiers — lipsticked mouth and hyper-feminine burlesque stage costume (evocative of Harvey Fierstein's prologue to *Torch Song Trilogy*) — are purposely not synched with the voice-over lyrics. Indeed, the images of her singing are not matched until the end of the song, when she not only seems to embody the lyrics but has unequivocally become the feminine object of a fashion photographer's camera/gaze.[23] By then, posing in costume, she angrily delivers lyrics which insist that the listener has no clue how it feels to be her.[24] While the lyrics alone might suggest that the video represents an argument between two lovers whose romance "is sinking," it also works as a challenge to unspecified audience members, who are positioned in the photographer's place. Passive viewers may not know how it feels to perform as an "embodied" woman, one whose body and voice are split from their "natural" state. However, lip-synchers, as the discussion below indicates, know exactly how it feels and enjoy this split.

This video display of "woman" as performative could be followed up on a playlist by RuPaul, a six-foot-four-inch, light-skinned African-American drag queen in a blonde wig who does "the runway thang," a performance mode that replaced voguing among many drag queens of color as a playful and performative means of effecting "genderfuck." RuPaul's drag performances celebrate and foreground gender/sexual/racial identities as crossover play between man and woman, straight and queer, Black and white. Indeed, the video rapidly produces a succession of images of RuPaul impersonating supermodels and Hollywood actresses (from Joan Crawford to Cindy Crawford), suggesting that a Black queer man is every white straight glamourpuss. Read in the context of MTV's dance video playlist, "Supermodel" problematizes a "straight" reading of Houston's "I'm Every Woman" in much the same way that the drag queens in Michael's video revamp the straight dance sequence as "too funky." As RuPaul sings, "it doesn't matter what you wear, they're checkin' out your savoir-faire."[25] In other words, it is not the simple assumption of gender masquerade, of dress and makeup, that is most important, but the performance, the attitude, the verisimilitude of the queer-styled crossdresser.

Lip-Servicing Queerness

Dance music videos featuring drag performers, however entertaining, offer only one mode of access to performative queerness within MTV's eclectic crossover programming. Another point of entry is the industry's standard practice of using lip-synchronized recordings in video song performances. Lip-synching is intended to insure a certain clarity of sound that would be quite impossible given some of the strenuous dance activity and the environmental noise present in the "real" performances being video-taped. Obviously, the recorded music industry wants the music video's sound to replicate the quality of sound on the album in order to foster higher sales; music videos are, after all, advertisements for the recorded music. But lip-synchronized performances have cultural effects as well, for they function as a kind of aural masquerade. Just as "transvestism is a space of possibility structuring and confounding culture,"[26] lip-synchronization is a *time* of such possibility.

While temporal displacements work more subtly than spatial ones, they still offer ways for audiences to participate in crossover identity play. Lip-synching indicates a slightly "off" performance between a *previously* recorded voice and a later recorded image that are then combined in the music video to *simulate* a "real," live voice/image recording. But no matter how many times a video is played, the gap between the previously recorded soundtrack and the image cannot be closed. These slightly "off" moments between a singer's voice and image comprise a time that audience members can slip into the text and crossover to other identity positions. Lip-synching to a music video grants them the same access as the singer to the singer's image. That is, their lip-synched voices allow them to occupy a body (image), often marked differently from their own in terms of gender, race, sexuality, or age. The temporal gaps of a lip-synching performance can therefore be as "troubling" to identity categories as the spatial drag of having a Black queer guy (RuPaul) performing in the identity space of a white straight woman. And given the commercial availability of music *everywhere at once* through market saturation, these queered subject positions are also accessible whenever and wherever participants lip-synch: with music television, the radio, film soundtracks, television soap operas, and shopping mall sound systems. Just as RuPaul's "supermodel" self appears everywhere — magazine covers, photo shoots, dressing rooms, city streets, even basketball courts — viewers of the "Supermodel" video can likewise produce their crossover selves everywhere at once.

Lip-synchronization works in still another way to effect a spatial/temporal form of drag, a crossing-over of subject positions. Because MTV's playlist policies make music videos constantly available to audience members, they can rehearse subject identities that are different from their own during repeated viewings. Participants can try on these commodified, styled identities, then exchange them for others in the video closet as yet another video offers different opportunities for lip-synching drag. Perfecting their performances through the repetition of the playlist suggests to them that they are producers of both the music and themselves. As Margaret Morse argues, the "constitutive rules of synchronization allow viewers to participate as well in the act of creating by synching along, inserting themselves as subjects in a pre-recorded world, inverting in play the act of reception into one of production."[27]

Some of MTV's non-music video programming takes full advantage of this inversion. Participatory programming such as "Lip Service" turn the audience's consumption of prerecorded, crossover music on its head, in that both "Lip Service" contestants and audience members (in the studio and in the living room) perform as though they are producing the music *and* its lip-synched subject positions. Indeed, lip-synching is so obvious a mode of cultural interpellation — a means of having consumers "buy into" the notion that they are producers in late-capitalist American culture — that MTV solicits viewers via an 800 number to compete in a lip-synching contest, the prize being a chance to star in their own music video. The winning performances are most often those in which contestants perform across gender, racial, and/or sexual lines to crossover dance music hits. Consider, for instance, the race and gender crossover performances of the "Lip Service" competition which aired during "Spring Break '93." Three of the winning teams consisted of one Asian and eleven white sorority "sistahs" performing songs by Black musical groups: En Vogue's "Free Your Mind," En Vogue's "Never Gonna Get It," and Heavy D and the Boys' "Now that We've Found Love." That these groups so comfortably performed in racial (and gender) drag indicates the extent to which the act of shifting subject positions is coded as style by MTV, the popular culture vulture. All three performances relied heavily on costuming — sexy dresses for En Vogue and B-boy rapper outfits for Heavy D and the Boys — so that music, fashion, and subject identities became fluid and interchangeable signifiers for crossover chic. As Madonna insists in her change-your-life-through-voguing instructional song, race and gender are irrelevant in the face of a strong beat.[28]

While it might appear that one need only dance, sing, and dress the part to pass as the Other on MTV, it becomes slightly more complex when the subject positions are specifically marked as queer. A more recent "Lip Service" performance (aired March 9, 1994) included a RuPauled performance by a Monmouth College team (known as "What Are We, Nuts?") consisting of two white men and one white woman. During the Scratch Factor portion of the contest (in which DJ Monie Love speeds up, slows down, and otherwise "queers" the audio to which contestants perform), the men crossdressed in blonde wigs and tacky silver lamé drag, the rather small woman in an oversized but chic brown suit and fedora. While her crossdressed reference was generic — any hip guy in a suit — the men's was specifically RuPaul. The guys' lamé impersonation (the woman had her moves down) meant that they ultimately lost to three Black women (called "Sistahs") from SUNY-Purchase, who lip-synched to En Vogue's still popular "Free Your Mind." However, their performance of "Supermodel" clearly passed on one level (the judges awarded them fifty-nine points out of a possible sixty, using such categories as "accuracy," "body mechanics," and "sass"). In fact, one of the judges, actress Parker Posey, conferred twenty points on the team, stating, "You dress in drag and you're sassy." Clearly, her remark indicates something about the ways in which we might read the Nuts team's "queer" performance. While "sass" is a category for judging this "Lip Service" contest, drag is not. Does this mean that "drag" somehow crosses over to the categories of "accuracy" or "body mechanics" (judged by rap artist "Father" and WWF wrestler "Sting"), that it is equivalent to "sass," or that it constitutes something else, something less categorizable?

Surely, their performance is not characterized as "accurate," as "passing" for RuPaul, in the sense that we mistake the two guys for RuPaul. Rather, their obvious "comic" interpretation of RuPaul's "Supermodel" video performance not only differentiates them from RuPaul but ironically comments on the constructedness of RuPaul's drag when one of the men removes an apple from his "breast" and bites into it. Here the categories of "accuracy" and "body mechanics" intersect, marking the Nuts team's ability to deconstruct queer RuPaul, while stalwartly not deconstructing themselves. The gesture's implication is that *they* have no detachable body parts. They can flaunt their white, male straightness by implying that their own body parts are "accurate." Posey's comment, "You dress in drag," suggests that the men are not playing with queered identities but dressing as RuPaul, who is the queer. They are *essentially* and unproblematically "straight men," whose drag is not a playful crossing-over among racial and sexual identities, but a purposely clumsy and distancing impersonation of a very specific identity: queer, Black RuPaul. The implication is that only "real" men (with "accurate body mechanics") would have the "sass" to dress in RuPaul drag.

In their badly choreographed and lip-synched performance, the two Nuts RuPauls pointedly refuse to acknowledge the ways in which lip-synching allows identity play; instead, they dramatize the gap between themselves and the drag personae they've doubly assumed. Passing for RuPaul, let alone passing for queer, is impossible if they continually misstep and flub their lyrics. Of course, one of the challenges of the contest is accommodating the disruptive effects of this "Scratch Factor" portion of the show. But the fact that their performance seems to purposely goof with Love's "scratching," widening the gap between their performance of "Supermodel" and RuPaul's "scratched" version, indicates to the audience that "authenticity" should not be confused with "accuracy" or "body mechanics." (Compare their performance to the more serious impersonation of En Vogue by Sistahs. Not only do they dance fluidly, but their own race/gender identities match En Vogue's). If there are two "RuPauls," there can be no mistaking an accurate match between their drag and RuPaul's, for reproducing "RuPaul" is yet another way of highlighting the constructedness of RuPaul's gender/sexual/racial identity while implying that their white, male, heterosexual identities are not constructed. And should viewers still have doubts, they need only note how the woman's graceful synching and fierce snapping more "accurately" convey RuPaul's performance while not conveying any sense of cross-gendered masculinity. Her male drag suggests the impossibility of performing straight masculinity, unless one "naturally" possesses "accurate body mechanics." The "you" who wears drag is the "authentic" het body.

Chillin' Queerness

If lip-synching allows for some playful gender/race/sexual crossover, the Nuts team's performance on "Lip Service" would seem to suggest that MTV (and its core straight white boy audience) displays considerable anxiety about playing with queer style. If queer drag problematizes the stability of all identity, then *comic* drag (that is, drag at the expense of drag queens) is a way of naturalizing identity. Comic drag attempts to divest queer drag of its radical power by suggesting that straight identity is stable, but "real" queer identity is not. In fact, the Monmouth team repeats a comic drag performance initiated by Pauly Shore during an interview with RuPaul on the "Chillin' with the Weaz" segment of "Spring Break '93." Repeatedly televised during weekends in March and April 1993, the show offered viewers a weekly opportunity to play out their queerphobia through Pauly's antics. Pauly, who performs as a het surfer dude, began his segment (taped live at Daytona Beach before a primarily white, middle-class, college-aged, male audience — the same audience to which his show appeals) by appearing in "comic" drag to the opening strains of "Supermodel." Renamed "RuPauly" for this segment, Pauly arrives in colorful Carmen Miranda–esque drag, full of racist and sexist overtones, while RuPaul dresses in a tasteful, no-nonsense, skin-tight white dress and blonde wig.

Pauly's drag, like the Monmouth team's, works to make RuPaul's appearance on the show (and on MTV's video playlist) less threatening by problematizing *RuPaul's* identity as mysterious, bizarre, queerer than queer. The first question of RuPauly's interview — "So what are you, man?" — is followed shortly thereafter by another inquiring whether RuPaul is transsexual (asked no less than four times throughout the interview). RuPaul addresses these questions by defining herself/himself[29] as "a drag queen," "a big ol' black man who likes to wear women's clothes," and "a transvestite," each time "educating" RuPauly and his rather quiet Daytona audience about gender masquerade and queer style, though clearly neither the audience nor Pauly are really getting it. As much as MTV promotes crossover as *style* (which RuPaul repeatedly confirms in her/his answers), RuPauly reads RuPaul's crossdressing as an essential sexual/gender transformation, an exchange of "body mechanics" that works to reassure the MTV audience that queer (drag) styling has nothing to do with them as long as their body mechanics are "accurate."

Such "accuracy" is again insured by the "Beauty and the Beach" competition. This "fabulous" body contest, in which women and men are paired for a runway striptease before the Daytona Beach crowd, immediately follows RuPaul's appearance on "Chillin' with the Weaz." With RuPaul serving as one of the judges, each contestant strips down to her/his non-queer basics, revealing not only a lot of skin but the "naturalness" of their female/male pairing off. Should we doubt the subtext here, the contest is intercut with commercials for Top Secret's pump-up bikini bra, which allows women to "fill the void," and Revlon cosmetics, with Cindy Crawford extolling their abilities to make one appear "natural." In combining the RuPauly interview with the "Beauty and the Beach" competition and its commercials, the "Spring Break '93" marathon seems virtually obsessed with drag, but it is an obsession that ultimately positions hetero-binary gender identities as normative and "natural." After all, it is the buff bodies of the "Beauty and the Beach" contestants, divested of their drag, that are applauded by the audience (and the complicit RuPaul). If drag works to signify queer style/identity in dance music videos, it works to stabilize straight subjectivity as "natural" during "Spring Break '93."[30]

Dance, Girl, Dance

The ability of the audience to "get it" is very differently configured on MTV's dance show "The Grind," which not only prominently featured RuPaul's video on the program (especially in early 1993), but had RuPaul appear as a guest performer the week following his interview with Pauly Shore. "The Grind," hosted by a hip-hop–talking white guy, Eric Nies (who first appeared on "The Real World" in its 1992 season), appeals to an entirely different audience than does "Spring Break." Like the participants on "The Grind" (auditioned in the New York City and Philadelphia areas through an 800 number), the viewing audience is urban-identified and fatally hip, making a point of dancing appropriately to all of the music videos. By this I mean they often adopt styles of dance generated within the videos themselves, synching their dance and vocal performances (many sing along) to the singer's. For the viewing audience, the show intercuts the music videos with shots of the dancers taken from a plethora of steadycam positions. Just as lip-synching provides access to multiple Other subject positions, the quick shots of multi-culti, twenty-something dancers allow viewers to fluidly dance their way into Other identities. And to the extent that many adopt clothing/piercing styles appropriated from queer s/m subcultures or dance in same-sex pairs and mixed-gender groups (resembling an ad for CK 1), these identities read queer, although the camera work tends not to foreground more blatantly queer references.

Free Your Mind: Revamping Identity and Desire

Free your mind and the rest will follow
(Why oh why must it be this way)
Be colorblind don't be so shallow
(Before you can read me you gotta learn how to see me)

Shot in high-contrast black and white with slanted camera angles and snappy editing, the music video for En Vogue's 1992 hit, "Free Your Mind,"[31] uses a type of postmodern visual representation that reprises high-art aesthetics and shots from quirky points of view.[32] The video's glossy aesthetics serve as a visual match for its location, the ubiquitous fashion show, and create a sense that "you are there," as much a part of the "to-be-seen" scene as the models. That the lyrics of "Free Your Mind" have nothing to do with fashion is hardly surprising or particularly remarkable; music videos are often narratively incompatible with the song's lyrics even while faithfully reproducing them. What "Free Your Mind" does have to do with, though, is how to "read," how to make sense of, cultural artifacts and the people who interact with them. The difficulty in reading, of course, lies in the reader's reliance upon cultural indicators that have no stable or fixed meanings. If cultural indicators are not "naturally" attached to a meaning, then readers must learn to assemble meanings from these indicators by way of a complex system of culturally agreed-upon interpretive moves. However, when there are several cultural groups using a range of analytical strategies, misreadings can occur.[33] Indicators created by one cultural identity position which are then read from another can produce the kinds of errors upon which prejudice thrives.

"Free Your Mind," in fact, frames itself as a polemical response to prejudice. The initial images of the video are voiced-over with the words, "Prejudice. Wrote this song about it. Like to hear it? Here it go," which are immediately answered by the sung refrain, "Free your mind." Thereafter, the lyrics specifically rely upon the cultural indicators of style to discuss the difficulties of reading. Lines such as "I wear tight clothing and high heel shoes," "I like rap music [and] wear hip hop clothes," and "Oh my please forgive me for having straight hair" clearly reference style — the intersection of fashion and popular culture — as a significant indicator of identity. By explicitly disavowing standard misreadings — through lyrics like "It doesn't make me a prostitute," "That doesn't mean that I'm sellin' dope," and "It doesn't mean there's another blood in my heirs" — the song acknowledges that the categories of sexuality, race, class, youth, and gender are likely to be misinterpreted or even criminalized. If, as it repeatedly suggests, "Before you can read me you gotta learn how to see me," then the music video offers the trope of runway vamping as a way of seeing, a way of reading the signs of intersecting cultural identities as wholly constructed, put on, strutted. It is this knowledge that will enable us to revamp our reading strategies and follow the directive to "free [our] mind[s]."

Such a revamping was precisely what MTV was after when it launched its two-year-long "Free Your Mind" Campaign. Designed to showcase issues of tolerance and diversity, to "open hearts and minds to other ways of thinking," the campaign included a series of hip public service announcements against sexism, racism, and homophobia; the "Free Your Mind Forum" sponsored by AT&T and Ford; and the inclusion of a number of relevant news stories on "The Week in Rock," the MTV news program. The campaign concerned three specific areas of intolerance and discrimination: the denial of gay civil rights, violent racial hatred, and sexual harassment.[34] Its primary audience was an eclectic and inclusive one. While it might be argued that MTV was particularly concerned with targeting the perpetrators of intolerance in an attempt to revamp their views, the campaign also worked to reaffirm the beliefs of viewers who were already relatively tolerant or who were themselves members of groups experiencing intolerance. One of the means by which this was achieved was a kind of rhetorical crossover: the issues were packaged as interconnected.

Like MTV's self-promotional spots, the campaign's PSAs were often pleasurable and always self-reflective moments for viewers to buy into MTV's ironic and eclectic sense of style. They relied on quick editing and fragmented imagery that assumed an intelligent and engaged audience willing to assemble the images and sounds into a coherent message. The PSAs were so successful that MTV invited viewers to submit their own ideas about "the power and potential of diversity" for a "Free Your Mind Commercial" contest, in which the winner traveled to New York to film her/his segment.[35] One PSA airing just prior to the "Free Your Mind Forum" adopted a montage technique popular with some contemporary documentary video/film makers. Intercutting flashes of text — "tolerance," "discrimination," "hatred" — with images of a guy wielding a baseball bat, the spot moves to "unity" and "truth," with an image of two people embracing, then to "pain" and "patience" and a KKK-ignited cross, to a final explosion of textuality that is impossible to read in one viewing. The PSA does not oversimplify the complexities of the issues by suggesting that one can move from "hatred" to "unity" in the linear fashion favored by situation comedies. Neither does it hierarchize acts of intolerance or oppression — by implying, for example, that gay-bashing is worse than other intolerant acts (such as cross burnings) — or simplify the solutions to intolerance. Instead, the PSA opts for the messy, contradictory, too-quick-to-grasp interconnections between acts of intolerance and "doing the right thing" that so well capture the present state of these issues in American culture.

Such interconnections were again evident (though less complexly) during the "Free Your Mind Forum" hosted by Tabitha Soren and Alison Stewart, in which eighty-five people of various sexual orientations, races, and genders in the age range of fifteen to thirty-one (MTV's target audience) were invited to express their opinions concerning lesbian/gay rights, racism, and sexual harassment. The initial segment on "homosexual issues" combined MTV News stories on "Gays in the Military" and Colorado's Amendment 2 with a debate among selected audience members. For the most part, the "Gays in the Military" issue was framed by straight-identified on-camera interviewees and audience members in terms of their levels of discomfort with the possibility of queer-identified service personnel openly expressing sexual interest in them. To be thought the object of queer desire provoked extreme anxiety for the male marines present, who seemed to spend an inordinate amount of time in the shower, and for a female audience member who was certain that lesbians were looking at her "funny." These opinions were countered by a gay sergeant's comment that he was not going to be attracted to a straight man and by a woman who had actively fought against the Colorado amendment, whose look of horrified disbelief signaled that a straight woman would not be the object of any dyke's desire. The anxiety here marks a space in which some straight-identified people fear being the objects of an unbridled queer desire, or that somehow they may be mistaken for, may "pass" as, queer themselves. As one intolerant audience member indicated, tolerance has a breaking point, which manifests itself in gay-bashing. His clear implication was that lesbians, gays, and bisexuals who "flaunt" their queerness invite violence from the "natural" order of heterosexuality.

Inside the Video Closet

Surely, these public interest forums indicate the extent to which "real" queer and queer-style positions come at a price. The Free Your Mind Forum was framed as a space in which to free one's mind through alternative (progressive) points of view, yet its effect was to contain tolerant views and legitimate intolerant ones. While the funky PSAs produced by MTV (and viewers) suggest the kind of crossover logic that exposes links between various forms of oppression, the forum clearly fails to do so, because it presents a debate "for" and "against" gays. Straight-identified white men and women shudder at queer desire, African-American men justify segregating gays in the military, and a Latino man denounces queers as immoral and therefore deserving to be gay-bashed. There are no coalitions built here, no playful performativity of subject positions, no listening to what others have said. Each speaks from his/her own fearfully entrenched positions, mind and body free only to reiterate an insistence on not crossing.

The forum provided a space for liberal pluralism that, like the "comic" drag of the RuPaul impersonators, was at odds with the discursive strategies of the PSAs, "The Grind," and some of the dance music videos privileging sexual/gender/racial play. And while these videos and some participatory shows may allow anyone to participate in a dress rehearsal of transgressive positions, they also effect an erasure of the cultural signifiers that mark one as "queer" by recirculating those signs as style, as detachable from queer identity and politics — precisely what was so glaringly absent from the forum. As bell hooks has argued in relation to the signs of Black nationalism, "meaningless commodification strips these signs of political integrity and meaning, denying the possibility that they can serve as a catalyst for concrete political action."[36] Her argument is no less true for queer identity politics, for MTV's video closet circulates queered positions as a style to be rehearsed in playful participatory programs — dance, lip-synching, beach parties — yet shut out of "real" exchanges. "Put on" as this moment's fashion within the music television closet, the political impact of queer performativity is diminished, though its "troubling" effects are still apparent to many straight-identified consumers. Insofar as consuming queer style on MTV protects one from some of the very real violent repercussions that might occur on the streets in a homophobic society, performing queer in the video closet can allow for a relatively safe crossing-over into queer territory.

But investing in queer style is not necessarily an investment in queer identity politics. Nor is it necessarily a disinvestment in hetero-norms, in the cultural laws that privilege heterosexuality. Recall, for example, the image of girl/guy pairing in the "Beauty and the Beach" segment. The contestants might have flounced on the runway in crossdressed signifiers — women in ties and hats, guys in skirts — but their commitment to queer style was quickly peeled off so that they might be paired off as hetero-couples. Thus what most needs revamping are the ways in which we as pop culture consumers so easily read crossdressing as "put on" and buy into the hetero-identity pairing as "natural." "Such collective disidentifications [with hetero-identities]," argues Judith Butler, "can facilitate a reconceptualization of which bodies matter, and which bodies are yet to emerge as critical matters of concern."[37]

All bodies wear drag; all bodies matter. Certainly some of MTV's eclectic programming allows its viewers to revamp their identities and thereby free their minds about how identities are produced. But insofar as MTV controls the codes of those identities and their repeated circulations through programming rotation, viewers have limited opportunities during which to cross-over, no matter how often they lip-synch/dance along with videos, are invited to submit ideas for PSAs, or join in the non-music programming. For as long as MTV and its viewers are more concerned with the styling of identities than with the very real queer(ed) bodies that assume these identities in everyday life, MTV will work as a closeted space in which queer style is divested of its queer politics.[38]

NOTES

1. Andrew Goodwin, *Dancing in the Distraction Factory: Music Television and Popular Culture* (Minneapolis: University of Minnesota Press, 1992), 138. For a history of MTV's music video programming prior to 1986, see E. Ann Kaplan, *Rocking around the Clock: Music Television, Postmodernism, and Consumer Culture* (New York: Methuen, 1987).

2. An extremely useful argument for thinking about the ways in which audiences interact "queerly" with popular culture texts is provided by Alexander Doty, *Making Things Perfectly Queer: Interpreting Mass Culture* (Minneapolis: University of Minnesota Press, 1993).

3. I'd be among the first to argue that there is no life outside of popular culture; what I mean to emphasize here are those areas which are not specifically constructed within MTV's borders in the ways that fashion and music are, however "real" their references (gangsta rap to South Central L.A., for instance).

4. I don't offer this enumeration of differences (and there are others) as a "politically correct" gesture, but to remind readers that "queer" is not limited to considerations of sexuality alone.

5. In March 1995, RuPaul was chosen to represent the MAC Glam Couture Color Collection

and serve as the honorary chairperson of the MAC AIDS Fund. Frank Toskan, cofounder of the company, "always thought it impossible to put a face to MAC because of what [they] stand for — all sexes, all races, all ages. But RuPaul is male, he's female and he's ageless. He fits the bill." Cited on the GLB-NEWS bulletin board.

6. For an extended discussion of these advertisements, see Lynda Goldstein, "Singing the Body Electric," in *Building Bodies*, ed. Pamela Moore (New Brunswick: Rutgers University Press, forthcoming).

7. I borrow Andrew Goodwin's incisive use of "incorporate" to mark MTV's impulses toward both inclusion and corporate profit, especially in relation to "countercultural and antiestablishment points of view." Goodwin, *Dancing in the Distraction Factory*, 154.

8. For a discussion of performativity and gender, see Judith Butler, *Gender Trouble: Feminism and the Subversion of Identity* (New York: Routledge, 1990), esp. 147.

9. Judith Butler, *Bodies That Matter: On the Discursive Limits of "Sex"* (New York: Routledge, 1993). For a different discussion of citationality, see Peggy Phelan, "Reciting the Citation of Others: or, A Second Introduction," in *Acting Out: Feminist Performances*, ed. Lynda Hart and Peggy Phelan (Ann Arbor: University of Michigan Press, 1993), 13–31.

10. Esther Newton, *Mother Camp: Female Impersonators in America* (Englewood Cliffs, NJ: Prentice-Hall, 1972).

11. Judith Butler, "Imitation and Gender Insubordination," in *Inside/Out: Lesbian Theories, Gay Theories*, ed. Diana Fuss (New York: Routledge, 1991), 21; emphasis in original.

12. Queerness is further evoked through the show's title, "House of Style," which references the voguing performances of the New York Black and Latino gays documented by Jenny Livingston's *Paris Is Burning* and Madonna's "Vogue," as well as the "insider" knowledge that Todd Oldham has employed male transvestites as haute couture runway models for years.

13. George Michael, "Too Funky," on *Red Hot + Dance* (Sony Music, 1992).

14. By "George Michael," I mean his ambiguous stage identities. See Will Straw, "Popular Music and Post-Modernism in the 1980s," in *Sound and Vision: The Music Video Reader*, ed. Simon Frith, Andrew Goodwin, and Lawrence Grossberg (New York: Routledge, 1993), 16–17.

15. Given Michael's rumored bisexuality, this alteration is especially interesting.

16. Jody Berland, "Sound, Image, and Social Space: Music Video and Media Reconstruction," in *Sound and Vision*, 25.

17. Ibid.

18. Ibid.

19. This unnaming is even extended to the "mystery" of the director, who is designated by a giant question mark at the end of the video.

20. RuPaul's dance hit single "Supermodel" includes a number of these models — Linda, Naomi, Christi, Cindy, Claudia, Nicki — in his list of those who had "better work it, girl."

21. Drag performances can be found in a number of music videos of all genres. For instance, metal/rock videos by Aerosmith ("Dude Looks Like a Lady") and Jane's Addiction ("Been Caught Stealing"), however conservative their politics, normalize the appearance of men in drag, while more progressive rock and alternative bands, such as Duran Duran ("Come Undone"), U2 ("One"), and Nirvana ("Smells Like Teen Spirit"), use drag to raise questions about the politics of gender.

22. Contrast this with Annie Lennox's "Little Bird" video, in which clones of her other performative selves vie for attention on the runway/thrust stage, ultimately working to obscure an enormously pregnant Lennox.

23. An alternative drag performance is offered in her "Walking on Broken Glass" video, in which men and women are rouged, coiffed, and encased in yards of satiny eighteenth-century costuming.

24. Annie Lennox, "Why," on *Diva* (Arista, 1992).

25. RuPaul, Larry Tee, and Jimmy Harry, "Supermodel," on *Supermodel* (Tommy Boy Records, 1992).

26. Majorie Qarber, *Vested Interests: Cross-Dressing and Cultural Anxiety* (New York: Harper Collins, 1993), 17.

27. Margaret Morse, "Postsynchronizing Rock Music and Television," *Journal of Communication Inquiry* 10, no. 1 (1986): 21.

28. Madonna and Shep Pettibone, "Vogue," on *The Immaculate Collection* (Warner Brothers, 1990).

29. While most drag queens refer to themselves using the feminine pronoun, many (lesbian) feminists reserve its use only for those whose "femininity" or womanhood is biological. For these reasons, I'm using "herself/himself" and "her/him."

30. The 1993 MTV Music Awards proved especially thick in its crossover intertextuality. Among the contenders for "Best Dance Video" were RuPaul's "Supermodel" and En Vogue's "Free Your Mind" (the winner), the award being presented by Shaquille O'Neal and Cindy Crawford. Embodying a combination of O'Neal's race and pro-basketball height with Crawford's supermodeling, RuPaul was later paired with vaudevillian Milton (Uncle Milty) Berle as presenters of the "Viewer's Choice" Award. A distinctly nasty on-screen shade-throwing exchange ensued. Obviously taking exception to Berle's quip, "Here we are, Wilt [Chamberlain] and Milt," RuPaul's testiness contends with Berle's crankiness in front of the noisy crowd. Berle later moves to grope RuPaul's breasts, which are level with his face (a move Jon Lovitz made with Jamie Lee Curtis during the 1995 MTV Movie Awards), and tells RuPaul that he likes her gown; she responds that he "should, queen, it's one of your old ones." Saying he's "beginning to feel like a 'straight' man," Berle moves into his scripted line that forty years ago, he too, wore dresses, to which RuPaul zings: ". . . that's funny, and now you wear diapers." Snap. Berle is visibly upset at RuPaul's ad-libbing and offers to "check [his] brains so [they'll] be even." So much for the happy combination of Mr. Television and Miz Thing.

31. Thomas McElroy and Denzil Foster, "Free Your Mind," on *Funky Divas* (Two Tuff-e-Nuff Songs/Irving Music, 1992).

32. These shots are not sight-matched or anchored to anyone in particular, but jump from relatively stable shots of En Vogue runway walking to quick, crisscrossed shots among audience members, so that there's a sense of everyone looking at everyone else at once, though longest at the models/En Vogue.

33. I'm using "cultural groups" in the broadest possible sense. While we generally think of cultural identities in terms of race or ethnicity, designators we essentialize as relatively fixed, they are often formed around more obviously arbitrary characteristics, such as age ("youth culture"), region ("southerners"), or sexual preference ("straight"). Each produces cultural artifacts — music, literature, film, etc. — that distinguish it from other cultural groups.

34. The latter two were prompted respectively by the increased visibility of youth participation in neo-Nazi skinhead groups and the 1991 Anita Hill/Clarence Thomas Senate hearings on sexual harassment prior to his confirmation as a Supreme Court justice.

35. The "commercialness" of these PSAs was hardly accidental. The "Free Your Mind" logo of a head in profile later circulated in Fruitopia beverage advertisements, crossing progressive multiculti politics with the utopia of multi-fruit drinks brought to you by Minute Maid/Coca Cola.

36. bell hooks, *Black Looks: Race and Representation* (Boston: South End Press, 1992), 33.

37. Butler, *Bodies That Matter*, 4.

38. Consider two new shows from the 1995 season. How might the hetero-privileging of "Singled Out," a dating game often involving a hundred participants each show, work against the MTV Weekend News program, hosted by Alison Stewart, which invites viewers to submit stories, some of which concern queer "bodies that matter" (a recent segment concerned a young gay man who graduated from college in full drag). In what ways do these shows foster play with crossover identities? Reinforce identifications with hetero-norms? Is MTV integrating queer style and politics or building a bigger closet?

chapter 15

Pages of Whiteness: Race, Physique Magazines, and the Emergence of Public Gay Culture

Tracy D. Morgan

Homosexuality, a much maligned category in U.S. social, political, and sexual life, is routinely assumed by the mainstream media, heterosexuals of all races, and white queers to be the province of white people. From IKEA television advertisements, to the kinds of gay issues considered worthy of news coverage, to the pronouncements of some Black religious leaders who see homosexuality as yet another genocidal white "import" into the Black community, the message is loud and clear: to be gay is to be white. Given the historical overidentification of Blackness with sexual perversion, this lapse in U.S. racial logic is decidedly odd. White men have historically hidden their own sexual "perversions" (the systematic rape of Black female slaves, for example) behind a fantastic projection of a shameless Black phallus, so why hasn't white men's homosexuality been similarly cloaked? What historical conditions, events, and discourses have enabled the all-but-complete erasure of Black gay men from discussions of gay male culture, sexuality, and community?

The premium that contemporary lesbian, gay, and bisexual organizations place on queer visibility makes the absence of Black gay men from the "gay family snapshot" especially disturbing. Clearly, Black gay men's invisibility is not a reflection of their organizing efforts, which, over the past ten years, have been extraordinary.[1] Instead, the discourse about race in the U.S., of which white queers are a part, must certainly shoulder some of the blame. Furthermore, as the cultural critic Jackie Goldsby has written, the low level of concern about racism among many lesbians, gay men, and other queers is derived, at least in part, from "the tight reins held by gay print media that have resisted and restricted the free flow of ideas on the subject of racism in the gay male community, proving once again that ignorance isn't innocent; it's organized."[2] Goldsby is right. Ignorance — the privilege of not having to know about something — is calculated. But white racial ignorance has an ever changing history, shaped by a multitude of forces over time; white racism at the end of the twentieth century, for example, is different from the white racism that proliferated at mid-century. Therefore, in order to see racism as a social product, it is important to know and historicize these differences.

In an effort to understand the "organization" of Black gay men's liminality, this essay will examine one of the very first gay print media in this country: male physique magazines. Looking at the period 1955–60, years which saw the founding of the Daughters of Bilitis, a lesbian organization, and the success of the Montgomery bus boycott and other civil rights actions, I will focus on the racial codes of some of these magazines and explore the implications of such coding for the creation of gay male community. To contextualize these publications, I inquire first into the erasure of Black gay men from the historical record of homosexuality in the U.S. The dominant cultural assumptions which consider Black men to be decidedly unfeminine or hypermasculine and which see gay masculinity as an oxymoron place these two identities — Black and gay — seemingly and, of course, falsely, at odds. After exploring gay historical paradigms and their racial ramifications, I will consider the legacy of male physique magazines in the formation of gay male community and identity in the postwar U.S. and raise some questions about how these publications might be read in ways that more productively explore the relationship between racial categories, representation, and homosexuality.

U.S. Homosexual History: A Few Questions

According to the dominant historical paradigm in U.S. lesbian and gay history, the seeds of the modern lesbian, gay, and bisexual rights movement were sown during the Second World War. Women and men in the service found themselves in sex-segregated environments, both at home and abroad, a situation that opened up myriad possibilities for the growth of gay communities. At the war's finish, lesbian, gay, and bisexual service people moved into the major urban centers of this country, and the modern gay ghettos of New York City's West Village, L.A.'s West Hollywood, and San Francisco's Castro District flourished.[3]

Many gay people, their services lauded during the war, found themselves dismissed from the military in peacetime, and when the House Un-American Activities Committee increased their postwar investigations, thousands of gay people lost their jobs with the federal government.[4] Just weeks after his 1953 inauguration, Eisenhower dispatched an executive order "barring gay men and lesbians from all federal jobs."[5]

Crackdowns on bars with a largely gay clientele dramatically increased in the 1950s. Police entrapment of men in cruising areas remained a problem as well. The rise of homosexual repression, coupled with a growing belief on the part of some gay people that they might be a "minority group," led to the formation of homophile political organizations, such as the Mattachine Society and the Daughters of Bilitis. These organizations worked toward gaining homosexual rights and freedoms in the U.S.[6]

They also provided their membership with various forms of support. Those who were arrested for solicitation or fired from their jobs as a result of being labeled "queer" could enlist the help of these emergent homophile groups. Annual conferences and regular social and educational events, including discussion groups, were instituted as strategies for changing public opinion about homosexuals and for changing the negative image that many homosexuals had of themselves. Of course, not all lesbians, gay men, and bisexuals were political. Most were terrified that membership in a political organization might publicly expose their sexual identities. Thus the lives of most lesbians, gay men, and bisexuals were probably informed less by the agenda of homophile organizations than by the social lives and worlds they created for themselves.

The less formally political gay world revolved around bars, house parties, bathhouses, jaunts to gay beaches, and other venues. This community also had its own form of print communication, which catered to gay men of a variety of political persuasions: the physique magazine. Available on newsstands and by subscription, these magazines helped to make men who were desirous of other men visible to each other, informing them about gay style, gay desire, and gay language.[7]

Questioning the Paradigms of Twentieth-Century U.S. Homosexual History

Unfortunately, the dominant historical paradigm in twentieth-century U.S. homosexual history fails to incorporate a, or possibly *the*, prevailing factor of social and political life during this segment of U.S. history: racial segregation.[8] In what follows, I want to elucidate some of the problems that a consideration of Black gay subjectivity inevitably poses for the current interpretation and periodization of postwar queer history.

As the historian David Roediger, in his book on the formation of the white working class, *The Wages of Whiteness*, has argued, "the pleasures of whiteness could function as a 'wage' for white workers. That is, status and privileges conferred by race could be used to make up for alienating and exploitative class relationships." In many ways, the same argument could be made regarding white lesbians, gay men, and bisexuals in the twentieth century. To better understand race and gay community formation in historical perspective, it is important to query how race privilege has been "useful" in assisting white gay people to attain greater social and cultural privilege. They may be outcasts, but are at least not racial outcasts in the dominant U.S. culture.[9]

Inarguably, white supremacist prerogatives have profoundly damaged efforts toward interracial community building and political organizing in homosexual organizations. In the short term, it might seem cost-effective to gloss over the meaning of white privilege in order to get the ear of those who might fund AIDS-related programs or overturn sodomy laws. Many gay groups, in their almost uniform whiteness, must look familiar, almost like family, to those who command power in the halls of government and business: they are, after all, largely "members" of the same race as those in power. In the long run, however, this strategy may cost the movement its very life. The failure of vision and will on the part of white lesbians, gay men, bisexuals, and their supporters is now being exploited by the religious right in their open courting of Black communities to oppose civil rights protections for lesbians, gay men, and bisexuals, as if lesbians, gay men, and bisexuals are not a part of Black communities. The current dynamics of racial segregation in the world of queer politics are rooted in the historical conditions in which that movement first emerged. For example, the lives of Black gay men were circumscribed by race in the very same arenas through which white gay men came to establish increasingly public lives: Jim Crow military service, housing patterns, and leisure activities. The roots of gay political activism and community building were thus nourished by the same soil in which racial segregation flourished.

Unearthing the Paradigm

According to historian Allan Bérubé, Black and white gay soldiers did not frequently socialize together, either on or off of segregated military bases, during World War II.[10] The gay bars frequented by white queer service men and women, for example, had racist door policies, mirroring the white supremacist practices of the dominant culture. And Black soldiers stationed stateside encountered sometimes murderous violence at the hands of their white colleagues.[11] In fact, the conditions for Black soldiers were sometimes so life-threatening that a few feigned homosexuality just to be released from their plight.[12] In short, the bonds of community, such as were forged by white gay service women and men, have yet to be adequately documented in Black gay history.

White gay people's race privilege enabled them to detach from their families of origin and form what today is known as *the* gay community. Restrictive covenants made it hard for Black homosexuals to do the same. Returning to their neighborhoods after the war, Black lesbians, gay men, and bisexuals did not disrupt the homophobically constructed geography of the U.S. urban sphere. Their queer identities were subsumed within the more dominant concept of "the Black community." They were also more fully integrated into the social fabric of the Black neighborhoods in which they resided. Recalling lesbian and gay life in the 1930s and 1940s, Black lesbian Harlemite Jeanne Flash Gray writes,

> There was a thriving Black Lesbian and Gay community within a thriving Black community. Harlem was alive with the life of her people. We lived there, played there and worked there. There were some who never had to leave for anything.... Before it was discovered by others that Black Lesbians and Gay Men had money to spend, there were many places in Harlem run by and for Black Lesbians and Gay Men.[13]

Unlike white homosexuals, Black lesbians, gay men, and bisexuals, at least in urban areas, might have actually had gay lives to come home to. "There were some who never had to leave for anything" could certainly not be said of the white lesbians, gay men, and bisexuals who fled their hometowns to live queer lives in New York, San Francisco, Los Angeles, and other cities.

Another major component of the mid-century paradigm for U.S. lesbian and gay history concerns the anti-homosexual purges of the federal government that were spearheaded by Senator Joseph McCarthy and his colleagues. Just as it would be inaccurate to describe the effects of the New Deal on the lives of Blacks in the U.S. as commensurate with its impact upon whites, there is little reason to believe that the ways in which Black lesbians, gay men, and bisexuals experienced McCarthyism mirrored the experiences of their white counterparts. The McCarthy anti-homosexual program included the ferreting out of homosexuals employed by the government. However, few

Black people were federally employed; in 1948, less than 200,000 Blacks worked for the government nationwide.[14] In Harlem, for example, the bulk of African Americans were employed in either personal services or manufacturing.[15]

This is not to imply that McCarthyism and the sexual politics of the Cold War had little impact on Black gays. After all, Black gay people were well integrated into most of the institutions of Black life — from churches to political organizations — and many of these institutions feared surveillance. Black civil rights organizations, such as the NAACP, were alert to changes in the political climate and concerned with being seen as un-American and/or subversive in their struggles for equality. For example, the NAACP journal, the *Crisis*, published many articles declaring that they were *not* a Communist organization and, if their review of James Baldwin's *Giovanni's Room*, a novel which depicts a homosexual relationship, is any indication, they had no more time for "faeries" than Senator Joseph McCarthy did. For, as James W. Ivy, the *Crisis* book reviewer, wrote, "It seems a pity that so much brilliant writing should be lavished on a relationship that by its very nature is bound to be sterile and debasing."[16]

To cite another example, Black civil rights mastermind Bayard Rustin, a gay man, was removed from a visible planning position for the 1963 March on Washington because Martin Luther King and other Southern Christian Leadership Conference organizers feared that "segregationists might try to smear the effort with histrionics about Rustin's leftist affiliations and homosexual proclivities."[17] Grappling with the very real questions surrounding integration, it was yet to be determined which Blacks would be supported by civil rights organizations in their efforts to be integrated into U.S. society at large. Sexual propriety would eventually play a key gatekeeping role. Thus the participation of Black gay men in the growing, exclusively gay urban enclaves was probably limited not only by white racism but also by the debates then taking place in Black communities regarding racial integration and sexual decorum.

Therefore, one must always be aware, as historian Nathan Huggins reminds us, of the racial silences imposed by historical master narratives.[18] In this instance, it would be a mistake to fully embrace the arguments being made about (white) lesbian, gay, and bisexual life in the mid-twentieth century and apply them with confidence to the lives of Black lesbians, gay men, and bisexuals during the same time period. To do so would be to miss significant and critical historical differences between the political and social formations of the two groups. For example, as white gay political organizations and neighborhoods were becoming more visible in New York City in the 1960s, Black lesbian, gay, and bisexual Harlemites found that their bars and clubs had either been burned to the ground or were inexplicably closing. How do we make historical sense of this information? How, when the current queer history paradigm understands the social patterns of urban lesbian, gay, and bisexual life as having led to the Stonewall rebellion, does information about the concomitant decline of community institutions in Harlem change the way this historical moment is understood? This is not to say that Black lesbians, gay men, and bisexuals were untouched by events that proved formative in shaping the lives of their white counterparts, such as the Second World War, anti-Communism, and the establishment of urban white gay domains. Rather, they were touched differently. The above example — one among many — highlights the importance of problematizing periodization and critically examining race in the writing of lesbian and gay history if we hope to avoid the construction of racially exclusive historical monoliths.

Masculinity in the 1950s: Race and the Politics of Being a "Real" Man

The relationship between masculinity, Blackness, homosexuality, and physique publications was negotiated within a culture marked by the special attention it paid to conformity. As Norman Mailer has written about the postwar U.S.,

> [O]ne could hardly maintain the courage to be individual, to speak with one's own voice. ... A man knew that when he dissented, he gave a note upon his life which could be called in any year of overt crisis. ... A stench of fear has come out of every pore of American life, and we suffer from a collective failure of nerve.[19]

In the often gender-rigid landscape of the 1950s, there were but a few popular models of masculinity. The businessman, in wing tips, white shirt, and tie, dominated images of manhood. His goals were to get married, rear children, manage a home, mow the lawn, and participate in the business of civilizing the "crabgrass frontier."[20] In 1957, the year Jack Kerouac's *On the Road* was published, "the man in the gray flannel suit" met his nemesis, the hipster or beat. The daring of the hipster, particularly his refusal to be tied down to a job or a woman, stood in stark contrast to the "suit." His was a different model of masculinity altogether. According to David McReynolds, "The hipster's ability to act spontaneously in a society which demands conformity [was] in itself an affirmation of the ability of the human being to will its own actions."[21]

The mid-1950s also signaled the beginning of a new epoch in the Black civil rights movement, which in the North was marked by expressions of Black masculinity that were often more righteous, race-conscious, and defiant than in previous decades. Aware of this transformation, Mailer took the hipster critique a step further, adding Blackness to the formula for white male rebellion; in an environment where "almost any kind of unconventional action ... takes disproportionate courage," he writes, "it is no accident that the source of Hip (the Beatnik) is the Negro."[22] In its quest for nonconformity, hip/beat maleness took seminal cues from urban Black masculinity. Thus, having filtered itself through Black maleness, hipsterism came to question the manhood of the conformist.

The 1950s were also marked by an increasing awareness of the lives of homosexuals. This complicated the revolt from conformity immeasurably. Men who continued to be devoted to wife and family were considered unmanly in some circles. Yet, if a man should leave his wife and kids, he might be accused of being "queer." To avoid this accusation, a man had to walk a virtual tightrope, careful not to do anything too suspect, like abandoning his eminently heterosexual role as breadwinner and husband. Guaranteeing that the critique of conformity remained within the socially acceptable confines of institutionalized heterosexuality, Barbara Ehrenreich writes that in 1950s popular culture, "the image of the irresponsible male ... blurred into the shadowy figure of the homosexual. So great was the potential overlap between the sexually 'normal,' but not entirely successful man, and the blatant homosexual that psychoanalyst Lionel Ovesey had to create a new category — 'pseudohomosexuality' — to absorb the intermediate cases."[23]

Moreover, a white man's inability to conform could also signify his failed masculinity, with the equation being *"I am a failure = I am castrated = I am not a man = I am a woman = I am a homosexual."*[24] The reassertion of a white hetero-masculinity that was neither conformist nor castrated nor queer depended upon an appropriation of the racist fantasy of Black male virility. Because of racist discrimination, "success" for Black men during the 1950s had an altogether different meaning than it did for their white counterparts. Few Black men had the opportunity to own suburban homes, play golf, or have jobs that required them to wear suits to work. Although Black masculinity was envied by some white men as more liberated, few Black men could have fulfilled the conformist ideal had they wanted to. Nonetheless, as articles written by Mailer and other men's magazine writers on the "white Negro" indicate, an attempt to celebrate the seemingly transgressive nature of Black masculinity was well underway. In a signature statement on the topic, Mailer writes, "Knowing in the cells of his existence that life was war, nothing but war, the Negro . . . could rarely afford the sophisticated inhibitions of civilization, and so he kept for his survival the art of the primitive."[25] Thus appropriated, negritude gave to white masculinity an unquestionably heterosexualized toughness and nonconformity that it had previously lacked. Representations of men in physique magazines — men photographed so as to arouse the desire of other men for them — were most certainly affected by the varied interpretations of 1950s masculinity.

Physique Magazines: Butch Bodybuilders and Friends of Plato

In the early 1940s, the photo studios of Bruce of Los Angeles and the Athletic Model Guild (AMG) founded what would eventually be known as "the physique movement." Both were run by gay men and sought muscular models to pose for photographs. Bob Mizer, the founder of AMG, "did all his recruiting personally, visiting local gymnasiums and male beaches" in his search for men who fit the Athletic Model Guild image, which included chiseled muscles, a cleft chin, and, by and large, white skin.[26] Initially, photos produced by these studios were part of a pinup mail-order business, but eventually, working with publishers in towns and cities as diverse as Metairie, Louisiana; Hollywood, California; Chicago, Illinois; Danville, Kentucky; and suburban Ridgefield, New Jersey, the photos were reproduced in pocket-size magazines. By the mid-1950s, well over twenty magazines served between sixty and seventy thousand readers, according to one estimate.[27] They could be purchased through subscription or, in some locales, at neighborhood newsstands.

According to Allen Ellenzweig, "Physique magazines, which for a half century had been variously marketed to health cultists and 'art appreciators' . . . began more strongly than ever in the 1950s to target a specifically homosexual audience."[28] Three types of physique magazines flourished. One used ancient Greece as its primary metaphor, filling its pages almost entirely with images of white men and Doric columns. The second popular type of physique publication focused more directly on the body and fitness, reflecting an actual boom in weightlifting competitions coming out of York, Pennsylvania, where the steel and barbell industries were centered. The third, according to Alasdair Foster, "served as early homophile publications."[29] For the purposes of this essay, I will concentrate primarily on two of the longest-running physique magazines. The first, which espouses the Grecian ideal, is the *Grecian Guild Pictorial*, and the second, which has a more "all-American" focus and represents the bodybuilding perspective, is called *Vim*. These publications are similar and yet have some differences worth noting.

The Greeks

Grecian publications frequently espoused a Protestant work ethic, encouraging their readers to labor diligently and to live by the supposedly Grecian ideals of honesty and moral uprightness. While full of scantily clad men, Grecian publications ran articles that focused primarily on the development of the mind and spirit rather than on the development of the body. This approach, stressing the relationship between a sound mind and a sound body, most certainly refers back to ancient Greece. According to cultural theorist Richard Dyer, referencing classical themes in physique publications "could be for [gay and bisexual] men a way of representing desire, both in the sense of imaging it to themselves and in the sense of arguing for it to the world; it could be both a form of desire and a defence of it."[30] Allusions to ancient Greece made homosexuality respectable and hence, representable. Even priests and ministers wrote articles for Grecian publications, offering religious approval of physique worship. What could be wrong with celebrating the contributions of ancient Greece? Quite little, it seems. Significantly, the Grecian publications, unlike those oriented toward bodybuilding, did not use the words homosexual or bisexual to refer to their readership. They did, however, devote themselves to a celebration of the male physique as a key to a more virtuous way of living.

The All-American Bodybuilders

"All-American" physique magazines, like Grecian publications, were full of photographs of scantily clad men. However, unlike the Grecians, bodybuilding magazines ran articles on exercises that promised to generate a washboard stomach or bigger biceps, and demonstrated less concern with their readers' virtuousness, publishing very few essays from religious clergy. Also prominently featured were photographs of weightlifting contests, which, unlike U.S. athletics in general during this period, were decidedly interracial. Generally, these magazines were more politically daring than their Grecian cousins, publishing articles, for example, on "by-sexuality" and racial discrimination in athletics. Maybe because they overtly attached themselves to an athletic and hence, a masculinized, discourse, rather than to the more feminized discourse of aesthetic physical appreciation, they were freer to address controversial topics.

Duplicity and Physique Culture

In the early 1950s, when the federal government launched an investigation into homosexuality among its employees, Harry Hay, cofounder of the Mattachine Society, started organizing. He took to the gay beaches of Los Angeles in the hope of finding political allies with whom he could fight this repression. Disappointingly, his efforts yielded little. "No one," according to historian John D'Emilio, "was willing to risk exposure of his sexual identity by joining a homosexual rights organization."[31]

Figuratively following Hay's footsteps in the sand, gay erotic photographer Bruce of Los Angeles probably trekked across some of the very same beaches, encouraging young, muscular men to venture out of the sun and into the studio for a photo shoot. His efforts, in contrast to Hay's, met with success. He was an integral part of the U.S. male physique industry, which began publishing magazines in 1945. Maybe because the physique industry had a longer history among these men, Bruce of L.A. had an easier time obtaining recruits. Unlike political organizing for homophile rights, these magazines were probably not unfamiliar to them, and most certainly were less risky to be involved with. Taking part in the physique culture of the 1950s did not necessarily mark one as homosexual.

The many men who agreed to be photographed by Bruce of L.A. probably did so for a variety of reasons, among them flattery, the opportunity for exposure, and the thrill of being a desired object. Given the anti-homosexual sentiment rampant in the dominant society, the physique world made it relatively safe for a man to be an object of other men's desires by maintaining a veneer of respectability. It also put him in touch with a wider homosexual public.

Photographs of men in g-strings, juxtaposed with textual appeals to the greatness of Greek society or the benefits of participating in the bodybuilding world, offered gay and bisexual readers both pleasure and safety. They could potentially look at and even celebrate these images without being labeled deviant. Gay journalist Alan Miller recalls first encountering physique magazines in 1960, when they "were thrown amongst the magazine collection at Top's Barber Shop . . . in Montreal. The six barbers were — or so I vaguely remember — not the least embarrassed at having these things about, let alone that a young boy would be flipping through them."[32]

Homosexuals, like Communists, were considered a major threat to postwar U.S. security. Physique magazines not only hid their homosexual content behind barbells and the pillars of ancient Greece but cloaked gay desire under an anti-Communist facade as well. What gave many of these magazines their respectability, their ability to traverse gay and straight worlds with little or no opprobrium, was their glorification of a particular kind of masculinity: patriotic, strong, and white. This was, after all, Cold War America. A perceived Communist threat, writes Barbara Ehrenreich, "kept masculine toughness in style long after it became obsolete in the corporate world and the consumer market-place." Maintaining U.S. security, she continues, "demanded ideological vigilance, crew-cuts, and a talent for rigid self-control."[33] Physique magazines exhibited the bodies of all-American men, which, if nothing else, demonstrated their strength, endurance, and discipline — all necessary qualities to combat the Russian threat to democracy. Furthermore, they promised that those bodies could be mobilized for the purposes of patriotism. As the *Grecian Guild* creed stated, "I pledge allegiance to my native land, ever willing to serve the cause of my country whenever and wherever she may need me; I seek a sound mind in a sound body that I may be a complete man; I am a Grecian."[34]

Bruce of L.A.'s photographs were printed in many male physique magazines, including *Grecian Guild Pictorial, Adonis, American Apollo, Little Caesar,* and *Olympians.* These photos appeared, for example, beside texts that asked, "Who are the Grecians?" and then supplied the answer: a Grecian is "somewhat individualistic, apt to be thoughtful — the type who 'figures life out.' "[35] Employing the democratic ideal of equality of opportunity, bolstered by the American dream of a classless society, the *Grecian Guild* described its readership as "drawn from all walks of life. Doctors, factory workers, [and] ministers are members."[36] Page after page of nearly naked men were threaded together by such reassuring phrases. Presumably, anyone could be a Grecian. But did that include Black men?

The Uses of Blackness in the Formation of White Gay Male Culture

Black men were generally underrepresented in physique publications in relation to their actual numbers in U.S. society during the years 1955–60. But, in a highly segregated society, the fact that they appeared at all, while not completely surprising (racism and sexual desire for "the other" are not mutually exclusive), calls for an explanation. The "all-American"–style physique magazines I surveyed included more than four times as many images of Black men as did the Grecian publications. In the latter category, in approximately twenty-six volumes published over a five-year period (1955–60), a paltry four images of Black men made it into print. This is hardly surprising; the image of ancient Greece in these magazines is coded racially as white. In contrast, the magazines oriented toward bodybuilding (I surveyed almost fifty volumes from the period between 1955 and 1960) included an average of one Black male image per issue, and often more.

Focusing on a harmoniously constructed past, the Greece-inspired physique magazines, as compared with the bodybuilding variety, were more fearful of directly acknowledging the gravity of the contemporary political situation in which they operated. For, in the U.S. during the McCarthy era, the continued publication of these magazines was hardly inevitable. According to John D'Emilio, the late 1950s witnessed myriad legal cases regarding charges of obscenity brought against physique publications, some even argued before the Supreme Court (*Manual Enterprises vs. Day*).[37] Aside from being called upon to defend in court the right of these magazines to exist, there were other perils of physique publishing. In September 1958, *Grecian Guild Pictorial* ran a letter to its readers which exclaimed "Danger Ahead!" The American News Company, distributor of many physique magazines, including the *Grecian Guild Pictorial*, had suddenly gone out of business. The fledgling *Guild* turned to its membership for help, declaring, "The future of most physique magazines is extremely dark."[38] A direct appeal for financial assistance, tinged with hysteria, was made to its readers: "Unless you support the physique magazine field NOW, the day may well come when you'll not be able to purchase physique magazines at all. . . . Imagine what a great void this would leave."[39]

It is telling that in its plea for financial assistance, the *Grecian Guild Pictorial* chose not to educate readers about the even greater threat to its existence: censorship. To mention the obscenity cases, however, would have broken the dominant code of the industry, which, in the mid-1950s, was never to mention homosexuality. In their stalwart refusal to address some of the most salient political topics of the decade, Grecian-style physique publications were often politically powerless to fight anti-homosexual prejudice. They instead maintained the complicated stance of denial in the face of extreme derision and denigration.

Their approach to racial politics was no more direct. In the mid-1950s, as Puerto Rican migration to "the mainland" increased and the *Brown vs. Board of Education* case was settled in favor of public school desegregation, "race mixing," for centuries a much-contested reality in the U.S., became even more conflictive. These changes, and the anxieties that accompanied them, were, not surprisingly, reflected in both types of physique magazine, with each choosing to perpetuate stereotypes of Black and Latino men. In their "Dossier on Black Masculinity," cultural critics Isaac Julien and Kobena Mercer comment on the racial matrix that anticipates representations of Black masculinity:

> [B]lack men . . . are implicated in the . . . landscape of stereotypes . . . organized around the needs, demands and desires of white males. . . . The repetition of these stereotypes in gay pornography betrays the circulation of "colonial fantasy," that is a rigid set of racial roles and identities which rehearse scenarios of desire in a way which traces the cultural legacies of slavery, empire and imperialism.[40]

In short, while some physique magazines may have violated 1950s homophobic morality, many paid deference to the Jim Crow laws then still in existence.

Observing the racial codes employed in contemporary gay men's personal ads, cultural critic Jackie Goldsby writes, "[A]n economy of desire . . . is invested in maintaining status quo racial politics; coming matters as much as overcoming the power dynamics that fix gay men of color into a peculiar status of (in)visibility, one that restricts them to being conspicuously consumed by the imaginings of gay male sexual culture."[41] The "economy of desire" regulating physique magazines in the 1950s was a bifurcated one. "Colored" bodies adorn the pages of bodybuilding publications in considerable numbers, but it is clear that Black and Latino men are only visiting Plato's world. If Black, they are en route from Africa to the New World as slaves. If Latino, they are framed as if in a postcard from the tropics. Both images are there to entice. However, in bodybuilding magazines, as opposed to their Grecian counterparts, representations of Black and Latino men, while stereotypical, were not limited to the recirculation of these racial stereotypes.

Nevertheless, in most physique magazines of the period, Black and Latino men are much more frequently photographed with props than are white men, who are generally posed au naturel. Often sporting thick, heavy chains and perched atop shipping crates, the representations of Black men in these publications call forth a haunting and historic image: the dangerous Middle Passage from Africa to the Americas, from freedom into slavery. Latino men, generally represented with fewer accouterments, occasionally don straw hats while surrounded by empty rum bottles. Either way, most of the representations of men of color abide by the rules of U.S. white supremacy. The photographs of Black and Latino men were reproduced to serve the interests of a white male readership whose desires and fantasies were circulated within the system of racial domination and subordination that was de rigueur in the dominant postwar U.S. culture.

Infrequently, images that are disobedient to the rules of racial hierarchy can be found; for instance, the images of equality between Black and white men at the often interracial weightlifting contests which were so popular in the period. Since many of the physique models were culled from weightlifting events, a conscious or unconscious decision has to have been made not to photograph, or at least not to publish, too many photographs of Black men. This decision needs to be further examined.

Earlier in this essay, I wrote about David Roediger's *Wages of Whiteness* thesis that the white working class found solace for its woes in white privilege. Roediger's idea may be usefully applied to the phenomenon of the missing Black male in much of photographed physique culture. These publications were among the first nationally circulated publications read by men who thought of themselves as gay or bisexual. As such, they were being consumed by a group of people living in a social order that sought to frighten them into postures of shame, self-abnegation, and suicide. It was bad enough for someone white to be queer; it would be even worse for someone white to be queer and reading interracial publications in a segregated culture. To be white and to share culture and community with Blacks — to be equal to "the other" — was then, as it is now, to lose a measure of personal esteem and social power. The absence of Black men from physique representations can be understood as a conscious or unconscious strategy employed by white publishers to remain connected to the connotations of class and quality generally associated with whiteness.

There is another element to the story behind the absence of Black male forms. Given the popularity of the gender-inversion model to explain homosexuality and the hypermasculinity attributed to Black men, the Black physique may have been difficult to represent as queer during the 1950s. In physique culture, Black men are typically shown as athletes, rather than depicted more directly as sexual objects. For example, their hands do not rest invitingly on their hips, and their eyes, unlike the eyes of their white counterparts, often avoid direct contact with the camera. Moreover, since women are very infrequently included in these publications, it is particularly significant that one of the few men photographed with "his wife" is a Black man.[42] Could the images of Black men have been included in an effort to "closet" the homosexual content of these publications, further reinforcing the sexuality of Black men as heterosexual?

The category "Black male" in antebellum and postbellum U.S. culture has provided an opportunity for the safe expression of white homosexual longing. Cultural theorist Eric Lott, in his book on minstrelsy, writes that Blackface was useful "in mediating white men's desire for other white men," ostensibly through hiding behind a hypermasculinized Black male figure which could not possibly be imagined as homosexual. For Lott, minstrelsy was a "process . . . in which [white] homosexual desire [was] deflected by identifying with potent [Black] male heterosexuality."[43] This is precisely my argument regarding physique magazines. The inclusion of the Black male physique can be understood as part of an unconscious strategy to protect physique publications from being queer-baited. The inclusion of "too many" photographs of Black men might run the risk of dehomosexualizing the publication completely, while too few might draw attention to the magazine's queerness. A fine line thus had to be maintained, and the representations of Black men were crucial to its maintenance.

Adonis, a publication headquartered in Jersey City, New Jersey, is one of the only Grecian-style magazines I found that indicated even a glimmer of recognition of the Black civil rights struggle then being represented in other media, such as the nightly news. Of Arthur Harris, a twenty-three-year-old African-American bodybuilder, who in 1953 was Mr. New York State, *Adonis* says,

> Of all the modern physique stars, we have followed Artie's career with greatest interest and admiration, for in true Alger tradition he has triumphed over adversities that would have destroyed lesser men, to reach heights of physical magnitude never achieved by anyone.[44]

This text, written in 1958, three years after the Montgomery bus boycott, never specifies the adversities over which Arthur Harris triumphed, but the reference to Horatio Alger implies that Harris started at the bottom and worked his way up, without receiving favors from anyone. *Adonis* adds, "Were it not for the hanky-panky of certain self-perpetuating officials who keep their greedy little pinkies in this particular pie, Arthur would have won the [Mr. America] title long ago."[45]

Physique magazines with a stated interest in bodybuilding grappled with the issues of homosexuality and Blackness in decidedly different manners. First and foremost, because they were associated with the masculine endeavor of building bulky bodies, they were often not seen as catering to "prurient" (homosexual) interests by the general public, despite the state's efforts to make this argument. Thus they could frequently acknowledge homosexual concerns within their pages. For example, in an article published in *Vim*'s July 1959 issue called "Males, Morals & Mores," author Jack Walters offered a frank discussion of the societal use of the homosexual as a scapegoat. He denied that homosexuality was contagious and then quoted the famous Kinsey study on male sexual behavior: "If all Americans who exhibit homosexual behavior at some time were to be treated according to the letter of existing law, a majority of the male public would be in prison and the unimprisoned would be too few in number to staff the penal institutions which would be required to hold them."[46] Other articles published in *Vim* between 1955 and 1960 that addressed sexual issues include "Are Bodybuilders Oversexed?" "The Sex Drive," and "The By-sexual Male, Parts I and II."

As stated previously, *Vim* and other physique magazines in the bodybuilding genre regularly included images of Black men. Nevertheless, *Vim*, like *Grecian Guild*, employed stereotypically racialized codes of representation: Black men's strength and power were commonly juxtaposed with implements previously used to control the use of that strength. However, *Vim* addressed contemporary issues that other publications avoided. They were, for example, much more explicit when explaining obscenity cases to their readers, and certainly they addressed the issue of homosexuality with aplomb. But, in terms of representing Black men, what is most unique about *Vim* is that of all the physique magazines I examined, it was the only one to put a Black man, Arthur Harris, on their cover, in June 1960.

From Margin to Center: Black Men Putting Black Men in the Frame

In the 1950s, far from Tucson or Chicago, where *Grecian Guild* and *Vim*, respectively, were published, an African-American gay man, Glenn Carrington, who was a major Black art collector, social worker, and newspaper writer, took amateur photographs — mostly of Black men.[47] His collection of well over two thousand photographic images includes shots of Black male couples seated on stoops — their hands resting casually on each other's thighs — or standing on street corners, presumably in Harlem or Bedford Stuyvesant, where Carrington, at different stages of his life, made his home. Other images created by Carrington include Black men in small groups, their bodies resplendent, relaxed, and at rest amidst heathery fields. Many of these photographs were turned into postcards, complete with a little box indicating where to place the stamp adjacent to Carrington's name, taking credit for the photograph on the flip side.

Then there are a series of small (three by three) studio photographs of Black men posed as if for a Grecian magazine. Of the collection, these images are unique because the men assume poses fully informed by the physique tradition. Carrington's Black models wear g-strings. They flex. They look right into the camera. In contrast to his non-studio photographs, these images do not seem to have been made into postcards.

Since Carrington's collection is the only one I have seen with so many photos of Black men taken by a Black gay man in this time period, it is obviously not possible to extrapolate from this evidence a community-wide strategy for (re)presentation. Still, because of the uniqueness of Carrington's position, his vision, or rather, re-vision, is worthy of further elucidation. Carrington was an active leftist in the 1930s, a reporter for the *Amsterdam News* for almost ten years, a psychiatric social worker, a friend of Langston Hughes and other gay and bisexual Black men, a world traveler, and a homosexual. The Carrington collection at the New York Public Library's Schomburg Center for Research on Black Culture, one of two such collections in this country (the other is at Howard University), is rich in correspondence with gay men from around the globe. In the 1920s, Carrington debated Freudian theories of homosexuality via letters with friends and lovers. By the 1940s, he frequently exchanged letters with Black gay men serving in the military during the war. In the 1950s, he received a letter of invitation to the founding meeting of the New York Mattachine Society, his name having been gleaned from the L.A. chapter's mailing list. In the 1960s, he kept a file containing the Village Theatre Club's suggested reading lists, which consisted entirely of gay material, as well as files on many Black leaders and organizations. In 1972, three years after the Stonewall rebellion, Glenn Carrington died. Throughout his rather exciting life, he documented the lives of his large circle of friends and acquaintances photographically.

Addressing the representation of Black masculinity historically, Isaac Julien and Kobena Mercer observe that "Black masculinity is a highly contradictory formation as it is a subordinated masculinity."[48] It is a masculinity that, to borrow postmodern phraseology, is always-already spoken for, determined, delimited. In short, Black masculinity is the opposite of what masculinity is supposed to be: self-determined, limitless, and self-possessed. Herein lies the value of Carrington's vision. Neither subordinated nor hypermasculinized, this collection of photos reconfigures one of the central modes of physique photography in the 1950s: the body in isolation. In almost every physique publication, the presentation of the male physique is rendered one man per page. Rarely do two men share the frame, except when there is an occasional interracial pairing. Contemporary gay male pornography has the same tendency, as Mercer and Julien note: "One major photographic code is to show single models in solo frames, enabling the imaginary construction of a one-to-one fantasy: but sometimes when models pose in couples or groups other connotations — friendships, solidarities, collective identity — can come to the surface."[49]

In contrast, Carrington's physique photographs, as well as his non-physique photos of openly gay and bisexual men, have a collective orientation: they are generally of duos and trios. Through this collectivity, they undermine an image of Black male subordination on the one hand, and Black hypermasculinity on the other.

To the best of my knowledge, Carrington's photographs were never published in any of the physique magazines of the 1950s and 1960s. But, in going through his papers, it is apparent that he read these publications. One folder contained photographs most likely purchased through the mail-order advertisements in the back of physique magazines: some were from Bruce of L.A. and others were gay erotic renderings by the artist Quaintance. The back of each image was stamped with a reminder that they could be traded in to physique photographers for a ten cent discount on the next photographs purchased.

As a leftist gay man, Carrington might have been dissatisfied with both the whiteness of physique magazines and the ways in which they tip-toed around political issues. Over time, physique magazines played an important part in the formation of a gay community, but the terms upon which this idea of community was built accommodated forms of discrimination and depersonalization that, in the end, ultimately destabilized it. Seeking normativity, physique publications reinforced codes of shame. Summoning forth white-skin privilege as a salve and smoke screen in their quest for respectability, physique magazines were part of a larger phenomenon within mid-twentieth-century gay community formation: they sought individualistic solutions to group problems.

Another African-American gay man, the writer Samuel Delany, recalls "the life" in the late 1950s, when he used to go to the piers by the Westside Highway in New York City for sex. One night, when approaching the pier, he encountered a raid:

> What frightened was, oddly, not the raid itself, but rather the sheer number of men who suddenly began to appear, most of them running. . . . That night policemen arrested maybe eight or nine men. The number, however, who fled across the street to be absorbed into the city was . . . perhaps as many as two hundred.[50]

For Delany the event was particularly significant:

> In the fifties . . . homosexuality was a solitary perversion. Before and above all, it isolated you. . . . What the exodus from the trucks made graphically clear . . . was a fact that flew in the face of the whole fifties image.[51]

Hundreds of men fleeing for their safety forced a recognition, or, at the very least, some small acknowledgment of the bare facts of shared political oppression. For Delany, "the first direct sense of political power comes from the apprehension of massed bodies." The men fleeing from the piers were just a tiny portion of a population, "not of hundreds, not of thousands, but rather of millions of gay men" for whom

> [i]nstitutions such as subway johns or the trucks, while they accommodated sex, cut it, visibly, up into tiny portions. . . . No one ever got to see its whole. These institutions cut it up and made it invisible — certainly less visible — to the bourgeois world that claimed the phenomenon deviant and dangerous. But, by the same token, they cut it up and thus made any apprehension of its totality all but impossible to us who pursued it. And any suggestion of that totality . . . was frightening to those of us who'd had no suggestion of it before.[52]

Physique magazines functioned similarly within a closeted gay male culture. They communicated zero-degree deviancy among those considered to be deviants, neutralizing the possibility for collective action or the drawing of parallels between African-American and homosexual oppression. Gay maleness became synonymous with whiteness. Black gay men became invisible: the representation of 1950s homosexuality demanded their erasure.

In Memoriam

This essay is dedicated to the memory of Marlon Riggs, recently dead from AIDS, who brought a Black gay male subjectivity unapologetically into homes across the U.S. with his brilliant, celebratory, and challenging documentary *Tongues Untied*. I never knew Riggs, but his work on Black gay men has inspired my own. It was his questioning of the absence of Black gay men from public discourse, coupled with my own emergent understanding of how white womanhood has historically informed racist interpretations of Black masculinity, that directly prompted the writing of this essay.

NOTES

Acknowledgments: An earlier version of this essay was published in *Found Object*, no. 4 (Fall 1994). I would like to thank the many friends and mentors who have read this article in its many stages. The steady encouragement and constant challenge of studying with David Nasaw has been of critical importance to me. John D'Emilio and Thomas Waugh shared their insights into the history of physique magazines and race in the gay community. Karen Sotiropoulos provided important perspectives on Black U.S. history and Black masculinity. The New York Public Library's curator of manuscripts, Mimi Bowling, and the archivist at the Schomburg Center, Amul Mohammed, directed me to the many sources I have cited here. Finally, thanks to Brett Beemyn, Heidi DeRuitter, Heidi Dorow, Lauren Kozol, Michael Rothberg, Todd Weisse, and the *Found Object* collective for their savvy commentary and editing of one version or another of this piece.

1. With the rise of the writing collective *Other Countries*, the production and wide distribution of Isaac Julien's *Looking for Langston* and Marlon Riggs's *Tongues Untied*, the establishment of monthly magazines such as *Colorlife!* in New York City and *BLK* in Los Angeles, and the ever increasing number of social, political, and cultural groups like Gay Men of African Descent, Black gay men are clearly putting forth their own agendas.

2. Jackie Goldsby, "What It Means to Be Colored Me," *OUT/LOOK* 3 (Summer 1990): 13.

3. This chronology is a mainstay of twentieth-century U.S. lesbian and gay history. See Allan Bérubé, *Coming Out under Fire: The History of Gay Men and Women in World War Two* (New York: Plume, 1990); John D'Emilio, *Sexual Politics, Sexual Communities: The Making of a Homosexual Minority in the United States, 1940–1970* (Chicago: University of Chicago Press, 1983); and Lillian Faderman, *Odd Girls and Twilight Lovers: A History of Lesbian Life in Twentieth-Century America* (New York: Columbia University Press, 1991).

4. D'Emilio, *Sexual Politics, Sexual Communities*, 41–44.

5. John D'Emilio and Estelle B. Freedman, *Intimate Matters: A History of Sexuality in America* (New York: Harper and Row, 1988), 293.

6. D'Emilio, *Sexual Politics, Sexual Communities*, 57–74, 92–107.

7. Indeed, they were included in the New York Public Library's groundbreaking exhibit, "Becoming Visible: The Legacy of Stonewall," as uniquely gay publications.

8. I am referring only to what has been *published* by historians. Currently, some interesting work that considers both race and homosexuality is underway. John D'Emilio has undertaken a biography of Bayard Rustin and Marc Stein's work on the lesbian and gay community in Philadelphia promises to be racially conscious. See his "Sexual Politics in the City of Sisterly and Brotherly Loves," *Radical History Review* 59 (Spring 1994): 60–93. However, I have only found one article that completely devotes itself to an historical consideration of Black gay subjectivity; Eric Garber, "A Spectacle in Color: The Lesbian and Gay Subculture in Jazz Age Harlem," in *Hidden from History: Reclaiming the Gay and Lesbian Past*, ed. Martin Duberman, Martha Vicinus, and George Chauncey, Jr. (New York: Meridian, 1989), 318–31.

9. David Roediger, *The Wages of Whiteness: Race and the Making of the American Working Class* (London: Verso, 1991), 13.

10. Bérubé, *Coming Out under Fire*, 79, 116.

11. Florence Murray, "Some Mutinies, Riots, and Other Disturbances," in *A Documentary History of the Negro People in the United States*, ed. Herbert Aptheker (New York: Citadel Press, 1990), 538.

12. Bérubé, *Coming Out under Fire*, 163.

13. Jeanne Flash Gray, "Memories," *Committee for the Visibility of the Other Black Women* 1, no. 1 (n.d. [early 1980s]): 3.

14. Manning Marable, *Race, Reform, and Rebellion: The Second Reconstruction in Black America, 1945–1990* (Jackson: University Press of Mississippi, 1991), 14. Furthermore, according to the United States Bureau of Labor Statistics, there were 670,000 Black people employed by federal, state, and local governments in 1956. The bureau is careful to point out that their "figures include all government service, including teaching and blue collar work done directly by government agencies." See United States Bureau of Labor Statistics, *Notes on the Economic Situation of Negroes in the United States* (Washington, D.C.: Government Printing Office, 1959), 10.

15. Harlem Youth Opportunities Unlimited, *Youth in the Ghetto: A Study of the Consequences of Powerlessness and a Blueprint for Change* (New York: Harlem Youth Opportunities Unlimited, 1964), 132.

16. James W. Ivy, "The Faerie Queens," *Crisis* 64 (February 1957): 123.

17. David Garrow, *Bearing the Cross: Martin Luther King, Jr. and the Southern Christian Leadership Conference* (New York: Random House, 1986), 280.

18. Nathan Irvin Huggins, *Black Odyssey: The Afro-American Ordeal in Slavery* (New York: Vintage Books, 1990), xi–lvii.

19. Norman Mailer, *Advertisements for Myself* (New York: Putnam, 1959), 338.

20. Kenneth T. Jackson, *Crabgrass Frontier: The Suburbanization of the United States* (New York: Oxford University Press, 1985).

21. Marty Jezer, *The Dark Ages: Life in the United States, 1945–1960* (Boston: South End Press, 1982), 253.

22. Mailer, *Advertisements for Myself*, 339.

23. Barbara Ehrenreich, *The Hearts of Men: American Dreams and the Flight from Commitment* (New York: Anchor, 1983), 24.

24. Ibid., 20, emphasis in original.

25. Mailer, *Advertisements for Myself*, 314.

26. Richard Dyer, *Now You See It: Studies in Lesbian and Gay Film* (New York: Routledge, 1990), 114.

27. Statistics on the potential readership of physique magazines come from the *Grecian Guild Pictorial* of September 1958.

28. Allen Ellenzweig, *The Homoerotic Photograph: Male Images from Durieu/Delacroix to Mapplethorpe* (New York: Columbia University Press, 1992), 123.

29. Alasdair Foster, *Behold the Man* (Edinburgh: Stills Gallery, 1988), 28.

30. Richard Dyer, *The Matter of Images* (New York: Routledge, 1993), 25–29.

31. D'Emilio, *Sexual Politics, Sexual Communities*, 63.

32. Alan Miller, "Beefcake with No Labels Attached," *Body Politic* (January 1983): 33.

33. Ehrenreich, *Hearts of Men*, 103–4.

34. *Grecian Guild Pictorial* (May 1957): 15.

35. *Grecian Guild Pictorial* (September 1963): 32.

36. Ibid., 32.

37. D'Emilio, *Sexual Politics, Sexual Communities*, 133.

38. *Grecian Guild Pictorial* (September 1958): 14.

39. Ibid., 14.

40. Isaac Julien and Kobena Mercer, "Dossier on Black Masculinity," in *Male Order: Unwrapping Masculinity*, ed. Rowena Chapman and Jonathan Rutherford (London: Lawrence and Wishart, 1988), 133.

41. Goldsby, "What It Means to Be Colored Me," 12.

42. *Vim* (July 1959): 2.

43. Eric Lott, *Love and Theft: Blackface Minstrelsy and the American Working Class* (New York: Oxford University Press, 1993), 54.

44. *Adonis* 7, no. 1 (1958): 10.

45. Ibid., 10.

46. *Vim* (July 1958): 2.

47. Carrington Collection, New York Public Library, Schomburg Center for Research on Black Culture, Photo Division.

48. Chapman, *Male Order*, 112.

49. Ibid., 135.

50. Samuel R. Delany, *The Motion of Light in Water: Sex and Science Fiction Writing in the East Village, 1957–1965* (New York: Arbor House, 1988), 173.

51. Ibid., 174.

52. Ibid., 174.

Choices and Chances: Is Coming Out at Work a Rational Choice?

M. V. Lee Badgett

Recently, public policy debates and academic attention have turned to the question of employment discrimination based on sexual orientation. On a policy level, the category of sexual orientation has been treated as another candidate for inclusion in antidiscrimination laws at the local, state, and federal levels. An emerging body of evidence demonstrates the existence of sexual orientation employment discrimination, as well as its economic harm to lesbian, gay, and bisexual people.[1] But, although the effects of discrimination against gay people are very similar to the economic effects of race or gender discrimination, sexual orientation differs in at least one significant way from some other protected categories: compared to race or gender, for example, sexual orientation is not an easily observable characteristic.[2] For a lesbian, gay, or bisexual worker, the disclosure of sexual orientation, whether voluntary or involuntary, is a necessary condition in most cases for direct discrimination to occur.

Some elements of the disclosure decision have been explored by researchers in other social sciences.[3] Beth Schneider has argued that lesbians' level of disclosure and their amount or quality of social contact with co-workers are interrelated.[4] James Woods has found that gay men reveal their sexual orientation to co-workers for various reasons, including friendship development, political goals, HIV-related health conditions, and personal ethics.[5] Neither of those studies was designed to fully capture the economic elements of disclosure, but employment discrimination was clearly a driving fear behind workers' nondisclosure. Numerous nonrandom surveys of self-identified lesbians and gay men have revealed that often more than half of the respondents either fear job-related discrimination if their sexual orientation were known or conceal their sexual orientation to prevent such discrimination.[6]

The connection between disclosure and discrimination, such as the possibility of employment or wage loss, suggests that powerful economic incentives are at work in LesBiGay workers' disclosure choices. An individual's weighing of the potential economic risk, however, does not mean that psychological, social, political, or ethical factors are unimportant in a LesBiGay worker's decision to disclose her/his sexual orientation. Rather, highlighting the elements of economic behavior — the kind of decision-making that economists classify as "rational" — is important, not simply because of economists' belief in rational behavior, but because of the implications of such behavior for research, politics, and policy-making.

This essay, then, focuses on the economic reasoning behind the voluntary decision to disclose one's sexual orientation, popularly known as "coming out of the closet," or simply, "coming out." In the next section, I will present an economic model of workplace disclosure in which LesBiGay workers are seen as wanting both income and disclosure. Workers then make their disclosure decisions to maximize their well-being (or "utility," in economic jargon), given the potential for workplace discrimination. The third and fourth sections discuss and test hypotheses from this model, using a detailed data set from a nonrandom sample of LesBiGay workers. In general, the statistical analysis shows that lesbian, gay, and bisexual employees working in low-risk workplaces — those with nondiscrimination policies or with well-treated, openly LesBiGay employees — were much more likely to be out to co-workers. This relationship between economic risk and coming out suggests an important role for rational decision-making, and in the final section of the essay I consider the implications of these findings, both for future economic research and for policy-making.

Rational Choice Disclosure Model

As part of the process of producing goods and/or services, work typically involves social interactions with bosses and/or co-workers.[7] In the course of those social interactions, workers choose which bits of personal information to reveal. Among other aspects of one's personality or life, individuals in this model are assumed to have a self-identified sexual orientation as being heterosexual, homosexual, or bisexual. A worker might or might not disclose his/her sexual orientation within the workplace.

Only one sexual orientation, heterosexuality, is considered legally and socially acceptable in most parts of the United States today. Public opinion polls, for example, demonstrate continuing disapproval of homosexuality. In one recent national poll, 53% of respondents stated that it is "wrong for two consenting adults to have a homosexual relationship."[8] The "other" sexual orientations, homosexuality and bisexuality, are stigmatized for deviating from heterosexuality. On a practical level, the stigma is evident in laws against same-sex sexual activity, in attempts to overturn existing laws that prohibit sexual orientation discrimination, in the difficulty of adding sexual orientation to existing civil rights codes, and in discrimination and violence against homosexual and bisexual men and women.[9]

Therefore, the choice to disclose one's sexual orientation is a benign one for heterosexual individuals, and heterosexuality can be considered the "default" assumption about individuals until disproven. The choice to contradict that default assumption can be a dangerous one for gay, lesbian, and bisexual workers. If co-workers and/or bosses disapprove of homosexuality and/or bisexuality (or the open discussion of one's homosexuality and/or bisexuality), then lesbian, gay, and bisexual workers who disclose their sexual orientations may be harassed, fired, or passed over for promotions. In many surveys, lesbians and gay men have reported workplace discrimination,[10] and recent research demonstrates that such discrimination may result in lower incomes for lesbian, gay, and bisexual workers.[11]

As with the impact of disclosure, the process or act of disclosure is likely to vary by sexual orientation. Heterosexuals may simply allow the default assumption to be maintained, or they may refer to legal spouses, children, dates with people of the other sex, or other information that typically implies a heterosexual orientation. Disclosure by LesBiGay workers must be more deliberate to dispel their presumed heterosexuality and may be quite explicit, like stating, "I am a lesbian." Any form of disclosure that is less explicit, such as a reference to someone of the same sex as being one's "partner," runs the risk of continued misunderstanding. Alternatively, involuntary disclosure might occur (as in "outing"), or co-workers and/or bosses might guess or presume that another employee is gay.

This discussion focuses attention on two important points. First, LesBiGay workers may face economic and social sanctions if they disclose their sexual orientations to disapproving co-workers or supervisors. In other words, disclosure of sexual orientation is a decision involving a trade-off between disclosure and possible loss of income. Second, disclosure, whether voluntary or involuntary, is often *necessary* for direct sexual orientation discrimination, since workers are likely to be considered heterosexual until circumstances suggest otherwise.

What, then, does it mean to think of disclosure as a rational choice? One way of thinking about it in economic terms is as a cost-benefit decision: if the benefits of disclosure outweigh the costs, then gay workers will disclose their sexual orientations. A more subtle decision-making process entails choosing from among various combinations of income and disclosure, each of which gives the worker some level of satisfaction, or utility. Individuals' preferences for disclosure may vary depending upon their political and ethical beliefs and the psychological costs to their self-esteem of nondisclosure, or "passing" as heterosexual. The psychological need for disclosure is likely to increase with the sociability of the workplace and the need for social interaction for career advancement.[12] LesBiGay workers are assumed to want both more income and more disclosure, and therefore, they may be willing to give up some of one for more of the other. At work, a trade-off is necessary because of the possible loss in income resulting from discrimination once a stigmatized sexual orientation is revealed. Given the options available in each worker's particular circumstances, LesBiGay workers choose the available combination of disclosure and income that provides the greatest satisfaction. In summary, this rational choice model involves workers weighing their desires for income and disclosure and making their decision knowing that disclosure might result in a lower income.[13]

The empirical strategy for testing this model, described in the next section, involved comparing the workplace disclosure decisions of people who were similar in some characteristics that might influence preferences for disclosure, such as race, age, sex, and a number of workplace characteristics. However, they faced different trade-offs between income and disclosure, either because of differences in apparent discrimination risk or differences in income. If the riskiness of their choice was an important determinant of individuals' disclosure decisions, then individuals were likely to be engaging in the sort of decision-making that economists call "rational."

Data Description and Measurement Issues

Data for this study came from mail-in responses to a survey published in the Spring 1992 issue of OUT/LOOK magazine, a "National Lesbian and Gay Quarterly" published in San Francisco. This particular survey, OUT/LOOK Survey no. 16, was one of a regular series of surveys published in the magazine. Out of a circulation of approximately 12,000,[14] 322 people returned surveys, resulting in a response rate of approximately 2.6%. Of those 322 respondents, 284 answered all of the questions needed for this study.

While the OUT/LOOK data is clearly not from a random sample of LesBiGay people in the U.S., the types of biases related to disclosure are fairly obvious. Table 1 describes the disclosure characteristics of the sample. Only a few respondents (6.5%) reported complete nondisclosure. In contrast, the only known study to examine disclosure rates using a national random sample of LesBiGay people found a much lower level of disclosure. This 1989 survey by Teichner Associates for the San Francisco Examiner interviewed 400 LesBiGay individuals (89% of whom were employed) through a process of random-digit dialing and screening of sexual orientation. In the Teichner survey, 54% of respondents answered yes to the question, "Have you told your co-workers about your sexual orientation?" If the Teichner survey respondents considered the question to mean either being out to at least one co-worker or being out to no co-workers, then it suggests that the OUT/LOOK respondents were almost nine times more likely to disclose their sexual orientations to at least one co-worker.

Table 1 shows that the degree of disclosure varied greatly among the OUT/LOOK respondents, even though this was a sample with a high frequency of disclosure overall. Almost two-thirds of the respondents have disclosed their sexual orientations to the majority of their co-workers, and slightly more have done so to their immediate supervisors. While the OUT/LOOK sample is biased toward LesBiGay workers who disclose, it is not clear how biased it may be toward LesBiGay workers with a very high degree of disclosure. Other sources of bias are also possible: this was a very well-educated group (see table 2), and readers of this magazine may have been likely to share the magazine's left-of-center political perspective. Thus the high degree of disclosure overall may have reflected, for example, the generally progressive political motivations of many OUT/LOOK readers. However, the degree of disclosure varied enough to warrant an analysis of the influence of other characteristics within this very "out" group.

The nature of the survey raised one other serious sampling issue. In their analysis of a different study of OUT/LOOK readers, Kenneth Sherrill, Scott Sawyer, and Stanley Segal found that OUT/LOOK readers were not only relatively liberal/radical but were also members of what they characterized as the "intelligentsia."[15] If such a group was predisposed to rational or analytical decision-making, this sample would be biased in favor of finding evidence of rational deliberation. In other words, the OUT/LOOK readers' disclosure decisions might not be representative of the decisions made by other lesbian, gay, and bisexual workers. This possibility will be considered further below.

Another issue with this data set concerns the causal connections between variables. The time frame for all of the questions used in this study was in the present, which means that a person might have come out after some constraining factors in the workplace had changed to their present condition. Thus causality cannot clearly be inferred, and the statistical techniques used might be more properly interpreted as uncovering correlations (or statistical relationships) between variables, rather than providing hard evidence for causal relationships between these variables. The uniqueness and depth of the questionnaire makes this a valuable data set, nonetheless.

Respondents provided several reasons for disclosure, such as personal ethics, changing attitudes (i.e., the education of co-workers), and reducing deceptive efforts, which indicate a positive preference for being out at work (table 1). The OUT/LOOK questions also included information about other factors that might have influenced a respondent's preferences for disclosure. The variables and their hypothesized effects on workplace disclosure are as follows:

> Age: Younger workers who have entered the work force after Stonewall and the emergence of the gay liberation/civil rights movements might be more committed to coming out as a political statement. The average age of the sample was 35.2 years.
>
> Sex: Occupational segregation and other gendered features of labor markets might change women's preferences for disclosure. In this sample, 56% of respondents were women.
>
> Race or ethnicity: This would measure cultural variation in preferences for disclosure, as well as racially and ethnically motivated differences in labor market treatment and outcomes, but the predicted effects are not clear. Of the OUT/LOOK sample, 8.5% were people of color.
>
> HIV-status: HIV-positive workers might require some accommodations by employers in case of illness and therefore might be more likely to be "out" about being HIV-infected. Or, HIV-positive workers might fear discrimination because of AIDS-phobia and therefore might be more likely to be "closeted" about their HIV status. Only 6% of the respondents reported being HIV-positive or having an AIDS diagnosis.
>
> Education: College-educated workers might have had more contact with LesBiGay social and political organizations that advocate a coming out political strategy. This was a well-educated sample, with 85.2% of respondents having at least a college degree.

In addition to the preference factors, the survey collected information on the respondents' workplace situations, providing some information that relates to what Schneider characterized as the social closeness of co-workers (the distribution of these characteristics is detailed in table 2):[16]

> Size of office: Smaller offices, defined here as having fewer than twenty-five employees, might demand more closeness.
>
> Occupation: Managerial or professional work may require social interaction for advancement.

Type of employer: Those who are employed by nonprofit organizations, for example, might
work in more liberal climates, and the often shared political values of these workers
might result in particularly close social bonding.

Supervision responsibilities: These may inhibit social closeness with subordinates.

And finally, several other variables provide some information that workers might use
to assess the riskiness of a coming out decision: having out gay co-workers, seeing out co-
workers being treated equitably, and being part of a company with a policy prohibiting
sexual orientation discrimination. All of these factors might lead a worker to expect fewer
negative sanctions for coming out. The survey also asked for respondents' income (from
all sources), but the potential impact of past disclosures, and therefore, the potential for
discrimination on current income, makes interpretation of the measured income effect
difficult.[17] Aside from the measurement issue, income could have divergent effects on
the coming out decision. High-income workers potentially have more to lose, but they
might also have more workplace authority to suppress negative peer and subordinate
reactions following disclosure. Unfortunately, the survey did not ask questions related to
the respondent's ability to find another job or what his/her alternative income might be.

Finally, measuring the degree of disclosure (the dependent variable in the model) is
not a simple matter. Disclosure can be considered binary: someone either knows or does
not know that a co-worker identifies as LesBiGay. (But, as noted earlier, disclosure may
be involuntary or may be tacit, disrupting the binary nature of "knowing"). Disclosure,
then, could be thought of as a series of bilateral decisions, or it could be measured
continuously as the number of co-workers who know the LesBiGay worker's sexual
orientation. But, at a certain point, if enough people know that someone is LesBiGay,
then other co-workers are likely to find out indirectly. Having reached some threshold of
general knowledge, the LesBiGay worker could be thought of as using a form of the
strategy that James Woods calls "integration," or "the authentic expression of a man's
[sic] sexuality," which could also be captured with a binary variable.[18] Although the
questions on the OUT/LOOK survey define several categories of disclosure, rather than
just "in" or "out" of the closet, they do allow a binary distinction between respondents
who are out to all/most co-workers and those who are out to some/few/none of their co-
workers.

Results

The basic statistical technique, the probit procedure in the LIMDEP statistical
package, involved sorting out the effects of the explanatory (or independent) variables
on the probability of being out at work to most or all co-workers. The coefficients from
the procedure measure the separate effect of each variable while holding all other
variables constant. In table 2, the first column lists the averages for the sample (some of
which were discussed above), the second column presents the raw probit coefficients,
and the third column gives the effects of each explanatory variable on the probability of
a respondent being out to most or all co-workers. The asterisks on the coefficients in the
second column indicate that the variable had a statistically significant effect on disclosure. With this statistical technique, figuring out the variables' effects on the probability

of being out requires some reference person. For this procedure, the "typical" person is a white, thirty-five-year-old lesbian with a college education who is working in a managerial/professional position for a company in a large office and making approximately $40,000. The third column shows the variables' impact on the probability of that reference person being out, but the general size and direction of the effect would be the same for other reference people as well.

The results clearly point out several characteristics that influence LesBiGay workers' disclosure decisions. Only one variable — race — stands out as reducing the probability of disclosure: LesBiGay white workers are less likely to disclose their sexual orientations at work. The third column shows that a lesbian, gay man, or bisexual of color with generally the same characteristics listed above would be 22% more likely to disclose their sexual orientations than a white lesbian, gay man, or bisexual. Most likely this difference results from the very small number of people of color in the sample (24), although it could also reflect more subtle choices of supportive workplaces than this study can pick up. None of the other variables with negative coefficients were statistically significant.

Two of the risk variables and one workplace variable had positive effects on disclosure. Gay workers who have seen out gay co-workers treated as well as or better than other co-workers and workers whose employers have a sexual orientation nondiscrimination policy are much more likely to disclose their sexual orientations. Being covered by a nondiscrimination policy increases the reference person's probability of disclosure by 21%, and having out gay co-workers who are treated fairly increases the probability by 18%. Gay workers employed in a not-for-profit organization are also more likely to disclose their orientations, perhaps because of a more liberal atmosphere.

Thus, overall, the data analysis provides strong support for the idea that the LesBiGay workers in this sample are exercising rational decision-making in their choices to come out when the economic risk is lower. The size and significance of the risk variables demonstrate that some of the other factors related to the workplace social environment, such as the size of the workplace and the extent of supervisory responsibilities, may not be as important in that decision.

Implications

As noted earlier, it may not be appropriate to generalize findings from a small, self-selected group of LesBiGay workers to the larger population of LesBiGay workers. Furthermore, we cannot tell if the nondiscrimination policies and the acceptance of out co-workers occurred before the worker's disclosure decision, so the causal links are unclear. For instance, out LesBiGay workers might be more likely to convince their employers to adopt nondiscrimination policies. Regardless of causation or representativeness, however, the findings demonstrate some empirical links between disclosure and risk characteristics that were only hypothesized previously, and those links are crucial for several reasons.

First, economists and other social scientists studying the effects of sexual orientation must take the disclosure decision into account to separate out the effects of direct discrimination against employees who are known or thought to be LesBiGay from the indirect discrimination that LesBiGay employees experience when they remain in the closet to avoid more direct discrimination. Incorporating the disclosure decision into comparisons of income based upon sexual orientation, for example, will require more subtle statistical techniques. In this sample, the incomes of those who were out to most or all co-workers were slightly lower (by $182) than the incomes of those who were not out, but this difference is not statistically significant and does not account for all possible effects of disclosure on income.[19] Unfortunately, data does not currently exist which considers both disclosure and income determination simultaneously, but the findings of this study suggest that future data collection efforts should include information on workplace characteristics and disclosure, as well as the more typical economic variables.

Second, LesBiGay workplace activists (and other political activists) should continue to question the disclosure decision more closely. The potential ambiguity of the causal links at work in this study could mean that either nondiscrimination policies have encouraged disclosure or that disclosure has encouraged nondiscrimination policies. But activists must deal with difficulties in both directions, and this study suggests that either or both of the following arguments could be true: (1) Employers who argue that sexual orientation nondiscrimination policies are unnecessary and will not help gay workers are ignoring the negative effects of no policy protection on the disclosure decisions (and possibly the psychological well-being) of their LesBiGay employees. (2) Closeted LesBiGay employees who come out can make a difference, both in promoting favorable employment policies and in serving as a positive example to their co-workers.

And finally, the debate over public nondiscrimination policies has often touched on the issue of disclosure. For instance, some legislators do not see the need for gay civil rights laws because "there are no gay people in my district." Given the findings of this study, those legislators might begin to realize that the very lack of legal protection for LesBiGay people probably explains their apparent absence. Also, the disclosure issue often arises in another context in policy debates: the disclosure-discrimination nexus serves as a distinction between sexual orientation discrimination and sex or race discrimination, since for most women and people of color, sex and race are characteristics that cannot be hidden. In that sense, it may seem as if many LesBiGay people can choose whether or not they wish to face the possibility of discrimination. One might thus conclude that eliminating sexual orientation discrimination is as simple as encouraging LesBiGay workers to resist the temptation to disclose their sexual orientations. This conclusion would be wrong, of course, since it allows heterosexuals to disclose their sexual orientation, but not homosexuals or bisexuals — a classic case of differential (i.e., discriminatory) treatment because of sexual orientation. In addition to the fairness issue, the results from this study suggest that disclosure is currently a complex and weighty decision, even for individuals who are highly educated and earning relatively high incomes. When LesBiGay workers choose to be more open about their sexual orientations, then, it suggests that they value disclosure enough to override the risk of discrimination. Pursuing policies of nondiscrimination would improve the lives and productivity of lesbian, gay, and bisexual workers by allowing and encouraging them to take the important step of coming out at work.

TABLE 1:   Workplace Disclosure and Factors Related to Disclosure

Variable	OUT/LOOK Survey
Are you "out" to other co-workers?	
All of them	38.8%
Most of them	24.8%
Some of them	17.7%
Few of them	12.1%
None of them	6.5%
Are you "out" to your immediate boss?	
Yes	68.3%
No	15.5%
Not sure	12.7%
No answer	3.4%
Which factors influenced decision to come out? *	
Include spouse/lover in company events	24.8%
Improve relationships with boss or co-workers	28.6%
Educate co-workers	57.1%
Help change company policy about lesbians and gays	22.4%
Feel more honest	83.9%
Avoid hassle of misleading co-workers	61.8%
N	322

SOURCE: Author's calculations.

NOTES: *Percent indicating that the factor had an influence.

TABLE 2:   Variable Means, Coefficients, and Effects on Probability of Disclosure

Variable	Mean (standard deviation) or percent	Probit coefficient (t-stat)[1]		Effect of variable on probability of being out[2]
Out to most or all co-workers	62.3%			
Constant		0.46	(0.9)	
Income	$41,623 (38,244)	-0.54×10^{-6}(0.2)		-1.7×10^{-7}
Female	56.0%	−0.24	(1.3)	−0.07
White	91.5%	−0.70 **	(2.1)	−0.22
Age (years)	35.2 (10.4)	−0.01	(0.7)	−0.002
Education:				
High School	12.3%	—		—
College grad	42.6%	0.32	(1.2)	0.10
Trade/Voc	2.5%	0.53	(0.9)	0.16
Grad degree	42.6%	0.25	(0.5)	0.08

Variable	Mean (standard deviation) or percent	Probit coefficient(t-stat)[1]		Effect of variable on probability of being out[2]
HIV-positive or AIDS/ ARC	6.0%	0.21	(0.5)	0.06
Company has non-discr. policy	45.4%	0.69**	(4.0)	0.21
Out co-workers	66.5%	0.02	(0.1)	0.01
Out co-workers treated fairly	53.9%	0.59**	(2.4)	0.18
Managerial or professional job	65.5%	−0.15	(0.8)	−0.04
Work in office with >24 employees	46.8%	0.02	(0.1)	0.01
Supervise >3 employees	15.8%	−0.28	(1.2)	−0.09
Type of employer:				
Self-employed	7.4%	0.28	(0.8)	0.09
Not-for-profit	17.6%	0.48*	(1.8)	0.15
Company	33.5%	—		—
Educ. institut.	22.5%	0.39	(1.6)	0.12
Gov't/milit./ other	19.0%	0.09	(0.4)	0.03
N	284	284		284

SOURCE: Author's calculations using LIMDEP.

NOTES: **Statistically significant at 5% level
*Statistically significant at 10% level

1. Dependent variable in probit model is whether respondent is out to most or all co-workers. The probit coefficient was not calculated for respondents with less than a college degree who worked for a company.
2. Effects on the probability of disclosure are calculated for a white woman with a college degree who works in a large corporate office.

NOTES

Acknowledgments: I thank James D. Woods and OUT/LOOK magazine for allowing me to use their survey data. This paper was prepared for presentation at InQueery/InTheory/InDeed, the Sixth North American Lesbian, Gay, and Bisexual Studies Conference, held at the University of Iowa on November 18, 1994, and I thank the participants for helpful comments and suggestions.

1. Whenever practical, I include all non-heterosexual people under the "lesbian, gay, and bisexual" umbrella, often abbreviated as "LesBiGay." Since no blanket term has achieved widespread acceptance, for convenience I occasionally refer to all three groups collectively as "gay." Evidence of economic harm comes from two studies: M. V. Lee Badgett, "The Wage Effects of Sexual Orientation Discrimination," Industrial and Labor Relations Review (forthcoming, 1995); and Marieka Klawitter and Victor Flatt, "Antidiscrimination Policies and Earnings for Same-Sex Couples," presented at the Research Conference of the Association of Public Policy and Management, October 1994.

2. In its immediate invisibility, sexual orientation is more like other protected categories, such as religion and some disabilities.

3. M. V. Lee Badgett, "Employment and Sexual Orientation: Disclosure and Discrimination in the Workplace," *Journal of Gay and Lesbian Social Services* (forthcoming, 1996).

4. Beth Schneider, "Coming Out at Work: Bridging the Private/Public Gap," *Work and Occupations* 13, no. 4 (1986): 463–87.

5. James D. Woods with Jay H. Lucas, *The Corporate Closet: The Professional Lives of Gay Men in America* (New York: Free Press, 1993).

6. Lee Badgett, Colleen Donnelly, and Jennifer Kibbe, "Pervasive Patterns of Discrimination against Lesbians and Gay Men: Evidence from Surveys across the United States," presented at the National Gay and Lesbian Task Force Policy Institute, 1992.

7. See Schneider, "Coming Out at Work," for a review of the sociological literature.

8. "Attitudes on Homosexuality," *Washington Post*, 25 April 1993, A18.

9. See, generally, William R. Rubenstein, ed., *Lesbians, Gay Men, and the Law* (New York: New Press, 1993).

10. See Badgett, Donnelly, and Kibbe, "Pervasive Patterns of Discrimination against Lesbians and Gay Men."

11. See Badgett, "The Wage Effects of Sexual Orientation Discrimination"; and Klawitter and Flatt, "Antidiscrimination Policies and Earnings for Same-Sex Couples."

12. See Schneider, "Coming Out at Work."

13. Mainstream economic models describe individuals' preferences and choices as "rational" as long as four simple criteria are met:

1. More income (or disclosure) is always preferred to less income (or disclosure), holding all else equal;

2. Preferences are consistent;

3. Each combination of items (such as an amount of income and a level of disclosure) can be compared to all other combinations of those items;

4. The more of one item an individual has, the less additional amounts of that item add to the individual's satisfaction.

14. Approximate circulation data is from a telephone conversation with Jeffrey Escoffier, publisher of *OUT/LOOK*, on February 25, 1994. *OUT/LOOK* ceased publishing in 1992.

15. Kenneth S. Sherrill, Scott H. Sawyer, and Stanley J. Segal, "Coming Out and Political Attitudes: The Experiences of Lesbians and Gay Men," presented at the annual meeting of the American Political Science Association, 1991.

16. Schneider, "Coming Out at Work."

17. Incorporating this feedback effect requires more sophisticated econometric techniques that will be explored in future research.

18. Woods, *The Corporate Closet*, 173.

19. The income of the out LesBiGay workers was $41,554; of those not out to most or all co-workers, $41,736.

Notes on Contributors

Feminist gender theorist *Amber Ault* finished a Ph.D. in sociology at the Ohio State University in the spring of 1995. She currently holds the position of visiting assistant professor in the Sociology Department at Beloit College in Beloit, Wisconsin. Her research interests include identities and social movements, violence against women, and the history of sex, gender, and sexuality in scientific discourses.

M. V. Lee Badgett is a labor economist and an assistant professor of public affairs at the University of Maryland, College Park. Her research focuses on the impact of race, sex, and sexual orientation in labor markets. Her studies on gay and lesbian earnings discrimination, domestic partner benefits, and public policy have been published in various academic journals, books, and magazines.

The co-coordinator of InQueery/InTheory/InDeed, *Brett Beemyn* is an A.B.D. in African American studies/American studies at the University of Iowa, where he is writing his dissertation, "A Queer Capital: Lesbian, Gay, and Bisexual Life in Washington, D.C., 1890–1955." His edited collection on lesbian, gay, and bisexual community studies is to be published in 1997 by Routledge. In his spare time, he is training to run a sub-three-hour marathon.

Warren J. Blumenfeld is coauthor (with Diane Raymond) of *Looking at Gay and Lesbian Life* (1988, second edition 1993, Beacon Press); editor of *Homophobia: How We All Pay the Price* (1992, Beacon Press); author of *AIDS and Your Religious Community* (1991, Unitarian Universalist Association Press); coproducer of the documentary film *Pink Triangles*; and editor of the *Journal of Gay, Lesbian, and Bisexual Identity*. He travels throughout the country facilitating diversity workshops and giving slide presentations on homophobia and LGBT studies. He is currently a doctoral candidate at the University of Massachusetts, Amherst.

Gregory Conerly teaches courses on African-American culture and the history of sexuality at Cleveland State University. His research currently focuses on socializing patterns among African-American gays and lesbians and representations of homosexuality in the black press.

Patricia L. Duncan is a Ph.D. candidate in women's studies at Emory University. Her writing focuses on the history of sexuality, postcolonial feminist theory, and queer culture. She plans to write a dissertation exploring racialized discourses and notions of the visible, particularly with regard to mixed-race subject positions in historical context.

Mickey Eliason is an assistant professor of nursing and psychology at the University of Iowa. Her research concerns the impact of negative attitudes toward lesbian, gay, and bisexual people on health care and lesbian, gay, and bisexual identity development. Her aspiration is to be a best-selling author of lesbian "Harlequin" romances.

Ruth Goldman has been a bi-queer activist for ten years. She is presently a doctoral student in the Communication Arts Department at the University of Wisconsin, Madison. Her area of concentration is the intersections between race and sexuality in popular culture, with a particular interest in MTV.

Lynda Goldstein teaches in the English Department and Women's Studies Program at a commonwealth campus of the Pennsylvania State University and doesn't watch nearly enough television.

Sherrie A. Inness is Assistant Professor of English at Miami University. Her research interests include nineteenth- and twentieth-century American literature, lesbian studies, popular culture, children's literature, and gender studies. She has published articles on these topics in a number of journals, including *American Literary Realism*, the *Edith Wharton Review*, the *Journal of American Culture*, the *Journal of Popular Culture*, the *NWSA Journal*, *Studies in Scottish Literature*, *Studies in Short Fiction*, and *Women's Studies: An Interdisciplinary Journal*, as well as in three anthologies. She is also the author of *Intimate Communities: Representation and Social Transformation in Women's College Fiction, 1895–1910*.

Christopher James is a writer, activist, and academic from Minneapolis, Minnesota. He is currently completing an M.A. at Iowa State University and was the recipient of the 1995 Associated Writing Programs' Introductory Award for creative nonfiction.

JeeYeun Lee is a graduate student in the Ethnic Studies Program at the University of California at Berkeley. She has been published in *Witness Aloud: Lesbian, Gay and Bisexual Asian/Pacific American Writings* (1993) and in *Listen Up: Voices from the Next Feminist Generation* (1995).

Michele E. Lloyd is an independent scholar and publisher of *The Decline of Civilization: News for the Paranoid*, a monthly newsletter.

Tracy D. Morgan is a Ph.D. candidate in American history at the City University of New York Graduate Center, where her work focuses on race, medicine, masculinity, and homosexual history. Her writing has been published in *Sisters, Sexperts and Queers*, edited by Arlene Stein; the cultural studies journal *Found Object*; various queer magazines; and ACT UP/New York's groundbreaking *Women, AIDS and Activism*.

Ki Namaste has a Ph.D. in semiotics from Université Québec à Montréal and has done research on transgendered people's access to health care and social services.

Vernon A. Rosario II, M.D., received his Ph.D. in the history of science from Harvard University and his M.D. from the Harvard Medical School–M.I.T. Program in Health Sciences and Technology. He is currently a visiting assistant professor in the History Department at the University of California, Los Angeles. He is coeditor with Paula Bennet of the anthology *Solitary Pleasures: The Historical, Literary and Artistic Discourses of Autoeroticism* (Routledge, 1995). Currently, he is completing *Science and Homosexualities* (Routledge, 1996) and *Sexual Psychopaths: Doctors, Patients and Novelists Narrating the Erotic Imagination in Nineteenth-Century France* (Oxford University Press, 1997).

Paula C. Rust, Ph.D., is an associate professor of sociology at Hamilton College, where she teaches lesbigaytrans studies. She is the author of *Bisexuality and the Challenge to Lesbian Politics: Sex, Loyalty, and Revolution.* She and her partner, Lorna Rodríguez, live in Rochester, New York, where they raise lettuce trees in their spare time.

Siobhan Somerville is an assistant professor of English and women's studies at Purdue University. She is presently completing a book on the interdependence of discourses of race and sexuality in late nineteenth- and early twentieth-century American culture, focusing on scientific, cinematic, and literary texts.

Amanda Udis-Kessler is a sociology doctoral candidate at Boston College. Her essays on sexuality, feminism, and stratification have appeared in seven books and a number of journals. She teaches on race, class, and gender inequality and is a trainer for the Gay/Lesbian/Bisexual Speakers Bureau of Boston. She is currently writing on dilemmas of bisexual identity.

Index

Printed in the United States
56709LVS00002B/111-122

9 780814 712580